MW00831555

Inside Patanjali's Words

EXPLORE THE HEART OF YOGA

A Sourcebook for the Study of the *Yoga Sutras of Patanjali*

Reverend Jaganath Carrera

ISBN 978-0-932040-05-3

Copyright © 2020 by Satchidananda Ashram-Yogaville,® Inc.

Library of Congress Control Number: 2019914297

Cover Design by Tim Barrall

Layout by Shiva Hervé and Cynthia Dailey

All Rights Reserved. Except as permitted under the U.S. Copyright Act of 1976, no part of this publication may be reproduced, distributed, or transmitted in any form in any form or by any means, or stored in a database or retrieval system, without the prior written permission of the publisher or the copyright holder.

Printed in the United States of America on recycled text stock.

Integral Yoga® Publications, Satchidananda Ashram–Yogaville®, Inc.

108 Yogaville Way, Buckingham, Virginia USA 23921

www.integralyoga.org

Contents

Foreword

Following in a Giant's Steps

Imagine what it would be like to follow a giant's directions for traveling from town to town. Strides, inconceivably longer than ours would span miles effortlessly. Striding from mountain top to mountain top, over rivers and lakes, we would miss many of the landmarks, so vital to us. In following a giant's directions, we certainly get the highlights, but not always the details.

That is what it is like studying the *Yoga Sutras of Patanjali*. Each sutra is the footprint of a spiritual giant. We see the imprint, but we can't always see how they got from point A to point B.

It's the same for the study of any sacred text, especially one like the *Yoga Sutras* with its terse aphorisms.

This text is an attempt to fill in the spaces between footprints, primarily by an in-depth examination of words. Words are the building blocks of ideas, each word adding nuance, richness, and detail. In many cases, we will gain a better grasp of what Patanjali might have intended by reflecting on his words, using them as launchpads for further exploration inside the *Yoga Sutras*.

Praise for *Inside Patanjali's Words*

Twelve years after his publication of *Inside the Yoga Sutras*, Reverend Jaganath gives us the much anticipated sequel, *Inside Patanjali's Words*. Both books should be studied together for a comprehensive grasp of the practice and meaning of Yoga as well as a focus for contemplation in order for personal insights to arise. Patanjali coded Yoga in riddles – comprised of words, which should be viewed as vehicles or metaphors for communication. Reverend Jaganath reminds us that "words are fingers pointing to the moon – they cannot contain truths, only point to them." But without *Inside Patanjali's Words*, we might not know where to look into the vastness of the sky to realize that a moon exists.

– Sharon Gannon, cofounder of Jivamukti Yoga Method

Reverend Carrera has written a beautiful companion guide for those who are curious. Have you read The *Yoga Sutras of Patanjali* and struggled with your ability to relate to the text? Have you found it dry, devoid of metaphor, irrelevant to modern life? This rendition breathes fresh life into this ancient text, providing illumination on this walk of life that we all traverse as human beings. It is a funny, warm, and unique addition to the books currently available regarding the *Yoga Sutras of Patanjali*. Pick it up, open to any page . . . see what happens.

– Carrie Owerko, senior Iyengar teacher

A ravishing and enriching contribution to the world! This new commentary of Sri Patanjali's *Yoga Sutras* – a text that has been around for thousands of years– has peaked my interest, awakened my curiosity, triggered my inquisitiveness and unpacked its meaning in a profound and poetic way. Jaganath Carrera's knack for word-for-word translation as well as his offering of the multitude of meanings a Sanskrit word can have is extremely helpful and refreshing. Some words have now hit home in a way they never had before! With Sanskrit being the source of all Indo-European languages, Carrera's translation also helps us connect to the source of our own language and understand how communication has spread throughout time. The Topic Index at the end of his commentary is a wonderful addition. If you are looking for a verse that covers the topic of forgiveness or curiosity for example, Carrera will direct you to it.

In summary, as a practitioner and teacher of Yoga, this fresh translation of the *Yoga Sutras* will be a manual and companion that I will cherish and carry with me always. It's a vehicle for gaining a deeper understanding of the subtle nuances the great sage Patanjali yearned to reveal.

– Rima Rabbath, Senior and Master Jivamukti Yoga Teacher

Inside Patanjali's Words, a new commentary on the *Yoga Sutras* by Reverend Jaganath Carrera, is an inspiring work and clearly the culmination of many years' worth of work, study and experience. Each sutra is broken down and easily explained through thorough analysis of the word and its roots. Stories and philosophies from many faith traditions are interwoven to help elucidate the text.

What I particularly love is the innovative architecture of the book. The writing and structure are similar to a "jungle gym" in a children's playground in which kids are swinging around in all directions, with options about which way to go and how to move. You are free to pick and choose where you would like to begin and delve into the text. The reader is also encouraged to work with another commentary of the *Sutras* to help provide a different light or a deeper depth and meaning to key concepts such as *nirodha.*

Inside Patanjali's Words is for the serious scholar, but ironically, is also for someone just setting out to study the *Yoga Sutras.* I love the detail, the commentary, the simple explanations, the parallels and similarities – all of it. Enjoy the journey. Each time you read it, whether in bite sizes or larger portions, settle down and uncover another golden nugget in your search for the truth.

– Beryl Bender Birch, developer and founder of Power Yoga

Overall, a wonderful companion piece, a treasure actually, to be used by students, teachers, and leaders of Teacher Trainings alike when teaching the *Yoga Sutras.* Easy to read, use, and teach from, full of insights, stories, and reflections, each Sanskrit word is broken down to reveal deeper meanings behind the sutras.

This book will give the teacher new insights into how to explain a concept or word and the student much to learn and ponder. It is a pearl except, in this case, a strand of pearls leading to One Truth.

– Rev. Amba Wallace, co-owner JaiPure Yoga
and co-leader of 200/500 Teacher Trainings

Dedication

This book is dedicated to all seekers who know and cherish the gifts of curiosity and wonderment; those who seek to know and experience the roots of abiding happiness; and those who value wisdom and the role it plays in the betterment of the world.

This book is also dedicated to those whose curiosity regarding the nature of Spirit and truth has been lit by the *Yoga Sutras of Patanjali.*

For me, no dedication is complete without offering my salutations and *pranams* to my revered spiritual master, Sri Swami Satchidananda Maharaj. It's one thing to read or hear about the exquisite teachings and practices of Yoga. It's quite another to see those teachings come to life in a realized master.

Acknowledgments

No book is ever created by one solitary person. This project is certainly no different. I am grateful to my wife **Reverend Janaki Carrera**, who is an ever-ready sounding board for all of the ideas that spring to my mind. She is unerring in her practicality and ability to get to the essence of the topic at hand.

Reverend Prem Anjali, Editorial Director of Integral Yoga® Publications, whose editing skills and oversight was akin to a loving adoption. Her care, encouragement, and keen eye brought this text to a higher level. **Reverend Paraman Barsel**, a great teacher of the *Yoga Sutras* and all things Vedantic and spiritual. He has a way with words that is unparalleled. **Tim Barrall**, a long time friend and yogi. He is generous beyond measure and his ability to convey the spirit of a project in images, fonts, and colors is amazing. To **Reverend Saraswati Lee**, who patiently read through the maze of words and definitions that make up this book, catching tons of typos. To **Reverend Amba Wallace** who repeatedly proofread the manuscript, peacefully accepting and correcting the almost constant stream of re-writes that I tossed her way. To **Satya Riggiola** for her invaluable legal expertise and guidance.

To all of the great luminaries who have inspired and taught me through their keen insights. I am humbled by their genius in giving life to an ancient text.

To the following yogis whose thoughtfulness and generosity helped fund this project. You are all great examples of selfless service.

Bashkari Browne
Shelly and Cory Douglas
Dee Duncan
Malati Shannon Elliot
Daya Lyn Francica
Mark Bhaktan Graceffo
Matthew Arjuna Grey
Reverend Nischala Lori Haytas
Janine Ilsley
Reverend Shanti and Andrew LeMaire
Reverend Narani Lisa Lorelli
Premadasi Zrinka K. Fudermuc Maler, Ph.D.
Amrita Kristin Mylecraine
Alex Scott
Siva Skroce
Reverend Lakshmi Vivian Susczcynski
The Harry Wadhwani Family
Reverend Amba Wallace

Finally, I have to acknowledge the many students to whom I have had the honor of sharing my experiences with the *Yoga Sutras*. Their comments and questions challenged me to go ever deeper into this incredible sacred text. There were many, many moments of shared joy and wonder. To say thank you is hardly enough. May they reap any sweet fruits come from this humble translation and commentary.

This is a Companion Text

This text is intended to serve as a companion alongside whatever other *Yoga Sutras* translations and commentaries you are drawn to study. Use the expanded word definitions to help clarify difficult sutras. Identify foundation themes that link together the entire *Sutra* text through the extensive cross-referencing, commentaries, and footnotes.

The Translation

The foundation of this text is the translation. Its objective is two-fold:

- Find language that better resonates with today's student of Yoga.
- To go beyond the definition of words to find their personality and a fresh look at the *Sutras*: Patanjali's words.

Paradoxically, this begins by going deeper into the words of the sutras, considering historical context, word roots, the myths, stories, and astrological, Ayurvedic, and linguistic conventions of Patanjali's day. A number of dictionaries, in print and online, were consulted along with dozens of translations and commentaries.

The viewpoints of Buddhism and Jainism, which preceded and influenced Patanjali have also been taken into account, along with the perspective of the *perennial tradition*.[1] The shared wisdom of all faith traditions often helps illumine the teachings of Patanjali.

More importantly, this translation is grounded on living the Yoga life, putting the teachings into practice in daily life, and sharing the fruits of the Yoga life with others.

No translation or commentary is complete or perfect. Each expresses the life, educational, and spiritual experiences of the author. Each has something of great value to contribute to our understanding. In spirituality, it is best not to be consumed with finding the one "right" way. This can lead to spiritual fundamentalism, which often ends up valuing ways to exclude others, rather than finding essential common truths and harmony.

[1] The perennial tradition or philosophy is based on the principle that there is one absolute truth from which evolves the source of the world's faith traditions. This principle is also found in the *Rig Veda*, the foundation shared by all spiritual traditions in India, as "Truth is one, paths are many."

What Your Journey Through the *Sutras* Will Reveal

Sometimes, the *Yoga Sutras* are described as only for renunciates, as being too strict or not appropriate for our times, or just too obscure.

This text attempts to counter these arguments. Here's what you can expect to find:

- A body of teachings that is filled with images of light and flow.
- A spiritual path that places great value on the beauties, abundance, and importance of nature.
- A philosophy that is permeated with images generally associated with feminine qualities: nurturance, gentility, love, and compassion.[2]

It is the grandest journey: a return to your essence and source, your home.

Are You Really Ready for the *Yoga Sutras*?

The *Yoga Sutras* are a holistic, multi-faceted approach to spirituality. Every aspect of who we are as human beings is embraced and included in a symphony of principles and practices. If you incorporate these teachings into your life, expect to change. Expect doubt, fear, envy, and other such disturbing emotions to decrease. Expect peace, joy, love, and compassion to increase.

You will find yourself being more forgiving of your own shortcomings, as well as those of others. Your knowledge of the world around you, and the ways of life, will grow exponentially. Your mind will be more focused, clear, and tranquil. You will be stronger and more courageous in the face of challenge. Your enthusiasm regarding life and Yoga will soar.

This is Yoga.

[2] Many of the key terms of the *Sutras* are in the feminine gender. See *buddhi*, discriminative faculty, as an example.

This is an Encyclopedia Designed for Discovery

No one believes until they discover for themselves.

In this text, you are free to indulge your curiosity regarding the mysteries of the mind, self, the purpose of life and nature, and ultimately liberation: the experience of your True Nature as pure consciousness, the higher Self or *Purusha.*

Discover how quirky, seemingly irrelevant word defintions can illuminate and expand your understanding of this text.

What does the word root for *mastery* have to do with...

Singing like a bird?

Dhyana, the Sanskrit term for meditation can be literally translated as, *placing in a womb*. How can that help deepen our meditation experience?

There *is* a connection and by understanding it, self-mastery and meditation will take on new, important, and practical dimensions.

This text invites you to discover for yourself the hidden depth and richness the *Yoga Sutras* have to offer.

The gates of wisdom yield to curiosity.

Never cease to stand like curious children before the Great Mystery into which we were born.
– Albert Einstein

Curiosity is lying in wait for every secret.
– Ralph Waldo Emerson

How To Use this Text

It's not necessary to read it from beginning to end – although benefit can be gained from doing so. Have it alongside your favorite translations and commentaries of the *Sutras* and use it to explore sutras that fascinate or perplex you, or to help in preparing a class. Or, dive in wherever you like, and let your curiosity and needs guide you.

Another option is to just simply read the commentaries and the footnotes. That alone will yield a wealth of food for growth.

You can also use this encyclopedia to:

- Discover the subtle dimensions of well-known sutras and those which are lesser known or ambiguous.
- Explore overarching themes through related sutras that are scattered throughout the text.
- Keep inspired and engaged in a path that leads to spiritual liberation and the end of suffering.

Words, Words, Words

The beginning of wisdom is the definition of words.
– Socrates

The Spirit Behind the Letter

Words are matchmakers. They introduce us to most knowledge, but they have limitations. Meanings change over time, and when taken out of their time and culture, we may miss essential subtleties.

For example, *terrible* and *terrific* share the same root. But at some point, their meanings diverged. Today, they are opposites. This phenomenon poses a challenge for anyone attempting to translate an ancient text. As an example, let's look at a key word in the *Sutras*, *tapas*.

It is usually translated as *austerity* or *asceticism*. Two thousand years ago, in India, the inferences of this word would likely have been well understood. Today, *austerity* and *asceticism* tend to conjure images of sad deprivation, or a dour disengagement with the joys and beauties of life.

The challenge is to find wording that keeps the spirit of the word and conveys that spirit to today's student and practitioner. Thus, in this text, *tapas* is translated as *self-discipline and accepting hardships and pain as a help for purification.* Commentary is still needed, but the expanded, interpretive translation hints at an attitude toward life that is not based on a clenched jaw resignation of deprivation. Instead, it is about sorting out priorities and values in life and accepting life's realities with equanimity, faith, and wisdom. *Tapas* teaches us how to convert hardships into times of growth and enrichment.

One Word: Many Definitions

In classic Eastern spiritual and philosophical traditions, the reader or listener is expected to consider most, sometimes all, of a word's meanings in their study. This was the world in which Patanjali taught.

Let's look at an example of how including alternate definitions of a word can enrich our understanding of a sutra:

Yoga means union, but it also means *spiritual disciplines*, *vehicle*, *device*, *remedy*, *meditation*, *fixing of an arrow to a bow string*, and some two dozen other definitions. Now think of all the times you have heard or read the word. How does including any of the above alternate definitions deepen or expand your understanding of what Yoga is?

A Little History Won't Hurt

Some of the terms in this encyclopedia include historical notes. We are all partially a product of our times. Values, priorities, challenges, technology, and methods of communication all affect our beliefs. There are instances when a bit of historical context reveals important subtleties of a sutra.

For example, notice how historical context enriches our understanding of sutra 4.3. Knowing a little about irrigation techniques in ancient India adds a fresh and practical dimension to the wisdom contained in this sutra.

Before Books There Was Group Study

Reading is a solitary process. Solitary study has benefits, but it does suffer from noteworthy weaknesses. It doesn't provide the communal experience of sharing questions and viewpoints that can uncover gaps in our knowledge. It can also lead to limited, personal interpretations based on personal wishes, fears, and life experiences.

It is often said that the sutra format exists to make memorization easier, a definite advantage in a time before books. But, in India, as in many other places, the oral tradition included the memorization of texts of far greater length than the *Sutras*, such as the *Vedas* and the *Bhagavad Gita*.

Instead, consider this: the terseness and ambiguity of the *Sutras* calls for expert guidance. Not only that, but the only way to learn them, the only source, was to find a master teacher who had memorized them.

In India, the transmission of spiritual teachings required a lengthy period of apprenticeship under the guidance of a Guru or adept. The master–apprentice relationship helps minimize the shortcomings of solitary study.

Fingers Pointing to the Moon

Words are launchpads, beginnings of study, tools to attain intellectual understanding, and vehicles for communication. But we should never forget that when speaking of things spiritual, they are always metaphors. They cannot contain truths, only point to them.

The words of spirituality and faith need to be integrated deeply within the mind and heart. The sacred space where this incredible transformation is silence, the silence to which the *Yoga Sutras* faithfully lead us.

However many holy words you read, however many you speak,
what good will they do if you don't act on them?
– The Buddha

Silence is the language of God. All else is poor translation.
– Rumi

Silence is more eloquent than words.
– Thomas Carlyle

Somewhere we know that without silence words lose their meaning.
– Henri Nouwen

Let words inspire us to lead the Yoga life, to be radiators of peace, harmony, and understanding and to turn our vision within to see that light that we already are.

What's in this Text

The Translation

The translation is new. It is also somewhat interpretive, meaning that a few words or phrases are added to the translation in order to reveal the essence of a sutra.

A Word-for-Word Dictionary

This provides the Sanskrit transliterations and English definitions for every word in the *Sutras*. Word roots for most terms used in Patanjali's text are also included.

Extensive Cross-referencing

Key words are cross-referenced to every instance they appear in the *Sutras*. This helps you see the web of principles and practices that link together the sutras. A deeper and more complete understanding of key terms is also gained.

Footnotes

Some terms benefit from brief side trips – a little extra information. These are contained in the footnotes.

Commentary and Reflections

Key terms and definitions include commentaries.

Note that a number of the commentaries refer to Buddhism. Buddhism, which preceded the *Yoga Sutras* by some five centuries, swept through India before Patanjali's time and influenced the traditions, philosophies, and practices of Hinduism. Although Patanjali's vision includes unique teachings, he was nonetheless influenced by Buddhism. However, some sutras also stand as countering certain Buddhist teachings.

A Continuous Translation

To better be able to perceive the flow of the text, and to help knit together the major themes of the *Sutras*, a continuous translation is included.

Topic Index

For many, this is the place to start. Subject matter directly covered by the sutras, or discussed in the reflections or footnotes is listed here. For example, as you scan the topics, you will find, forgiveness and with it, the pertinent sutra to refer to for more information.

Quotes

Sprinkled through the text are quotes from great spiritual masters of different faiths, philosophers, and other great thinkers and luminaries to help illustrate the topic at hand.

The Format

The text is formatted to help you locate the information you need. Examples are given below.

The word-for-word translations and definitions use a standard, academic style, with diacritic marks (dots and lines on certain letters).

The English translations and the commentaries employ a nonstandard method of transliteration. The reason is to help give a sense of the pronunciation. It is admittedly not always consistent, but represents my familiarity with translations and Sanskrit pronunciation.

Sample:

First, the sutra in English:

1.3 When this mistaken perception ends, the Seer (pure, unchanging, eternal consciousness) stands free as the true[3] Self.

Then the Sanskrit transliteration with the diacritic marks. This can be helpful when doing research in Sanskrit dictionaries:

tadā draṣṭuḥ svarūpe' avasthānam

A few sutras will include commentary here, after the Sanskrit. This commentary refers to the sutra as a whole, not on an individual word. It is in this font.

[3] The word "true" in much of Eastern sacred wisdom, is better not thought of as the opposite of false. That kind of binary thinking makes understanding sacred texts difficult. Instead, think of true as meaning essential, fundamental. The Self is our ground and essence. It is not that our human nature is somehow false. It is not. What is false is thinking that this body-mind self is only who we are, when in fact, it is only a small (although important) aspect of self-identity. Our human nature is not false, just falsely perceived and experienced as the root of who we are. The aspect of who we are, that is unchanging, eternal, ground, and essence of who we are, is the Self – *Purusha, Atma.*

The sutras will be broken down into individual words with their definition like below:

tadā = when

then, at that time, in that case

draṣṭuḥ = seer

from ***dṛś*** = to see, perceive, understand, to wait on, to visit, to see with the mind, learn, understand, notice, care for, try, examine, to see by divine intuition, think, find out

the ***Purusha*** – Seer, pure, omniscient consciousness, one who sees, beholder, one who sees well, onlooker, judge, one who examines or decides in a court of law

Any commentary on the individual word, historical or other information relevant to the word under examination, will be in this font. For example, under *draṣṭuḥ* you will find this:

The Seer is the *Purusha*. In the *Sutras*, *Purusha* is also referred to as Self, Owner.

Reflection

Some words include a reflection, a side trip to topics that increases our understanding of the subject under discussion or expand it to matters that are pertinent to the Yoga life.

If a quote is included, it is in this font below:

May Patanjali's words of light and wisdom inspire and enrich your every step on the path to the great silence that leads to liberation.

Chapter One

Samadhi Pada

The Chapter on Absorption

The goal of Yoga is to have an easeful body, a peaceful mind, and a useful life.
– Swami Satchidananda

1.1 Now is the time for Yoga.

atha yoga-anuśāsanam

atha = now

auspicious beginning, expressing the beginning of an action, an interrogation or inquiry into a doubt, after this, next, a condition, as in "after then, now"

Atha traditionally implies an auspicious beginning, a call to attention that something important, delightful, or beneficial is about to happen.

yoga = left untranslated

act of yoking, joining, attaching, harnessing, vehicle, conveyance, employment, use, application, performance, equipping or arraying (of an army), fixing (of an arrow on a bow string), putting on (of armor), a remedy, cure, a means, device, way, manner, method, a supernatural means, charm, incantation, magical art, a trick, strategy, fraud, undertaking, business, work, acquisition, gain, profit, wealth, occasion, opportunity, partaking of, possessing exertion, endeavor, zeal, diligence, industry, care, attention, application or concentration of thoughts, abstract contemplation, meditation (See 1.1–1.2, 2.1, 2.28)[4]

from ***yuj*** = union, unite, join, connect, employ, use

Yoga was a word that was in usage in India in such areas as farming and the military, where it referred to the yoking ("the yoga") of a horse to a plow, or a team of horses to a chariot. In fact, the chariot itself came to be called a "yoga."

[4] Other words in the *Sutras* that contain the word *Yoga* in them:
- yogin (4.7)
- yogyatā (3.54)
- yogyatva (2.41)
- samyoga (2.17, 2.23, 2.25)
- samprayoga (2.44)

The first usage of the word Yoga in its spiritual sense is in the *Katha Upanishad*, a sacred text in which a young boy is instructed in the theories and practices that lead one to liberation from suffering.[5]

Although Yoga can be translated as union, it also includes any and all means that are employed to attain or experience union: all of one's spiritual practices and lifestyle. This implies that Yoga includes much more than the practice of postures, breathing techniques, *mudras*, and *bandhas*.[6] These practices were dubbed *hatha*, meaning *forceful*, to differentiate them from practices, such as meditation, in which the body was not the center of practice.

Yoga, taken in its fullest sense, is holistic, helps to purify body, mind, and spirit, in order to attain an "easeful body, a peaceful mind, and to lead a useful life," as Swami Satchidananda often explained. These benefits combine to bring the seeker to spiritual liberation (*kaivalya*), also called: enlightenment, Self-realization, *samadhi*, nirvana. Regardless of what the final goal is named, it refers to nothing less than the destruction of ignorance and the suffering it brings.

anuśāsanam = (refers to the knowledge of Yoga that will be imparted)

instruction, direction, teaching, knowledge imparted only after the student is ready, command, precept, a follow-up to something else that has formerly occurred or existed, to teach what has been taught before within an existing tradition

from ***anu*** = after, with + ***śāsana*** = teaching, instructing, instructor, government, rule over, an order, command, edict, decree, any written book or work of authority, scripture, from ***śas*** = chastise, correct, restrain, teach

Here's one revealing way of translating this sutra using the roots of the words as a guide:

After our previous knowledge and experience of Yoga, there now arrives this auspicious time when instruction in Yoga is offered, with correction of misperceptions and the removal of doubt.

[5] Steady control of the senses and mind is called Yoga. Those who attain this are freed from delusion. However, once this control is attained, the yogi must be careful, for this state of Yoga can be acquired and then lost. *Katha Upanishad*, 6.11

[6] *Mudras* and *bandhas* are ways of concentrating *prana* (vital energy). *Mudras* are seals, positions, or gestures that focus *prana* and influence the mind. *Bandhas* are locks that concentrate *prana*, binding it to specific areas of the body to direct benefits there.

1.2 Yoga ends the misperception that the Seer/Self is the same as the mind's usual tangle[7] of whirling excursions of thought (*vrittis*)[8].

yogaś citta-vṛtti-nirodaḥ

A full, clear understanding of this sutra is vital if we are to get the most out of our study and practice of Patanjali's sutras, so commentary here will be longer than anywhere else in this text.

yoga = left untranslated: (1.1 – 1.2, 2.1, 2.28)

Refer to 1.1 for more on Yoga.

citta = mind

consciousness (see commentary below), reason, intelligence, noticed, longed for, visible, thinking, reflecting, imagining, pure thought, intention, aim, the heart, the mind, memory, to perceive, attend to, notice, aim at, longed for (*Chandogya Upanishad*), appeared, visible (*Rig Veda*), care for, observing, thought (*Rig Veda*), wish (*Rig Veda*), the need to care for, to cure (to attend to and to cure are related) (See 1.2, 1.30, 1.33, 1.37, 2.54, 3.1, 3.9, 3.11–3.12, 3.19, 3.35, 3.39, 4.4–4.5, 4.15–4.18, 4.21, 4.23, 4.26)

from ***cit*** = to know, observe, perceive, think, be aware, fix the mind upon, attend to, be attentive, take notice of, to aim at, intend, design, be anxious about, care for, resolve to, to understand, comprehend, to become perceptible, instruct, teach, to form an idea in the mind, be conscious of, remembering

[7] Tangle is a perfect word to describe the state of our mental affairs. Tangle = a confused mass of something twisted together; a confused or complicated state. See 2.24, where the confusion of the Seer and seen is identified as being caused by ignorance.

[8] There is one vital point we need to understand from the start. *Nirodha*, usually translated as cessation or restraint, should not be reduced to a one-dimensional meditation practice comprised entirely of forceful attempts at stilling the mind, of stopping all mental activities. Instead, *nirodha* is attained through redirecting one's life focus to the cultivation of a tranquil, powerful inner-directed awareness, acceptance of life's realities, devotion to the sacred, acquisition of reliable knowledge, and following universal moral precepts.

Citta is the individual's mind. It is through *citta* that we experience the world, our life, and build self-identity. It is comprised of three aspects or functions:

- Mind – *manas*, the recording faculty
- Ego sense – *ahamkara*, the sense of individuality
- Intellect – *buddhi*, the discriminative faculty; associated with the will.

Citta is also referred to as *antahkarana*, the inner organ. Although consciousness is present in the *citta*, that consciousness is not innate to it. It is "borrowed," like borrowing the light of the sun in a mirror to brighten a room. In this case, it is the *Purusha* that is the source of light.

Like any other manifestation of nature, the *citta* consists of three fundamental qualities or forces (*gunas*): balance, activity, and inertia. What we experience as consciousness occurs when an object and consciousness (*Purusha*, Seer) "meet." In other words, our individual consciousness is a function of the relationship between *Purusha* and *prakriti*.

It is in this sense that *citta* is perhaps better understood not as a noun, but a verb, a busy center of sensory input, will, memory, moods, feelings, and reason. The *citta* sustains self-identity through the influence of ignorance and, as part of material nature (*prakriti*), it is subject to constant change (see *parinama*, 2.15). This contrasts with the *Purusha* (our Essential Self, True Nature, Self, Seer) which is nothing but pure unchanging, omnipresent, eternal consciousness.

In Hindu astrology, *citta* is the 9th mansion (six stars in the constellation of Hydra), the female water snake whose name, Ashlesha, means the entwiner. It is called the clinging star, and desires to embrace or entangle the object on which it is focused. On the other hand, its deity, *ahi*, is the *naga* or serpent of wisdom whose primary motivation is *dharma* – truth, righteousness. This sign also represents *kundalini*.[9] This indicates that *citta* has two competing potentials: it can entwine and obstruct or it can lead to wisdom through *dharma*.

[9] *Kundalini* = the primordial life force, or cosmic energy, that lies coiled in the root *chakra* (one of the centers of energy in the subtle body) of every individual.

vṛitti = whirling excursions, life focus

rolling, mode of life, conduct, course of action, behavior, moral conduct, kind or respectful behavior or treatment, common practice, character, disposition, mode of being, nature, condition, occurring or appearing in, practice, business, devotion or addiction to, occupation with, activity, function, mood of the mind (Vedanta), a commentary, comment of explanation

from **_vṛt_** = turn, revolve, roll, move, being, conclusion, end of a list, to turn, turn round, revolve, roll (also applied to the rolling down of tears), to move or go on, get along, advance, proceed, take place, occur, be performed, to be, live, exist, be found, remain, stay, abide, dwell, to not be in one's right mind, to dwell or be turned or thought over in the mind, to be of most importance, to live on, subsist by, to depend on, condition, be engaged in or occupied with, to be intent on, attend to, to act, conduct one's self, behave toward, to act or deal with, follow a course of conduct, employ, use, act in any way, toward, to act under another's command, to mind one's own business, to tend or turn to, be alive or present, such continues my opinion, continue in force, be supplied from what precedes, to originate, arise from, to become, to have illicit intercourse with, to cause to turn or revolve, whirl, wave, brandish, hurl, to produce with a turning-lathe, to cause to proceed or take place or be or exist, do, perform, accomplish, display, exhibit (feelings), spend, pass, lead a life, live, enter upon a course of conduct, conduct one's self, behave, to set forth, relate, recount, explain, declare, to begin to instruct, to understand, know, learn (See 1.2, 1.4–1.5, 1.10, 1.41, 2.11, 3.44, 4.18)

Vritti is a term that graphically describes the nature of the mind's fundamental functioning: a constant whirl of activity meant to help us make sense of life and the world around us.[10] This constant whirling means that despite our subjective experience of clear rational thought, human consciousness is a series of fleeting thought excursions.

These thought excursions are for the purpose of discovering which thoughts, words, and actions produce pain and which produce pleasure. The mind is trying to chart a safe, secure course through life. Single thoughts are woven into concepts (also called *vrittis*) and many of these thoughts and conceptions sink into the subconscious where they remain functional as subliminal activators – again *vritti* activity, but on a subconscious level.

[10] This activity continues except in higher contemplative states and deep sleep.

Of particular importance to yogis are the five types of *vrittis* listed in sutra 1.5 and expanded on in sutras 1.6–1.11. The mind is the ship we use for our inner exploration. Knowing the character of these fundamental categories well helps us navigate through life and toward spiritual maturity safely.

It is perhaps best not to limit our understanding of *vrittis* as categories of thoughts. They are much more than that. *Vritti* activity is the conduct, likes and dislikes, values, and priorities – the personality and character – of the mind (*citta-vritti*). It is only when we understand *vritti* well that we can understand the next, all-important term: *nirodha*, a term that will follow us throughout the *Sutras*.

nirodha = ends

to obstruct, restrict, arrest, avert, support, confinement, locking up, imprisonment, investment, siege, enclosing, covering up, restraint, check, control, suppression, destruction

from ***ni*** = down, into, leading, guiding, into, within, inward, back + ***rodha*** = sprouting, growing, moving, upwards, ascending, stopping, checking, obstructing, impeding, suppressing, preventing, confining, surrounding, investing, besieging, blockading, from ***rudh*** = obstruct, arrest, avert, desiring, covering (See 1.2, 1.12, 1.51, 3.9)

Look at the roots of *nirodha*, *nir* and *rodha*:

ni = leading or guiding, down, into inward, back, within

rodha = sprouting, growing, moving upwards, ascending

from *rudha* = desiring, covering, obstruct, arrest, avert

From these roots, we can discern a translation of this word which can read something like:

To *lead or guide within, in order to grow and ascend to the spiritual heights.*[11]

[11] There are many terms in Sanskrit and English that refer to the highest spiritual heights. Here, it is especially appropriate to look to sutra 4.34. The term in that sutra is *citi-shakti:* the power of the highest consciousness.

We will go into this all-important word in some depth since having a clear grasp of the vital nature of *nirodha* is essential to a proper understanding of the *Yoga Sutras of Patanjali*. In the process, we will be referring to sutras that span all four sections of the *Sutras*.

Although *nirodha* is usually interpreted as the cessation of thought, we will find that this definition limits the real and practical intent of the word.

The clearing of all mental activity is the means, not the end. The goal is the cessation not of thought activity, but of the misperception of body-mind as Self, Seer, Spirit, pure infinite, eternal, consciousness.

Nirodha: How it is Cultivated

In sutras 1.12–1.16, we find the ground for the development of *nirodha*: practice and nonattachment. Practice is defined as regular, repeated efforts to break free from misperception of the mind as Self/Seer. For practice to bring benefits, it needs to be carefully nurtured for a long time, engaged in faithfully, with inner reflection, and fervor.

Nirodha's sweetest fruits arise when practice is paired with nonattachment, self-mastery and freedom from craving. Nonattachment naturally arises when the love of the attainment of liberation from ignorance, and the suffering it brings, becomes stronger than the desire for sense-satisfaction and self-centered thoughts of status and acknowledgment. Craving for objects seen, heard, or described in sacred tradition, pale in comparison to inner discoveries made by the yogi. Sense pleasures can still be enjoyed, but they cease to be the center of life.

Can you imagine a life without fear, envy, anger, or hatred – a life permanently rooted in joy and unconditional loving kindness? Spiritually mature yogis don't have to imagine it. They live it.

Nirodha: A State, a Process, a Way of Life

In its final manifestation, *nirodha* is a state in which the mind has become utterly steady, clear, one-pointed, and free from selfish attachment. It is the state of mind that brings about Yoga: union, harmony, and integration of all aspects of the individual and of the individual with nature. It is *kaivalya* – liberation from suffering brought by ignorance.

As a process, *nirodha* is multileveled and multifaceted. For most seekers, it usually begins with a contemplative practice, such as meditation or prayer. These practices alone bring great benefit, but to attain the ultimate goal of Self-realization or spiritual liberation, a comprehensive approach is needed. As evidence of this, you will see that the path recommended for the cultivation of *nirodha* spans the entire text.

For the sincere seeker, the development of *nirodha* is not just about getting better at meditation. *Nirodha* is also a turning point in life. It is adopting a fresh, vibrant way of life that is grounded in timeless wisdom while adapting to today's needs.

This turning point, to be authentic, is preceded by clear, honest self-examination, and a reassessment of goals and priorities. This deep introspection could follow a time of stress or challenge, or by an experience or experiences of great upliftment of mind and heart. Usually it is only great suffering or great joy that provokes the kind of fundamental changes we have to accomplish to truly grow in Spirit.

The main question boils down to this: Who owns your heart? Is it the world with its emphasis on material success, status, and acknowledgment, or the experience of the Highest Truth, Spirit – what we call God?

Nirodha's Adversary: *Vyutthana*[12]

Vyutthana, externalization of the mind, is the predominant characteristic of ordinary consciousness. The temptation might be to characterize *nirodha* as a mind in meditation and *vyutthana* as a mind tempted by distractions of the outside world. While this is true, it is not the whole story. The difference between the two mindsets is more comprehensive.

Vyutthana, as a mindset, is not necessarily evil or wrong, but is based on an allegiance to the priorities and values that work against, or that can hinder, Self-realization.

[12] This activity continues except in higher contemplative states and deep sleep.

The symptoms of *vyutthana* include:

- Pursuing status
- Nurturing or ignoring craving for happiness or security through material acquisitions
- The need to be acknowledged or praised, and resentment when we are not
- Low self-esteem that needs constant affirmation of worth – all these, and more, are symptoms of *vyutthana*

When we sit to meditate or find time for quiet self-examination, we most likely encounter what seems like a haphazard assortment of thoughts, habits, images, and emotions. These are not simply a random collection of mental artifacts. Most are aligned with one organizing principle: *vyutthana*.

Egoism and ignorance may be the bedrock of the self-identity, but *vyutthana* provides an externalized orientation that easily appeals to the mind. *Vyutthana* is strengthened by:

- Societal values that measure success, status, and happiness by material gain
- Lack of curiosity regarding the True Nature of self and life
- Deeply ingrained habits formed under the influence of ignorance that sustain unwanted attitudes and behaviors

Like Darth Vader to Luke Skywalker or Dracula to Van Helsing, *vyutthana* is the arch opponent to *nirodha*.

A mind caught in *vyutthana* always looks outside itself for satisfaction, for shelter from fear, loneliness, anger, and hatred. It also blames the outside world for its pains, too rarely looking within honestly to see how our own ideas and actions have contributed to our discomfort and unhappiness. In short, force of *vyutthana* resists probing within for the deep and abiding source of peace and happiness.

In sutra 3.9, we find that *nirodha* is presented as the remedy for *vyutthana*. If *vyutthana* is a centrifugal force ever urging our attention away from our center, then *nirodha* is the centripetal force, moving the mind toward its source and essence. Every moment of *nirodha*, or of inward reflection, every mantra repeated, every instant spent clarifying and strengthening our understanding of what is truly precious and worthwhile in life, creates a counterflow, an inwardly directed movement that leads to enlightenment. The movement inward – *nirodha* – is the journey of all journeys.

Degrees of *Nirodha*

Think of *nirodha* as degrees of success in countering *vyutthana*. Let's look at the stages of *nirodha* as outlined in the *Sutras*, how they relate to some of the practices included in the text.

You can attain *nirodha* over *vrittis* (conceptions and conceptualizing), *pratyaya* (single thoughts that comprise *vrittis*), *samskaras* (subconscious impressions) and complete *nirodha* over all states of mind. How *nirodha* is attained over these states of mind is from gross to subtle:

Vritti Nirodha – countered by *dharana*/concentration
Conceptions, our biases, and personal interpretations of reality, begin to unravel.

Pratyaya Nirodha – countered by *dhyana*/meditation
Vritti activity of creating concepts from combining single thoughts is suspended. The mind experiences its first moments of deep, steady, focused attention. Inner obstacles are reduced, the mind becomes clear and cheerful, and the senses begin to come under control.

Samskara Nirodha – countered by *samadhi*/absorption
Samadhi is the yogi's prime investigative tool to explore life, the universe, self, and Self and arises when the mind becomes deeply absorbed in the object of contemplation.

Subconscious impressions gradually diminish in power and number from the first stages of *samadhi: samprajnata samadhi*. Intuitive insights are attained.[13] One gains full knowledge of gross aspects of the object of meditation, then the subtle factors that brought the object into existence. This is followed by the bliss of a steady mind, and then the experience of the pure ego sense.

[13] Refer to 1.17 and 1.41.

A deeper *samadhi, asamprajnata*, gradually arises in which conscious activity is quieted and only subconscious impressions remain (1.18). In sutra 1.23, *asamprajnata samadhi* can also be attained through *Ishvara pranidhana*, devotion to God.

Nirvichara samadhi: Insights into even the most subtle aspects of the object of meditation are completed. The luminous, tranquil clarity of the Self shines forth. This state is truth-bearing, granting intuitive insights into the deepest realities of existence, self-identity, the mind, and the universe. The purpose of this insight is to end false identification with *prakriti* by discerning the Seer from the seen. The *samskaras* from this *samadhi* displace all other *samskaras* (See 3.9 – 3.12).

When even this *samskara* is transcended, *nirbija samadhi* arises – the technical term for Self-realization or liberation.

> *Sarva nirodha – dharmamegha samadhi/cloud of dharma samadhi*: What can be left after attaining *nirodha* over concepts, thoughts, and subconscious impressions? The subtlest thought of all – the individual ego sense. When all the other facets of the mind are transcended, what's left is the one thought that binds all mental experiences together, the "I" sense. Continuous discriminative discernment of the highest level – *dharmamegha samadhi* – is required to reach this stage.

We might also wonder why Patanjali only mentions attaining *nirodha* over the *vrittis*. For one, *vritti* activity, and the conceptions it creates, comprise the bulk of our conscious life and more importantly, our understanding of realities and experiences. They are a major influence regarding what we consider important, essential, desirable, and undesirable. Another reason why only *vrittis* are mentioned might be because once mastery over *vrittis* is attained, self-effort begins to recede as the core of practice. Refer to sutra 3.2, the sutra that defines meditation. Look at the Sanskrit. You will not see the word *vritti* there. Instead, it describes a state of unbroken attention toward a single thought – a *pratyaya*. *Vritti* activity is no longer a factor when the mind reaches the state of meditation proper. Remember that meditation is a state of effortless attention, even though in the beginning, that effortless flow may only continue for a few seconds.

Nirodha as the Root of Intuitive Insight

One of the major themes in the *Sutras* is the ability to distinguish between the mind, even the completely tranquil mind - and the Self, our True Nature. This ability is called *viveka* (discriminative discernment) or *Yoga pratyaksha* (yogic vision). It is first presented in sutra 2.26 as the requirement to overcome ignorance. *Viveka* can be cultivated by following the eight limbs of Yoga (2.29).[14] Together, these eight limbs keep the mind focused and moving toward our center.

Although *Yoga pratyaksha* is not mentioned in the *Sutras, pratyaksha* - direct perception - is given as one of the means to attain reliable knowledge. *Yoga pratyaksha*, the highest order of direct perception, occurs without the aid of the senses.[15] This degree of insight is needed to distinguish between the calm, clear mind - which is still founded on a quiet subtle ego - and the Self. The good news is that *Yoga pratyaksha* is developed through a multi-faceted collection of practices and lifestyle changes. Small, definite steps lead to great accomplishments in Yoga.

Nirodha and the Moral Life

Nirodha is turning toward what is real and abiding, our essence and source, the root of all experiences of peace and happiness. Patanjali's Yoga takes this into account by offering principles and guidance for cultivating *nirodha* in and through everyday life. The main observances are:

Yamas and *niyamas*: the moral and ethical foundation of Yoga. (See 2.29–2.45)

Pratipaksha Bhavanam: the cultivation of a counterforce as an aid to following the *yamas* and *niyamas* and to counteract the unsettling influence of any disturbing thought. (See 2.33–2.34).

The Four Locks and Four Keys: ways to attain and maintain a tranquil mind under all circumstances (See 1.33).

[14] *Yama, niyama, asana, pranayama, pratyahara, dharana, dhyana, samadhi.*

[15] The term is common to both the Nyaya and Vaisesika schools of philosophy and was likely first used by the sage Prasastapada in his commentary on the *Vaisesika Sutras* in 6 BCE.

There is one more principle to explore before we leave *nirodha*: *pratiprasava*, returning to the source.

Nirodha is a Return to Our Source

The word, *pratiprasava* only occurs twice in the *Sutras*[16] but it is a central theme.

The process that began with turning inward – away from the *vrittis* and the externalized state of mind – then continued with the single thoughts, *pratyaya*, and finally the subconscious impressions, finds its culmination with *pratiprasava*. Nature, which has been the good, reliable teacher and guide, has finished her job of transformation of the individual.[17]

The idea of nature returning to its source needs a bit of explanation, since as a feature of spiritual growth, it represents a personal, subjective experience. It is the gradual ending of the differentiation of matter into objects – the stilling of all physical activity for the yogi. Once completely quieted, the yogi experiences the Self/*Purusha* – it now stands apart from the dance of Spirit and nature. We can use the phenomenon of sound as an example.

Sound requires two factors: something to vibrate that generates the sound waves and a medium, like air, to propagate the sound. Think of a church bell ringing. The striking of the bell creates the vibration/sound. The components and particles in the air then transmit that vibration, spreading the sound. Without any further stimulus, the sound of the bell fades, but its reverberations continue for a while as the sound waves travel through the air. The distance the sound travels, depends on how strong the original vibration was and the amount of obstacles the waves encounter that dissipate the sound waves. Eventually, we return to quiet. The bell and the air continue to exist, but they have returned to their source: potentiality.

---

[16] In sutra 2.10, *pratiprasava*, returning to the source, is another way of referring to *nirbija samadhi*, the highest *samadhi*. It is described as the state that overcomes all obstacles even in their subtle form. In *sutra* 4.34, the last sutra, *pratiprasava*, is the transcendence of all the limitations of nature in order to experience the pure power of the highest consciousness.

[17] See 2.18: the seen (nature) consists of the elements and sense organs and has the qualities of illumination, activity, and inertia. Its purpose is to provide experiences and liberation.

Similarly, for advanced yogis, the inwardly directed one-pointed focus removes all stimuli allowing for the mind to return to its source: *Purusha*. For the yogi, nature (*prakriti*) has finished its job.

We can infer a final stage of spiritual development. Fully matured yogis don't remain sitting in the deepest of meditative states. They are still human beings. The final stage of liberation remains: to integrate the experience of Self-realization into the physical world in order to be of service to others. This is what is known as becoming a *jivanmukta* - one who is fully liberated while still in the physical body.

1.3 When this mistaken perception ends, the Seer (pure, unchanging, eternal consciousness) stands free as the true Self.[18]

tadā draṣṭuḥ svarūpe' avasthānam

tadā **= when**

then, at that time, in that case

draṣṭuḥ **= seer**

from ***dṛś*** = to see, perceive, understand, to wait on, to visit, to see with the mind, learn, understand, notice, care for, try, examine, to see by divine intuition, think, find out

The Seer is the *Purusha*. In the *Sutras*, *Purusha* is also referred to as Self, Owner, or *Atma*.[19]

svarūpe **= true Self**

true, nature, one's own form or shape, the form or shape of, own condition, peculiarity, character, nature, having one's own peculiar form or character, having a

[18] The word *true*, in much of Eastern sacred wisdom, is best not limited to meaning the opposite of false. That kind of binary thinking makes understanding sacred texts difficult. Instead, think of *true* as meaning *essential*, fundamental. The Self is our ground and essence. It is not that our human nature is somehow false, as in the sense of wrong. What is false, is thinking that the body-mind self is only who we are, when in fact it is only a small (although important) aspect of self-identity. Our human nature is not false, just falsely perceived and experienced, as the root of who we are. Our source, origin, and essence is the unchanging, eternal Self – *Purusha, Atma.*

[19] *Purusha* = pure, omniscient consciousness, one who sees, beholder, one who sees well, onlooker, judge, one who examines or decides in a court of law

like nature or character, a particular relation, similar, like (in Samkhya philosophy), kind, sort, occurrence, event, pleasing, handsome, wise, learned, in reality, by nature, the state of one's nature, the True Nature of being, the essential nature of Reality (*Brahman*): *sat-cit-ananda* (existence, awareness, bliss) (See 1.3, 1.43, 2.23, 2.54, 3.3, 3.45, 3.48, 4.34)

from ***sva*** = own, self + ***rūpa*** = form, nature, body, visible thing

Although this term can be translated in various ways, its fundamental spirit is the essential nature or form of something, or, as in this sutra, the essential or True Nature of the individual – the Seer or Self.

avasthānam **= stands free**

stands, dwells, standing, taking up one's place, situation, condition, residing, stability, train station

from ***ava*** = off, away, down + ***sthanā*** = stand, from ***sthā*** = stand, to stand out, stand firmly, to be distinctive, be prominent, attract attention, be noticeable, conspicuous, be striking, be obvious, be conspicuous, endure, continue, get upon, take a position on, remain, stay, continue with any action, to remain occupied or engaged in, depend on, to arise from, strengthen, confirm, support, to fix, to give in marriage, to preserve, be intent on, make a practice of, persevere in any act, to exist, to be present, to belong to

Avasthanam in this context can have many shades of meaning, all appropriate to the sutra. Many translations read something like: *Then the Seer rests (or abides) in its True Nature*. This may suggest that our essential Self is fatigued or subject to change. This is not the case. What this word is indicating is that as a seeker progresses on the spiritual path, glimpses of a self that transcends all former notions of self-identity begin to emerge. In the beginning they come and go. With continued practice, they increase in depth, breadth, and length until a direct, ever-stable experience of the Self that is always present, always infinite, beyond space and time is realized. In other words, the experience of the Self becomes stable – it rests.

This leads us to a subtler understanding of what is meant by the Seer *standing apart*. Our conceptions of the Seer, Self, Cosmic Consciousness, or God is part reason, part faith, part experience, but largely projection. When we say that the Seer stands apart, we mean the Seer experienced as it is – free of the overlay and colorations of our biases, hopes, fears, and conceptions. We gradually learn to allow God to be God, to resist shrinking the highest reality to fit our limited ego's vision. This understanding resonates with sutra 2.5, which discusses the major, most impactful manifestations of ignorance. Four are listed: regarding what changes as changeless, what is impure with what is pure, what brings pain as that which brings contentment, and lastly, regarding the non-Self as the Self. This last one – projecting our conceptions onto Reality – is what we are discussing here. These manifestations of ignorance are what stand between every seeker and Self-realization. They permeate every corner of our minds, every moment of our lives. To correct our perception, to transform our minds so that the Self/Seer can be realized, takes a holistic approach, the kind of approach typified by Yoga. That is why Yoga is not just about the formal practices, but how we live our lives.

Avasthanam also resonates with a fundamental theme found in the *Sutras*: to identify or discern the difference between the mind (especially, a clear, tranquil mind) and *prakriti*. That is why one good translation of *avasthanam* is: *to stand away from, or stand apart from*. This definition suggests the freedom that arises from experiencing the Seer as different from, or liberated from, the seen.[20] The Seer doesn't fully express in an individual until the confusion between the pure, eternal consciousness that is the Seer and the seen, as body-mind is removed. Removing this confusion is the end goal of all Yoga practice and theory. (See 2.17, 2.23, 2.25)

1.4 Otherwise, the mind continues to mistake the whirling excursions of thought (*vrittis*) as the Self.

vṛitti-sārūpyam itaratra

vṛitti = left untranslated

whirling excursions (See 1.2, 1.4–1.5, 1.10, 1.41, 2.11, 3.44, 4.18)

Refer to 1.2 for more on *vritti*.

sārūpyam = mistake

takes the form or likeness, similarity of form, proper, suitable, fit, assimilation

[20] Patanjali calls this state *kaivalya*, independence or isolation.

to or conformity with the deity, resemblance, identity of appearance, one of the grades of *mukti* or beatitude (*Bhagavata Purana*).

from ***sā*** = with, junction, together, along with, having, possessing, accompanied by + ***rūpya*** = any outward appearance or phenomenon or color, form, shape, figure, in the form of, to assume a form, formed or composed of, feature, marker, sign, symptom, likeness, image, stamped, impressed, in the possession of, or possessed by, proceeding from or originating with, impressions in the possession of, from ***rūpa*** = form

The mind mistakes the forms the *vrittis* take as being the Self.

itaratra **= otherwise**

at other times, elsewhere, on the other hand

1.5 There are five types of *vrittis*. Those that are afflicted by ignorance of one's True Self bring pain. Without the influence of ignorance, they are painless.

vrittayah pañcatayyaḥ kliṣṭa-akliṣṭa

vrittayah **= left untranslated**

mental excursions (See 1.2)

pañcatayyaḥ **= five kinds**

fivefold, having five parts

from ***pañc*** = five + ***taya*** = fold

kliṣṭa **= afflicted**

painful, molested, distressed, wearied, hurt, injured, troubling, being in bad condition, connected with pain and suffering (see 2.3, the *klesas*, which share the same root)

from ***kliś*** = torment, distress, to cause pain, afflict

In Buddhism *klishta* means *trouble, defilement, passion.* It refers to all the properties that dull the mind, and are the basis for all unwholesome (*akushala*) actions and thus bind people to the cycle of rebirth.

In the *Visuddhi Magga*, ten are listed: craving, hate, delusion, pride, false views, doubt, rigidity, excitability, shamelessness, lack of conscience.

***aklișța* = without influence of ignorance**

not afflicted, untroubled, painless, undisturbed

from ***a*** = not + ***klișța*** = afflicted

1.6 The five types are:

- **Reliable knowledge**
- **Unreliable knowledge**
- **Knowledge based on words without substance**
- **Sleep**
- **Remembering**

pramāṇa-viparyaya-vikalpa-nidrā-smṛitayaḥ

pramāṇa* = *reliable knowledge

valid cognition, correct notion, right perception, measure scale, proof

from ***pra*** = before, forward + ***māna*** = means of proof, demonstrating, from ***mā*** = to measure, display, prepare, standard, measure of any kind (size, extent, circumference, length, distance, multitude, quantity, duration, etc.), measure in music, dancing in harmony with music, measure of physical strength, capital as opposed to interest, right measure, authority

The essence of *pramana* is knowledge that has been demonstrated to be true, valid, and reliable by one of the methods Patanjali will list in the next sutra (direct perception, inference, authoritative testimony).

Pramana stands as a reminder that regardless of the source, only knowledge that has been tested and proven can dependably and consistently be used by the yogi.

We can also understand *pramana* as processes for acquiring knowledge in which thought and senses are not deceived. Compare *pramana* to *viparaya* – unreliable knowledge (sutra 1.8) – in which knowledge is attained through faulty perception, inference, memory, or inaccurate or incomplete data.

Reliable knowledge allows us to make wise, informed decisions that advance us to our spiritual goals.

Reflection

We think of knowledge mostly as a collection of facts, ideas, and images. That's only partly true. The root of knowledge is a force that is like fire. Reliable data is like feeding a fire with good dry wood. If the data digests well, the fire blazes hotter and gives off more light. More light equals more wisdom, more insight.

This means it is important not only to feed your knowledge fire with reliable data, but also to absorb and integrate it into your life through contemplation and practice.

Undigested knowledge and unreliable knowledge (see *viparayaya*, next), chokes the fire, leading to sustaining ignorance, misperception, and confusion.

viparyaya = unreliable knowledge

misconception, error, misapprehension, reversed, inverted, perverse, contrary to, turning around, revolution, running off, coming to an end, transposition, change, alteration, inverted order to succession, opposite of, change for the worse, reverse of fortune, calamity, misfortune, change of purpose or conduct, enmity, hostility, mistake, shunning, avoiding, forms of intermittent fever

from ***vi*** = asunder, away + ***pari*** = around

Viparyaya is the opposite of *pramana* (1.7). It is knowledge based on misperception. It happens when we are misinformed, underinformed, or completely ignorant of a subject, occurrence, or person.

Knowledge can also be corrupted by the passage of time, by biases, or when our judgment is hampered by self-centered desires, greed, fear, or anger.

***vikalpa* = knowledge based on words without substance**

conceptualization, imagination

from ***vi*** = asunder, away + ***kalpa***, from ***klp*** = correspond, in accordance with, suitable to

Yogis are called on to be well aware of the ways of the world. Until intuitive insight gives rise to the expanded capacity to discern the subtle realities imperceptible by the senses, our beliefs need to be validated. The yogi is very careful not to be influenced by words alone, without any trusted, independent source to validate them. The next sutra details the means of corroboration.

***nidrā* = sleep**

from ***ni*** = down + ***drā*** = sleep

***smṛitayaḥ* = remembering**[21]

memory

from ***smṛ*** = to recollect, bear in mind, think of, be mindful of, to hand down from memory, by heart, teach, declare, to recite

1.7 *Vrittis* bring reliable knowledge – knowledge that is trustworthy and useful – through:

- **Information obtained from the senses' direct contact with sense objects**
- **Inference properly applied**
- **Authoritative testimony**

pratyakṣa-anumāna-āgamāḥ pramāṇāni

Let us enter into the house of knowledge of ourselves.
– St. Catherine of Siena

[21] The term "remembering," is used here instead of the more common "memory" since, being a *vritti*, it is an activity, not simply a storehouse of subconscious impressions.

***pratyakṣa* = direct contact with a sense object**

direct perception, apprehended by the senses, present before the eyes, visible, perceptible, clear, distinct, manifest, direct, immediate, actual, real, ocular evidence

from ***prati*** = against, back, in the direction of, in the presence of, near to, upon, to go to meet, to resort or apply to, recognize, to make clear, to prove, to try to understand + ***akṣ*** = eye, sense of sight, or to reach, penetrate, embrace

Pratyaksha can be translated as in the *presence of sight or to reach the presence of.* It is considered a valid means of acquiring knowledge by all schools of philosophy in India.

There is another, higher form of *pratyaksha*: *yoga pratyaksha*. Born of a spiritually mature mind that has attained a high degree of one-pointedness and nonattachment, *Yoga pratyaksha* is direct perception of subtle realities beyond the reach of the senses.

***anumāna* = inference**

consideration, reflection, permission, consent, the act of inferring or drawing a conclusion from given premises, reflection, guess, conjecture, a means of attaining valid knowledge

from ***anu*** = along, after + ***māna*** = means of proof, demonstration, from ***mā*** = to measure, prepare, display

***āgamāḥ* = authoritative testimony**

traditional doctrine or precept, a sacred work, wisdom that has come down from tradition, revealed scripture

from ***ā*** = hither, unto, toward + ***gama*** = going, from ***gam*** = to go, more

We can see that *agamah* suggests *movement toward*, theories and practices that advance seekers toward their goal.

The most common understanding of *agamah* is scripture or sacred wisdom that has been handed down from teacher to pupil through the ages. The teachings of the Guru are considered to have the same weight as scripture.

Traditionally, *agamah* is concerned with four topics:

- Temple construction
- The making of sculpted dieties and other holy objects
- Philosophy
- Meditative practices and methods of worship

pramāṇāni **= reliable knowledge** (See 1.6)

A *pramana* is an instrument, means, or method for reaching a valid grasp (*prama*) of a state, condition, fact, or object.

1.8 Knowledge is unreliable when based on errors in perception, which result in false information regarding the True Nature of an object or event.

viparyayo mithyājñānam atad rūpa-pratiṣṭham

viparyaya **= unreliable knowledge**

error, misapprehension, reversed, inverted, perverse, contrary, turning around, revolution, running off, coming to an end, transposition, change, alteration, inverted order or succession, opposite of, exchange, barter, buying and selling, trade, change for the worse, reverse of fortune, calamity, misfortune, perverseness, change of purpose or conduct, enmity, hostility, mistake, shunning, avoiding.

from ***i*** = to go, flow, or get about + ***vi*** = asunder or away + ***pari*** = around

Viparyaya is perceiving an object as different from what it actually is (Refer to 1.6 for more on *viparyaya*).

mithyājñānam **= false information**

unreliable or false knowledge

from ***mithya*** = to conflict with or dispute, inverted, contrary, wrongly, improperly, falsely, deceitfully, untruly, to no purpose, fruitlessly, personified as the wife of ***adharma*** + ***jñāna*** = to know, knowledge, knowing, becoming acquainted with, higher knowledge derived from meditation, conscience, from ***jñā*** = to know, have knowledge, perceive, apprehend, experience, recognize, ascertain, investigate, regard or consider as, take possession of, to visit as a friend, examine, to conjecture

Mithya suggests that the perception is neither entirely real nor unreal. Since there is perception involved, the object perceived must exist. However, it is understood or perceived improperly. Ordinarily, perception is a complex event that includes the object being perceived, the senses, the mind (with its memories, biases, and limitations), and the experience of sensing itself.

Any one of these factors has limitations or can be corrupted by mental error and can result in *mithyajnanam*, false information.

The most fundamental form of false information is regarding the instrument of knowing (the mind) with the principle of consciousness (*Purusha*).

atad = *(refers to errors in perception)*

not that

This word implies that what is being perceived is not the true essence or nature of the object.

rūpa = nature

form, appearance, figure, likeness, shape, feature, any outward appearance, phenomenon, or color

pratiṣṭham = based on

standing firmly, steadfast, point of support, center or base of anything

from ***prati*** = down upon, near to, in opposition to + ***sthā*** = to stand

This is the first of fifteen words that contain the root *stha, to stand.* The root has one of the longest lists of meanings in the *Sutras*. What follows are most, but not all of the definitions: *to stand, to stand firmly, station one's self, stand upon, to take up a position on, to stay, remain, continue in any condition or action, to remain occupied or engaged in, be intent on, make a practice of, keep on, persevere in any act, to continue to be or exist, endure, to be present, be obtainable or at hand, to be with or at the disposal of, belong to, abide by, be near to, be on the side of, adhere or submit to, comply, serve, obey, stop, halt, wait, tarry, linger, hesitate, to behave or conduct oneself, to be directed to or fixed in, to be founded or rest or depend on, to rely on, confide in, resort to, arise from, to remain*

unnoticed, be left alone, to affirm, settle, determine, direct or turn toward. (See 1.8, 1.13, 1.35, 1.41, 2.18, 2.35–2.37, 2.39, 2.46, 3.38, 3.45, 3.53, 4.34)

1.9 Words without substance refers to knowledge that is based on words alone without any tangible reality to verify it.

śabda-jñāna-anupātī vastu-śūnya vikalpaḥ

śabda **= expressed in words**

based on sounds, oral, verbal, resting on or enjoined by sacred sound, relating to sound, verbal testimony, oral tradition

jñāna **= knowledge**

becoming acquainted with, knowledge (especially higher knowledge), conscience, engaging in, perception, investigation, to acknowledge, to allow (See 1.9, 1.38, 1.42, 2.28, 3.16–3.19, 3.22, 3.26, 3.28–3.29, 3.36, 3.53, 3.55, 4.31)

Reflection: Knowledge vs. Wisdom

Jnana**, defined here as knowledge, is also frequently translated as wisdom. In general, the words can be interchangeable, although, in this text, they have been assigned slightly different meanings.**

Knowledge, as the *Oxford Dictionary* defines it, is facts, information, and skills; the theory of a subject. In philosophical circles, knowledge is defined as that which is true; justified belief; to have certainty in what is understood, as opposed to opinion.

Wisdom, according to the *Oxford Dictionary*, is having experience, knowledge and good judgment; the quality of being wise; the wise application of knowledge. This last definition is also how wisdom is used in this text. It is the result of intuitive insight (*prajna*), a direct experiential grasp of truths rather than understanding based on reasoning alone.

anupātī **= based on**

following as a consequence or result, to fall after, to follow, derived from

from ***anu*** = after + ***pāt*** = to fall (this is the same root as in the name, Patanjali = ***pat*** (the falling to earth of) ***anjali*** (grace)

vastu = tangible reality

object, item, natural disposition, house, becoming dawn, morning, the seat or place of, the real, the right thing, a valuable or worthy object, subject matter, the pith or substance of anything, any real existing or abiding substance or essence, matter, seat or place, theme, the thing in question, affair, existential property

from ***vas*** = live, dwell, remain, abide

śūnya = without

void, empty, barren, destitute of, possessing nothing, hollow, having no certain object or aim, distracted, wholly alone, having no friends, free from, missing, void of results, ineffectual, free from sensitivity or sensation, bare, naked, innocent, indifferent, a deserted place, absolute nonexistence, space, heaven, atmosphere

from ***śū***, ***śvā***, or ***śvi*** = to swell

vikalpaḥ = conceptualization

alternation, alternative, option, variation, combination, variety, diversity, contrivance, difference of perception, distinction, indecision, doubt, hesitation, false notion, fancy, imagination, calculation, (in grammar) the admission of an option or alternative, the allowing of a rule to be observed or not at one's pleasure

from ***vi*** = asunder or away + ***kalpaḥ***, from = ***klp*** = to correspond, in accordance with, suitable to

Refer to 1.6 for more on *vikalpah*.

Vikalpah implies that the mind creates a reality according to its imagination. This is not always a bad thing. *Vikalpah*, as creativity and imagination, is an integral aspect of the arts. *Vikalpah* is also used in creating metaphors (as in the *trapdoor* of depression) and similes (as in *brave* as a lion). This demonstrates that *vikalpah* can include a statement that is meaningful, even though it is without an external reality.

But, in the realm of Yoga and spirituality, for knowledge to be considered reliable, there needs to be an actual object of experience (*artha*) to corroborate it or there needs to be corroboration by an accomplished teacher or other generally accepted authoritative source, such as scripture.

1.10 Deep sleep occurs when the waking and dreaming states (*vrittis*) are naturally overcome by inertia.[22] There is only awareness of the thought of non-existence.

abhāva-pratyaya-ālambanā vṛitti nidrā

abhāva **= overcome**

absence, non-existence, annihilation, non-entity.

from ***bhāva*** = being, becoming, from ***bhū*** = to be

Abhava, non-becoming, is the desire to get rid of something.

In deep sleep, the mind's waking and dreaming activities are absent because they are overcome by *tamas*.

In Buddhism, *bhava* is a process of becoming conditioned by the mind's identification with the factors that make up our sense of individuality. It is related to craving.

pratyaya **= the mind's waking and dreaming activities**

fundamental notion or idea (Buddhism, Jainism), cognition, thoughts, firm conviction, intention, basis, the content of individual consciousness, cooperating cause (Buddhism), motive, cause (see 1.19), trust, belief, certainty of, solution, explanation, ground, the image of an object imprinted on the mind[23] (See 1.10, 1.18–1.19, 2.20, 3.2, 4.27)

from ***prati*** = against, back + ***aya*** = going, from ***i*** = to go forth

Like many of the terms in the *Yoga Sutras*, *pratyaya* has a number of definitions making it difficult to determine which one best fits or best captures the sense of the sutra.

In the *Yoga Sutras*, *pratyaya* can generally be understood as an idea or condition of mind. It is the content of individual consciousness at any

[22] *Tamas*, one of the three qualities of nature: *sattva* (balance), *rajas* (activity), and *tamas* (inertia).

[23] The powers behind the five senses (*jnanendriyas*, the organs of knowledge) flow out through the senses, with the mind as the internal organ (*antahkarana*) to grasp their objects and then imprint images of these objects on the mind, which presents them to *Purusha*.

given moment. It can also be regarded as the thought that immediately arises when the mind is impacted by a stimulus.

Comparing *pratyaya* with *vritti,* we can say that *vritti* is an underlying mental process, the fluctuation of individual awareness as the mind searches for what brings pleasure and what threatens it with pain and suffering. *Pratyaya* provides both the content of *vrittis*, and their significance (including ideas of self-identity) as well. Together, *pratyaya* and *vritti* constitute the primary mode of consciousness that absorbs our time and attention on a daily basis.

For Buddhists and Jains, *pratyaya* is a fundamental notion or idea. Buddhism also regards *pratyaya* as a cooperating cause of individual consciousness.

ālambanā = there is

support, depending on, based on, resting on

Perception is a three-part process that requires a perceiver, the act of perception, and an object (or support) of perception. The supporting object in deep sleep is the dormant mind.

vṛitti = *left untranslated*

seesaw whirling excursions of the mind, fluctuations of individual consciousness, modifications of the mind, the mind's attempt at understanding life experiences – looking for what is beneficial or pleasurable and trying to avoid that which is not (See 1.2, 1.4–1.5, 1.10, 1.41, 2.11, 3.44, 4.18)

***nidrā* = deep sleep**

sleepiness, sloth, the budding state of a flower

from ***ni*** = back, in, into, within, down + ***drā*** = to sleep

1.11 Remembering is the recollection of objects and occurrences that have been experienced.

anubhūta-viṣaya-asaṃpramoṣaḥ smṛitiḥ

***anubhūta* = experienced**

perceived, understood, apprehended, resulted from, followed as a consequence, tasted, tried, enjoyed

***viṣaya* = objects**

that which is experienced through the senses, condition, sphere of activity or concern

from ***viṣ*** = to be active, or from ***vi*** = asunder, away + ***si*** = extend

***asaṃpramoṣaḥ* = remembering**

not forgotten, not escaping, not being stolen, not allowing to be carried off, refraining from acquiring objects that are not yours

from ***a*** = not + ***sam*** = together + ***pra*** = before, forward + ***moṣa*** = to steal, rob, theft, from ***muṣ*** = to steal

Sam is an important prefix. We see it in key terms such as *samadhi* (absorption, contemplation) and *samyoga* (conjunction). Its meanings include: *along, with, together, union, thoroughness, intensity, completeness*.

The word "remembering" is used in this translation because it suggests it is part of a process of collecting, storing, and recollecting past mental impressions, while memory implies only the storehouse of past impressions.

***smṛitiḥ* = recollection**

memory, awareness, desire, tradition, mindfulness, handed down, taught, prescribed, enjoined by traditional law, declared or propounded in law books, declared as, passing for, styled, named, recollection, remembrance

from ***smṛta*** = remembered, recollected, called to mind, thought of, mentioned

1.12 The ingrained habit of mistaking the *vrittis* as the Self ceases by practice and nonattachment.

abhyāsa-vairāgyābhyām tan-nirodhaḥ

Be suspicious of what you want.
– Rumi

abhyāsa **= practice**

reaching to, pervading, the act of adding anything, reduplication, repetition, multiplication, repeated or permanent exercise, discipline, use, habit, custom, repeated reading or study, inculcation of a truth conveyed in sacred writings by means of repeating the same word or the same passage, the effort of the mind to remain in its natural *sattvic* (clear, balanced) condition

from ***abhi*** = toward, over, upon, going toward, approaching, for the sake of, with regard to, in front of, it may even express one after the other, severally (each in turn, as in tree after tree) + ***āsa*** – seat, from ***ās*** = sit quietly

Abhyasa **implies motion, movement toward a goal. This suggests perseverance and repetition. Successful Yoga practice begins with setting clear goals, deciding on a course of action, and then following through.**

The heart of success in Yoga is regularity. Habits are formed through repetition. Through *abhyasa*, good habits gradually replace harmful ones.

vairāgyābhyām **= nonattachment**

dispassion, freedom from worldly desires, renunciation

from ***vi*** = without + ***raj*** = color, to be moved, excited, attracted + ***bhyam*** = with

or, from ***vai*** = not + ***raj*** = be attracted or excited + ***bhyam*** = with

Nonattachment is one of the great pillars of Yoga theory and practice. It is paired with practice (as in the *Bhagavad Gita*, 6.35) since they harmonize, balance, and support each other.

It is important not to mistake nonattachment for not caring or indifference. Nonattachment is a clear, objective, unbiased state of mind. A mind firmly established in nonattachment is not without emotion. Instead, it is clear, unbiased, and loving.

Patanjali's description of nonattachment can be found in sutras 1.15–1.16.

tat = (*refers to vrittis*)

those

nirodha = ceases

to obstruct, restrict, arrest, avert, support, confinement, locking up, imprisonment, investment, siege, enclosing, covering up, restraint, check, control, suppression, destruction

from ***ni*** = down, into, leading, guiding, within, back + ***rodha*** = sprouting, growing, moving, upwards, ascending, stopping, checking, obstructing, impeding, suppressing, preventing, confining, surrounding, investing, besieging, blockading, from ***rudh*** = obstruct, arrest, avert (See 1.2, 1.12, 1.51. 3.9)

Refer to 1.2 for more on *nirodha*.

1.13 Of these, practice is the regular repeated effort to break free from this misidentification by cultivating steady resolve and a tranquil focused flow of awareness.

tatra sthitau yatnah abhyāsaḥ

Refer to sutras 3.9–3.12, which discuss the development of *nirodha*, *samadhi* and one-pointedness (*ekagrata*) which expand on the progressive development of a tranquil flow of attention. This reminds us that Yoga does not ask us to forcefully pin down the mind. Instead, we gain skill in guiding the mind by creating conditions in which our attention will naturally flow toward a state of one-pointedness.

tatra = of these

there, in that place, to that place, in that case, on that occasion, under those circumstances, then, therefore

sthitau = steady

steadiness as opposed to going, sitting, or lying, standing firm in battle, resting, abiding, remaining, being or remaining or keeping in any state or condition, engaged in, occupied with, intent upon, engrossed or addicted to, performing, protecting, conforming to, following, lasting, firm, constant, invariable, settled, established, fixed upon, determined, firmly resolved to, faithful to a promise or agreement, prepared for, existing, present, close at hand, ready, belonging to, leading to, perseverance on the right path, standing upright or firmly, not falling, staying, residence, a temporary stay in or on or at, permanence, station, high position, rank, settled rule, fixed decision, maintenance of discipline, establishment of good order, devotion to, intent on, firm conviction, stability, manner of acting, behavior, procedure, virtuous conduct, maintaining discipline, manner of acting

from ***sthā*** = to stand (See 1.8, 1.13, 1.35, 1.41, 2.18, 2.35–2.39, 2.46, 3.52, 4.34)

Steadiness of mind is not necessarily the complete cessation of *vritti* activity. *Sthitau* in this context implies that all *rajasic* (restless, attachment-based) and *tamasic* (false, negative) *vrittis* have quieted. The mind can now engage in one-pointed reflection on an object.

The mind, stable and free from *rajasic* turbulence and *tamasic* delusions, is prepared to experience *samprajnata samadhi* (See 1.17).

***yatnah* = resolve**

aspiring after, effort, activity of will, volition, performance, work, exertion, energy, zeal, trouble, pains, care

from ***yat*** = to marshal, to march in step, to be in line, to vie with

***abhyāsa* = practice, repetition**

near, imminent, vicinity, in the neighborhood, addition, reduplication, practice, application, repeated recitation, multiplication, discipline, habit, custom, study, the instilling of a truth conveyed in sacred writings by means of repeating the same word or same passage, the effort to remain in the *sattvic* state

from ***as*** = to be, live, exist, be present, to happen, take place, dwell, abide, to belong to, to sit quietly, to tend to any result + ***abhi*** = as a prefix to verbs and nouns, expresses, to, toward, into, over, upon. As a prefix to verbs of motion, it expresses the notion of going toward, approaching. As a prefix to nouns not derived from verbs, it expresses superiority, intensity.

Repetition sounds boring. The mind – usually in a state of restlessness – looks for distraction or variety in just about everything. Such a mind is not patient. It may have only rarely experienced – or forgotten – the variety that is inherent in deep contemplative experiences. As we dive deeper within in meditation, we discover corners of our minds and hearts where wonderful and essential aspects of life and the world around us are revealed. These deeper experiences require some effort and time, but the results are more satisfying and rewarding. They ring with meaning and nourish the mind and heart with peace, joy, and fulfillment.

This doesn't mean that we can't have variety in our practices, but the core of our daily routine should become stable after experimentation, study, and introspection. This is when practice really begins to yield its sweetest fruits.

1.14 Practice becomes fully integrated into one's life when it is carefully nurtured for a long time and engaged in faithfully, with inner reflection and fervor.

sa tu dīrgha-kāla-nairantarya-satkāra-āsevito dṛdhabūmi

Thus with patience I will strive with careful and persistent effort,
For in such diligence enlightenment is found.
If no wind blows, then nothing stirs,
And neither can there be merit without careful and persistent effort.

That, if they bring forth the strength of perseverance,
Even bees and flies
And gnats and grubs will gain
Supreme enlightenment so hard to find.
– Shantideva

***sah* = (*refers to practice*)**

this, that, it

***tu* = (*refers to a further explanation of abhyāsa*)**

but, now, then, moreover

dīrgha **= long time**

deep, lofty, high, tall

Dirgha can mean long in space or in time.

kāla **= time**

a fixed or right point of time, a period of time, the time of the world (*yuga*), time as leading to events (the causes of which are imperceptible to the mind), destiny, fate, time as destroyer of all things (personified as the god Yama)

from ***kāl*** = to calculate or enumerate

nairantarya **= faithfully, inner reflection**

without break, without interruption, close succession, continuousness

from ***nair*** = a form of ***nir*** = out, away from + ***antar*** = interior, between, in the middle, amongst, within + ***ya*** = restrain, go or come, to cause, to depart, moving, walk, flee, to find out, to intend, proceed, behave, withdraw, implore, advance

This word could be literally translated as: *without leaving* the interior (of the self or of the path).

satkāra **= fervor**

enthusiasm, kind treatment, honor, favor, reverence, hospitable treatment, feasting, festival, religious observance, care, attention, consideration of or regard for a thing

from ***sat*** = right + ***kāra***, from ***kṛ*** = to do, make, perform, cause, prepare, undertake, to do for the benefit of another, to take by the hand, making, doing, working, author, an act or action, effort, exertion, religious austerity, master, Lord, act of worship, song of praise

In Advaita Vedanta, a similar principle, *mumukshutva*, is revered as one of the four qualifications of a seeker to attain enlightenment.

The four qualities are:

- Discriminative discernment (*viveka*)
- Nonattachment (*vairagya*)
- The six virtues:
  - Equanimity of mind
  - Regulation of the senses

  - Fully experiencing the limitations of sense pleasures
  - Endurance
  - Faith in the Guru, the sacred teachings, and in oneself
  - Cultivating a mindset steadfastly focused on the highest Truth or Reality (*Brahman*)
- Fervor (*mumukshutva*)

***āsevitah* = carefully nurtured**

well attended to, frequented, practiced assiduously (great care and perseverance)

from ***ā*** = hither, unto + ***sev*** = to stay near, inhabit, honor, dwell, to be taken care of, to be honored

dṛdhabūmi = fully integrated

firm ground

from ***dṛdha*** = fixed, firm, hard, strong, solid, massive, firmly fastened, shut tight, whole, complete, difficult to be bent, steady, resolute, persevering, confirmed, established, certain, sure, intense, mighty, violent, stronghold, fortress, very well + ***bhūmi*** = the earth, soil, ground, territory, country, district, a place, situation, position, posture, attitude, floor of a house, stage of Yoga, the ten stages Buddhists must go through to attain Buddhahood

1.15 Nonattachment is self-mastery and freedom from craving. It manifests when love of liberation (from ignorance and the suffering craving brings) awakens due to the recognition of the beguiling[24] and captivating nature of craving for objects seen, heard, or described.

dṛṣṭa-anuśravika-viṣayavitṛṣṇasya vaśīkāra-samjñā vairāgyam

Without nonattachment there cannot be any kind of Yoga.
Nonattachment is the basis of all the Yogas.
– Swami Vivekananda

[24] Beguile = to charm or enchant someone, sometimes in a deceptive way.

***dṛṣṭa* = seen**

observed, perceived

from ***dṛś*** = to see

***anuśravika* = heard, described in sacred tradition**

according to what is heard

from **anu** = after or along + ***śrava*** = hearing, hearsay, desire of praising, from ***śru*** = to hear (referring to the Vedic tradition), acquired by repeated hearing, resting on tradition

***viṣaya* = objects**

condition, an object of the senses, anything perceptible to the senses, any object of affection or concern or attention, any special worldly object or aim or matter or business, sensual enjoyments, sensuality, any topic or subject matter, a religious obligation or observance, a lover, husband, semen, virile
from ***viṣ*** = to be active + ***aya*** = going

***vitṛṣṇasya* = freedom from craving**

nonthirst, not clinging to

from ***vi*** = without + ***tṛṣ*** = to be thirsty, long for, strong desire

***vaśīkāra* = self mastery, to master by love**

control (See 1.15, 1.40)

from ***vaṣi*** = to will, to subjugate, fascination, bewitching, from ***vaṣ*** = command, desire, wish, long for, be fond of, willing, glad, obedient + ***kāra*** = making, doer, an author, doing, working, religious austerity, from ***kr*** = to make, to do, make, perform, accomplish, to place in one's heart, love, cause, effect, prepare, undertake, to do anything for the advantage or injury of another, carry out (as an order or command), to manufacture, work at, elaborate, build, to form or construct one thing out of another, to employ, use, to compose, describe, to cultivate, bring to completion, spend, to place, put, lay, bring, lead, take hold of, to take to one's own side or party, to take by the hand, marry

In the context of the holistic approach of the *Sutras*, *vasikara* (mastery) should not be understood as being born from brute willpower, but from love of liberation. It is freeing of oneself from attachments by cultivating love of liberation until it is greater than craving objects of attachments.

This love is nurtured through practice, discernment, and introspection. Zeal for liberation gradually eclipses attachments.

This understanding of mastery is based on nurturing the innate harmony between the individual, with the forces of nature, and the ways of the world. When *vasikara* is attained, the *gunas* (constituents of nature) continue their natural functions but no longer obscure our intrinsic Self-identity. The result is freedom from misidentification with *prakriti*, a misperception that is based on the limited perspective of self-interest.

Vasikara is a state of mind that corrects all former life imbalances. Nature, instead of being a source of misperception, is experienced as a source of joy, wisdom, and liberation.

The different possible roots for *vas* are varied and can expand our understanding of the nature of mastery. Let's look at a few:

1. *Vas* = to will, command, to desire, wish, long for, be fond of, to maintain, affirm, declare for, to get in one's power
2. *Vas* = to roar, howl, bellow, bleat, low (the deep sound made by a cow),[25] sing like a bird
3. *Vasa* = *a)* will, wish, desire, power, control, dominion, to fall into a person's power, by force of, on account of, by means of, birth, origin, willing, submissive, obedient, dependent on; b) cloth, clothes, garment, abiding, dwelling, abode, habitation, perfuming, perfume, to take up one's abode, place or seat of, situation, condition
4. *Vasi* = to ensnare or to enthrall

The sense of *vasikara* that emerges is to *control, subdue, or subjugate the mind* – to become its master. We form an image in which the mind obediently responds to the will of the individual without hesitation. This interpretation is certainly correct and applies to the *Sutras* concerning

[25] Cows are known to employ two separate pitches when they low. The lower pitch is for calling calves that are close by; the higher is for those that are further away. In addition, the mother cow has different melodic phrases for each calf. In the context of the sutra under discussion, we could envision that the disciplines of Yoga are like calling the calf to come back to its mother, the place of its birth and origin (look again at the third definition, above and note Patanjali calls this *pratiprasava*; see sutras 2.10 and 4.34).

nirodha (cessation, restraint). In this light, we can understand self-mastery as the essence of developing *nirodha*. Though accurate, this understanding may be a bit one-dimensional.

However, we know that the human mind is not one-dimensional. Attaining self-mastery, then, should not be cultivated in a one-dimensional way. Willpower begins with a combination of a desirable and compelling goal, knowledge of the benefits of that goal, and the ability to set a clear intention. In addition, we need to factor in our own limitations, an understanding of how habits are formed, the obstacles the mind projects when trying to create new habits, and the strength to persevere until the goal is reached. The above factors can be summarized as knowledge, love, and strength.

Each of the four possible roots of *vasikara* has at least one definition that expresses an emotional content not captured by subjugation or obedience. Note, for example:

1. To be fond of, to maintain, to affirm
2. Sing like a bird
3. Dwelling, abode, perfume, to take up one's abode
4. To enthrall, ensnare, a sage without selfish attachments.

One conclusion we can draw from this is that there is a dual goal behind mastery: steadiness and delight. We find this from words like *maintain, dwelling, perfume, enthrall,* and from phrases like *to take up one's abode and to sing like a bird.*

Mastery should bring delight – not just in its final stage. While it brings delight, it also brings challenge, as a process that engages mind and heart in its quest to find meaning and joy in life. Thus, *vasikara* means to guide the mind gently but surely, through wisdom and resolve, to generate steadiness of mind and freedom from selfish attachment, with the objective of finding delight in life. Try on this definition of *vasikara*: *To guide the mind's transformation in order to maintain steadiness so that life is a delight.*

The gist is that mastery does require discipline and effort – practice for a long time, without break, and with fervor (see 1.14) – but it is fueled and accompanied by a vision of a goal that is poetic, beautiful, and attainable. There is a very tasty carrot at the end of the stick of practice: a mind that sings like a bird, that is home and a delight to the individual and to the world.

samjñā = awakens the recognition

to know, recognize, to agree together, be of the same opinion, be in harmony with, to appoint, assign, intend (for any purpose), to acknowledge, own, to acknowledge or claim as one's own, to take possession of, to think of, to know well, understand, to watch, to appease, satisfy, to cause to understand, to make to be known, to make anything known by signs, command, enjoin, instruct, consciousness, clear knowledge or understanding or notion or conception, a sign, token, gesture, signal, a track, footstep, the name of anything thought of as standing by itself

In Buddhism, *samjna* is the psychological faculty of perception or discernment. It is said to recognize the distinctive characteristics of things, for example, by identifying different colors. Sometimes the term is used simply in the sense of *idea or concept*, especially in lists of meditation topics (for example: *anitya-samjna*, the concept of impermanence or *anitya*).

Buddhism also identifies *samjna* as one of the five aggregates: form, sensation, perception, subconscious impressions, and consciousness. These constitute what is generally understood as the personality. The aggregates are frequently referred to as aggregates of attachment since craving or desire attaches itself to them and attracts them to itself. This makes them objects of attachment that bring suffering.

vairāgyam = nonattachment

from ***vi*** = without + ***rāj*** + color, to be moved, excited, attracted, or from ***vai*** = not + ***raj*** = be attracted or excited (See 1.12, 1.15, 3.51)

Refer to 1.12 for more on *vairagya*.

1.16 The highest nonattachment arises when the *Purusha* is correctly discerned as the True Self. This realization ends all craving and the compulsive urge to find lasting satisfaction from any sense experience that can be provided by nature (*gunas,* the constituents of nature).

tat param puruṣa-khyāteḥ guṇa-vaitṛṣṇyam

Be aware of the ephemeral nature of material things. Lose your attachment to them.
– Shui-ch'ing Tzu

tat **= that**
param **= highest**

supreme, best, above, beyond, farther on, high degree, greatly, completely (See 1.16, 1.24, 3.36, 3.50, 3.56, 4.18, 4.34)

from ***para*** = higher, supreme, from ***pṛ*** = to surpass, excel

puruṣa **= left untranslated**

true Self, Spirit, highest Self, soul, animating principle, pure consciousness, man, human, primeval man as the original source of the universe, the inactive witness (in Samkhya) of creation, people, an officer, functionary, attendant, servant, a friend, a follower of Samkhya philosophy, a representative of a race or generation, the pupil of the eye, the personal animating principle in humans and other beings, the Supreme Being

from ***puru*** = a being connected with the sun, or ***pṝ*** = to fill, make complete

Purusha can simply mean person, or something more lofty: Seer, Self, and Owner. There are no capital letters in Sanskrit. The meaning is inferred from context. *Purusha* is the highest Self, Spirit, pure consciousness, the eternal witness of all phenomena. Its counterpart is *prakriti*, matter that is devoid of consciousness.

In Samkhya philosophy - and in Patanjali's Yoga - *Purusha*, (consciousness), is one of two eternal realities, the other being *prakriti*, matter. Strictly speaking, in this tradition, *Purusha* refers to the individual soul as distinct from the universal one. This means that every person has his or her own *Purusha*, each identical.

This differs from the philosophy of Advaita Vedanta, which is based on a nondual vision: there is only one Reality, with all names and forms we see around us as the product of ignorance, of misperception. Therefore, there is no difference between the individual Self and the Supreme Self.

In practical terms, the difference between Samkhya and Advaita Vedanta makes little impact on day-to-day living or in spiritual pursuits. Both are a combination of tradition, logic, and most importantly, subjective experience of truths – realities – that can essentially not be expressed in words. Think of it: we can't even explain the taste of a banana to someone who has never had one. How can we convey in words the subtlest essences of the universe we live in, the nature of the mind, and of enlightenment? However, we can be told where to find bananas, that they need to be yellow to be tasty, and that they need to be peeled before eating. That is the true heart of spiritual teachings, especially Yoga, with its primary focus on practice. Keep in mind, regardless of the philosophical tradition, two important points: 1) That we suffer due to ignorance, and 2) That there is a way out of ignorance.

The first and most fundamental priority in spiritual life is to remove ignorance, selfishness, fear, and every artificial limitation imposed by the ego. The way we subjectively understand and describe the absolute, unchanging, eternal Truth – after that experience – will vary according the culture, language, and beliefs of the individual.

khyāteḥ = discernment

knowledge, or vision

from ***khyā*** = to see, to be known, to be named, to make known, promulgate, proclaim, to relate, tell, say, declare, betray, denounce

Another form of the word is *khyati = declaration, opinion, view, idea, assertion, perception, knowledge, renown, fame, celebrity*

guṇa = constituent of nature

a single thread or strand of a cord or twine, rope, garland, a bow string, a sinew, the string of a musical instrument, co-efficient, subdivision, species, kind, a secondary element, subordinate or unessential part of any action, a quality, peculiarity, attribute or property, the property or characteristic of all created things, good quality, virtue, merit, excellence, merits of good composition (consistency, elegance of expression) (See 1.16, 2.15, 2.19, 4.13, 4.32, 4.34)

The word is from roots that mean cow sinew. Cow sinew was most often used for making ropes and as a backing for bows. The sinew was both strong and able to stretch and store energy better than wood alone, which prevented the bow from breaking. These characteristics are perhaps part of why the word *guna* was used to describe the forces or qualities that make up the material universe.

In Samkhya philosophy, the *gunas* are regarded as ingredients or constituents of *prakriti*.

There are three *gunas*:

- *Sattva* – balance, tranquility, harmony, luminosity
- *Rajas* – activity, restlessness, passion
- *Tamas* – dullness, inertia, lethargy

The *gunas* are also understood as attributes of the five elements:

- Ether
- Air
- Fire or light
- Water
- Earth

The *gunas* and spiritual knowledge are also related. Think of true or reliable knowledge as discovering bits of the Absolute (the Self, God, Cosmic Consciousness). This category of knowledge is attained when the mind is *sattvic* – tranquil, clear, and focused. These tidbits of reality are like appetizers that nudge the seeker ever deeper into contemplative practices and selfless service.

Knowledge that is colored by attachment, selfish desires, or restlessness often results in partial or misunderstood truths. This category of knowledge is marked by a predominance of *rajas* – restlessness and craving.

Knowledge that is rejected or mutated into its opposite is dominated by a *tamasic* – dull, inert, obstinate – state of mind.

It would not be incorrect to regard the goal of Yoga to be cultivating a *sattvic* state of mind. Once that is achieved, individual effort ends and the seeker now allows and receives grace, which carries her or him to liberation. (See 4.25–4.26)

vaitṛṣṇyam **= end craving and compulsive urge**

no thirst, freedom from desire. It is a strengthened form of *vitrsna* (See 1.15)

from ***vi*** = divided, asunder, apart + ***tṛṣ*** = thirst, long for, strong desire, desire as the daughter of love

1.17 When practice and nonattachment strengthen, intuitive insight (*samprajnata*) arises. As this insight deepens, it reveals four increasingly subtle levels of nature (*prakriti*), bringing complete and accurate knowledge of the object of contemplation.

The four levels are:

- *Vitarka (investigation into the gross form of objects)*: The mind investigates and gains knowledge of the gross aspect of an object.
- *Vichara (knowledge of subtle essences)*: The factors that brought the object into existence are revealed.
- *Ananda (bliss of a sattvic mind)*: At this level, attention naturally turns to awareness itself. Devoid of a gross or subtle object, *manas* – the part of the mind that constantly seeks objects to grasp – becomes clear and tranquil, resulting in the experience of joy.

- *Asmita (ego sense)*: The direct experience of the ego sense, pure I-am-ness.[26]

The duality of mind and object remains in all these states.

vitarka-vicāra-ānanda-asmitā-anugamāt-samprajñātaḥ

vitarka **= investigation**

discursive thought, deliberation, conjecture, supposition, guess, fancy, imagination, opinion, doubt (YS[27]), uncertainty (YS), a dubious or questionable matter (YS), reasoning, consideration, purpose, intention, a teacher, instructor in divine knowledge, knowledge obtained by reason and argument rather than intuition

from ***vi*** = apart, away, divided, different, asunder. It can be similar in meaning to the English dis or de (which is not necessarily negation) and can mean reversal or removal, separate, or take apart. This prefix can sometimes refer to a negation. At other times, ***vi*** simply sorts things out, as in delineate. ***Vi*** can also be an intensifier. In which case, it does not imply negation + ***tark*** = conjecture, reason, speculation, reasoned investigation, conjecture, inquiry, doubt, system or doctrine founded on speculation, logic, cause, motive

This sutra is important. It introduces us to the state of contemplative absorption, *samadhi*, which marks the beginning of a new way of understanding, experiencing, and responding to life, self, and life's realities. It is the transcending of a mindset that understands life only by comparing, contrasting, and dissecting. This mindset, virtually the only way things are known to us, is obsessed with being right – right being defined as that which is in agreement with our own biases, desires, and fears. We rarely enjoy the great benefit of knowing an object or event in itself, free of our

[26] *Asmita*, defined here as the ego sense, is also called *ahamkara*. While both terms can mean a sense of individuality, *asmita* is also used to designate a larger sense of ego – the cosmic sense of "I" – the very principle of individuation. This ego transcends the individual mind. It is the principle that makes the more limited body-mind ego possible.

While the ego sense is often treated as the primary foe in spiritual life, it is more accurate to state that it is not the sense of ego, but an ego that has been colored by ignorance and selfish attachments. When we hear or read Yoga masters talk about ridding ourselves of the ego, it is mostly in this sense that they are speaking. At the same time, the highest enlightened state – liberation or Self-realization – consists in completely transcending the confines of ego: selfish and selfless, in order to experience the authentic Self. After liberation, the ego resumes its function, but without losing the experience of liberation. To be liberated while living – a *jivanmukta* – is the goal of a yogi for this lifetime.

[27] YS means that the definition is particularly associated with the *Yoga Sutras*.

expectations, plans, and ideas of what's right and wrong. *Samadhi* opens the path to experiencing the deepest realities. It brings us to the peace of the Self that lies within each of us. Let's take a look at some of the specifics of this sutra.

Vitarka describes a state of mind that is discursive, suggesting that the mind, although in deep contemplation, still digresses from subject to subject or from one aspect of the subject to another. The mind still oscillates or indulges in internal dialogue.

Look at the list of definitions for *vitarka*. They center around doubt, implying that the acquisition of spiritual wisdom is preceded by *not knowing*. In general, in the context of spiritual pursuits, it is perhaps more useful to understand the state of not knowing as refined, directed curiosity.

In this stage, the reduction of the conceptualizations that color perception begins. It is the beginning of applying the totality of the mind to the object of contemplation.

vicāra = subtle knowledge

subtle awareness, sustained absorption

from ***vi*** = apart, away + ***car*** = go, move, motion

As deep, steady attention is sustained, the mind naturally begins to probe the object of contemplation revealing subtler aspects of its nature. The roots of the word suggest this probing movement – from the gross manifestation of an object to its subtler components.

Vichara is a more peaceful, focused state than *vitarka*.

ānanda = bliss

joy, happiness, enjoyment, sensual pleasures, pure happiness, one of the three attributes of *Brahman* or *Atma* (sat-chit-ananda; existence, knowledge, bliss)

from ***ā*** = hither, unto + ***nand***, to rejoice, be glad. The prefix, long a, ā, denotes emphasis. If ***nand*** is joy, ***ānanda*** is extreme joy.

Ananda is connected to the expansion of an individual's consciousness. It is uncreated joy, not connected with any attainment of possessions or status, or any external circumstances or conditions.

In theatrical dramas, *ananda* is the thing wished for or expected, the climax of the drama, the point at which all aspects of the drama are resolved. *Ananda* is also a kind of house, suggesting a sense of security.

Ananda is also traditionally used to designate the hours between 2–6 p.m. and 2–6 a.m., times of high creativity and hours when the mind moves quickly – good times to meditate.[28]

asmitā = ego sense

the sense of 'I' before it takes on identifications

from ***as*** = to be + ***tā***, a suffix suggesting to have the quality of

Ahamkara is the *power of asmita* to take on identifications.

anugamāt = associated with

following, going after in life or death, imitating, approaching (See 1.16)

from ***anu*** = after or along, near to, toward, next + ***gama*** = going, riding on, course, road, march, intercourse with a woman, removal, going away from

The idea of *anugamat* as intercourse is interesting. The analogy of two people becoming one, through love and yearning, is an interesting parallel with the mind of the meditator and the levels of *samprajnata*. It brings love and fervor into the equation for success in meditation. This helps remove notions of meditation as being an unfeeling calculating exercise in sheer willpower.

samprajñātaḥ = intuitive insight

with consciousness, cognitive, distinguished, discerned, known accurately

from ***sam*** = with, together, entirely, wholly, perfectly, absolutely + ***prajñā*** = to know, understand, discern, distinguish, know about, be acquainted with, to find out, discover, perceive, learn, to show or point out the way, to summon, invite, wisdom, intelligence, knowledge, wisdom personified as the goddess of arts and eloquence (Saraswati)

[28] The perennial tradition or philosophy is based on the principle that there is one absolute truth from which evolves the source of the world's faith traditions. This principle is also found in the *Rig Veda*, the foundation shared by all spiritual traditions in India, as "Truth is one, paths are many." Many of the key terms of the *Sutras* are in the feminine gender. See *buddhi*, discriminative faculty, as an example.

prajñā, from ***pra*** = forward, in front, placed in front, the front part of anything (like the bow of a ship), called out as a warning, onward, forth, fore (before in time) + ***jñā*** = knowing, intelligent, perceive, apprehend, seize, grasp, understand, experience, recognize, ascertain, investigate, regard or consider as, to acknowledge, approve, allow, to visit as a riend, to recognize as one's own, to engage into, to wish to know, to request, having a soul, wise, the thinking soul (purusa)

The roots of *samprajnata*, intuitive insight, reveal a lot about its meaning. *Prajna* can be translated as *before (in time) knowledge*. In other words, insight that occurs before the arrival and influence of intellectual knowledge.

Jna, as you can see, has many meanings. An interesting one that seems particularly relevant to the study of the *Yoga Sutras* is *to apprehend*. The word apprehend is related to apprentice. In apprenticeship, much of what is learned is not from books, but by emulation and guidance of a master teacher. The main idea is that knowledge is not static – a collection of data – but a dynamic process of learning, self-transformation, and growth.

The four levels of consciousness in this sutra are usually referred to as *samadhis*. While this is technically true, the word is not mentioned in the sutra itself. One possible reason is that Patanjali was seeking to convey the mind's ability to probe and discover, rather than attain (and perhaps, rest in) states, a more static way of looking at this subject.

In Buddhism, *prajna* is consciousness or insight. It refers to the intuitive wisdom that cannot be conveyed by concepts or in intellectual terms. The ultimate moment of *prajna* is insight into emptiness (*shunyata*), which is the True Nature of reality. It is often equated with enlightenment and is one of the essential marks of buddhahood. *Prajna* is also one of the perfections (*paramita*) attained by a *bodhisattva* in the course of his or her development.

1.18 Another, deeper insight manifests with the sustained practice of quieting all conscious thoughts, intentions, and expectations until only subconscious impressions (*samskaras*) remain.

Since there are no objects in the conscious mind to investigate and therefore, no insights to be had, this experience is referred to as *asamprajnata*[29] *samadhi*, beyond insights (or beyond discerning).

virāma-pratyaya-abhyāsa-pūrvah saṃskāra-śeṣo' nyah

virāma **= quieted**

standstill, complete cessation, to stop, pause, cease, termination, end, abstention from

from ***vi*** = asunder, away, divided, apart, different + ***ram*** = stop, to set at rest

pratyaya **= conscious thoughts**

firm conviction, intention, basis, the content of consciousness at any given moment (See 1.10, 1.18–1.19, 2.20, 3.2, 4.27)

from ***prati*** = against, back + ***aya*** = going, from i = to go

Refer to 1.10 for more on *pratyaya*.

abhyāsa **= sustained practice**

repeated exercise, discipline, study (See 1.12)

from ***abhi*** = to, unto, toward + ***āsa*** = seat, from ***ās*** = to sit quietly

Attaining *asamprajnata samadhi* takes time and practice. Since it is beyond the highest *samprajnata* insight, *asmita* (ego sense), it includes even going beyond the ego-based desire to still the mind. That means that the *asamprajnata* state is beyond effort. The mind is effortlessly still and clear and nonattachment has reached higher levels.

Note that enlightenment is a process of moving from doing to being.

pūrvah **= manifests**

preceded by

[29] It was the great sage and classic commentator on the *Yoga Sutras*, Vyasa, who originally referred to this state as *asamprajnata*. The word does not appear in the sutra itself, but it is widely known and used in this sutra.

saṃskāra **= subconscious impressions** (See 1.18, 1.50, 2.15, 3.9–3.10, 3.18, 4.9, 4.27)

from ***sam*** = with, together, wholly + ***kṛ*** = to do, make, or cause

No thought, word, or action disappears completely. The mental modifications associated with them sink to the bottom of our mental lake (the subconscious), where they become like sandbars that cause ripples on the lake's surface (the conscious mind).

Most of what we call mind is on the subconscious level. That is why we find ourselves sometimes compelled to act in ways we know are not beneficial. Yet, we feel driven to continue with our bad habits. These "invisible" activators to action are *samskaras*, subconscious impressions.

Acts that produce strong impressions or evoke strong emotions, or acts that are repeated, create most of the *samskaras* that affect our conscious mindset and choices. The implication for yogis is evident: repeated practice, especially when engaged in wholeheartedly, produce strong yogic *samskaras*, accelerating progress in Yoga.

śeṣaḥ = remain

from ***śiṣ*** = to remain

anyaḥ = another

the other, inexhaustibleness, other, different, opposed to, the one

1.19 Unresolved or unexpressed feelings and intentions can cause the individual to become melded with *prakriti* (through thoughts of continued existence) and subject to rebirth. This can be true even for celestial beings who are without gross physical bodies.

bhava-pratyayo videha-prakṛti-layānām

bhava = continued existence, unresolved or unexpressed feelings and intentions

being, becoming, coming into existence, spirit, emotion, nature, manner, mindset, inclination, tendency, disposition of mind, sentiment, birth, nature, existing, well-being, contemplation, origin, thing or substance from ***bhū*** = to become, exist, be, to come into being, be found, live, stay, abide, occur, to be on the side of, assist, serve, devote oneself to, thrive or prosper, be of consequence or useful, attain to, be successful or fortunate, place of being, space, world, universe, the planet earth, ground

In this sutra, *bhava* refers to an ingrained mindset marked and driven by attachment to continued existence, the continued desire for physical life, and the sensations and experiences it offers.

Bhava has many other meanings in Hindu philosophy, especially in *Bhakti Yoga*, the path of devotion to a name and form of the Divine that one is drawn to. In general, *bhava* can be thought of as a mindset, or mental environment that influences reactions, responses, and perceptions of events.

In Buddhism, *bhava* refers to continuity of life and death and the spiritual maturation that ultimately results from these experiences. It is also the clinging desire for further life and sense experiences. In Buddhism, *bhava* can also mean a mood or feeling that is unexpressed. If we apply this understanding to this sutra, we can see how unexpressed or unresolved subconscious impressions – desires, fears, etc. – can lead to rebirth.

pratyaya = intention

thought, belief, presented idea, notion, firm belief, conviction, faith, assurance or certainty of, proof, ascertainment, conception, assumption, notion, idea, (with Buddhists – fundamental notion or idea), consciousness, understanding, intelligence, intellect, analysis, solution, explanation, definition, ground, basis, motive or cause of anything, an oath, religious meditation, content of the mind at any given moment (See 1.10, 1.18–1.19, 2.20, 3.2, 4.27)

Refer to 1.10 for more on *pratyaya.*

videha = without bodies

to be separated from the covering that is the body, incorporeal, deceased, dead, form, shape, mass, bulk, person, individual, appearance, manifestation, of a country

from ***deha***, from ***dih*** = to plaster, mold, fashion, smear, anoint

The beings who are without physical bodies (*videha*) are comprised of two categories. The first category is the *devas*. They are celestial beings (*deva* = being of light), something like angels. Many are thought to be evolved yogis who have left their bodies. The term is also applied to any of the higher or lower class of gods.

The second meaning of *videha* includes those whose self-identity is not based on the physical body but who, instead, identify with subtler aspects of *prakriti*: subtle elements, ego, or *buddhi* (pure intellect), for example.

prakṛiti = *left untranslated*

making or placing before or at first, the original or natural form or condition of anything, original or primary substance, origin, nature, character, disposition, pattern, model, the material world (consisting of the three *gunas*), nature, fundamental form, the personified will of the Supreme in the creation, the organ of generation, a woman or womankind (See 1.19, 4.2–4.3)

from ***pra*** = before, forth, forward, in front, away + ***kṛ*** = to do, create, make, accomplish, cause, effect, prepare, undertake, to do anything for the benefit or injury of another, to manufacture, work at, elaborate, build, to make one thing out of another, to make use of, to cultivate, to bring to completion, bring, lead, to direct the mind toward any object

Prakriti is the active, creative aspect of reality as opposed to the *Purusha*. It is composed of, and inseparable from, the three *gunas*. In Samkhya philosophy, it is regarded as the original producer of all things and the power to create. It is eternally coexistent with *Purusha*, the unchanging Seer, Self, Pure Consciousness.

layānām = melded to

to merge, making the mind inactive or indifferent, dissolution, diversion, rest, a place of rest, dwelling, disappearance or absorption in, mental inactivity, extinction, delight in anything, destruction, melting, pause, death, time, house

from ***lī*** = to melt, cling

1.20 Others, aware of how attachments hinder progress, continue to strive to attain (the highest) *samadhi*, a state preceded by:

- Faith
- Courage to face obstacles and the persistence to carry on
- Remembrance of life's lessons and repeated recollection of the truths of sacred wisdom traditions
- (lower) States of contemplative absorption (*samadhi*), a clear, tranquil, one-pointed mind
- Intuitive insights that remove ignorance

śraddhā-vīrya-smṛti-samādhi-prajñā-pūrvaka itareṣām

We can understand this sutra not only as a list of separate practices and observances that help bring the intuitive insight, *asamprajnata*, but as an interconnected series in which each item engenders and/or supports the others.

śraddhā = faith

from ***su*** = bright, pure, clean + ***hṛd*** = heart + ***dhā*** = to hold or place

Shraddha literally means, *to hold or rest in a pure heart.* It is the state of being that results from a heart filled with light or wisdom. *Duhkha* – persistent pervasive anxiety, dissatisfaction, and suffering – would not find a hospitable home in such a heart.

Since it is a convention in Hindu philosophy to place the most important item on a list first, the central importance of faith in Patanjali's Yoga is emphasized.

Reflection

Reflecting on matters of faith often brings up questions about free will. Is it possible to reconcile free will with the surrendering of our will to God? – "Thy will be done."

Our will is always a matter of choice. We can give over our will to an individual, group, organization, or faith tradition out of fear, greed, or when we seek stability, comfort, prosperity, or other limited desires. Our will then molds to the requirements of the situation. In these cases, the motive for the giving over of our will is based on self-interest, thus a strong sense of the limited ego remains.

In spirituality, will is wedded to faith and faith is wedded to things eternal and timeless. Such faith is natural and ever-renewing, like love. It is like lover and beloved naturally and joyfully giving themselves to each other.

In a loving, giving relationship your will, your freedom, is never lost. Paradoxically, you find and enrich yourself. It is the same in a relationship with God and Guru. There is never a sense of loss, only gain, only finding oneself by losing oneself. It is a theme which we have all heard in some form: we have to lose our limited self to find our ultimate freedom in the Self or God.

"Thy will be done," may not feel like a decision, but it is. It is not a one-time decision book-ended by external circumstances, but a loving gift we freely give – out of clear understanding, faith, love, and in a quiet, nurturing joy.

vīrya = courage, persistence

manliness, valor, strength, power, energy, heroism, virility, splendor, luster, dignity, consequence

For a better understanding of *virya*, we turn to Ayurveda – the ancient healing system of India – which describes *virya* as the intrinsic factor in an herb, or other remedy, that gives it its healing power. It is the factor that makes things happen, proceeding from potential to realization.

In Buddhism, *virya* = exertion, energy, will power, untiring pursuit in transforming the impure to pure.

It is one of the seven factors of attaining enlightenment:

- Mindfulness (*smriti*)
- Distinguishing right from wrong according to the teachings
- Energy and exertion in the practice
- Joy concerning the teachings
- Overcoming passions
- Equanimity
- Freedom from discrimination

smṛti = remembrance, recollection

authoritative tradition, thinking of, calling to mind, awareness, mindfulness, wish

from ***smṛ*** = to remember

Memory, properly used, keeps us from living in the past, repeating mistakes, and caught in guilt, regrets, and fears. Memory of painful events can also sensitize us to pain and suffering and can thus awaken and deepen compassion.

To remember is not simply to relive the past. It involves extracting lessons from them and storing them as an inner reference library of important beneficial lessons learned.

Hatred finds a comfortable home in unexamined or improperly used memories. Living firmly planted in the present, but with lessons learned and remembered, we build toward a future that can be a valuable inheritance we leave for family, friends, and community.

samādhi = *left untranslated*

bringing into harmony, settlement, joining with, intense absorption, attention, joining or combining with, whole, accomplishment, conclusion, concentration of mind, union, concentration of thoughts, profound meditation, bringing into harmony, intense application of the mind on, attention, completion (See 1.20, 1.46, 1.51, 2.2, 2.29, 2.45, 3.3, 3.11, 3.38, 4.1, 4.29)

There are three possible derivations for *samadhi*:

1. ***sam*** = entirely, wholly, perfectly, absolutely, with, together + ***adhi*** = eagerness, longing, care:

Complete longing for union.

2. ***sam*** = wholly, entirely, perfectly, together + ***a*** = near, toward, up to + ***dhi*** = receptacle:

To progress toward a perfect receptacle.

3. ***am*** = together + ***dha*** = to put, place, or hold (***dhi*** is the feminine form) + ***a*** = into joining or combining together, union, whole, bringing into harmony, intense application or fixing the mind on, attention, completion, profound meditation:

To bring together in perfect union.

In *samadhi*, there is a merging of subject (the individual) and the object of attention. *Samadhi* naturally arises when the mind is made peaceful, clear, and one-pointed. A nonattached attitude greatly facilitates, accelerates, and deepens the experiences of *samadhi*.

The *Yoga Sutras* identify a number of *samadhis* that fall into four categories. They are, from most gross to most subtle:

1. *Samprajnata* (cognitive *samadhi*)
   - *Savitarka* (with examination)
   - *Nirvitarka* (beyond examination)
   - *Savichara* (with insight)
   - *Nirvichara* (beyond insight)
   - *Ananda* (joy)
   - *Asmita* (pure I-am-ness)
2. *Asamprajnata* (noncognitive *samadhi*)
3. *Dharmamegha samadhi* (considered as a subcategory of *asamprajnata*)
4. *Nirbija samadhi* (seedless *samadhi*; the highest state that brings liberation)

It is perhaps more practical and beneficial to think of these *samadhis* as means for the exploration of subtle realities rather than static states. The insights gained from *samadhi* enable yogis to perceive the subtlest of principles and realities. This capacity is called *yoga pratyaksha*: yogic vision.

To attain the higher *samadhis*, we need to let go of craving for advancement (See 3.51). Instead, there is joy in, and fervor for, the practice

itself, an inner environment of stillness, acceptance, and openheartedness that allows *samadhi* to arise.

prajñā = intuitive insight

judgment, intelligence, knowing, true wisdom, awareness, to find out, discover, learn, clever, a wise or learned person, a person worthy of being revered, intelligence dependent on individuality, one who can correctly discern, intuitive knowledge conducive to attaining liberation, wisdom attained by intuitive means beyond normal cognition (See 1.20, 1.48–1.49, 2.27, 3.5)

***Prajna* is wisdom gained in states of *samadhi*, from deep inspired study, profound and tranquil introspection, devotional practices, and the forgetting of personal desires in selfless service. These are all ways of acquiring spontaneous insights that are not dependent on the usual routes of sense contact or rationality. In Western religious terms, we could equate *prajna* with revelations. Essential scriptural principles are derived from *prajna*. The wisdom insights gained from *prajna* are considered true and are capable of advancing one's progress toward liberation.**

pūrvaka = preceded or accompanied by

earlier, former, previous, prior, first, connected with, consisting in

from ***pūrva*** = being before or in front, first, eastern, to the east, former, prior, preceding, previous to, earlier than, accompanied by, attended with, mentioned before

itareṣām = of the others

from ***itara*** = low, vile, expelled, rejected, the other, the rest, this-that, another, remaining one of the two, different from

1.21 Success is near for those whose resolve is unrestrained – fervent and unwavering.

tīvra-saṃvegānām āsannaḥ

tīvra = fervent

keen, intense, strong, extremely energetic, intense ardor

from root ***tu*** = strong, to have authority, severe, intense, hot, pervading, excessive, ardent, sharp, acute, pungent, horrible

saṃvegānām = fervent, unrestrained, unwavering

intense or vehement, intent, violent, agitation, excitement, flurry, vehemence, intensity, high degree, desire for emancipation

from ***sam*** = with, together + ***vega*** = to be agitated, shock, a stream, flood, current (of water, tears), rush, dash, impetus, momentum, vehemence, haste, speed, velocity, the flight of an arrow, outbreak, outburst (of passion), agitation, emotion, semen

Success – enlightenment, liberation – is near for those whose practice is *samveganam*. This important term suggests an attitude, practice, and lifestyle found in one who has addressed their doubts and is filled with, and driven by, enthusiasm for Yoga's ultimate objectives.[30]

Samveganam is intensity, without attachment. When *samveganam* arises, success in Yoga is near; enlightenment will soon dawn, and with it, the eradication of suffering.

Look at the roots of *vega*. It includes *agitated, shock, flood, vehemence, speed, the flight of an arrow, outbreak, outburst of passion, semen*. Taken at face value, it would seem that success in Yoga is for those who are about ready to explode emotionally. Instead, think about these words in the context of a passionate relationship. When we meet the one we love, the one who we have faith in, we naturally wish to commit to that person for life. In this, there is an elation, a sense of rising above all our troubles, and a joyful natural focus trained on the one we love.

Samveganam is free from fear, anxiety, doubt, or craving. It is fueled by curiosity to gain knowledge regarding the self, the Self, and life in this universe. It is a quiet fire fed by increasingly deeper insights and experiences. It is like a cosmic dinner composed entirely of appetizers (usually the best part of a meal), that stokes our digestive fire, never leaves us in a food coma, but inspires us to keep eating shamelessly and with joy.

In practice, *samveganam* also expresses as simplicity. It involves assessing the use of personal time, effort, and resources, looking for

[30] One of the roots of *samveganam*, *vega*, can mean "current of tears." This suggests both the tears of the suffering and the persistent, pervasive feelings of precariousness (*duhkha*) that made us look to Yoga as a remedy, and the tears of joy that follow finding it due to the transformations and fulfillment its practice brings.

harmony of purpose. Activities, possessions, and aspirations that occupied large swaths of time and expenditures of energy either naturally dwindle or are systematically and conscientiously dropped. As our excess baggage reduces, our burden lightens, and the journey to enlightenment is easier and quicker.

The ultimate reward for a life permeated with focus, energy, enthusiasm, and simplicity is liberation from ignorance and the suffering it brings.

Samveganam is all heart and purpose. It is the joy of a journey – a pilgrimage – that can only end in peace, joy, love, light, and harmony

Success in Yoga is assured for those whose practice is like an arrow, flying free, and heading inevitably toward the bull's-eye.

āsannaḥ = near

very quick, seated down, set down, proximate, reached, obtained, occupied

from ***ā*** = hither, unto + ***sanna*** (set down), from ***sad*** = to sit.

1.22 Understanding the power of resolve, one can infer that nearness of success depends on the degree of its steadiness and intensity: mild, moderate, or fervent.

mṛdu-madhya-adhimātravāt tato'pi viśeṣaḥ

A glad spirit attains to perfection more quickly than any other.
– St. Philip Neri

The meaning of this sutra is that, having understood that there is an ultimate degree of intensity in Yoga practice, we can infer that there are lesser degrees of intensity.

mṛdu = mild

soft, delicate, tender, mild, gentle, weak, feeble, slight, moderate, slow, pliant

from ***mṛd*** = trample down

madhya = moderate

medium, the middle (of a place, thing, or concept), center, average, standing between the two

may be related to ***mā*** = to measure out

adhimātravāt = fervent

extreme, above measure, excessive, literally, beyond the measure

from ***adhi*** = above, over, on + ***mātra*** = measure, quantity, from ***mā*** = measure + ***tva***, a suffix meaning to have the quality of

tatah = understanding this

thence, therefore, due to that, from that, resulting from that, then

api = (*refers to the previous sutra*)

indeed, also, very

viśeṣaḥ = depends on its steadiness and degree

distinction, difference, peculiarity, to define, apart from, special, superiority, extraordinary, definite, individualization, variety, peculiar merit, characteristic difference, special property, various objects, individual essence, the earth as an element

from ***vi*** = asunder, away + ***śeṣa*** = remainder, from the root ***śiṣ*** = leave

1.23 Or *asamprajnata samadhi* can be attained by wholehearted devotion and dedication to God (*Ishvara*) which displaces self-centered personal desires and naturally fosters contemplative absorption.

īśvara-praṇidhānā vā

īśvara = left untranslated

Lord, king, master, able to do, capable, God, supreme soul, Supreme Being, the god of love, the energies (*shakti*) of a Goddess (See 1.23–1.24, 2.1, 2.32, 2.45)

from ***iś*** = to rule, to own, to command, to be valid or powerful, to be master of, to reign, to behave like a master, supreme spirit + ***vara*** = valuable, eminent, choicest, suitor, lover, most excellent or eminent, better than, from ***vṛ*** = to choose

Ishvara is a term found in many sacred texts of India, including the *Upanishads* and the *Bhagavad Gita*. A good general understanding of *Ishvara* is that it is the reflection of the Absolute (*Brahman*) on the purest aspect of *prakriti* (*sattva*, that which has the nature of pure beingness) – like the sun reflecting on a perfect mirror. We see the sun. We can benefit from its light and even feel some of its heat. The mirror allows us to experience several real characteristics of the sun.

In Hinduism, interpretations of what *Ishvara* is may differ but they share the sense of *Ishvara* as the cosmic governing force and intelligence of the universe – master and Lord over all that is valuable. The Lordship of *Ishvara* extends to the individual self as well as to the entirety of the universe. Any name and form of the Divine can be taken as *Ishvara* for the sincere devotee.

Within the hearts of all beings resides the Supreme Lord (Ishvara)
and by the Lord's power, the movements of all beings are orchestrated
as if they were figurines on a carousel.
– Bhagavad Gita, 18.61

Ishvara serves as a role model for seekers who strive to manifest within themselves *Ishvara's* innate freedom from ignorance, obstacles, karma, and subconscious impressions.

Devotion to *Ishvara* harnesses the power of a loving, devoted heart to one's spiritual quest. Devotion and dedication directed to *Ishvara* have the power to awaken selfless love, the perfect inner environment for attaining self-mastery and which is also a natural counterforce to all vices and limitations. Selfless love generates a force that brings the devotee to liberation. Look ahead to sutra 2.45:

By wholehearted dedication to Ishvara,
perfection in samadhi is attained.

It is noteworthy that Patanjali gives no physical description of *Ishvara*. There is no one name and form assigned to *Ishvara*, although many Hindu deities are called by that name. Think of *Ishvara* as a screen upon which any name and form of the Divine can be projected. Wherever the devotee perceives the qualities of *Ishvara*, that is *Ishvara* for him or her (See 1.24). That is why even one's Guru can be taken as a form or expression of *Ishvara*.

Please note one more important aspect of *Ishvara pranidhanam*. Namely, Patanjali affirms the importance of not allowing the limited ego to be the beginning, middle, and end of life. We flourish and find peace and meaning in life when we have a reference point – a transcendent reality – outside of a private "I."

In other words, *Ishvara pranidhanam* helps prevent an individual from becoming her or his own personal god. Instead, Yoga (and all faith traditions) teaches the value of humility, and of being able to embrace the paradox of being fully human and fully divine. If we never learn to comfortably embrace this paradox, we can never know the inner workings of harmony and peace.

praṇidhānā = devotion, dedication, displace self-centered personal desires

to hold within and in front of, profound religious meditation, vehement desire, attention paid to, laying on, fixing, applying, access, entrance, exertion, endeavor, respectful conduct, abstract contemplation of, vow

from ***pra*** = before or in front + ***ni*** = down into or within + ***dhā*** = place, put, or hold

The essence of this very important word is to put something (or someone) first, before oneself. Reading through the various definitions, you can see that the term also implies strong intent and steady focus. This resonates with *Matthew 6:33*:

But seek first the kingdom of God and His righteousness,
and all these things will be added unto you.

Pranidhana is about cultivating priorities, focus, intention, and action – all based on love and reverence. It is describing an intimate relationship with that which is transcendent and that wields the power of self-transformation. It can also be described as nurturing an intimate relationship with the Great Mystery of life itself.[31]

[31] The Great Mystery is a phrase that encompasses eternal questions, such as: What is the purpose of life? Who am I? Why was I born? Why is there suffering? What brings happiness? What is God? Does God exist? The only satisfying answer to these questions is not to be found by finding just the right words, but by having the right relationship with the Source and Essence of life, the governing force and Cosmic Consciousness that pervades all creation, yet is also beyond it all.

Looking at the roots of *pranidhana*, we can see how it implies a heart-centered mindset: *to place down within and before.* It suggests a state of loving reverence. True love naturally promotes a selfless state of mind, a mindset where the object of love is always in the forefront of awareness. In *Ishvara pranidhanam*, the object of love is God.

Contemplating *Ishvara pranidhanam* and attempting to live it in our lives, we inevitably confront a vital question, a question rooted in our need to be appreciated, acknowledged, and loved. First, let's look at how hard we work to fulfill these needs by being good at what we do and by being a good person – both noble pursuits. We also look for signs of our worth, usually by status and possessions. In short, we feel we need to earn the right to be loved. Here's the question:

Do we look to the world or to God for love and for our worth?

Ishvara pranidhanam nudges us to look to *Ishvara*/God. It is here that we find that we have always been loved and that we need not do anything to earn that love. Our worthiness is innate in us. Nothing else is needed. This transformative realization is the basis of *svadharma*, our unique purpose for being.

Our worth – to ourselves and to others – and our discovery of our purpose for being all begins with dedication, our wish to find our ever-existing roots and connection to our True Self. Consider this quote:

The dedicated immediately enjoy an unbroken state of supreme peace.
– Bhagavad Gita 12.12

The final and sweetest fruit of dedication to *Ishvara* is enlightenment. We can interpret this sutra as being about surrender to God or Source. But, for many of us, surrender implies a slavish loss of freedom. True surrender is not. It is readiness to serve combined with trust in the fact that we are loved by that Source and Essence that gave and gives us life. Even for those who are not of a devotional nature, readiness to respond to life with, trust in its innate wisdom, is a vital aspect of spirituality.

The trust that we are loved unconditionally, arises when our suffering has reached its limit and we have nowhere else to turn except to God or

Guru, or when we are the object of complete, unconditional forgiveness. It is from this trust that gratitude grows, from gratitude comes faith, and from faith, a readiness to serve. This is the essence of surrender from a spiritual perspective.

In Buddhism, *pranidhana* is part of *bhadracharya pranidhana* (Vows of Good Conduct)[32] that includes: inexhaustible service to all buddhas, learning and obedience to all teachings of all buddhas, lamentation with the intention of calling forth all buddhas to descend into the world, the teaching of the *dharmas* (universal truths) and the *paramitas* (transcendental virtues) to all beings, the embracing of all universes, the bringing together of all The Buddha's lands, the achievement of The Buddha's wisdom and powers to help all beings, the unity of all *bodhisattvas*, and the accommodation of all sentient beings through the teaching of wisdom and *Nirvana*. These are *bodhisattva* vows, meant to express a mind directed toward enlightenment. In Mahayana Buddhism, this vow is taken by laypersons as well as monks and nuns.

va = or

either, on the one side – or on the other, either-or, to blow (as the wind), to procure or bestow anything by blowing

The word *va*, or, appears in this sutra for a reason.

The implications suggested by this simple word casts an interesting light on the process of choice. *Va* is also the root of the Vayu, the Hindu god of wind. *Vayu* is regarded as the breath of the cosmos, as Spirit, and as the mantra, OM (See sutra 1.27 on *pranava*). *Vayu*, as cosmic wind, saturates, shatters, and cleanses. *The Book of Psalms* and the *Koran* equate winds with angels – God's messengers.

Travelers know well that it is much easier to go with the wind at their back than facing it. Just as we hope to travel with the wind at our backs, we hope to travel the spiritual path in harmony with the flow of nature (*prakriti*) that exists to give experiences and liberation to the individual. (See 2.18)

[32] *Bhadracharya* = *bhadra* = good, dear, excellent, happy, pleasant, blessed, skillful in, blessed, great, auspicious, beautiful + *carya* = to be practiced or performed, going about, concern for, roaming about, conduct

Could it be that "or" is only meant to simply present us with two choices to mull over, or could it be a subtle call to attempt to tune into which direction the "spiritual wind" is blowing? A clear, meditative mind can often trace the subtle movements of life that have been and are shaping us. Could "or," in a yogic context, suggest that seekers should strive to put God's will above self-will?

In the spiritual arena, choice is not solely based on personal preference or on financial or social advantage. Choice includes assessing the impact of our options on our spiritual growth and on its impact on others and our planet.

Look at this sutra again. In the previous two sutras, Patanjali tells us that intense practice brings the realization of the goal of Yoga quickly. First, we get a picture of mastery over the mind and senses that arises through intense, sustained practice. Then we are presented with another option: we can explore devotion as a source of deep, powerful support for our practices. No emotion is stronger than loving devotion. The path of exertion of willpower and of heartpower is an example of Patanjali's holistic approach.

1.24 *Ishvara* is a unique *Purusha*. It is never touched by the root causes of suffering (*klesas*), the entanglements created by actions, their reactions (*karma*), and the subconscious impressions (*samskaras*) produced by these actions.

kleśa-karma-vipāka-āśayair aparāmṛṣṭaḥ puruṣa-viśeṣa īśvara

kleśa = root causes of suffering

pain, affliction, distress, pain from disease, anguish, wrath, anger, worldly occupation, care, trouble (See 1.24, 2.2–2.3, 2.12–2.13, 4.28, 4.30)

from ***kliś*** = to be troubled, to suffer distress

In some Hindu scriptures, the *klesas* are referred to as *viparaya* = error or misperception. This is because the root of the *klesas* is ignorance of our True Nature, the Seer. All suffering (*duhkha*) stems from this basic misperception of self as Self. (See 1.8)

Ignorance (*avidya*) is common to all human beings until liberation (*kaivalya*). This is much like what Christians refer to as original sin, which all human beings bring with them at birth. Why this is so, no one can give an answer that satisfies the intellect. The great faith traditions accept spiritual ignorance (not-knowing the Self) as a fact of human existence and instead focus on ways to become free of it and the suffering it brings in its wake.

In Buddhism, the *klesas* are considered to be the properties that dull the mind's perceptive abilities. They are the cause of all nonvirtue and suffering. As in the *Sutras*, the *klesas* are also the cause of rebirth. All the *klesas* are eliminated by the attainment of pure insight. Meditation is stated as the practice that gradually evaporates the *klesas*.

Refer to 2.3. The five *klesas* are listed as: ignorance, egoism, attachment, aversion, and clinging to bodily life.

karma = actions

performance, business, special duty, occupation, obligation, any religious act or rite (especially with the hope of future recompense and as opposed to speculative religion or knowledge of spirit), product, result, effect, fate (as the certain consequence of acts in a previous birth)

from ***kṛ*** = to do, act, or make (See 1.24, 2.12, 3.22, 4.7, 4.30)

In the West, we know karma as the universal law of cause and effect: we reap what we sow. However, the same word has an older meaning. Karma was used to designate the acts performed during rituals. Later, the *Upanishads* (fundamental scriptures discussing principles of Advaita Vedanta) expanded the understanding of karma to include any act performed by a human being.

Karma as action and reaction and karma as ritual acts have an important principle in common. Both present the power of *human actions* – not the powers of gods or other celestial beings – to determine destiny. The person who engaged in ritual acts expected rewards to come from their ritual sacrifices. It was believed that ritual could control the gods. In this way, rites performed perfectly – according to sacred tradition – were believed to determine one's future.

The law of karma, as we know it now, is the final stage in the development of the understanding of karma as the power to create, change, and determine how destiny is determined.

Here's India's historical development of karma:

The power lies with the gods who control everything. Ritual (sacrifice, *yajna*) is a way to appease or please them to attain what is needed and desired.

Religious rituals and rites have the power to control or influence the gods.

The power to create destiny rests in individuals themselves. Here is where karma and free will meet. This last stage leads to the next rather large leap of understanding:

For the mystic or yogi, the ultimate sacrifice or rite is not something performed at a temple or altar or by a priest but is the sacrifice of ignorance and selfish attachments at the altar of wisdom.

Reflecting on the above, we can see that there was a dramatic shift in the understanding of karma. When it was limited to the actions – the rites – performed only by priests, the divine powers and grace that could change lives for the better were only in the hands of priests. When karma evolved to a more general notion of action and reaction, it was democratized. The power to affect the experiences of our lives and to change are now in the individual's hands.

It is important not to reduce the law of karma to a fixed destiny. On the contrary, it is about the freedom to make decisions and to learn from the consequences of those choices. Karma is about how we learn, grow, and create our destiny ourselves.

In Jainism, karma is considered a subtle form of matter. The seeker needs to be freed from karma in order to attain liberation.

vipāka = reactions

ripe, mature, effect, result, the consequence of actions in the present or former births

from ***vi*** = away + ***pāka***, from ***pac*** = to cook, cooking

āśayair = storehouse

accumulation, receptacle, storage, or deposit of *samskaras*, residue, stock, balance of fruits from past actions

from ***a*** = hither, unto + ***śaya*** = lying, resting, abiding, from ***śī*** = rest, lie

aparāmṛṣṭaḥ = untouched

from ***a*** = not + ***mṛṣ*** = to touch or stroke + ***parā*** = other, another, subsequent, away, off, aside

puruṣa = *left untranslated*

soul, spirit, human being, humankind, witness of *prakriti*, Seer (passive spectator of *prakriti*; the term most used by Patanjali), knower within, indwelling form of God, cosmic person, the pupil of the eye, the first human and source of the universe, Supreme Being, a member or representative of a race or generation, officiant, servant, an officer

possibly from ***pur*** = the body, the stronghold of spirit, or ***puru*** – a man, male, human being (See 1.16, 1.24, 3.36, 3.50, 3.56, 4.18, 4.34)

viśeṣa = unique

distinct, difference between, characteristic difference, peculiar mark, special property, excellence, superiority, individuality, essential difference, individual essence, extraordinary, abundant (See 1.22)

***Ishvara* is a unique *Purusha*. What does this mean? We are all *Purushas*; all beings are *Purushas*, individual sentient beings. *Ishvara* is also a *Purusha*, an individual sentient being, but unique, distinct, special, extraordinary, abundant. There is a beautiful and important paradox here. *Ishvara* is divinity, but not the highest Divinity.[33]**

[33] *Ishvara* still has traits. It is the Seer as experienced from within *prakriti*. The reality of the Seer is beyond all description.

This sutra suggest that *Ishvara* is a *Purusha* like us, yet *Ishvara* stands apart, is unique. In the next sutra, Patanjali will begin to describe the ways in which *Ishvara* is unique.

īśvara = *left untranslated*

Lord, God (See 1.23–1.24, 2.1, 2.32, 2.45)

1.25 There, in *Ishvara*, is the seed of omniscience, which surpasses all other sources of knowledge and ideas of omniscience. It is beyond what is known by gods, clergy, and philosophers.

tatra niratiśyaṃ sarvajña-bījam

This sutra describes *Ishvara* as the ultimate "other." While this may make *Ishvara* seem like a distant reality, there is a powerful use in this. The paradox is that only when we fully embrace *Ishvara* as the ultimate other, can we experience the utter harmony/unity between *Ishvara* and self.

We need to grapple with conceiving the inconceivable in order to mature spiritually. The ego most often seeks to keep God at arm's length – at a safe distance – in the hope that it can sit at a safe distance, worshipping without deep connection. Love seeks union. Ultimately, we are that which we worship with faith and devotion.

tatra = there

niratiśyaṃ = surpasses

perfect, extremely, very, exceedingly, go beyond, beyond, over and under

from ***nir*** = out, away from + ***ati*** =over, beyond, past + ***śaya*** = lying, resting,

from śi = to rest, lie

sarvajña = omniscience

all-knowing, a buddha

from ***sarva*** = all + ***jñā*** = knowledge

This word is associated with gods, human beings, and especially ministers and philosophers.

bījam = seed

semen, any primary cause or principle, source, origin, truth (as the seed or cause of being), grain, matrix (an environment in which something develops), analysis, anything serving as a receptacle or support, seed sounds

From an uncertain origin:

The seed of omniscience is also found in every individual. The imagery of a seed calls to mind the cycle of regeneration: from seed, to plant, to fruit, and back to seed. The suggestion is that the seed of omniscience is potent and eternal.

The word *seed* could also be translated as matrix, a place within which something originates and develops.

1.26 Not bound by time, *Ishvara* is the Guru of even the most ancient Gurus.

pūrveṣaṃ api Guruḥ kālena anavachchedāt

The teacher provides spiritual energy!
Just like roots provide nutrients to the flowers.

– Master Choa Kok Sui

pūrveṣaṃ = the most ancient

the ones who came before, the previous ones

from **pūrvam** = before, formerly, hitherto, previously, former, being before or in front, prior, preceding, previous to, earlier than, ancient, old, an ancestor

api = even

expresses placing near or over, uniting to, annexing, reach to, proximity, and, also, moreover, besides, surely, as well as. Often used to express emphasis: very, even now, this very day

In this context, *api* is used to emphasize that *Ishvara* is not limited or conditioned by time and that the teachings, guidance, and wisdom of all Gurus are a reflection of the omniscience of *Ishvara*.

The focus of this sutra is on the omnipresence of wisdom and that the same wisdom, found in even the most ancient of Gurus, still flows through the spiritual masters of today, waiting to be fully awakened in us.

One benefit of this understanding is to keep the mind from longing for a past age of wisdom or of past great masters, now lost. Spiritual truths and the path to their realization, like love, eternally pierce through the layers of ignorance that veil every age and every place. *Ishvara* is the source of all redemptive knowledge and practices.

The same enlightening, redemptive wisdom found in the great Gurus is within all beings. Once kindled, this light continues to expand and grow brighter, purifying the mind and heart of ignorance.

Guru = *left untranslated*

heavy, weighty, heavy in the stomach with food, difficult to digest, great, large, extended, long, high in degree, vehement, important, serious, valuable, highly prized, venerable, respectable, any venerable or respected person, spiritual preceptor, pregnant

from ***gur*** = to raise, lift up, to make an effort, or from ***gri*** = to invoke, to praise

It is important to realize the central place the Guru holds in Indian thought, and in all mystic traditions, East and West. The Guru is not what many today imagine. The Guru is not just a master teacher or speaker. Some Gurus spoke little or not at all. The Guru is not just the intelligence of an individual or the knowledge accumulated from years of study. The Guru is a conduit or embodiment of the qualities of *Ishvara* listed in the past two sutras. In fact, historically, great enlightened individuals were addressed as *Ishvara*, a practice that continues to this day.

Especially before the widespread use of books, the teachings and guidance of a Guru were by far the most important sources of wisdom teachings. To this day, in India, the words of great spiritual masters are valued over the written word.

The bond between the Guru and disciple is a powerful, respectful, and loving relationship. It is through the disciple's dedication and willingness to be guided that the door to enlightenment swings open. The deepest and most transformational teachings are conveyed nonverbally through a process like osmosis. Words point to these truths, but are not themselves the truths. Too subtle for language, they are conveyed through example and the principle of spiritual resonance. The *Guru Gita*, a sacred text that details the nature of the Guru and the Guru-disciple relationship, presents this teaching as: *only a lit candle can give light to an unlit one.*

In this light, we can better understand why the great Gurus – past and present – were and are revered in the Yoga tradition.

Still, it is legitimate to question the need for a Guru in this day of easy to attain information, the multitude of Yoga centers, Yoga retreats, and Yoga teachers with impressive biographies all around us. No doubt, there have been those, called or considered Gurus, who have had either weaknesses or impure motives exposed. And there are those sincere seekers who have concerns with the idea of becoming a follower. The show of reverence to what obviously is a human being, doesn't sit well with them. They see devotion to a Guru as a loss of freedom. But one important spiritual truth should not be ignored: for those who are lost, guidance is freedom.

Anyone who feels that they have the means and wisdom to navigate through life without guidance doesn't need a Guru, or at least they won't be attracted to that relationship. But those who wish to make sense of what seems senseless in life, who wish to overcome fear, resentment, greed, anger, who suffer from these emotions even though they engage in regular practice, may find freedom in being shown direction and given support from an experienced guide.

kālena = by time

from ***kāl*** = drive forward, produce

anavachchedāt = not bound

not limited, not cut or separated, unconditioned

from ***an*** = not + ***ava*** = down, from, away, favor, off + ***cheda*** = cutting off, interrupting, from chid = cut, amputate

1.27 *Ishvara* expresses as the primordial sound OM, also known as *pranava.*

tasya vācakaḥ praṇavaḥ

tasya = that - (*refers to Ishvara*)

vācakaḥ = expresses

speaking, saying, telling anything, speaking of, treating of, declaring, expressive of, expressing, signifying, expressed by words, a significant sound or word, a messenger

from **vac** = to speak

praṇavaḥ = OM

from **pra** = to give, offer, bestow, before, forward + **nava**, from **nu** = sound, shout, exult

from **av** = to support or protect

OM is a word of solemn affirmation and respectful agreement, sometimes translated as *yes, verily, or so be it.* In this sense, it can be compared with Amen. It is placed at the beginning of most Hindu works.

Traditionally, it may be quietly repeated at the beginning and end of a reading of the *Vedas* or to begin any prayer.[34] OM is also used as part of an auspicious salutation (Hail!).

In the *Upanishads*, OM appears as a powerful mantra that is the object of profound meditation. OM represents the entire *Veda*[35] and since the *Veda* is considered one with *Brahman*, OM is regarded as the equivalent of *Brahman*.

OM is comprised of three letters in Sanskrit: *a, u, m*. In later Hinduism, it embodies the powers of the Hindu triad of gods, representing the union

[34] The reason for the quiet repetition is so that it is not overheard by those who are not pious.

[35] *Veda*, or *The Vedas*, are the most revered scriptures in Hinduism. They are four in number: *Rig, Atharva, Yajur*, and *Sama*. They are texts founded on the profound intuitive insights – revelations – of great sages. The *Upanishads* comprise the final portions of the *Vedas* and are considered the highest spiritual teachings in Advaita Vedanta, the philosophical school of nondualism.

of the three gods: a = Brahma, the creator; u = Vishnu, the sustainer; and m = Siva, the dissolver.

1.28 Repeat it with focus, devotion, and right understanding and the purpose of this practice is revealed.

taj japaḥ tad artha-bhāvanam

OM stands for the Supreme Reality. It is a symbol for what was, what is, and what will be. OM represents also what lies beyond past, present and future.
– Mandukya Upanishad

taj = that (*refers to OM*)

japa = to repeat

muttering, whispering, to repeat in a murmuring tone, passages from scriptures, mantras, or names of a deity

The word *jap* is quite common in the *Brahmanas*.[36] It refers to the priest's low muttering of mantras and sacred texts during ritual sacrifice. *Japa* is considered a form of *tapas*[37] in the *Dharma Sutras*[38]. The *Bhagavad Gita* lists *japa* as the greatest sacrifice.

Japa, then, is the interiorization of ritual sacrifice, a significant development toward the mystical or contemplative practices found in many faith traditions.

Tradition teaches that silent *japa* is one thousand times more powerful than outward sacrifice.

Svadhaya (study) and *japa* (repetition) are closely related. This emphasizes that study is more than collecting information. It is about the

[36] The *Brahmanas* are liturgical texts that give guidelines for performing sacrificial rites. They give rules for the use of mantras or hymns at various sacrifices, with detailed explanations of their origin and meaning. Each *Veda* has its own *Brahmana*.

[37] *Tapas* = hardship, self-discipline. See 2.1 for more on *tapas*.

[38] The *Dharma Sutras* are scriptures that are inspired by the *Vedas* and detail guidelines for proper conduct. They include rules regarding governance, diet, religious duties, and relationships between castes. The most important is the *Manu-smriti*, the Laws of Manu.

transformation of the individual. Old habits have to be transcended and new ones created, hence, the importance of repetition.

tat = (*refers to the purpose of the practice*)

that

artha = purpose

meaning, aim, cause, motive, reason, advantage, use, utility, wish, relating to a thing or object, material, means of life, true sense, occurrence (event), profit, object of desire, advantage, utility, and reason (See 1.28, 1.32, 1.42–1.43, 2.2, 2.18, 2.21–2.22, 3.3, 3.17, 3.36, 4.23–4.24, 4.32, 4.34)

Artha is difficult to reduce to a single English word. Its meanings vary widely and sometimes seem contradictory. *Artha* may best be described as the pursuit of any activity and the use of any means to create a peaceful, joyous life, and to foster harmony, without causing harm to anyone.

It is also described as the attitude and capacity necessary to make a living, remain alive, and thrive. *Artha* includes attaining prosperity, security, and health – the necessities of life.

Of particular interest, in the context of the *Sutras*, is *artha* as *true sense, occurrence (event), profit, object of desire, advantage, utility, and reason.* The practice of *japa* reveals the True Nature of OM, its spiritual utility, its benefits, and cultivates realization of the object of desire: realizing our connection with *Ishvara* and attaining the wisdom pointed to by *Vedic* scripture.

Some ancient Indian texts suggest that *artha* is anything that enables the satisfaction of desires, protecting what is already acquired, and increasing what is valuable. At the same time, it is required that, in acquiring possessions, none of the principles of *dharma*[39] should be violated.

bhāvanam = focus, devotion, right understanding

reflection, feeling of devotion, faith in, right conception or notion, thought, emotional intent, causing to be, manifesting, mind development, producing,

[39] One of the best definitions of *dharma* is from Sri Swami Sivananda: that which brings harmony.

displaying, promoting or affecting one's welfare, mental discipline, imagining, fancying, teaching, forming in the mind, conception, apprehension, supposition, meditation, direct one's thought to, (in logic) that cause of memory which arises from direct perception, furthering, nature, essence (See 1.28, 2.2, 2.33–2.34)

from **bhāv** = becoming, being, existing, occurring, appearance, transition into, continuance, continuity of existence through successive births, state, condition, rank, state of being anything, true condition or state, truth, reality, manner of being, nature, temperament, character, manner of acting, conduct, behavior, any state of mind or body, way of thinking or feeling, sentiment, opinion, disposition, intention, passion, emotion, conjecture, supposition, meaning, love, affection, attachment, the seat of feelings, heart, soul, mind, any living creature, the world, universe, the Supreme Being, advice, instruction, contemplation, meditation. From **bhū** = to become, exist, causing to be, affecting, producing, manifesting, displaying, contemplation, condition, inherent qualities of mind, feeling (in *Bhakti Yoga*) + **ana** = the act of doing and the vehicle for doing it

Bhavana is the emotion with which the work is being done,
the real motive with which the first move into the activity was made.
Bhavana is the most basic factor of all activity.
– Sri Swami Santananda Saraswati

Bhav, bhava, and bhavana, all different forms of the root, *bhu*, occur seven times in the *Sutras*.[40] As you can see above, the meanings of *bhavana* are vast and varied. That's because, *bhu* – existence or becoming – encompasses the essential nature of life: being and becoming, consciousness and matter, thinking and feeling.

Bhavana can refer to the act of contemplation as well as the "mental environment" in which thoughts appear.

When we come across this word in the *Sutras*, or in any Sanskrit text, it would be wise to pause and reflect on what the author might be trying to communicate. It's not likely that any English word captures the richness of this family of definitions. Yogis can consider that *bhavana* carries the sense of being absorbed emotionally and mentally in a practice, a practice that is informed with the right knowledge of theory and its goal.

[40] Note that the suffix, *ana* brings an emphasis of action to *bhav*. *Darsh* = to see. *Darshana* = the process of seeing, all that is needed to facilitate the act of perceiving.

In Buddhism there are two types of *bhavana*: the development of tranquility and the development of clear perception. The first leads to the second; it refers to development of the mind.

For the Jains, the word is used to mean to reject conceptualizations.

1.29 From this practice, awareness attains focus and naturally turns within. Not only that, obstacles that distract the mind and obstruct practice vanish.

tataḥ pratyak cetanā-adhigamo'py-antarāya-abhāvaś ca

tataḥ = from this

pratyak = within

in the opposite direction, backwards

from ***prati*** = as a prefix = toward, near to, against, in opposition to, back, again, in return, down upon. Before nouns, it also expresses likeness or comparison + ***ac*** = to bend

Awareness turning within is another way of describing the development of *nirodha*. (See 3.9–3.10)

cetanā = awareness

consciousness, understanding, visible, conspicuous, distinguished, excellent, sentient, intelligent, soul, mind

from ***cit*** = to perceive, know, appear

adhigamah = attains

result, gain, the act of attaining, acquisition, mastery, study, knowledge

from ***adhi*** = above, on, over and above, besides + ***gama*** = going, riding on, intercourse, going away from, a road

The meanings of this word suggest movement (*riding on, going away from, a road*) and also something that is primal and powerful – that leads, or better yet, beckons us – to satisfaction and creation (*intercourse*).

What we can discern is that as we attain the goal of the practice of mantra *japa* (and by extension, other yogic practices), our lives are more and more characterized by the fullness of life: movement, zeal, and vigor. Gradually, higher and more expansive states of consciousness arise in us.

api = not only that

also, even

antarāya = distracting obstacles

impediment, hindrance, intervention (See 1.30)

from ***antar*** = within, between, amongst, in the middle or interior, internal + ***āya***, from ***i*** = to go

abhāvaḥ = vanish

disappear, absence, non-existence, annihilation, death

from ***a*** = not + ***bhāva*** = being, from ***bhu*** = to be, exist

ca = and

1.30 The obstacles that distract the mind and disrupt practice are:

- **Disease**
- **Dullness, complacency, narrow-mindedness**
- **Doubt**
- **Carelessness**
- **Laziness**
- **Addiction to sense experiences**
- **Confused, false, or shifting views on principles of life, wisdom teachings, and practice**
- **Failure to reach firm ground**
- **Slipping from the ground gained**

vyādhi-styāna-saṃśaya-pramāda-ālasya-avirati-bhrānti-darśana-alabdha-bhūmikatva-anavasthitatvāni citta-vikṣepās te'ntarāhaḥ

vyādhi = disease

disorder, ailment, any tormenting, frustrating, or annoying person or thing

from ***vi*** = asunder, away + ***ā*** = hither, unto + ***dhi*** from ***dhā*** = put, place[41]

Disease in Patanjali's time included more than the disorders we know today. Disease was understood as any imbalance of the subtle energies[42] or humors that cause anxiety, restlessness, low energy, and physical discomfort.

styāna = dullness

apathy, grown dense, coagulated, stiffened, become rigid, soft, bland, unctuous, thick, bulky, gross, idleness, sloth, to grow dense, massiveness

from ***styā*** = to stiffen, to sound or echo: what is heard when a solid is struck, a dull thud or echo, a reverberation generated by the nature of the material struck

saṃśaya = doubt

indecision, uncertainty, irresolution, hesitation, doubt, a doubt about the point to be discussed

from ***sam*** = together + ***śaya*** = lying, sleeping, from śī = to rest, lie

The roots of this word suggest that a *tamasic* (lethargic, inert) state is fertile ground for the development of dullness. So doubt is not just the result of lacking sufficient information to make a decision, or of having too many choices, conflicting goals, or desires, but it is born from a mind that lacks clarity and insight – a mind that has lost focus. We will see that lack of mental focus, which disables the mind's ability to probe the object of its attention, is the root of almost all of the obstacles.

[41] The roots, *dhi* and *dha*, are the roots of *dharana* and *dhyana*, concentration and meditation. This tells us that these obstacles are those that take us from, or oppose, the meditative state of mind.

[42] This refers to the three *doshas*: *vata, pita*, and *kapha*, which are condensed and composed of the five elements: ether, air, fire, water, and earth.

pramāda = carelessness

negligence, lack of commitment, intoxication, madness, insanity, carelessness about, negligence, an error or mistake, to revel or delight in

from ***pra*** = forward, in front + ***mad*** = to be exhilarated, intoxicated

Pramada **suggests a state similar to intoxication or a form of mental imbalance. It can follow misuse, overindulgence, or abuse of the senses. Since it is listed as following doubt, we can imagine it as a state of discouragement with oneself or with the results of practice.**

ālasya = laziness

idleness, sloth, lack of energy

from ***a*** = not + ***lasa*** = to shine, to be lively, moving about, from ***las*** = shine, flash, play, frolic

Look at the root, *las*. It suggests that what is translated as laziness can be interpreted as not feeling like playing or frolicking, a loss of the joy of life.

avirati = addiction to sense experiences

sensuality, incontinence, intemperance, lack of self-restraint

virati = cessation, pause, stop, end, to not abstain or desist, from ***a*** = not + ***vi*** = asunder, away + ***rati*** = pleasure

The word suggests the inability to stay away from indulging the senses.

bhrānti = confused, false, shifting

moving around, staggering, wandering about, doubt, perplexity, error, quivering, false opinion, reeling

from ***bhram*** = wander about, waver

darśana = view, philosophy

philosophical system, knowing, exhibiting, showing, looking at, teaching, seeing, perception, way of looking, apprehension, observation, aspect, act of seeing, inspection, contemplating, vision, observing, visiting, audience, meeting, experiencing, discernment, understanding, intellect, intention, doctrine, the eye, becoming visible or known, presence (See 1.30, 2.6, 2.41, 3.33)

from ***dṛś*** = to see, perceive

Refer to 3.33 for more on *darshana*.

In this sutra, *darshana* refers to philosophies of life and spirituality. The combination of *darshana* with *bhranti* (*confused, false, shifting*) forms an image of a mind that is uncertain about what is true, and which teachings, principles, and bits of knowledge are reliable (See 1.7).

Uncertainty leads to not delving sufficiently into teachings. This can lead to a tendency to find fault in teachings that are true and proven by time and experience instead of looking within for our own shortcomings or gaps in understanding.

Our ability to perceive (*darshana*) subtle truths is wedded to a clear, one-pointed, unbiased (*sattvic*) mind. Such a state of mind gives rise to *yoga pratyaksha*, yogic perception. *Yoga pratyaksha*, a central principle in Yoga, is unmediated perception that transcends sense perception.[43] It is what enables seers to apprehend the truths of self and existence, since it transcends the distortion caused by the senses, ignorance, and ingrained mindsets and beliefs. Other forms of cognition, even if valid and reliable, are inferior to *yoga pratyaksha*.

The knowledge gained from *Yoga pratyaksha* is the basis of the wisdom of Vedic sages, yogis, and *siddhas* (see *siddha* in this sutra).

alabdha = failure

not obtained, not having attained

from ***a*** = not + ***labh*** = to take, seize, catch

bhūmikatva = ground

groundedness, stage, place, step

from ***bhūmi*** = earth, position, stage + ***ka*** = having + ***tva*** = quality

[43] Unmediated refers to perception without the means of – that bypasses – the senses.

The words, *alabdha* (above) + *bhumikatva* combined, mean the failure to reach firm ground or the absence of initiative.

anavasthitatvāni = slipping from ground gained

inconstancy, unsteadiness, instability, not abiding

from ***an*** = not + ***avasthita*** = standing near, placed, abode, continuing to do anything, engaged in, following, practicing, obeying or following, giving oneself up to, contained in, firm, fixed, determined, steady, trusty, to be relied on

This word suggests a withdrawing or pulling back of the mind: *to not be fixed* and *to not follow*. But maybe the most telling definition is *to not give oneself up to* – something like an emotional withdrawal from a love affair.

The results we experience from our Yoga practice is a harmonious symphony consisting of the yogic lifestyle and exercises along with the degree of inspiration, devotion, joy, faith, and optimism we bring to the practices.

citta = mind

individual consciousness (See 1.2)

vikṣepā = distract, disrupt

the act of throwing asunder or away or about, scattering, discharging, moving to and fro, waving, shaking, tossing, letting loose, indulging, letting slip, neglecting, inattention, distraction, confusion, perplexity, a kind of disease

from ***vi*** = away, asunder + ***kṣepā*** = throwing, casting, from ***kśip*** = throw, send

Vikshepa can be understood as the opposite of *samyama*: the practice of concentration, meditation, and absorption on any one object. (See 3.1-4)

Vikshepa as shaking or moving to and fro, when seen in light of the three functions of mind, can offer an interesting insight into the inner mechanics of these obstacles...

Manas: the recording faculty.

When it shakes, misperception, partial perception, or nonperception of an event, thought, image, or feeling occurs.

Buddhi: the discriminative faculty.

When our ability to discern falters, we miss important facets or implications of events, thoughts, images, or feelings.

Ahamkara: the ego sense.

When the ego is unstable, it is also unclear. Its appropriate function is hampered by feelings of lack of worth, guilt, and self-doubt. In some cases, it can also lead to an inflated sense of worth and a compulsive need to dominate or control.

te = these

antarāya = obstacle

intervention, impediment, hindrance

from **antar** = between, within, in the interior, amongst, into + **āya**, from ***i*** = to go

As a suffix, *aya* strengthens the word it is attached to. The implication is that these are deeply rooted inner obstacles that are not easy to overcome.

1.31 These distracting obstacles are accompanied by:

- *Duhkha*: dissatisfaction, sorrow, suffering, and a pervasive, persistent feeling of precariousness
- Frustration from not having desires fulfilled
- Restlessness or trembling of the body
- Agitated or labored inhalation or exhalation

duḥkha-daurmanasya-angam-ejayatva-śvāsa-praśvāsāḥ vikṣepa-sahabhuvaḥ

When the mind wanders in its focus or resolve, the obstacles appear accompanied by any or all of these accompaniments.

duḥkha = pervasive, persistent uneasiness or dissatisfaction

discontent, distress, anxiety, stress, pain, uneasiness, difficulty, sorrow, trouble, to cause or feel pain, unpleasant (See 1.31, 1.33, 2.5, 2.15–2.16, 2.34)

from ***duṣ*** = difficult, wicked, bad, inferior + ***kha*** = axle hole, cavity, hollow, cave

The essence of *duhkha* – often translated as pain, sorrow, or suffering – is more than that. It is grounded in a persistent sense of never-ending precariousness, a baseline of uneasiness or anxiety that forms the backdrop of our lives. *Duhkha* is a feeling or belief that life is flawed; that it can't be trusted. *Duhkha*, manifesting as suspicion, is the pathology of ignorance.

Duhkha, in its most insidious form, is a background of quietly screeching violins seeming to warn us of possible pain behind the closed door we are about to open (or decisions or plans, or relationships). *Duhkha* is born of fear, uncertainty, ignorance of our True Nature, and attachments to our dreams or personal visions of our future.

The opposite of *duhkha* can be said to be *suhkha*, pleasure or happiness. But, it might be more accurate, or at least more helpful, to think of trust as the opposite of *duhkha*. We see in sutra 2.28, that the entire universe exists to give us experiences and liberation. It would not be incorrect to understand this as an act of love. Out of love, the universe manifests and acts. When we learn to trust that we are loved and that the universe is a benevolent place, then – and only then – are we truly free to accept and to give love. This trust in life also eradicates greed, lust, fear, anger, and resentment.

How do we develop this trust? Through cultivating gratitude, by daily remembering all the gifts we have been freely given: our mind, our friends, the sun, the scent of a rose, the thirst for knowledge, laughter, song, a tasty

peach, the great sages and saints of all faith traditions.[44] Gratitude ripens into devotion and devotion into trust, which is faith.

daurmanasya = frustration

despair, depression, dejectedness, melancholy, sorrow from having a desire frustrated, a deep, pensive and long-lasting sadness, it is a form of mental agitation

from ***daur*** = a strengthened form of ***duṣ*** = difficult, inferior, bad + ***manasya*** = have in mind, think, from man = to think, conjecture

angam = body

limb

ejayatva = trembling, restlessness

unsteady, shaking

from ***ej*** = stir, move, tremble

Agitated or labored breathing is implied from *ejayatva*.

śvāsa = inhalation

from ***śvas*** = to pant, to breathe, draw breath, to sigh, groan, to cause heavy breathing

praśvāsāḥ = exhalation

from ***pra*** = before, forward + ***śvāsa*** = inhalation, breath

vikṣepa = distracting obstacles

dispersion of intents and resolves of the mind, the act of throwing asunder or away or about, scattering, dispersion, discharging, moving to and fro, waving, shaking, tossing, letting loose, indulging (the opposite of *samyama*), letting slip, neglecting, inattention, distraction, confusion, perplexity, a kind of disease

from ***vi*** = away, asunder + ***kṣepa*** = throwing, casting, from ***kṣip*** = throw, send

[44] Why use the phrase "faith traditions," instead of faiths or religions? The phrase encompasses the two major aspects of the culture, history, and teachings of all spiritual paths. What they have in common is faith: in something beyond the material universe that is our essence and source. What differs is their traditions: myths, rituals, holy days, language, etc. In the phrase "faith traditions," we can see the essential teaching: "Truth is one, paths are many," to quote Sri Swami Satchidananda.

sahabhuvaḥ = accompany

appearing together, counterpart of

from ***saha*** = together with + ***bhuva*** = from ***bhū*** = to be or exist

1.32 In order to prevent the distracting obstacles and their accompaniments, commit to the teachings and practices of one path.

tat-pratiṣedha-artham eka-tattva-abhyasa

This sutra adds another facet or option to the methods for overcoming the distracting obstacles presented in sutras 1.30 and 1.31.

Here, we are given the importance of regularity and of maintaining our efforts within an established, proven tradition. For example, sporadic repetition of a mantra, outside the supportive practices and lifestyle of an established yogic path, usually does not produce the desired or optimal results. Even a regular practice can greatly benefit from the cohesiveness and time-and-effort-saving teachings within a yogic tradition, a lineage or school of thought, with its built-in checks and balances.

Changing approaches and techniques whenever the mind feels bored or disappointed can aggravate the obstacles (1.30), all of which are based on restlessness of mind.

tat = (*refers to the distracting obstacles and their accompaniments*)

these, them

pratiṣedha = prevent

counteract, keeping back, warding off, prevention, repulsion (of a disease), refusal, denial, contradiction, exception, negation

from ***prati*** = against, back + ***sedha*** = driving away from, from ***sidh*** = repel

artham = in order to

purpose, meaning, aim, purpose, cause, motive, reason, advantage, use, utility, relating to a thing or object, material, resulting from or based on the possession of a thing

eka = one

single

When we talk about sticking to one path, we are talking about the focus, harmony, holism that is found in any proven school of thought and practices.

Even though in the beginning, it is usually best to experiment with different spiritual paths, it is recommended to stick to the path or tradition that resonates most deeply for us. It is better to dig deeply in one place to find water than to continually dig shallow wells, as Yoga Master Swami Satchidananda often reminded us.

Though the superficial characteristics of every genuine path may differ, in essence, they are the same. Every faith tradition is about evaluating what's important in life, seeking what brings peace and harmony and what brings pain; it's about turning from selfish cravings and toward selfless service; it's about transcending spiritual ignorance.

As seekers approach Me, so do I receive them. All paths, Arjuna, lead to Me.
– Bhagavad Gita 4.11

And Peter opened his mouth and said, "Truly I perceive that God shows no partiality, but in every nation anyone who fears him and does what is right is acceptable to him."
– Bible, Acts 10:34 – 35

Confucius said... "In the world there are many different roads but the destination is the same. There are a hundred deliberations but the result is one."
– I Ching, Appended Remarks 2.5

At any time, in any form and accepted name, if one is shorn of all attachment, that one is you alone. My Lord! You are one although variously appearing.
– Anyayoga-Vyavaccheda-Dvatrimsika of Hemacandra (Jainism)

tattva = teachings

subject, true or real state, truth, reality, principle, the essence or substance of anything, an elementary property of existence, that-ness, a category of cosmic existence (the elements and essences of *prakriti*, for example)

from ***tat*** = that + ***tva*** = the quality of something; literally, that-ness

Tattva refers to the principles that make up a school of theories and practices. The *Yoga Sutras* are the *tattvas* (the principle teachings) of Patanjali.

abhyasa = practices (See 1.12)

1.33 The mind becomes calm, clear, and bright when it cultivates and abides in the unconditional virtues of friendliness, compassion, delight, and equanimity in conditions, respectively, of happiness, distress, virtue, and absence of virtue.

maitrī-karuṇā-muditā-upekṣānām sukha-duḥkha-puṇya-apuṇya-viṣayāṇām bhāvanātaś citta-prasādanam

Be a rainbow in someone else's cloud.
– Maya Angelou

This sutra is not just specific techniques to be deployed in situations of happiness, unhappiness, virtue, and nonvirtue. More importantly, it is about cultivating an intimate relationship with friendliness, compassion, delight, and equanimity.

The focus is on practice and lifestyle rather than belief. Belief is a matter of accepting ideas. Practice and lifestyle are about self-transformation and direct experience of realities of life and Spirit. We see this here and in other sutras, such as 2.1 and 2.29.

We have come to understand faith traditions as emphasizing belief. Yoga, and all deep spirituality emphasizes practice...

How we behave is much more important than what we believe.

This is one reason why so much attention is given to this sutra in this text.

maitrī = friendliness

friendship, benevolence, good will, close contact or union, equality, similarity, a feeling of approval or support from ***mid*** = to love, feel affection, to melt, to adhere

The main idea is to cultivate a mindset that projects – and is led by – friendliness in situations, and toward people, where happiness is perceived. Ultimately, it is about making friends with happiness and training the mind to recognize it wherever, and in whomever, it expresses.

In Buddhism, *maitri* is often translated as lovingkindness.

karuṇā = compassion

mercy, pity, mournful, lamenting, in the *Rig Veda*, *karuna* is considered a holy work or action

From ***kṛ*** = to do, or ***kṛ*** = to pour out, scatter

Karuna, compassion, is the deep hope that the suffering of others will be reduced. It's not only a nice sentiment. Compassion is a powerful generator of a clear, focused, peaceful mind that naturally leads to selfless actions performed for the benefit of others. Science has recently affirmed that the happiness that is innate in giving is greater than the happiness derived from receiving.

Compassion is always associated with some sort of action. It's not just feeling pity or empathy. But, to act – to reach out in compassion to someone who is suffering – can be difficult when confronting a person who we have issues with, who we might not like, or who has hurt us or those we love. That is why for the full transforming power of compassion to manifest, forgiveness is necessary.

Reflection

We need to extend forgiveness to ourselves, as well. We need to extend our compassion to our own shortcomings and mistakes. The danger is that if we can't forgive and extend compassion to ourselves, the darker sides of who we are retreat to ever more deeply hidden recesses of the mind, only to come back with redoubled force.

The need for forgiveness also applies to *mudita* (See page 92). How can we delight in a virtue we see in someone we have issues with? In fact, without the ability to forgive, we might miss perceiving the virtue altogether. Let's take a closer look at forgiveness.

We can understand forgiveness as the restoration of belonging in a relationship. We argue, feel a break or fracture (minor, middling, or great) in a relationship. The sense of trust and belonging is damaged. When forgiveness arrives, the sense of belonging is restored.

What about the guilt we carry for past wrongdoings? So many of us are in need of being forgiven. The fracture caused by guilt – or believing that we are not good enough – in some way, can be so deep that virtually no one we know can heal it with their forgiveness and acceptance of who we are.

Sacred wisdom teaches that consciousness, Spirit, *Purusha*, is omnipresent. We also read in the *Sutras* that nature exists to give us experiences that lead to liberation. Put together, these truths lead us to a vital and true conclusion: we belong. We are children of the universe here for a purpose, and to grow and find our spiritual freedom. We belong. We don't need to ask the universe or God for forgiveness. We are already forgiven because we belong – to God, to the universe, to life. We are participants in the dance of life, not just observers. We belong.

When we ask God, Guru, or others for forgiveness, it is for the sake of experiencing a restoration of the feeling of belonging in the relationship. Asking for forgiveness opens our hearts and makes us vulnerable to the forgiveness that was, is, and always will be ours.

A final thought regarding forgiveness. Life can be hard. So many changes and unwelcome and unexpected challenges arise. We can see arrayed before us every manner of injustice and unexplainable atrocities. Yet, if we can't embrace all of life, we can never know its essence and source. We are caught in a thought habit of: If it doesn't make sense to me, then it is senseless. How can a God that "allows" all these terrible events be wise, loving, and merciful? We can't understand it. This amounts to seeking a God that is just a tiny bit less intelligent than we are, a God we can understand with our limited intellect. This is a symptom of believing that we should and can control life or God by our thoughts, words, and deeds. It never works. What are we to do? One way to begin is by forgiving God for not living up to your standards. The absurdity of this practice helps reconcile us to the ways and wisdom of life. We are released from the need to be in control of everything and, in a healthy way – that is not resignation – surrender to universal cosmic life, truth, love, and light. The answer to some questions just has to be lived out. The question of the sense or senselessness of life is one of them.

muditā = delight

happiness, gladness, joy with others

from **mud** = be merry, glad, happy, rejoice, delight in, sympathetic joy, a kind of sexual embrace, happiness at another's success, a particular kind of servant

Mudita is the happiness that comes from expanding our vision of life and our concerns to include caring about and working for the happiness and welfare of others. When we extend our goals and desires to include caring for the welfare of others, we experience an expansion of joy.[45]

Mudita is also happiness connected to a view of life that anticipates – even perceives – the beauty, benefit, and inherent rightness of an object or event even before those benefits have fully emerged. It's not a simple state of optimism, but an enhanced or expanded vision of life that experiences the harmony behind (and as the motive force of) all events and objects. For example, it is like appreciating a flower before it reaches its full bloom – before it manifests its colorful petals and releases its fragrance. *Mudita* requires faith, knowledge, and a more refined ability of perception.

Mudita counters distrust, suspicion, and the tendency to reject happiness from things that are short-lived, a *"What's the point? It will only last for a moment"* attitude.

The practice of *mudita* lifts the heart out of its anxieties over not having enough of what we think we need to be happy and secure. The heart, unburdened by these concerns, discovers new and greater gratitude and a powerful natural inclination toward generosity.

[45] The more we make for "others" in our hearts, the happier we become.

Mudita should not be mistaken for the excited state that many regard as happiness. *Mudita* is grounded in peace and faith.

Mudita is born in a selfless, grateful, giving heart that desires and works for the welfare of others. *Mudita* rejects jealousy and envy. It seeks to break down all artificial barriers that separate us from each other and nature. It rejoices in the good fortune and happiness of all.

Mudita is an eagerness and ability to support the joy and expanding spirit of others.

The Buddha taught that one of our challenges is to cultivate *mudita,* even in a world full of misery.

There may be no more powerful practice in Yoga than *mudita*.

upekṣānām = equanimity

the act of disregarding, overlooking, indifference, not doing, omission, care, circumspection

from ***upa*** = to go near, toward + ***ikṣā*** = to look at or on

Look at the roots of the word. We could literally translate *upeksha* as, going near to look at. This give us the key to cultivating *upeksha*. When confronted with any nonvirtue, yogis are asked to not turn away, to not jump to conclusions (a technique of avoidance of discomfort), but to remain clear, focused, and centered in order to correctly perceive the event and its ramifications. Clear perception and a tranquil mind also foster creative solutions where none were apparent before.

Upeksha strengthens our capacity to accept life as it is, allowing us to work with, and not against, inevitable change. It allows us to accept that nonvirtue exists, has a course, and may have roots and impacts on many levels. It is a state of mind that is not overwhelmed by ignorance, selfish egoism, dullness, agitation, hatred, or greed. *Upeksha* helps us to serenely accept loss and gain, praise and blame, sorrow and happiness. Because of this, *upeksha* helps overcome fear.

Upeksha accepts, with equanimity, (not with resentment or reluctance) that all people have shortcomings and make mistakes. It helps us avoid condemning others. Instead, we come to rightly perceive, accept, and love others in their entirety, faults and all. We come to embrace all people regardless of their beliefs, behavior, or origin.

Through *upeksha*, we come to see how our own thoughts, words, and deeds may have contributed to hardships, tensions, and other nonvirtuous situations. This helps develop compassion.

Upeksha replaces both an overly sentimental and an overly pessimistic view of life with a powerful insight: All thoughts, words, and deeds, and all events have "side effects." Some are obviously pleasant and beneficial, some cause hardship and troubles. Yet, somehow, they have a purpose.

Since we can't eliminate or avoid negative situations and people, *upeksha* teaches us the limits of self-effort. This helps cultivate humility, which softens the grip of the selfish ego on the mind which, in turn, helps cultivate:

- Forgiveness
- Gratitude
- Cooperation
- Generosity

Upeksha helps open the heart. The spiritual heart is a sensitive organ. It is the home of the Self, the Divine within. It is powerful, yet it closes easily to avoid getting hurt. The equanimity and fearlessness generated by *upeksha* encourages the heart to open.

Upeksha is also the remedy for resentment. There can be no joy where there is resentment. Resentment is a reaction; a feeling of hostility or anger that arises as a result of a real or imagined wrong done. It is from the Latin, *sentire*, to feel. *Re* is an intensifier that also means to return. Resentment is an injured ego striking out in anger. *Upeksha* teaches us to stand firm in our center, knowing who we really are. Who we are is not determined by what others think of us or how we are treated. Although we should attentively and sincerely listen to the criticisms and observations others have of us, we need to develop an inner sense of who we are. Knowing that we are living a virtuous life as best we can, engaging in practices that uplift us and bring us ever closer to our source and essence helps a lot.

When viewed from this vantage point, and armed with compassion, discernment, and inner tranquility, instances that once caused resentment lose their power to disturb our inner peace.

In Buddhism, *upeksha* means to discern clearly; to view justly. It is one of the most important virtues. It is a state of neither excitement nor suffering, but is independent of both. It arises in a mind that is in equilibrium and that transcends all distinctions. It is considered one of the seven factors of enlightenment.

We can also think of *upeksha* as having the attitude of a scientist, a mind bent on discovering realities not readily discernable. When yogis confront any unpleasantness, they don't shrink from it. Instead, they examine it, looking for its roots and ramifications.

sukha = happiness

running swiftly or easily (applied to cars or chariot), easy, pleasant (rarely with this meaning in the *Vedas*), agreeable, gentle, mild, comfortable, prosperous, virtuous, pious, the sky, heaven, In Hindu mythology, *sukha* is the child of *dharma* (righteousness) and *siddhi* (accomplishment, perfection, power). (See 1.33, 2.5, 2.7, 2.42, 2.46)

from ***su*** = well, good, fine + ***kha*** = axle hole, state

The intent of cultivating friendliness toward the happy is, of course, to extend our compassion and energies to those who are experiencing happiness, but there is another level of benefit suggested here. It is to help heal any sense of envy or separation with those who are experiencing the smooth ride (*sukha*) as opposed to *duhkha* in their lives. The healing of what separates us (gender, religion, race, etc.) is central to every faith tradition.

The yogi is asked to generate the attitude of happiness regardless of the source of happiness.[46] There are essentially two paths we can take to experience happiness.

First, and the one we are most familiar with, is the attempt at lining up pleasurable experiences as tightly as possible with the hope of shutting out disappointments and preventing anxieties from creeping in and spoiling our happiness. The happiness we experience from this way of generating *sukha* is a fleeting form of happiness. Its roots are not deep and are very susceptible to damage.

The second source of *sukha* is within and is intrinsic to our nature. It is like an underground river of joy that flows regardless of our state of mind and external circumstances. Because of its special nature, it is often called joy or bliss, rather than happiness. The mind may be suffering, but bliss, a river that flows deeply within the heart, is unaffected. This means that it is possible to know joy beneath and beyond challenge and hardship. The joy we experience is far more vast and will feel more real and true than our sadness or anxiety.

Furthermore, we shouldn't limit our understanding of bliss to being a personal possession. It is not stored in the mind like a gift in a box. It is a mighty river that flows in, around, and through us. It is experienced in a tranquil mind and loving heart. It is a particular joy that cannot be taken away because it has no cause. It just is. It is a manifestation of our True Nature.

duḥkha = distress

uneasy, uncomfortable, unpleasant, difficult, pain, sorrow, trouble, to cause or feel pain, discontent, anxiety, stress, a persistent background of dissatisfaction (See 1.31, 1.33, 2.5, 2.15–2.16, 2.34)

from ***duṣ*** = prefix implying evil, bad, difficult, hard, slight, inferior + ***kha*** = axle-hole

Refer to 1.31 for more on *duhkha*.

[46] This doesn't include happiness derived from unethical or nonvirtuous means. Instead, we look to equanimity toward the nonvirtuous.

puṇya = virtue

merit, righteousness, goodness, auspicious, deserved reward, to earn or deserve, right, pleasant, purity, holy, propitious, fair, virtuous, sacred, moral or religious merit (See 1.33, 2.14)

from ***puṇ*** = to act piously or virtuously, to collect or accumulate, or ***pu*** = cleansing, purifying, to make clean and bright, to purge, clarify, illumine, or ***puṣ*** = thrive, cause to prosper + ***ya*** = from

Punya, virtue, is always understood in the context of thoughts, words, and deeds that are for the benefit of others. Virtue is that which brings the greatest happiness to the greatest number of beings. As such, virtues are not simply rules or codes of conduct, they are ways of perceiving and being, qualities that are integrated into one's heart and mind that help foster the well-being and happiness of all beings.

Note that the root word of *punya* means to *thrive; to cause to prosper.* Virtue is not about ideas of holiness that the mind has constructed. Virtue is anything that brings harmony, that breaks down artificial barriers that separate us – it is about anything that fosters lovingkindness.

apuṇya = absence of virtue

impure, wicked (See punya, above and 1.33, 2.14)

In Patanjali's text, the opposite of virtue, strictly speaking is not evil or wickedness. *Punya* = virtue; *apunya* = the absence of virtue. It's like darkness. Darkness isn't a thing, but the absence of something – light. Therefore, we can understand nonvirtue as a state of mind and being that ignores the unhappiness and suffering of others. A state of inner darkness also allows someone to engage in thoughts, words, and deeds that bring harm to others.

viṣayāṇām = conditions

sphere of influence or activity, dominion, kingdom, territory, region, district, country, abode, scope, compass, horizon, range, the reach (of ears, eyes, mind), period of duration, fitness, toward (experiences of)

viṣayā = an object of senses, anything perceptible by the senses, any object of affection or concern or attention, any special worldly object or aim or matter or business, sensual enjoyments, sensuality, an object, a fit or suitable object, the subject of an argument, category, the subject of comparison, a religious obligation or observance, a lover, husband, virile, auspicious, propitious, fair, pleasant, good, right, virtuous, meritorious, pure, holy, sacred, good work, moral or religious merit, religious ceremony (especially by a wife to retain her husband's affection and to obtain a son)

from ***viṣ*** = to act or from ***vi*** = asunder, away + ***si*** = to extend

bhāvanātaḥ = cultivate

to project

from ***bhāvanā*** = demonstration, argument, ascertainment, feeling of devotion, faith in, reflection, contemplation, infusion, steeping, finding by combination or composition, from ***bhū*** = to become (See 1.28, 2.2, 2.33–2.34, 4.25)

Bhavanatah **suggests the place where anything is produced, gives birth, and grows. It is related to *bhavana, a state of being or mind, abode, home, site, receptacle,* and to *bhava, being, nature, disposition, feeling* (this last definition is mostly found in *Bhakti Yoga*).**

Home is where you have comfort, support, and safety. Birth implies emergence. The virtues listed in this sutra need to be birthed, and nurtured by contemplation and reinforced by action until they become our foundation, innate qualities of our inner spiritual home.

citta = mind

consciousness, field of consciousness (See 1.2)

prasādanam = calm, clear, bright

rendering clear, soothing, cheering, gratifying, rendering gracious, tranquility, grace, a gift from God, to be satisfied (the opposite of *duhkha*), to be kind, gracious (See 1.33, 1.47)

from ***pra*** = before, forward + ***sādana*** = to cause to settle down, offer, grace, from sad = to sit, dwell

Reflection

This sutra, beautifully called the "*Four Locks and Four Keys*" by my spiritual master, Sri Swami Satchidananda, presents the same principles known as the *Brahma Viharas* in Buddhism.

Vihara translates as a place of rest and peace. It is also the term for temple and monastery – the residence of monks – and a place where they can go for meditation.

Definitions of Brahma include: *holy, relating to sacred knowledge, that which is divine, Supreme Spirit, the absolute*. The suggestion is that these principles offer a place to find peace, clarity, knowledge, and wisdom.

In Mahayana Buddhism, these teachings, also known as the Four Immeasurables, are regarded as perfect virtues. Their practice is required in order to help bring all beings to liberation. They are to be meditated on in the following manner:

The meditator generates these mindsets to all beings in all directions:

- Limitless lovingkindness
- Limitless compassion
- Limitless sympathetic joy
- Limitless equanimity

Here are two examples of using the locks and keys as the focus of a meditation practice from the Buddhist tradition:

1. Sit with a mind filled with compassion, kindness, sympathetic joy, and equanimity. Radiate these virtues first in one direction, then a second, then a third, and then a fourth; above as well as below, and all around and feeling connected with everything everywhere. Fill the whole world with kindness, sympathetic joy, compassion, and equanimity. Let your mind be expansive, serene, unconfined, and free from malice and resentment.

2. These four virtues should be practiced by taking each one in turn and applying it to oneself, then to others nearby, to everybody in the world, and to everybody in all universes.

1.34 Or by smooth, regulated exhalation and by retention of the breath.

pracchardana-vidhāraṇābhyāṃ vā prāṇasya

pracchardana = exhalation

emitting, vomiting

from ***pra*** = to come forth, before, forward + ***chṛd*** = to vomit, expel, eject

vidhāraṇābhyāṃ = retention

holding, restraining

vidārana = tearing, breaking, splitting, piercing, a tree or rock in the middle of a stream to which a boat is fastened, opening the mouth wide

from ***vi*** = asunder, apart, different, away + ***dhārana*** = to hold, keep, bear, from ***dha*** = to hold + ***abhyām*** = to advance violently against, pain, hurt

vā = or

This word generally comes immediately following the word to which it refers.

prāṇasya = of the breath

life

from ***pra*** = before, forward + ***ana*** = breath, respiration

1.35 Or clear steadiness of mind is attained when focus on a sense object causes a subtle sense perception to arise.

viṣayavatī vā pravṛitti utpannā manasaḥ sthiti-nibandhanī

viṣayavatī = sense object

having a condition, involved in a sphere of sense activity, taking up an object of desire

from ***viṣaya*** = object, condition, dominion, sphere of activity or concern (See 1.11 and 1.23) + ***vati*** = feminine form of a suffix indicating possessive adjective

vā = or

pravṛitti = subtle sense perception

activity, moving onward, cognition, advance, progress, coming forth, appearance, manifestation, rise, source, origin, activity, exertion, efficacy, function, active contemplative devotion (defined as consisting of the wish to act, knowledge of the means, and accomplishment of the object), conduct, behavior, practice, continuance, fate, lot, destiny, news, tidings, cognition (See 1.35, 2.26, 4.5)

from ***pra*** = before, forward, in front of, forth + ***vṛitti*** = a commentary, comment, gloss, explanation (especially of a sutra), being, existing, occurring or existing in, common practice, rule, mode of being, nature, kind, character, disposition, mode of conduct, mood of the mind, devotion or addiction to, working, activity, function, rolling, rolling down, business, practice, behavior, course of action, from ***vṛt*** = to turn, twirl, whirl

Pravritti **can mean spiritual engagement and creating a self-identity based on material, tangible factors.**

Nivritti **means spiritual disengagement from worldliness and self-identity based on that which transcends the world. Yoga teaches a balance, or better yet, the intrinsic harmony between these two apparently conflicting orientations.**

utpannā = arise

risen, gone up, born, produced, appeared, come forth, ready, mentioned

from ***ut*** = up, forth + ***panna*** = fallen, gone, from ***pad*** = fall

manasaḥ = the mind

organ of cognition and perception

from ***man*** = think, believe, conjecture

Manas**, most often translated as mind, does not represent the totality of the mind (*****citta***** is the word for the totality of the mind). *****Manas*****, closely associated with the senses, is one of the three basic functions of *****citta*****. It is that aspect of individual consciousness that takes in impressions as part of *****citta's***** effort to discover which objects and situations are pleasant and which bring pain and suffering.**

The impressions taken in by *manas* are directed to the *buddhi* (intelligence, discriminative faculty), which categorizes the impressions it receives. When the mind is peaceful, clear, and one-pointed, *buddhi* acts as the intuitive faculty, revealing insights into subtle aspects of the universe and self.[47]

The third aspect of the mind is *ahamkara*, the ego sense. This faculty of mind constructs our sense of self by claiming thoughts and accumulated memories and subconscious impressions as the self. The self created by *ahamkara* is not the Self, Seer, or *Purusha*, but the body-mind misperceived as the Self.

In Buddhism, *manas* is considered almost like a sixth sense that is suited for rationality – the quality of being able to think logically – and the ability to reason. It is similar to the tongue being suited for taste, the ears for sound, etc.

sthiti = steadiness

standing upright, staying (See 1.13, 1.35, 2.18, 3.52)

from ***sthā*** = to stand, to stand firmly, station one's self, stand upon, to take up a position on, to stay, remain, continue in any condition or action, to remain occupied or engaged in, be intent on, make a practice of, keep on, persevere in any act, to continue to be or exist, endure, to be, exist, be present, be obtainable or at hand, to be with or at the disposal of, belong to, abide by, be near to, be on the side of, adhere or submit to, acquiesce to, serve, obey, stop, halt, wait, tarry, linger, hesitate, to behave or conduct oneself, to be directed to or fixed in, to be founded or rest or depend on, to rely on, confide in, resort to, arise from, to remain unnoticed, be left alone, to affirm, settle, determine, direct or turn toward (See 1.8, 1.13, 1.35, 1.41, 2.18, 2.35–2.39, 2.46, 3.52, 4.34)

nibandhanī = attains

hold, bind, causing

from ***ni*** = down, into + ***bandh*** = to bind

[47] What we experience as a mind that is peaceful, clear, and one-pointed is one in which *manas* is free from lethargy or restlessness, and in which the ego is free from selfish attachments. This leaves *buddhi* unencumbered, enabling its discriminative capacity to flourish.

1.36 Or by contemplating the supreme radiant[48] light in the heart that is beyond sorrow.

viśokā vā jyotiṣmatī

Lead me from the unreal to the real,
From darkness to light,
From the fear of death to the knowledge of immortality.
– Brihadaranyaka Upanishad

viśokā = beyond sorrow

blissful

from ***vi*** = not + ***śoka*** = sorrow, from ***śuc*** = to burn, heat, glow, sorrow, affliction, anguish, pain, trouble, grief

vā = or

jyotiṣmatī = the supreme radiant light

sacred light, spiritual, pure, brilliant, sun, the world of light, star-illumined, luminous, having light

from ***jyotiṣ*** = light (of the sun, dawn, fire, lightning), brightness (of the sky), the light that illumines the three worlds, flash of lightning, moonlight, eye-light, the eye, astrology, celestial world, intelligence, light as the divine principle of life or source of intelligence, human intelligence, highest light or truth, light as a type of freedom or bliss or victory + ***matī*** = devotion, prayer, worship, hymn, sacred utterance, thought, design, intention, resolution, determination, inclination, wish, desire, purposely, to set the heart on, make up one's mind, notion, idea, mindful, respect, perception. As a suffix, it indicates the possessive adjective.

Light is a universal symbol of wisdom, knowledge, the soul, the Absolute, and God. We experience light as that which allows us to see objects, people, and physical pathways. That same light, but on a much subtler level, is consciousness, allowing us to perceive our thoughts. It would certainly be correct to frame the entire Yoga life and its practices as a way of discovering our innermost self – the Seer – as light.

[48] Radiant = sending out light, shining or glowing brightly.

Vedic sources present the idea that there are three suns: in the sky, in the eye, and in the heart. There are a number of interpretations that can be derived from this: one is that all three suns are manifestations of the principle of awareness, the power of perception. The sun and eye allow us to perceive physical objects, the heart allows us to "see" - understand, feel, communicate, connect, and hold spiritual truths.

We can interpret *jyotishmati* as the *Purusha*, the light in the heart that is beyond sorrow - *duhkha*. (See 2.20)

1.37 Or by contemplating the state of a great soul's mind that is free from attachments to sense objects.

vīta-rāga-viṣayaṃ vā cittam

vīta = free

gone, released, gone away, departed, disappeared, vanished, without, lost, approached, desired, liked, loved, straight, smooth, trained, quiet, the driving or guiding of an elephant, a useless horse or elephant

from ***vi*** = asunder, away + ***ita*** = from ***i*** = go

rāga = attachment

any feeling or passion, affection, love, affection or sympathy for, vehement desire, act of coloring or dyeing, color, hue, tint, red color, inflammation, delight in, loveliness, beauty, seasoning, condiment

from ***rañj*** = reddened, be attracted

viṣayaṃ = state, sense objects

condition (See 1.11)

vā = or

citta = mind (See 1.2)

1.38 Or by contemplating knowledge revealed through:

- **A dream**
- **The tranquility of deep sleep**
- **The sense of individuality that persists through the states of wakefulness, dreamless sleep, and dreams**

svapna-nidrā-jñāna-ālambanaṃ vā

The state of sleep provides three objects for meditation:

- A dream with an impact that is striking and remains in the mind upon awakening. It could be a teaching or the experience of the visitation of a divine being.

- The tranquility that we experience from a good deep sleep that is recalled on awakening. This tranquil state provides a taste of the peace of the Self.

- The sense of individuality that persists through deep sleep and the other states of awareness: the dream and the waking states.

There is a fourth state of consciousness, *turiya*, the superconscious state experienced in the highest *samadhi*.

svapna = dream

sleep, relating to sleep

from ***svap*** = sleep

nidrā = deep sleep

sleep, slumber, sleepiness, sloth, the budding state of a flower, a mystic, a moment of sleep, approaching the time of sleep, blind with sleep, dead asleep, fast asleep, a state of deep meditation which resembles sleep, long sleeping

from ***ni*** = down, into + ***drā*** = sleep

jñāna = knowledge

knowing, becoming acquainted with, conscience, engaging in, higher spiritual knowledge (See 1.9, 1.38, 1.42, 2.28, 3.16–3.19, 3.22, 3.26, 3.28–3.29, 3.36, 3.53, 3.55, 4.31)

Refer to 1.9 for more on *jnana*.

ālambanaṃ = revealed

resting on, depending on or from, that on which one rests or leans, support, prop, receptacle, asylum

from ***ā*** = hither, unto + ***lambana*** = hanging down, pendant, dangling, hanging by or down to, long, large, spacious, from ***lamb*** = to hang, dangle, sink

vā = or

1.39 Or by meditating on any suitable object that inspires you.

yathā abhimata-dhyānād vā

yathā = any

whichever way, according as, like, for instance, namely

abhimata = suitable, inspires

per choice, something thought to be fit or right, approved, honored, esteemed, respected, longed for, wished, desired, loved, dear, allowed, supposed, thought, believed, imagined, understood, regarded or considered as, taken or passing for, liked, intended, belief, doctrine, purpose, knowledge

from ***abhi*** = a prefix to nouns and verbs = to, toward, into, over, upon + ***mata***, from man = to think, believe, imagine, suppose, conjecture, to regard or consider anyone or anything, to set the heart or mind on, to agree, to think of (as in prayer and meditation), declare, invent, to offer, present

dhyānāt = by meditating

meditation, thought, reflection (especially profound and abstract religious meditation), the mental representation of the personal attributes of a deity, attention, appreciation, contemplation, lost in thought, insensibility, dullness, mindfulness (See 1.39, 3.2, 3.11, 3.30, 4.6) from ***dhyai*** = to meditate, think of, contemplate, imagine, call to mind, recollect, from ***dhā*** = to hold, maintain, to put, place, lay on or in, bestow, have, cause, a name of the god Brahma

related to ***dhi*** = to perceive, think, reflect, wish, desire, religious thought, devotion, prayer, understanding, intelligence, wisdom, science, art, disposition, intention, splendor

Reviewing the roots of the word, we find an image of holding and maintaining. Meditation really begins in earnest when the mind learns to embrace, hold, and nurture the object of meditation. Refer to sutras 3.1–3.12 for information detailing the progressive stages of meditation.

vā = or

1.40 When any meditation practice is mastered, the mind is freed from the distracting obstacles. Then the mind is able to focus its attention on anything from the smallest particle to the greatest magnitude.

parama-aṇu-parama-mahattva-anto'sya vaśikāra

paramaṇu = smallest particle

atom, the smallest particle of sunlight, the passing of a sunbeam past an atom of matter

from ***parama*** = extreme, most, from ***pṛ*** = surpass + ***aṇu*** = smallest particle, minute, small. *Parama* is the superlative form (expressing the highest degree or quality) of *para* (more or better)

paramamahattva = greatest magnitude

great size or extent

from ***parama*** = greatest, most + ***mahattva*** = magnitude, great size or extent, magnitude, violence, intensity, moral greatness, from ***mah*** = to magnify + ***tva*** = suffix indicating the essence of

Magnitude indicates great in size, extent, or number.

anta = anything from

indicates from ___ to ___, end, limit, boundary, term, conclusion, end of life, death, destruction, pause, certainty, whole amount, outskirt, nearness, proximity, presence, inner part, inside, condition, nature, at last, in the inside

asya = (*refers to the meditation techniques that preceded this sutra*)

of this, for all these acts, of that, of this one, its, of it, his, of this man, for him

vaśikāra = mastery

bringing into subjection, subjugating (See 1.15, 1.40)

from ***vas*** = to will, command, to desire, wish, long for, be fond of, willing, eager, zealous, obedient, charming, lovely, to aver, maintain, affirm, to cause to desire, to get in one's power + ***kṛ*** = to make, to do, to act, perform, business, action, work, a religious rite or ceremony, sacrificial act, study, means, to take by the hand, marry, to place in one's heart, love

Refer to 1.15 for more on *vasikara*.

1.41 With regular practice and nonattachment, the whirling excursions of thought (*vrittis*) dwindle, weaken, and cease. As a result, the faculties of the mind become absorbed on the object of contemplation. The mind becomes like a naturally flawless transparent crystal that assumes the shapes and colors of objects nearby. This experience, called *samapatti* (or *samadhi*), is the union of knower, the object known, and the act of attaining knowledge.

kṣīna-vṛitter abhijātasya-iva maṇer grahītṛ-grahaṇa-grahyeṣu tat-stha-tad-añjanatā samāpattiḥ

Then the soul is in God and God in the soul,
just as the fish is in the sea and the sea is in the fish.
– St. Catherine of Siena

kṣīna = dwindle, weaken, cease

waned, diminish, wasted, expended, lost, destroyed, worn away, waning, weakened, injured, broken, emaciated, feeble, delicate, slender, poor, miserable

from ***kṣī*** = to decrease, destroy, make an end to

vṛitteḥ = left untranslated

whirling excursions of thought, fluctuating thought patterns, shifting mental activities (See 1.2, 1.4–1.5, 1.10, 1.41, 2.11, 3.44, 4.18)

abhijātasya = flawless

naturally pure, precious, born, produced, noble, well-born, fit, proper, wise, learned, high birth, nobility

from ***abhi*** = superior, to toward + ***jāta*** = to be born, from ***jan*** = be born

iva = like

maṇeḥ = crystal

jewel, gem, pearl, any ornament or amulet, globule, crystal, bell, magnet, loadstone, the hump of a camel, glans penis, clitoris, large water jar

grahītṛ = knower

grasper, taker, experiencer

from ***grabh*** = to seize + ***tṛ***, a suffix that indicates agency

grahaṇa = act of attaining knowledge

knowing, grasping, seizing, holding, act of experiencing

from ***grabh***, to seize

grahyeṣu = object known

to be grasped, seized, or taken, that which is experienced, knowledge

from ***grabh*** = to seize

tatstha = the mind becomes

similar

from ***tad*** = that + ***stha*** = to stand, to stand firmly, station one's self, stand upon, to take up a position on, to stay, remain, continue in any condition or action, to remain occupied or engaged in, be intent on, make a practice of, keep on, persevere in any act, to continue to be or exist, endure, to be, exist, be present, be obtainable or at hand, to be with or at the disposal of, belong to, abide by, be near to, be on the side of, adhere or submit to, acquiesce in, serve, obey, stop, halt, wait, tarry, linger, hesitate, to behave or conduct oneself, to be directed to or fixed in, to be founded or rest or depend on, to rely on, confide in, resort to, arise from, to remain unnoticed, be left alone, to affirm, settle, determine, direct or turn toward (See 1.8, 1.13, 1.35, 1.41, 2.18, 2.35–2.37, 2.39, 2.46, 3.38, 3.45, 3.52, 4.34)

Literally, the mind *abides like that*; like the object placed before the crystal.

tad = by that

añjanatā = assumes the shapes and colors

made clear, anointed, caused to appear

from ***añj*** = applying ointment or pigment, saturation, to smear, anoint (in the East the entire body is anointed with oil after bathing), ointment + ***tā*** = indicating a quality of

The words, *tat-stha-tad-anjana-ta, mean standing there,* or *standing there being anointed.* The mind, like a pure crystal, just "stands" there – it simply is, and it is anointed by whatever object is near it. This is a state of effortless absorption.

samāpattiḥ = left untranslated

coming together, meeting, encountering, accident, chance, falling into any state or condition, getting, becoming, assuming an original form, completion, conclusion, yielding, giving way (See 1.41–1.42, 2.47, 3.43)

from ***sam*** = together + ***a*** = hither, unto + ***pat*** = fall, fly

Samapatti, a synonym for *samadhi*, indicates a state of unity or integration between the knower, the object known, and the act of knowing. It is a state that arises when there is a merging of the meditator, the object of meditation, and awareness of the act of meditation.

The roots of the word – *to fall* or *fly together* – affirm that it is also an effortless state.

In Buddhism, *samapatti* refers to the four states of absorption or formlessness.

1.42 There are levels of *samadhi*. In the first, mingling of the word, form, and knowledge regarding the object of contemplation persist. This is known as *savitarka samadhi*, or *samadhi* accompanied by concepts (of the object).

tatra śabda-artha-jñāna-vikalpaiḥ saṃkīrṇā savitarkā samāpattiḥ

tatra = (refers to samāpatti)

there in that place, therein, in that case, on that occasion, under those circumstances, then therefore

śabda = word

name, sound, noise, voice, tone, speech, language, verbal communication or testimony, oral tradition, verbal authority or evidence

artha = object

meaning, aim, purpose, cause, motive, reason, advantage, use, utility, thing, object of the senses (hence the number five), substance, wealth, property, opulence, money (See 1.28, 1.32, 1.42–1.43, 2.2, 2.18, 2.21–2.22, 3.3, 3.17, 3.36, 4.23–4.24, 4.32, 4.34)

Artha is personified as the son (result or conjunction) of *dharma* (form) and *buddhi* (intelligence), a reference to the interdependence of object and the ability of the mind to perceive.

Refer to 1.28 for more on *artha*.

jñāna = knowledge

ideas (See 1.9, 1.38, 1.42, 2.28, 3.163.16–3.19, 3.22, 3.26, 3.28–3.29, 3.36, 3.53, 3.55, 4.31)

Refer to 1.9 for more on *jnana*.

vikalpaiḥ = *(refers to the conceptual knowledge of word, form, and ideas of an object as stated in 1.41)*

assumptions, alternative, option, variation, concepts, combination, variety, diversity, difference of perception, distinction, indecision, doubt, hesitation, statement, false notion, fancy, imagination, calculation, thinking (See 1.6)

Jnana (see page 110) + *vikalpaih* indicate that our ideas (our knowledge) regarding objects are at least partially formed of assumptions and imagination.

samkīrṇā = mingling

mixed, full of, poured together, confused, polluted, disordered, sprinkled, diffused, narrow, born of a mixed marriage, combined with, spread, crowded with, impure, adulterated, kind of riddle

sam = with, together, completely, absolutely + ***kṛ*** = scattered, thrown, cast, filled with, full of, covered, hidden, stopped up, given, injured, hurt

savitarkā = accompanied by concepts

thought, cognition, accompanied with reason or thought, thoughtfully

from ***sam*** = with + ***vi*** = asunder, away + ***tarka*** = debate, conjecture, reasoning, cogitation, speculation, inquiry, cause, confute, supposition, logic, wish, desire, a doctrine or system founded on speculation or reasoning

Savitarka samadhi literally translates as *samadhi* with *tarka* (debate, conjecture, reasoning). At this stage, the mind is probing the object of contemplation (an object perceivable by the senses), diving deeper and deeper into its subtle nature. It is a state of mind that is focused on investigating the truth of the object or of opinions. It can also mean inquiry into metaphysical contradictions.

In all *samadhis*, there is a high degree of absorption on the object of contemplation, but at the *savitarka* stage, the mind is still somewhat actively engaged in reasoning or discursive thought.

Savitarka has also been translated as *deliberation, cogitation, reasoning, supposition, philosophical curiosity, consciousness of sentience,* and *analysis of a gross object*.

In the next sutra, the probing – the *tarka* – of the perceivable object ends.

samāpattiḥ = samādhi

unity, integration (See 1.41–1.42, 2.47, 3.43)

Samadhi is used in this translation instead of *samapatti* since most students of Yoga are more familiar with this term. (See 1.20, 1.46, 1.51, 2.2, 2.29. 2.45, 3.3, 3.11, 3.38, 4.1, 4.29)

Refer to 1.20 for more on *samadhi.*

1.43 On the next level, the memory is completely cleared of all words, forms, knowledge, and concepts regarding the object of contemplation. It's as if the mind gives up its own intentions and identity so that only the object of contemplation shines forth in its own nature. This is called *nirvitarka samadhi*, the *samadhi* free of any concepts associated with the object.

smṛti-pariśuddhau svarūpa-śūnyā-iva-artha-
mātra-nirbhāsā nirvitarkā

smṛti = memory

remembered knowledge, reminiscence, thinking of or upon, calling to mind, the entire body of sacred tradition or what is remembered by teachers as opposed to *sruti* (that which is heard) (See 1.6)

pariśuddhau = cleared

well-purified, cleaned, pure, acquitted, discharged, diminished by, that from which a part has been taken away

from ***pari*** = abundantly, around, about, fully, beyond, away + ***śuddha*** = to purify, cleanse, clear, free from, bright, white, free from error, faultless, right, correct, accurate, exact, complete, entire, unqualified, unmitigated, unequalled, tried, examined, sharp, the bright fortnight (in which the moon increases), anything pure, pure spirit

svarūpa = its own nature

one's own form or shape, the form or shape of, own condition, peculiarity, character, nature, peculiar aim, kind, sort, similar, like, wise, learned (See 1.3, 1.43, 2.23, 2.54, 3.3, 3.45, 3.48, 4.34)

from ***sva*** = own, one's own, + ***rūpa*** = form, appearance, figure, peculiarity, trace of, drama, rereading a book, image, beauty, play, likeness, way, dreamy or phantom shapes, mode

Refer to 1.3 for more on *svarupa*.

śūnyā = gives up its own intentions and identity

empty, without any, void, blank (See 1.9)

This refers to the *citta* emptying itself of its own *form* – its sense of identity.

iva = it's as if

as it were, like, in the same manner as, in a certain manner, in some measure, a little, perhaps, nearly, almost, about, so, just so, just, exactly, indeed, very (especially after words which involve some restriction), just a little

artha = object

purpose, meaning (See 1.28, 1.32, 1.42–1.43, 2.2, 2.18, 2.21–2.22, 3.3, 3.17, 3.36, 4.23–4.24, 4.32, 4.34)

Refer to 1.28 for more on *artha*.

mātra = only

simply, merely, amounting to, sheer, being nothing but, possessing as much as or no more than, an element, elementary matter, measure, quantity, sum, size, duration, measure of any kind,the whole or totality, the one thing and no more

from ***mā*** = to measure

nirbhāsā = shine forth

is apparent or illumined

from ***nir*** = outward, away, without, out, forth + ***bhāsa*** = to be bright, light, luster, brightness, impression made on the mind

nirvitarkā = cleared of words, forms, knowledge, and concepts

beyond conceptualization, thought, cognition

from ***nir*** = without + ***tarka*** = debate, conjecture, reasoning, cogitation, speculation, inquiry, cause, confute, supposition, logic, wish, desire, a doctrine or system founded on speculation or reasoning

Nirvitarka samadhi answers these two questions: What is the true, intrinsic nature or essence of an object, when perception is freed from all learned knowledge, conceptualizations, and memories of that object? What is the reality of the object when it stands free from any influence of personal experience or the colorings of the ego and ignorance?

In *savitarka samadhi*, the exploration of the object was begun. In *nirvitarka samadhi*, the exploration is completed. The object is now known in its essence. Since the knowledge this brings is without the support of any conceptualizations, it stands alone, radiating its innate nature.

1.44 The next two levels of *samadhi* are deeper, but can be explained in the same way as the previous two. They are practiced on the subtle nature of objects and are known as *savichara*, with insight, and *nirvichara*, beyond insight.

etayā-eva savicārā nirvicārā ca sukṣma-viṣayā vyākhyātā

etayā = previous

refers to that which precedes, in the same way, in this manner, by this, thus, so at this time, now

from ***etad*** = this, this here, here (especially referring to pointing to what is nearest the speaker)

eva = same way

only, so, just so, thus, exactly so, indeed, truly, really, very, alone, merely, still, already, course, way, going, moving

Eva strengthens the idea of the word it is associated with. In this instance, it strengthens *etaya* (previous). This not only implies that the two *samadhis* referenced here can be explained in the same way as the previous two (*savitarka* and *nirvitarka*), but that the four *samadhis* are part of a continuum.

savicārā = with insight

with reflection, consideration

from ***sa*** = with + ***vi*** = asunder, away + ***cāra*** = to move oneself, go, walk, stir, roam about, wander, to spread, be diffused, pervade, go along, follow, to behave, conduct oneself, act, live, to be engaged in, occupied or busy with, to undertake, undergo, practice, do or act in general, make, observe vows, to send, direct, turn, to doubt, to try to have intercourse with

The word *vichara* (shared by both of the *samadhis* mentioned in this sutra) suggests a progressive movement. The mind progresses from the gross (perceivable by the senses) aspects of objects to the five subtle elements (*tanmatras*) and the ego, which is the immediate cause of the subtle senses.

With this *samadhi*, perception becomes clearer, more light-filled, deeper, and broader revealing subtler levels of matter.

nirvicāra = beyond insight

super or beyond reflection or consideration

from ***nir*** = without + ***cāra*** = to move oneself, go, walk, stir, roam about, wander, to spread, be diffused, pervade, go along, follow, to behave, conduct oneself, act, live, to be engaged in, occupied or busy with, to undertake, undergo, practice, do or act in general, make, observe vows, to send, direct, turn, to doubt, to try to have intercourse with

***Nirvichara* brings knowledge that is not bound by space or time.**

ca = and

sūkṣma = subtle

minute, small, fine, thin, narrow, short, insignificant, unimportant, acute, keen, exact, precise, atomic, intangible matter, subtle all-pervading spirit, Supreme Soul, marrow, the Vedanta philosophy from (perhaps) ***siv*** = to sew

viṣayā = objects

objects that are experienced through the senses (See 1.11)

vyākhyātā = can be explained

from ***vi*** = asunder, away + ***ā*** = unto + ***khyā*** = to be named or announced, to make known, proclaim, to relate, tell, say, declare, betray, denounce

1.45 The subtlety of objects for contemplation ends only at what is undefinable: the unmanifest state of matter (*prakriti*). At this level, since matter has no distinguishing characteristics, there are no objects to perceive. There is just the primordial soup of *prakriti*.

sūkṣma-viṣayatvaṃ ca aliṅga-paryavasānam

sūkṣma = subtlety

minute, small, fine, thin, narrow, short, insignificant, unimportant, acute, keen, exact, precise, atomic, intangible matter, subtle all-pervading spirit, Supreme Soul, marrow, the Vedanta philosophy (See 1.44)

viṣayatvaṃ = objects

condition, nature of a condition or object.

from ***viṣaya*** = that which is experienced through the senses + ***tva*** = suffix indicating the nature of

ca = and

aliṅga = undefinable

having no marks, absence of marks, without designation, having no gender, undifferentiated ***prakṛti***

from ***a*** = without, not + ***liṅga*** = sign, mark, emblem, characteristic, from ***liṅg*** = paint, change

paryavasānam = ends

termination, conclusion, end only at

from ***pari*** = around + ***ava*** = down + ***sāna***, from ***sā*** = bind

1.46 These four *samadhis* still carry the seeds of subconscious impressions (*samskaras*).

tāḥ eva sabījaḥ samādhiḥ

tāḥ = these

they

eva = still

all, only, so, just so, exactly so, indeed, truly, really, very, same, alone, merely, already, course, way, going, moving (See 1.44)

sabīja = carry subconscious seeds

with seed

from ***sa*** = with + ***bīja*** = seed, semen, any germ, element, primary cause or principle, origin, caused or produced by, truth (as the seed cause of being), the essential syllable of a mantra

samādhi = left untranslated

absorption, superconscious state (See 1.20, 1.46, 1.51, 2.2, 2.29, 2.37, 2.45, 3.3, 3.11, 4.1, 4.29)

Refer to 1.20 for more on *samadhi.*

1.47 As *nirvichara samadhi* fully matures, the luminous[49] tranquil clarity of the supreme inner Self shines forth.

nirvicāra-vaiśārdye' dhyātma-prasādaḥ

nirvicāra = left untranslated

super or non reflective, beyond reflection, beyond insight (See 1.44)

vaiśārdye = clarity, fully matures

experience, skill, expertness, wisdom, clearness of intellect, infallibility

[49] Luminous = full of or shedding light. Although this word is a good fit for the subjective experience of the yogi, it should be remembered that the Self is pure light – unbounded consciousness – itself.

from ***vai*** = used to express emphasis or affirmation + ***śārad*** = autumnal sunshine, growing in autumn, mature

One of the roots of *vaisardye* is *sharad*, autumn sunshine. Autumn is the time to enjoy the fruits of the harvest, the result of planting and nurturing the seed. For the yogi, the harvest is the light of the Self manifesting more fully and bringing with it a transcendent peace of mind.

In Buddhism, this word can refer to The Buddha's confidence in himself.

adhyātma = supreme inner self

authentic, inner being, own, belonging to the self, transcendental, concerning self or individual personality.

from ***adhi*** = superior, above, over, from above, from, from the presence of, after, for, on, at, in comparison with, concerning + ***ātma*** = self, from ***an*** = breathe or ***at*** = move

prasādaḥ = tranquil, shines

clearness, brightness, purity, calmness, graciousness, kindness, favor, aid, meditation, free gift, well-being, welfare, to grow clear and bright, become placid and tranquil, to become clear or distinct (See 1.33)

from ***pra*** = filling, fulfilling + ***sad*** = to sit, especially at traditional rites of sacrificial worship, to wait for

The roots of the word suggest the fulfillment (*pra*) of attentive (*sad*) worship. *Prasada* also suggests that grace is part of the process at this stage of attainment. The yogi experiences the grace of the Self, lifting and refining awareness to a level that self-effort alone cannot accomplish. (See 4.25–4.26)

1.48 This state is truth-bearing. It grants intuitive insights into the cosmic order – the deepest realities of existence: self-identity, the mind, and the universe.

ṛitaṃ bharā tatra prajñā

ṛitaṃ = truth, cosmic order

bearing the truth in one's self, intellect or knowledge which contains the truth in itself, possessing the knowledge of the previous sutra, *dharma*, proper, right, fit, suitable, able, brave, honest, worshipped, respected, enlightened, luminous, rule (especially in religion), sacred or pious action or custom, faith, divine truth, to go the right way, the underlying truth of reality

Ritam is the underlying flow of life: creation, evolution, and dissolution. It is the cosmic order of all life and creation. It includes all objects, ethics, morals, and spiritual truths. *Ritam* also includes the law of karma, the subtle ways of justice and learning.

The fundamental gist of *ritam* is that the universe is not made up of senseless or meaningless accidents. All the diverse and disparate aspects of life – the changes, comings and goings, successes and failures, good times and bad – are part of a grand cosmic symphony. Usually we only hear a part of it. *Nirvichara samadhi* awakens the power of refined inner awareness that allows the yogi to "hear" the cosmic truths and relationships that form the cosmic symphony.

In Hinduism, *ritam* also represents the victory of light against darkness and good over evil. It is the ultimate emergence of righteousness and beauty in life. This is one reason why Hindu deities are, with a few exceptions, represented as beautiful and benevolent.

Ritam is the same essential principle as the Tao (the Way) of Taoism. We also find essentially the same teaching in the *New Testament* in Romans 8:28: "*We know that all things work together for good for those who love God, to those who are called according to His purpose.*" This quote has three parts:

1. The principle that *all things work together for good.*
2. *For those who love God.* This can be understood as those who love God know from direct experience that all things work for good.
3. *Who are called according to His purpose* is essentially the same as the Hindu and yogic principle of *svadharma*, one's ultimate purpose in this life.

bharā = bear

carrying, bringing, bestowing, granting, supporting, maintaining, gain, prize, a large quantity, great number, abundance, excess, shout or song of praise

Bhara suggests that this experience not only carries truth, but that the truth, manifesting in its fullness, is so abundant that it overflows, displacing all other subconscious impressions. Such an experience could certainly evoke songs of praise (a definition of *bhara*).

tatra = this

prajñā = insight

wisdom, knowledge, intelligence (See 1.20, 1.48–1.49, 2.27, 3.5)

from ***pra*** = before, forward + ***jñā*** = to know

Refer to 1.20 for more on *prajna*.

1.49 The purpose of this insight is different from the insights gained from inference or from hearing sacred wisdom teachings. Its unique purpose is to end false identification with the seen (nature, *prakriti*) by being able to discern the Seer (Self, *Purusha*) from the seen. (See 1.2–1.4)

śruta-anumāna-prajñābhyāṃ anya-viṣayā viśeṣa-arthatvāt

śruta = sacred wisdom teachings

scripture, heard, listened to, taught, orally transmitted or communicated from age to age, knowledge as revealed to holy people

from ***śru*** = to hear

The word *sruti* refers to revealed knowledge of scripture and tradition. In Hinduism, it traditionally refers to the *Vedas* and *Upanishads*.

anumāna = inference (See 1.7)

prajñābhyāṃ = from insights

from wisdom (See 1.48)

anya = different from

other, opposed to, another

viṣayā = (*refers to prajñā of the previous sutra*)

object, condition (See 1.11)

viśeṣa = distinct

different from, special, specific, or particular, peculiar mark, specialty, a kind, species, special property, peculiar merit, excellence, superiority (See 1.22, 1.24, 1.49, 2.19, 4.25)

This word refers to the specific qualities that make an object distinct, its essential individuality. In the context of this sutra, it suggests the growing capacity to make the distinction between the True Self, and the misperceived, limited self (the reflection of the Self on the mind).

In sutra 1.24, *Ishvara* is said to be a distinct *Purusha*.

Refer to 1.22 for more on *visesa*.

arthatvāt = purpose

because of its aim, suitable to the object, fitting, full of reality, real, significant, according to a purpose (See 1.28)

from ***artha*** = purpose, utility, aim, as its object + ***tva*** = having the quality of (See 1.28, 1.32, 1.42–1.43, 1.49, 2.2, 2.18, 2.21–2.22, 3.3, 3.17, 3.36, 4.23–4.24, 4.32, 4.34)

1.50 The subconscious impression (*samskara*) born of this insight displaces all other *samskaras.*

taj-jaḥ saṃskāro'nya-saṃskāra-pratibandhī

tad = by this

that

jaḥ = born of

arisen, sprung

from ***jan*** = to generate, beget, produce, create, cause, to assign or procure, to grow, to be born as, to be by birth or nature, destined for, to become, to be changed to, to take place, to be suitable

saṃskāra = subconscious impression

mental impression or recollection, acts performed in a former lifetime, putting together, forming well, making perfect, accomplishment, embellishment, adornment, purification, cleansing, making ready, preparation, refining of metals, polishing of gems, rearing of animals, cleansing the body, attire, forming the mind, training, education, correction, purity, making sacred, consecration, a sacred or sanctifying ceremony (which purifies one from sin contracted in the womb) (See 1.18, 1.50, 2.15, 3.9–3.10, 3.18, 4.9, 4.27)

Refer to 1.18 for more on *samskara*.

anya = all other

different, other, opposed to, another, different from

saṃskāra = left untranslated

subconscious impression (See above and 1.18, 1.50, 2.15, 3.9–3.10, 3.18, 4.9, 4.27)

Refer to 1.18 for more on *samskara*.

pratibandhī = displaces

overcome, contradiction, objection, obstruct, prevent, impede

from ***prati*** = in opposition to, back, again, in return, down upon, upon, on, to go toward or against, go to meet (as friend or foe), to come back, to receive, accept, admit, recognize, be certain of, to trust, believe + ***bandh*** = to bind, tie, fix, fasten, to catch, take or hold captive, to rivet the eyes, ears, or mind on, to arrest, hold back, restrain, suppress, stop, shut, close, offer, sacrifice, to join, unite, put together or produce anything in this way, construct a dam or bridge, to cause, affect, make, bear fruit, to be affected by, to cause to be built or constructed, a suffix indicating possession

1.51 When even this impression (*samskara*) stills, all mental processes – conscious and subconscious – are stilled. This is the seedless (*nirbija*) *samadhi*, the state that transcends ignorance and brings liberation.

tasya api nirodhe sarva-nirodhān nirbīja samādhiḥ

tasya = this

of that, of it

tad = it, that, this, this world, there, in that place, to that spot, then, at that time, in that case, in this manner, for that reason, therefore, consequently, because, various, different

api = even

also, expresses placing near or over, uniting to, annexing, reaching to, proximity, and also, moreover, besides, assuredly, surely, perhaps.

The word is often used to express emphasis, in the sense of *even, also,* or *very*. Sometimes, it is simply an expletive.

nirodhe = stills

restricted, suppressed (See 1.2, 1.12, 1.51, 3.9)

It is important to keep in mind that this complete stilling of the mind is not achieved through force, but from focusing and redirecting attention – a persistent, fervent, but gentle and guiding of the mind through the yogic practices and lifestyle. It cannot be accomplished directly through effort. Patanjali suggests that grace is the final factor in this attainment. (See 4.25–4.26)

It is also important to note that the cessation of all mental processes is not permanent. The mind re-emerges to function on the physical plane, most often to engage in active service to others who suffer.

What is permanent is the cessation of the misidentification of Self as body-mind. Ignorance has been overcome and one can rest in their True Nature, their essence and ground: the Self or *Purusha*. (Refer to sutra 1.2 for more on *nirodha*.)

sarva = all

nirodhāt = stilled

restrained, from being restricted (See 1.2, 1.12, 1.51, 3.9)

Refer to 1.2 for more on *nirodha*.

nirbīja = seedless

without seed (See 1.46)

samādhi = left untranslated

absorption, superconscious state (See 1.20, 1.46, 1.51, 2.2, 2.29, 2.45, 3.3, 3.11, 3.38, 4.1, 4.29)

Refer to 1.20 for more on *samadhi*.

Chapter Two

Sadhana Pada

The Chapter on the Purpose of Practice

2.1 *Kriya Yoga*, the three elements that form the foundation of the Yoga life are:

- ***Tapas*: self-discipline and accepting hardship and pain as a help for purification**
- ***Svadhyaya*: repeated, deep study of sacred wisdom and the introspective search into the nature of the self; mantra repetition**
- ***Ishvara pranidhanam*: wholehearted devotion and dedication to *Ishvara***

tapaḥ-svādhyāya-īṣvara-praṇidhānāni kriyā-yogaḥ

tapaḥ = left untranslated

austerity, self-discipline, creative heat, consuming by heat, causing pain or trouble, distressing, religious austerity, penance, intense meditation, excellence of devotion, the efficacy or potency of devotion, tormented by, warmth, an attendant of Lord Siva (See 2.1, 2.15, 2.32, 2.43, 4.1)

from **tap** = to burn, to make hot, to shine (as the sun), to shine upon, to consume or destroy by heat, to suffer pain, to repent of, to torment oneself, to practice austerity, to become purified by austerities

There are uses to adversity, and they don't reveal themselves
until tested. Whether it's serious illness, financial hardship,
or the simple constraint of parents who speak limited English,
difficulty can tap unexpected strengths.
– Justice Sonia Sotomayor

There are two basic categories of *tapas*:

- The pain, suffering, and sorrow that is generated by the inevitable appearance of unpleasant events in life
- The effort and challenges that are an essential part of cultivating self-discipline through spiritual practices and lifestyle choices

Tapas, like any heat source, can illumine and it can purify. A campfire produces both light and heat. The light illumines the campsite revealing objects and people within its reach. One of the definitions of the root, *tap*, suggests that as a result of *tapas*, an individual can shine upon – benefit in some natural way – others. But, if engaged in, in an unbalanced way, it is just a way to torment oneself.

Some people perform stern austerities that are not enjoined by the scriptures,
but rather motivated by hypocrisy and egotism. Impelled by desire and
attachment, they torment not only the elements of their body,
but also I who dwell within them as the Supreme Soul.
Know these senseless people to be of demoniacal resolves.
– Bhagavad Gita, 17.6

Heat also has the power to purify. The classic example is the purification of gold ore. The ore is heated until the impurities float to the top where they are skimmed off. This process is repeated a number of times until no impurities remain. What's left is pure 24-karat gold.

Tapas, as both light and heat, explains why, when Patanjali arrives at the sutra that describes the fundamentals that underpin all Yoga practice, the first word (*tapas*) brings to mind light and heat. In this one word, we see that the very foundation of the Yoga life rests on understanding that challenge and hardship are not mere uncomfortable experiences, but occasions that can help us break through the manifestations of ignorance allowing pure light to illumine us.

The yogi learns to regard hardships as opportunities for purification from negative states of mind such as anger, impatience, or jealousy. *Tapas* is not simply grimly enduring pain and suffering. Adversities, encountered with the proper yogic attitude of acceptance, equanimity, and mindfulness, can become times of discovering or developing strengths and virtues that we never suspected we had.

Tapas holds one more great benefit. Heat can also unite. How often have we witnessed the unity of communities when challenged by a natural disaster? Political, religious, social status, and gender all recede into inconsequentiality when we must endure a common struggle. Empathy and compassion rise quickly and, with great unifying power, allow us to nurture hope and behold examples of the beauty of human nature when it is freed from self-interest.

Cultivating the attitude of *tapas* helps us convert experiences that bring only suffering – burning – into a heat that purifies and unites, and a light that enlightens.

svādhyāya = left untranslated

study, self-study, study of sacred texts, reciting, repeating or rehearsing to one's self, repetition or recitation of the *Vedas* in a low voice to one's self, recitation or study of any sacred text (See 2.1, 2.32, 2.44)

from ***sva*** = one's self, ego, soul, one's own, one's own goods (property, wealth, etc.), + ***adhi*** = to go over or on, to turn something over in the mind repeatedly, to recite until memorized and absorbed

Svadhyaya could refer to study of the self or to integrating the teachings learned from scripture and the Guru into oneself.

To more adequately define *svadhyaya* and reveal the full power of its transformative capacities in the yogic context, we can look to the roots of two words: *study* and *research.*

Study

From the Old French, *estudier = to strive toward, to devote oneself to, to cultivate.* The sense is to thrust or press forward. In Yoga, the focus of study is on the mindset of the one who studies rather than the information to be accumulated. We can say that study produces the best results for one who nurtures an intense enthusiastic curiosity[50] regarding knowledge and practice.

However, the word study alone lacks the sense of experimentation, discovery, and the replication of results that are central to scientific research, but that form an essential element of *svadhyaya.*

[50] Don't undervalue curiosity. Too few seekers, believers, or people of faith have it. It is well worth cultivating. Here's one of the many quotes on curiosity from Albert Einstein: *"The important thing is not to stop questioning. One cannot help but be in awe when he contemplates the mysteries of eternity, of life, of the marvelous structure of reality. It is enough if one tries merely to comprehend a little of this mystery every day. Never lose a holy curiosity."*

Research

Research literally means to search and search again. It is from the Latin *circare, to wander*, which is in turn, from *circus = circle, ring, orbit*. The prefix *re* is an intensifier.

From this, we can see that research suggests a focused search - within a circle or orbit of knowledge - and to search and search again and again. Each fact or lesson learned also opens a new horizon to explore. Recall that *adhi*, a root of *svadhyaya* means *to go over* or *on, to turn something over in the mind repeatedly.*

The word *research* helps us get beyond the image of burying our heads in books. Although this is certainly part of study, it's only one aspect of it. Look at the following criteria for scientific research to see how the *Sutras* portrays an understanding of study that shares the same framework as scientific research.[51]

Research begins with a clear statement of its objectives. In Yoga, as in any faith tradition, the objective is to eradicate suffering born from ignorance. In Yoga, as in any research, the results need to be able to be replicated by others following the same essential methods.

The researcher (in our case the student of Yoga) needs to remain unbiased, in order to refrain from wishful thinking and to assess the benefits of Yoga honestly for themselves.

Research also requires that the researchers have sufficient and appropriate resources. For yogis, this requirement is satisfied by the wealth of tried and true fundamental teachings and practices.

Those who design research studies should have a full understanding of the subject. This resonates with sutra 1.7, which states that one of the methods for cultivating reliable knowledge is *agama*, authoritative testimony. This includes scriptural testimony and, in Yoga, the teachings and guidance of a spiritual master.

[51] Much of this scientific material was paraphrased from a document published by the National Academies of Science, Engineering, and Medicine.

The body and mind of the yogi are the laboratory for this experimentation.

Certainly, *svadhyaya* includes the kind of study we did in school to pass our exams: gathering knowledge, analyzing it to understand its import, relating new information to other pertinent teachings, and memorizing key facts. But *svadhyaya* also includes probing into the causes behind effects, and expanding our research results by seeing how they relate to other principles and experiences.

As we have seen, the roots of *svadhyaya* suggest repeated effort. This repetitiveness is not just for the sake of memorization of principles, but for fully engaging in the Yoga life until a new way of perceiving and being arises. The higher goal of study in Yoga is to clarify and deepen perception, so that insight (*prajna*) is cultivated and can be used as an enhanced exploratory tool of perception that extends beyond the reach of rationality.

The enhanced super perception possessed by evolved yogis is also known as *yoga pratyaksha*, yogic vision. In sutra 1.7, *pratyaksha*, defined as direct perception, is listed as one of the sources of reliable knowledge. But *Yoga pratyaksha* goes well beyond the reach of normal sense perception and logic. It enables the yogi to perceive subtle realities of the universe, the ways of life, and the self.

Mantra repetition (mantra *japa*) is also included in study since it is a powerful way to refine perceptual powers, and since the process of *japa* naturally includes encountering subtle facets of self-identity that dwell in the subconscious mind.

We can summarize the goal of study as bringing the light of wisdom into the darkest and most unvisited corners of our minds, hearts, and lives.

īṣvara = left untranslated

Lord, king, God, master, able to do, capable (See 1.23–1.24, 2.1, 2.32, 2.45)

Refer to sutra 1.23 for more on *Ishvara*.

praṇidhānāni = left untranslated

to hold within and in front of, laying on, fixing, applying, access, entrance, exertion, endeavor, respectful conduct, attention paid to, profound religious meditation, abstract contemplation of, vehement desire, vow (See 1.23, 2.1, 2.45)

from ***pra*** = before or in front + ***ni*** = down into or within + ***dhā*** = place, put, or hold

Refer to 1.23 for more on *pranidhana*.

Anyone who truly loves God travels securely.
– Saint Teresa of Avila

kriyā = lifestyle

doing, performing, occupation with, act, action, undertaking, work, bodily action, exercise of the limbs, medical treatment or practice, applying a remedy, cure, a religious rite or ceremony, sacrificial act, sacrifice, rites performed immediately after death, purificatory rites, religious action, worship, study

from ***kṛ*** = to do or make

Kriya Yoga, simply defined, is Yoga in action. For the yogi, action consists of the practices, resolves, decisions, conduct, and lifestyle that are conducive to growth, transformation, and the transcending of ignorance.

In Saiva Siddhanta (a path followed by devotees of Lord Siva predominant among the Tamils of Sri Lanka and South India), *kriya* refers to a stage that is preparatory to liberation, to attain nearness to God.

yoga = left untranslated

union, connection, joining, yoke, attaching, harnessing, equipping an army, fixing of an arrow to a bow string, a remedy, cure, a means, manner, a supernatural means, incantation, stratagem, undertaking, to agree or consent, mixing of various materials, partaking of, arrangement, suitability, exertion, zeal, diligence, care, attention, with all one's powers, application or concentration of the thoughts, abstract contemplation, meditation, any act conducive to Yoga or meditation, union of the individual soul with the universal soul (See 1.1–1.2, 2.1, 2.28)

from ***yuj*** = unite, join, connect, employ, use

Refer to 1.1 for more on *Yoga*.

2.2 Their purpose is to cultivate *samadhi* and to weaken and diminish the root causes of suffering (*klesas*).

samādhi-bhāvana-arthaḥ kleśa-tanú-karaṇa-arthaś ca samadhi

Thus walking on this way with an awakened heart, not only do we escape the heavy cares of this world, but we are uplifted above ourselves and do taste of the divine sweetness.
– Blessed Angela of Foligno

samādhi = *left untranslated*

bringing into harmony, settlement, joining with, intense absorption, attention, joining or combining with, whole, accomplishment, conclusion, concentration of mind, union, concentration of thoughts, profound meditation (See 1.20, 1.46, 1.51, 2.2, 2.29, 2.45, 3.3, 3.11, 3.38, 4.1, 4.29)

Refer to 1.20 for more on *samadhi*.

bhāvana = cultivate

causing to be, manifesting, mind development, producing, displaying, promoting or affecting one's welfare, mental discipline, imagining, fancying, teaching, forming in the mind, conception, apprehension, imagination, supposition, thought, meditation, direct one's thought to, (in logic) that cause of memory which arises from direct perception, furthering, nature, essence (See 1.28, 2.2, 2.33–2.34)

from ***bhū*** = to be

Refer to 1.28 for more on *bhavana*.

artha = purpose

to get into (See 1.28, 1.32, 1.42, 2.2, 2.18, 2.21–2.22, 3.3, 3.17, 3.34, 3.36, 4. 23–4.24, 4.32)

Refer to 1.28 for more on *artha*.

kleśa = *left untranslated*

pain, affliction, distress, pain from disease, anguish, wrath, anger, worldly occupation, care, troublesome, causing pain (See 1.24, 2.2–2.3, 2.12–2.13, 3.11, 3.44, 3.50) from ***kliś*** = to be troubled, to suffer distress

Refer to 1.24 for more on *klesa*.

tanū = diminish

attenuated, lessened, weakened, slim, small, minute, delicate

from ***tan*** = stretch, spin out

karaṇa = (*refers to diminish*)

causing, doing, making, affecting, instrument, means of action, a field

from ***kṛ*** = to do, make

arthaḥ = purpose (See 1.28, 1.32, 1.42–1.43, 2.2, 2.18, 2.21–2.22, 3.3, 3.17, 3.34, 3.36, 4. 23–4.24, 4.32)

Refer to 1.28 for more on *artha*.

ca = and

samādhi = left untranslated

bringing into harmony, settlement, joining with, intense absorption, attention, joining or combining with, whole, accomplishment, conclusion, concentration of mind, union, concentration of thoughts, profound meditation (See 1.20, 1.46, 1.51, 2.2, 2.29, 2.45, 3.3, 3.11, 3.38, 4.1, 4.29)

Refer to 1.20 for more on *samadhi*.

2.3 The root causes of suffering (*klesas*) are ignorance, egoism, attachment, aversion, and clinging to bodily life.

avidyā-asmitā-rāga-dveṣa-abhiniveśā kleśa

avidyā = ignorance

nonwisdom, delusion, unlearned, unwise, foolish, not educated, spiritual ignorance (See 2.3–2.5, 2.24)

from ***a*** = not + ***vid*** = to know, feel, experience, being, existing, obtaining, to declare to be, understand, seize, visit, discover, recognize

Avidya, ignorance, translates literally as *not-knowing*. While there is almost always a negative connotation associated with the word *ignorance*, regarding it as *not-knowing* reveals shades of meaning pertinent for the seeker:

1. To be unaware of the spiritual nature of self, suffering, and the transcendent Self. In this case, these truths are not ignored, they are not known. You can't consciously turn your back to something you don't know exists.

2. The truths are known but the individual is not inspired to engage them. There could be a lack of understanding of the importance or benefits of a spiritual lifestyle. Or, the individual could be swayed by friends and family who disapprove, or have little or no interest in spirituality.

3. One might not be open to, or might actively oppose, principles of faith. In these cases, ignorance could stem from a past hurtful experience with a faith tradition or its followers, or misunderstanding the true meaning and depths of spiritual truths.

4. Ignorance also pertains to a sincere seeker who engages in a yogic lifestyle, but has not yet attained liberation. While progressing and gaining wisdom in many things, the seeker is ignorant of – has not yet known/experienced – Self-realization.

When a superior person hears of the Tao,
She diligently puts it into practice.
When an average person hears of the Tao,
she believes half of it, and doubts the other half.
When a foolish person hears of the Tao,
she laughs out loud at the very idea.
If she didn't laugh,
it wouldn't be the Tao.
– Tao Te Ching

Avidya is the ultimate cause of all suffering. It is not just any kind of not-knowing. In spiritual contexts, *avidya* refers to the continued, deeply ingrained misperception of one's essential identity as the body-mind, instead of the Seer/Self.

The root, *vid*, suggests that ignorance is not a simple state of not knowing facts, but it is, in some way, a state of not being engaged with life: *avidya* is not feeling, experiencing, discovering, or recognizing. *Avidya* is a passive state, a way of being that withdraws from the fullness of life.

Without proper moral, ethical, and mental training (i.e., introspection, contemplation, selfless service), the mind, out of fear and habit, not only retreats from truth and engages in distractions and denials, but misses the harmony and wonders of life and self.

In Buddhism, *avidya* is often equated with not being aware of the Four Noble Truths (suffering is inevitable, it is caused by selfish desire, the cause of suffering can be removed, and it is removed by following the Eightfold Path).

We can see the same essential teachings of the Four Noble Truths in Patanjali's sutras:

2.15: All life is suffering to those who have deeply investigated the truths of life.

2.16: Suffering can be avoided.

2.17 and 2.24: The cause of suffering is ignorance, or not discerning the difference between the Seer and seen.

2.26: Unwavering discriminative discernment removes ignorance.

2.28: By practice of the limbs of Yoga, unwavering discriminative discernment can be cultivated.

Buddhist teachings offer other wonderful insights into ignorance that are a perfect fit for yogis.

Ignorance is:

- The root of everything unwholesome
- The state of mind that does not correlate to reality
- The taking of the phenomenal world as the only reality
- The veil that obscures the True Nature of the world and self and is responsible for constructing the illusory appearance of reality

asmitā = egoism

literally, I-am-ness, the fundamental sense of "I" before it takes on identifications (See 1.17)

from ***asmi*** = first person singular indicative of as (be) + ***ta*** = feminine suffix = meaning to have the quality of

There is often confusion between the terms *asmita* and *ahamkara*. Ahamkara, the I-maker, is not mentioned in the *Yoga Sutras*, although it is considered to be one of the three aspects of the *citta* (mind-stuff), along with *manas* and *buddhi*.

Although the terms are often used interchangeably, they can hold slightly different meanings. While *asmita* is the sense of individuality, *ahamkara* can be more specifically defined as the *power of asmita* to build self-identity. For example, *ahamkara* is the power that makes our identification with gender, occupation, intellect, body, etc. possible.

Ahamkara, the I-maker, creates the many versions and variations of our self-identity. It is our misidentification with the body-mind that makes *asmita* a *klesa*. *Asmita* can also be a *samadhi* (See sutra 1.17) but, in this case, the ego is purified.

rāga = attachment

any feeling or passion, affection, love, or sympathy for, vehement desire, act of coloring or dyeing, color, hue, tint, red color, inflammation, delight in, loveliness, beauty (See 1.37)

from ***ranj*** = reddened, be attracted

dveṣa = aversion

repulsion, hatred, dislike

from ***dviṣ*** = hate

abhiniveśā = clinging to bodily life

desire for continuity, application, intentness, study, affection, the determination to realize a purpose or attain an object, tenacity, adherence to

from ***abhi*** = to toward + ***ni*** = down, into + ***veśa***, from ***viś*** = enter

kleśa = *left untranslated*

obstacles, pain, affliction, distress, pain from disease, anguish, wrath, anger, worldly occupation, care, trouble (See 1.24, 2.2–2.3, 2.12–2.13, 3.11, 3.44, 3.50)

Refer to 1.24 for more on *klesa*.

2.4 Ignorance is the origin of the other root causes of suffering (*klesas*), whether they are dormant, weakened, interrupted, or fully active.

avidya kṣetraṃ uttareṣaṃ prasupta-tanu-vichchinna-udārāṇām

avidya = ignorance

not-knowing, delusion, nonwisdom (See 2.3–2.5, 2.24)

Refer to 2.3 for more on *avidya*.

kṣetraṃ = origin

field, ground

from ***kṣi*** = possess

uttareṣaṃ = of the others

prasupta = dormant

fallen, asleep, inactive, latent

from ***pra*** = before, forward + ***supta*** = from ***svap*** = sleep

tanu = weakened

feeble, attenuated, lessened, diminished, small, thin

from ***tan*** = stretch, spin out

vichchinna = interrupted

intercepted, suppressed, overpowered

from ***vi*** = asunder, away + ***chinna***, from ***chid*** = cut

udārāṇām = fully active

engaged, sustained, aroused

from ***ud***= up, forth, out + ***āra***, from the root ***ṛ*** = go

2.5 Ignorance is rooted in misperception. It is due to experiencing:

- **What changes as unchanging**
- **What is impure, colored by bias, and nonvirtuous as pure, free of bias, and virtuous**
- **What brings pain, restlessness, dissatisfaction, and distress as that which brings serenity, contentment, fulfillment, and happiness**
- **What is not the Self as the Self**

anitya-aśuci-duḥkha-anātmasu nitya-śuci-sukha-ātman-khyātir avidyā

Real knowledge is to know the extent of one's ignorance.
– Confucius

The doorstep to the temple of wisdom is knowledge of our own ignorance.
– Benjamin Franklin

anitya = changes

impermanent, transient, fleeting, not everlasting, occasional, nonessential, unimportant, uncertain

from ***a*** = not + ***nitya*** = eternal, from ***ni*** = lend

The definitions of this word suggest that ignorance is not just concerned with black and white, true or not true situations. It is simply getting whole swaths of life wrong: regarding what is nonessential as essential, unimportant as important, what is uncertain and can't be counted on, as trustworthy. This nuanced look at one of the contributory factors of ignorance helps keep us from simply identifying our big mistakes and shortcomings as born of ignorance. Ignorance most often is a silent killer of happiness, found in misperceiving or having a dysfunctional relationship[52] with the minutia of life.

We need to always keep in mind that clinging is out of step with the rhythms of life.

[52] As in expecting or treating what is bound to change as changeless, etc.

aśuci = impure

from ***a*** = not + ***śuci*** = pure, from ***śuc*** = gleam

duḥkha = pain, restlessness, dissatisfaction, distress

dissatisfaction (to feel that life is flawed in our eyes), discontent, anxiety, stress, pain, uneasiness, difficulty, sorrow, trouble, to cause or feel pain, unpleasant (See 1.31, 1.33, 2.5, 2.15–2.16, 2.34)

Refer to 1.31 for more on *duhkha*.

anātmasu = not self

from ***an*** = not + ***ātman*** = self

nitya = unchanging

permanent

śuci = pure

shining, glowing, gleaming, radiant, bright, white, clear, clean, pure, honest, virtuous, holy, a true friend, the condition of a religious student, untainted

from ***suc*** = to gleam, glow, burn, suffer violent heat or pain, be absorbed in deep meditation

The yogi seeks to think, speak, and act without selfish attachment. This gradually thins and ultimately overcomes the power that fear, lust, greed, anger, hatred, obstinacy, and laziness have to obstruct the inner Light.

Essential to purity is clarity of intentions and acknowledgment of our strengths and weaknesses. It is a balanced mind, free from bias and the limited self-interest that can cloud our innate capacity for good judgment and for serving the common good.

sukha = happiness

pleasure, joy, well being, running swiftly or easily (applied to cars or chariots), easy, agreeable, gentle, mild, comfortable, happy, prosperous, virtuous, pious, the sky, heaven (See 1.33, 2.5, 2.7, 2.42, 2.46)

Refer to 1.33 for more on *sukha*.

ātman = self

the principle of life and sensation, the individual self, soul, essence, nature, character, peculiarity, the person or whole body considered as one as opposed to the separate members of the body, the body, the understanding, intellect or mind, the highest personal principle of life, effort, firmness, the sun, fire, a son (See 2.5, 2.21, 2.41, 4.13, 4.25)

from the verb root ***at*** = to breathe, or the verb root ***ap*** = to pervade or reach up for, or from ***at*** = to move

This word has several meanings. The two most common uses in Hindu spiritual contexts are *atma* as the individual self or soul, and *Atma* as the Supreme Self or the spark of Divinity within. Since capital letters are not part of Sanskrit, the only way to tell which meaning is intended is by context, and even then, it can be a tricky.

One way of understanding *Atma* is that it is *Brahman* (the highest attributeless Reality) as viewed from within the individual; the Self or Seer within each individual. This understanding is found in the philosophical school of nondualism, Advaita Vedanta.

Yoga and its related philosophical sister, Samkhya philosophy, tend to regard the *Atma* as identical with self-luminous, omnipresent consciousness.

Experiencing the non-Self as Self refers to the mind's tendency, under the influence of ignorance, to try to define the Self. The nature of the mind is to persevere in its attempts to limit the pure Self, assign it attributes, and somehow bring it under the control of the ego. This is perhaps why the moment that best depicts the objective of Patanjali's Yoga comes in sutras 4.25 and 4.26 This is where it states that once the seeker is able to distinguish the *Atma* from the mind, thoughts of the mind as *Atma* cease forever and the seeker experiences the pull of the Absolute toward liberation (*kaivalya*).

A similar idea is presented in sutra 3.50, which states that when an individual can discern the difference between the pure *sattvic* mind and the *Purusha* (Self, Seer), there arises all knowledge and knowledge of all states of being.

The other sutras that contain the word *atma*:

2.25: One symptom of ignorance is regarding the non-Self as the Self

2.21: The seen exists (*atma*) for the sake of the Seer

2.41: By purification, one attains (among other benefits) fitness of Self-realization

4.13: Characteristics that form the nature (*atma*) of the *gunas*

Other texts state that the *Atma* is the ultimate essence of the universe, as well as the vital breath in human beings.

Buddhism denies the reality of the *Atma* as intrinsically real.

khyātir = regarding

seeing, identification, asserting, viewing (See 1.16)

avidyā = ignorance (See 2.3–2.5, 2.24)

not-knowing, nonwisdom

from ***a*** = not + ***vid*** = to know, feel, experience, being, existing, obtaining, to declare to be, understand, seize, visit, discover, recognize

2.6 Egoism arises from confusion, regarding the power of the Seer and the power of the instrument of seeing (mind/intellect) as the same thing.

dṛg-darśana-śaktyor eka ātmatā iva asmitā

Doesn't the Bible say "Blessed are the pure in the heart, they shall see God?" When? Only when there is purity in the heart; a heart peaceful and free from egoism – the "I" and the "mine." Purity of heart and equanimity of mind are the very essence of Yoga.
– Sri Swami Satchidananda

dṛg = seer

discerning (See 2.20)

from ***dṛś*** = to see perceive

darśana = instrument of seeing

what is seen, philosophy, view, knowing, exhibiting, showing, looking at, teaching, seeing, perception, way of looking, apprehension, observation, aspect, act of seeing, inspection, contemplating, vision (See 1.30, 2.6, 2.41, 3.32)

from ***dṛś*** = to see, perceive

Refer to 1.30 for more on *darsana*.

śaktyor = powers

ability (See 2.6, 2.23, 2.34, 3.21, 4.34)

from ***śak*** = to be able

Shakti is the term for power. It is especially associated with the force within and behind creation. All movement, all force, all power, is an expression of *shakti*. It is regarded as feminine and often depicted as a goddess.

In Hinduism, even the gods are depicted as needing *shakti,* which is why Hindu gods are associated with goddess consorts – their *shakti*. Without this feminine energy, the god is powerless. This imagery is a way to depict the natures of *Purusha* (pure consciousness, but without agency) and *prakriti* (matter and change).

When viewed as the latent force of evolution within every individual, it is referred to as *kundalini shakti,*[53] the coiled force that rests at the base of the spine in the subtle body.

In this sutra, *shakti* is in the dual tense, referring to two powers: the power of the Seer and the power of the seen.

eka = identical

the same, one, alone, solitary, single, one and the same, singular

[53] *Kundalini* literally means *coiled.* In addition to being envisioned as a goddess, the *kundalini* is thought of as a sleeping serpent coiled three and a half times (a reference to the Sanskrit OM symbol which has three curves). When this energy is awakened in a pure heart and focused mind, it rises to the crown of the head, bringing the experience of Self-realization.

ātmatā = selfness

nature, essence

from ***ātma*** = self + ***tā*** = a suffix meaning having the quality of, of a single self

This refers to the ego's ability to cause a fundamental confusion of self-identity by assigning the power of consciousness (*atmata*, selfness) to the body-mind.

iva = as

as if, as it were

asmitā = egoism

I-am-ness, sense of individuality, the sense of "I" before it takes on identifications (See 1.17, 2.3, 2.6, 4.4)

from ***as*** = to be + ***tā***, a suffix suggesting to have the quality of

Refer to sutra 2.3 for more on *asmita*.

2.7 Attachment arises from clinging to pleasurable experiences.

sukha-anuśayī rāgah

sukha = pleasurable

pleasant (See 1.33, 2.5, 2.7, 2.42, 2.46)

Pleasure, in spiritual contexts, is understood as enjoyable experiences that are temporary. Pleasure, as nice as it is, should not be mistaken for true happiness, which is an uncreated experience.[54] We often substitute the words "joy" or "bliss" to differentiate this experience from happiness. Pleasure is called a created form of happiness because it requires the convergence of a desire with its object.[55]

[54] The root of the word suggest the condition for enjoyment based on the fulfillment of a desire.

[55] The object of desire can include any number of requirements for happiness. A picnic could be the obvious desire. But for it to bring happiness, we might require it to be a nice day, with a certain person, at a certain park, at a certain place in that park, at a certain time, with certain food, and with certain things said. When all of the conditions are met, we find happiness – a created happiness manufactured from a coming together of factors that we largely cannot control.

Take away either of the factors needed to experience it and it falls apart, often becoming some form of dissatisfaction or suffering (*duhkha*).

True happiness arises independent of external and mental circumstances. It is the light of the Self, shining unhindered on the mind – unobstructed by attachment and ignorance. It cannot be created; any external force also cannot destroy it. It is uncreated joy. It exists and persists in us as our True Nature.

Refer to 1.33 for more on *sukha*.

anuśayī = clinging to

resting on, follows.

from **anu** = along, after + **śaya**, from the root **śi** = to rest

After resting with, could be a literal translation for *anusayi*. It is used to denote the close connection between an act and its consequences. It is also used to refer to the cause of rebirth.

In Buddhism, *anusayi* means tendencies or passions that lay dormant, a fitting notion when considering that often the pain-bearing nature of attachments is not realized immediately, but only when the object of attachment is lost to us.

The most important point here is to note that clinging is out of step with the nature of life, which is constant change. We cling when we feel and fear change. To cling is to resist life. It is to hold onto hopes, images, and a limited understanding of self and life. Many of life's lessons and beauties are missed when we cling.

Pleasurable experiences depend on circumstances that inevitably change, and the nature of most change involves some degree or type of loss. And with the loss of whatever brought us pleasure, the pleasure itself leaves. The fear of loss leads to the clinging to the pleasurable experiences mentioned in this sutra.

The yogic attitude is to enjoy pleasurable things when they arrive and peacefully send them off when it is time for them to move on. Enjoy the beauty of a sunset while it lasts, but don't ask for or hope that the sun won't drop below the horizon. Let the mind enjoy the flow of life. Let the joys of life – large and small – nourish your mind and soul. Clinging to them is not the best strategy for happiness.

The happiness that arises when the mind is peaceful, clear, and one-pointed is a deep happiness, but it is still a facsimile of the unbounded, eternal happiness of the Self. It is the happiness of the Self or Seer reflected on a *sattvic* mind. To attain the highest enlightened state, attachment to even this rarified happiness needs to be transcended.

From the *Bhagavad Gita*, 14.6, on this subject:

Although the sattva guna is pure, luminous, and without obstructions,
still it binds you by giving rise to happiness and knowledge
to which the mind readily becomes attached.

rāgah = attachment (See 1.37)

The subject of attachment is central to any discussion of the theory and practices of Yoga. Ignorance, the source of all the other *klesas*,[56] is difficult to identify directly. Attachment, aversion, and clinging to bodily life are more easily perceived and therefore more readily addressed.

The nature of attachment includes:

- Craving for pleasure based on sense satisfaction
- Loss of perspective and objectivity
- The expectation that what does bring satisfaction will never change
- The conviction that some object or situation is absolutely necessary for happiness; the search for happiness in externals

[56] See 2.4.

2.8 Aversion arises from clinging to painful experiences.

duḥkha anuśayī dveśaḥ

duḥkha = painful

dissatisfaction (See 1.31, 1.33, 2.5, 2.15–2.16, 2.34)

Refer to 1.31 for more on *duhkha*.

Recall that *duhkha* is a pervasive, persistent feeling of precariousness. This is fertile ground for fears to grow.

anuśayī = clinging to

resting on, follows (See 2.7)

dveśaḥ = aversion

hatred, dislike, repugnance, enmity to, distaste (See 2.3, 2.8)

from ***dviś*** = foe, enemy

No one spends their lives seeking painful experiences, but this sutra is not about the painful situations themselves. It is about aversion to them.

The original meaning of the English word, *aversion*, can give us an insight into why it works against our intentions and efforts in Yoga: *to turn away* or *avert one's eyes*. When we close ourselves off or back away from inevitable challenges and hardships – a major part of life experiences – we are in danger of losing the opportunities to learn and grow from them. A state of aversion brings with it anxiety. However, anxiety does not have to be understood as a form of fear.

Anxiety is from a root that means "narrowness" or "tightness." Anxiety results from being in a difficult situation, one that demands courage, faith, creativity, or persistence to move through. Situations that feel tight, trapped, and with, few – if any – options are part of the challenges we face in life. But, our response to anxiety need not necessarily include fear. By understanding this, by eliminating anxiety-producing situations from the list of fears, we free the mind of a great burden. We experience less threat and more challenge. We are more likely to perceive the challenge accurately and call on our creative impulses to resolve the problem and summon our faith to endure it with tranquility.

Fear, on the other hand, is a type of mental paralysis. It is always a reaction against a possible future loss. It is a mind taken out of the present and, instead, contemplates what dire, painful consequences may be coming our way. Fear feeds imaginary fates. Faith is the best antidote for both fear and anxiety.

The word for faith in Sanskrit is *shraddha*, literally *to hold in a pure heart*. Through Yoga, we learn to have increasing trust in the ways and wisdom of life. When we are in a tight spot we pause, collect ourselves, and return to our clear center. Often, creative options begin to arise.

Faith is a bird that sings when the dawn is still dark.
– Rabindranath Tagore

Faith is taking the first step even when you don't see the whole staircase.
– Martin Luther King, Jr.

Faith is the strength by which a shattered world shall emerge into the light.
– Helen Keller

The same equanimity we have learned to apply to nonvirtuous situations can be used here. (See 1.33)

2.9 Clinging to life arises even in the wise and learned. It persists because it is innate.

svarasa-vāhī viduṣo api tathā rūdha abhiniveśaḥ

svarasa = innate

by its own potency, own inclination, natural or peculiar flavor, instinct for self preservation, agreeable or pleasant to one's taste

from ***sva*** = own + ***rasa*** = inclination or taste, from ***ras*** = taste

Literally, with its own juice or essence.

vāhī = persists

carried, flowing, sustained, borne

from ***vah*** = to flow, carry, sustain

Svarasa + vahi **indicate that the will to live (or fear of annihilation) is carried from birth to birth by its own power. In other words, it is a fear that is considered as part of human nature.**

viduṣo = learned

wise person, sage, one who knows, educated, very learned, knowing, perfectly educated, advanced in spiritual knowledge, one who knows the inconvenience of material existence, learned philosophers, scientists, politicians, those learned in Vedic knowledge, to be completely aware of a fact

from ***vid*** = to know

Let's unpack *viduso* to get a better sense of the richness of this sutra. *Viduso* is a form of the word: *vidvan* or *vidwan*. It refers to an expert and the term has the sense of a doctoral degree. More importantly, for our studies, it refers to one who is an expert in the *Vedas* or who has a highly developed discriminative capacity. This drives home the point that clinging to life is impervious to book learning and philosophical prowess.

api = even

also

tathā = because

thus, so, in that way

rūdha = arises

exists, sprung up, produced from, sprouting, rooted, established

from ***rūh*** = ascend, rise, spring up

abhiniveśaḥ = clinging to life

desire for continuity, persistence, determination, application, intentness, study, affection, the determination to achieve a purpose or attain an object, tenacity, adherence to, application, intentness, study, affection, with devotion, tenacity, adherence to (See 2.3) from ***abhi*** = to toward + ***ni*** = down, into + ***veśa***, from ***viś*** = enter, dwell to enter toward and then into

The *abhi* here is the same as the root for *abhyasa*, practice, which implies repetition. *Abhinivesah*, the desire for continuity of life, pops up repeatedly. It is the major source of existential angst.[57]

2.10 The root causes of suffering (*klesas*) are overcome in their subtle form (subconscious impressions) when the mind returns to its original, pure state. (See 1.45, 2.4, 4.34)

te pratiprasava-heyāḥ sūkṣmaḥ

te = (*refers to the klesas*)

these

pratiprasava = return to its original state

resolving back into their cause, return to the original state, disassociation from the creation process, counter-order, inverse propagation, to resolve to a more elementary form, withdrawal from manifestation (See 2.10, 4.34)

from ***prati*** = against, back + ***prasava*** = creation, beginning, pressing out, setting or being set in motion, impulse, course, rush, flight, stimulation, pursuit, begetting, procreation, generation, conception, delivery, birth, augmentation, from ***pra*** = before, forward + ***sava*** = pressing out, from ***su*** = generate, impel

Nothing in any of the Hindu philosophies admits to nonexistence. Something that exists, that manifests, eventually returns to the unmanifest state from which it arose. Matter never becomes nonexistent. The same is true for the mind, which is subtle matter. This means that the essence of the mind can never be truly nonexistent, but it can return to its source. This returning to the source is *pratiprasava*.

***Pratiprasava* is the end game of spirituality, the mind resolving back into its source, unmanifest matter. It is again described in sutra 4.34, but in**

[57] Existential angst has a lot in common with *duhkha*. It is described as anxiety over the possible meaninglessness of life, a nameless dread – even terror – without an identifiable cause. It is an emotion that never really passes away, although we try to distract ourselves from it. It pervades all aspects of life and nothing seems to overcome it. But Yoga, *viveka*, and faith, in particular, can.

a more cosmic sense in which the entire universe – all of the *gunas* – return to their origin, a state of equilibrium.

Pratiprasava does not describe the end of the universe. Instead, it is a personal transcendent experience in which the mind, by ending its misidentification with *prakriti*, is resolved or returns to its origin – unmanifest *prakriti*. *Pratiprasava* is the transcending of self-centered mentality. Ignorance, egoism, attachment, aversion, and clinging to bodily life are overcome when the *gunas* (manifested as the mind) return to a state of equilibrium. This is a state in which the need to find support, comfort, guidance, and self-value through the acquisitive nature of the world is transcended. The yogi has learned that gaining worldly position and possessions are, in and of themselves, powerless to give the depth of meaning, fulfillment, and happiness that we seek.

This is not a rejection of the world, but a state of freedom in which both the joys and challenges of life are put into perspective. This same principle is echoed in the *New Testament, Matthew* 11:28, *"Come to me, all you that are weary and are carrying heavy burdens, and I will give you rest."* Rest should not be misinterpreted as a break. It is a coming home to Source, a direct experience of one's source and essence. Self-realization is usually preceded by knowing well the weariness of the burdens that we carry, burdens born of hopes and of expectations that *prakriti* cannot deliver.

Our discussion of *pratiprasava* has focused on the recognition of the grand cycle from the source of creation to emergence or birth, to evolution and then back to source. There is also a personal dimension to *pratiprasava* that expresses as gratitude. As we become aware of the gifts we have been given in this life: intelligence, kindness, friends, life partners, health, prosperity, a rewarding career, etc., the only proper response is gratitude. Appreciation should not be limited to verbal thank yous, but should express as the good we can do in this world. We bless others as we have been blessed.

A life grounded in gratitude puts us in harmony with the subtle and grand cycles of creation and forms a lifetime foundation for our spiritual pursuits. Scientists who study happiness note that gratitude is one of the most important predictors of a happy life.

heyāḥ = overcome

destroyed, to be avoided, to be gone, to be left, quieted or abandoned, to be rejected, to be avoided, to be subtracted

from ***ha*** = to leave, desert, avoid, abandon, quit, forsake, shun, lay aside, give up, renounce, refrain from, to lose, escape from, to disregard, to come to an end

sūkṣmaḥ = subtle

minute, small, fine, thin, narrow, short, insignificant, unimportant, acute, keen, exact, precise, atomic, intangible matter, subtle all-pervading spirit, Supreme Soul, marrow, the Vedanta philosophy (See 1.44)

2.11 In their gross, active manifestations they can be overcome by meditation. (See 2.2)

dhyāna-heyās tad-vṛittayaḥ

dhyāna = meditation (See 1.39, 3.2, 3.11, 3.29, 4.6)

Refer to 1.39 for more on *dhyana*.

heyās = overcome

Refer to 2.10 for more on *heyas*.

tad = they

that, those

vṛittayaḥ = active state

fluctuations of individual consciousness, the whirling excursions of the mind (See 1.2, 1.4–1.5, 1.10, 1.41, 2.11, 3.44, 4.18)

Refer to 1.2 for more on *vritti*.

The active state referred to is the typical state of *vritti* activity functioning under the influence of ignorance. Meditation helps quiet the endless turning of thought. The root causes of suffering begin to lose their hold over our state of mind through meditation.

2.12 The residue of karma, the latent impressions produced by past actions, is rooted in the *klesas*. The effect of these impressions is experienced in present or future births.

kleśa-mūlaḥ karma-āśayo dṛṣta-adṛṣta-janma-vedanīyah

kleśa = *left untranslated*

root obstacle (See 1.24)

mūlaḥ = rooted

firmly fixed, lowest part or bottom of anything, basis, foundation, cause, origin, beginning, derived from, a temporary owner

from ***mūl*** = to be rooted or firm

karma = left untranslated

actions and reactions (See 1.24, 2.12, 3.23, 4.7, 4.30)

Refer to 1.24 for more on karma.

By knowing that life experiences are caused by our own thoughts, words, and deeds, our struggle for happiness and fulfillment becomes an internal one, largely independent of external circumstances. This also means that we always have and have had the keys to peace, harmony, and happiness within us.

In Yoga theory, the fruits of previous acts are stored in the mind in the form of subconscious seeds of merit or demerit. They remain there, inactive, until the appropriate circumstances allow them to ripen and bloom as experiences of social status, length of life, and enjoyment. (See 2.13)

The most important lesson taught by karma is that our fate is ultimately in our own hands. This knowledge neutralizes mindsets of victimhood, resentment, and hatred.

āśayaḥ = residue

reservoir, resting place, bed, seat, place, abode, retreat, receptacle, any vessel in the body, the seat of feelings and thoughts, the mind, heart, soul, thought, meaning, intention (See 1.24)

dṛṣta = seen

present (See 1.15)

adṛṣta = unseen

future (See 1.15)

janma = births

existence, life

from ***jan*** = to beget, to be born, come into existence

vedanīyah = experienced

to be felt, to be known

from ***vid*** = to know

2.13 As long as ignorance, the source of the root causes of suffering (*klesas*) exists, karma produces fruits in the form each birth takes, its life span, and its experiences.

sati mūle tad-vipāko jāty-āyur-bhogāh

sati = exists

being, occurring

from ***as*** = to be

In Buddhism, meanings of *sati* include memory, awareness, skillful attentiveness, a recollection of purpose, a constant affirmation, or renewal of direction. Looking at this sutra through the lens of this understanding of *sati* suggests that an act or acts of will are the primary source of ignorance's continued existence.

mūle = root (See 1.12)

tad = it

that

vipākaḥ = fruits

fruition (See 1.24)

jāti = birth

production, rebirth, the form of existence (as man, animal, etc.) determined by birth, position assigned by caste, family, rank, lineage, or race, natural disposition, genuine or true state of anything

from ***jam*** = to beget, to be born

āyuḥ = life span

vital power, life, health

from ***ā*** = hither, unto + ***yuḥ***, from ***i*** = go

bhogāh = experiences

enjoyment, eating, any winding or curve or coil (life is not a straight line – experiences are the curves), the expanded hood of a snake, the body, application, use, sexual enjoyment, enjoyment of the earth, feeling, perception of pleasure or pain, profit, utility, advantage, delight, possession

from ***bhuj*** = to enjoy

2.14 These fruits can be either sweet or bitter – pleasurable or painful – depending on whether they were caused by virtuous or nonvirtuous acts.

te hlāda-paritāpa-phalāh puṇya-apuṇya-hetutvāt

te = (*refers to the sweet and bitter fruits*)
they, these

hlāda = pleasure

joyful, delightful, pleasurable

from ***hlād*** = to bring delight, joy, to refresh

paritāpa = pain

agony, grief, sorrow, glowing, scorching, heat

from ***pari*** = around, about, fully, beyond, away + ***tāp*** = to burn, heat, shine upon, to consume or destroy by heat, to suffer pain, to torment oneself, self-mortification, practice austerity, to cause pain, damage, spoil, to be purified by austerities, to suffer, trouble, distress, great anxiety

phalāh = fruits

consequence, result

from ***phal*** = to produce fruits, to ripen

The fruits referred to here are the ones listed in 2.13.

puṇya = virtuous

merit, auspicious, propitious, pure, holy

from ***puṇ*** = to do good

Refer to 1.33 for more on *punya*.

apuṇya = nonvirtuous

demerit

from ***a*** = not + ***puṇ*** = to do good

Refer to 1.33 for more on *apunya*.

hetutvāt = caused

impulse, motive, reason for

from ***hetu***, from ***hi*** = impel, incite + ***tvat*** = composed by you, suffix indicating the quality of

2.15 Those who investigate the ways of life find that pain, sorrow, dissatisfaction, and a feeling of persistent, pervasive precariousness are surely a part of all experiences. This is *duhkha*. It is due to:

- **Fear over losing what is gained**
- **The impermanence of all things**
- **Subconscious habit patterns (*samskaras*) created under the influence of ignorance that sustains craving and ignorance**

• Changes of mood and mindset due to the interplay of the forces of nature (*gunas*)[58] that vie for dominance in the mind

pariṇāma-tāpa-saṃskāra-dukḥair guṇa-vṛitti-vīrodhāc ca duḥkḥa eva sarvaṃ vivekinaḥ

And so . . . castles made of sand melt into the sea, eventually.
– Jimi Hendrix

pariṇāma = change

alteration, transformation, evolution, development, ripeness, maturity, digestion, consequence, result (See 2.15, 3.9, 3.11, 3.13, 3.15–3.16, 4.2, 4.14, 4.32–4.33)

from ***pari*** = around, fully, abundantly + ***nam*** = to bend or bow

As is evident by the number of cross-references for *parinama*, it is a central principle in the *Yoga Sutras*. Always associated with dynamism and energy, it is the principle of evolution or transformation, the changes in the form of an object, the passage of time, and the emergence of latent qualities in objects and beings.

The oak tree is latent in the acorn. Due to external circumstances, such as weather and the passage of time, the acorn eventually sprouts and grows. Its growth – tall and straight or crooked – are determined by its innate impulse to grow modified by external circumstances.

Parinama also applies to attaining liberation. That which we seek is already fully present within each of us. The application of Yoga theory and practice creates the optimum environment for this evolution to take place.

tāpa = sorrow, anxiety

pain, angst, hardship (See 2.1, 2.15, 2.32, 2.43, 4.1)

from ***tap*** = to burn, be hot

Refer to 2.1 for more on *tapa*.

[58] The *gunas* are the three fundamental qualities of nature: *sattva* (purity, light, balance), *rajas* (activity, passion), and *tamas* (dullness, inertia, ignorance). They manifest in different quantities and percentages in all created objects, including the mind. They determine the inherent characteristics of all created things.

saṃskāra = *left untranslated*

subconscious impression left by action (See 1.18, 1.50, 2.15, 3.9–3.10, 3.18, 4.9, 4.27)

Refer to 1.18 for more on *samskara*.

duhkḥair = *left untranslated*

dissatisfaction, pain (See 1.31, 1.33, 2.5, 2.15, 2.16, 2.34)

Refer to 1.31 for more on *duhkha*.

Character cannot be developed in ease and quiet. Only through experience of trial and suffering can the soul be strengthened, ambition inspired, and success achieved.

– Helen Keller

guṇa = *left untranslated*

qualities of nature, strand, thread, quality

Refer to 1.16 for more on *guna*.

vṛitti = *left untranslated*

fluctuation, modification, turning, referring to the *gunas* (See 1.2, 1.4–1.5, 1.10, 1.41, 2.11, 3.44, 4.18)

Here, *vritti* can be understood as the mind being subject to mood changes. (Refer to 1.2 for more on *vritti*.)

vīrodhāt = contradictory

conflict, opposition, hostility, adversity, strife between, hostile contact of inanimate objects (like planets), inconsistency, incompatibility, hindrance, prevention, misfortune, an apparent contradiction or incompatibility, an impediment to the successful progress of a plot

from ***vi*** = away, asunder + ***rudh*** = to stop, obstruct

ca = (*Refers to the items in the list*)

and

duḥkḥa = pain

dissatisfaction, a persistent, pervasive feeling of precariousness (See 1.31, 1.33, 2.5, 2.15–2.16, 2.34)

Refer to 1.31 for more on *duhkha*.

eva = surely

indeed, thus

sarvaṃ = everything

all, entire, every, of all sorts, various, different, completely

possibly from ***sara*** = stretching out, extension, or from ***sa'ra*** = substance or essence or marrow or heart, or the essential part of anything

vivekinaḥ = investigate

discrimination, discernment, distinguishing, right knowledge, wise, separated, kept asunder, examining, judicious, prudent (See 2.15, 2.26, 2.28, 3.53, 3.55, 4.26, 4.29)

from ***vi*** = asunder + ***vekin***, from ***vic*** = divide, asunder, distinguish, sift + ***in*** = possessive suffix

Viveka, in the context of Yoga, is the mental state, that is capable of discerning what is true from what is false, what is permanent from what is fleeting, what brings suffering from what does not.

In its highest state, *viveka* is the ability to discern the Self from the self – the power to separate the invisible Spirit (consciousness, *Purusha*) – from the visible world (*prakriti*). It is having clear, objective vision – the ability to distinguish and classify things according to their real properties.

Patanjali will tell us in sutra 2.26 that *viveka* is the method to remove ignorance and the pain it causes. We might think that such a vital piece of information would appear much earlier in his text. Most likely, it appears here because to attain the necessary discernment to realize that *duhkha* is a pervasive persistent fact of life is not easy. It requires that the mind:

- Has been well-informed (right knowledge, 1.7)

- Has attained some degree of nonattachment (1.15–1.16)
- Has learned to deal with obstacles (1.32, 2.3)
- Has become grounded in attitudes that cultivate clarity of awareness in daily life (1.33)
- Has attained a good measure of contemplative focus (1.34–1.39)

This approach to attaining *viveka* is expanded beginning with sutra 2.28, the prelude to the eight limbs of Yoga.

2.16 The *duhkha* that has not yet come can be avoided.

heyaṃ duḥkham anāgataṃ

heyaṃ = avoided

destroyed (See 2.10)

from ***ha*** = to leave, desert, avoid, or abandon

duḥkha = dissatisfaction, pain

a persistent, pervasive feeling of precariousness (See 1.31, 1.33, 2.5, 2.15–2.16, 2.34)

Refer to 1.31 for more on *duhkha*.

anāgataṃ = not yet come

not arrived, future, not attained, not learned, unknown

from ***an*** = not + ***ā*** = unto + ***gam*** = to go

Suffering is a short pain and a long joy.
– Blessed Henry Suso

2.17 The dissatisfaction and suffering (*duhkha*) that can be prevented is caused by confusing the nature of the Seer with that of the seen.

draṣṭṛ-dṛśyayoḥ saṃyogaḥ heya-hetuh

draṣṭṛ = Seer (See 1.3)

dṛśyayoḥ = seen

that which is visible

from ***dṛṣ*** = to see

saṃyogaḥ = confusing

union, correlation, joining, combination, connection, sexual union, absorption with, a kind of alliance or peace made between two kings with a common objective

from ***sam*** = together, with, completely, absolutely + ***yoga*** = union, junction, addition, total, partaking of, putting on, application or concentration of thoughts, wealth, team, lucky conjuncture, diligence, strategy, disposition, device, any act conducive to concentrating the mind, combination, application, work, discipline, attaching, devotion, vehicle, original meaning of a word, contact with, from ***yuj*** = yoke (See 2.17, 2.23, 2.25)

This apparent – not real – union of Seer and seen is not a permanent, irreversible state. A coming together now means falling apart in the future. In nature, all things formed from a combination of elements, eventually return to a more fundamental state – the elements separate. It is important to understand that the contact, union, or conjunction referred to here is like the contact of a stone with water. The water cannot pervade the stone, yet the water does obscure the stone's nature. We can't truly know the qualities of the stone until it is viewed out of water. Similarly, the Seer is never polluted or changed by its conjunction with the seen, but we need to be able to experience the Seer, without the distorting lens of the seen.

In Ayurveda, the traditional healing modality of India, disease is defined as *duhkha-samyoga*: contact with physical and mental unpleasantness.

heya = that can be avoided

to be avoided, to be ended, to be gone, to be subtracted, to be left behind, to reject (See 2.10)

hetuh = cause

motive, reason (See 2.14)

from ***hi*** = impel, incite

Spiritual traditions such as Yoga contain the remedy that ends the confusion of Seer and seen. This ends *duhkha* and leads to liberation.

2.18 The seen consists of the five elements and sense organs and has the qualities of translucence, activity, and inertia. Its purpose is to provide experiences and liberation.

prakāśa-kriyā-sthiti-śīlam bhūta-indriya-ātmakaṃ bhoga-apavarga-arthaṃ dṛśyam

Life is a succession of lessons which must be lived to be understood.
– Ralph Waldo Emerson

prakāśa = translucence[59]

illumination, light, splendor, brightness, pure consciousness, visible, clear, manifest, open, public, expanded, universally noted, before the eyes of all, appearance, display, manifestation, diffusion, laughter, it is the principle by which everything else is known, the principle of self-revelation

from ***pra*** = before, forward + ***kāśa*** = from ***kaś*** = to shine, appear

***Prakasa* is an innate quality of the Divine or Absolute Truth. The word is also used to describe a quality of *sattva*.**

kriyā = activity

doing, performing, work (See 2.1)

sthiti = inertia

remaining inert, standing

from ***sthā*** = to stand, to stand firmly, station one's self, stand upon, to take up a position on, to stay, remain, continue in any condition or action, to remain occupied or engaged in, be intent on, make a practice of, keep on, persevere in any act, to continue to be or exist, endure, to be, exist, be present, be obtainable or at hand, to be with or at the disposal of, belong to, abide by, be near to, be on the side of, adhere or submit to, acquiesce in, serve, obey, stop, halt, wait, tarry, linger, hesitate, to behave or

[59] Translucence = allowing light to pass through, referring to the *sattva guna*. *Sattva* – having the quality of *sat* or existence/consciousness – lets the light of the Seer through. The mind becomes luminous and capable of experiencing subtle insights into reality.

conduct oneself, to be directed to or fixed in, to be founded or rest or depend on, to rely on, confide in, resort to, arise from, to remain unnoticed, be left alone, to affirm, settle, determine, direct or turn toward (See 1.8, 1.13, 1.35, 1.41, 2.18, 2.35–2.39, 2.46, 3.52, 4.34)

śīlam = qualities

character, nature, natural or acquired way of acting, conduct, disposition, form, shape, beauty. Or, good behavior, right discipline, morality, self-restraint, giving of one's self, desisting from all sinful acts

from ***śīl*** = serve, act

In Buddhism *sila* is one of the six ideals, obligations, precepts, or virtues (*paramita*). These virtues guide and assist the seeker on the path to perfection. They have three stages and are six in number: ideals for the worldly life, ideals for the mental life and ideals for the spiritual life.

- *Dana* = Charity and Love
- *Sila* = Good Behavior
- *Ksanti* = Patience
- *Virya* = Zeal
- *Dhyana* = Meditation
- *Prajna* = Insight

These guidelines help regulate the behavior of monks, nuns, and lay persons. They constitute the preconditions for progress on the path. As morality, *sila* is part of the eightfold path: right speech, right action, right livelihood.

bhūta = the five elements

earth, water, fire, air, space, constituents of the manifest universe

indriya = sense organs

power; derived from the Vedic god named Indra, it means agreeable to Indra.

from ***Indra*** = ruler, chief, mighty, powerful

Indra is the *Vedic* god of the atmosphere and sky as well as of rain, who rules over the deities in the mid-region of heaven, and fights against and conquers demons and the forces of darkness with his thunderbolt. He rides an elephant, a symbol of strength and the ability to remove obstacles. He holds his hands in gestures of protection and the granting of boons. Sometimes, he is depicted with eyes all over his body.

Over time, his position as the great god weakened and he was only king of the lesser gods and the Lord of heaven. He loves to drink *soma*, the intoxicating nectar of immortality, of which he drinks enormous amounts. Stimulated by its exhilarating qualities, he goes forth to fight against his foes, and to perform his other duties. He was worshipped and loved, especially in *Vedic* times for his generous nature as the bestower of rain and the cause of fertility, yet was also feared as the ruler of storm and the sender of lightning and thunder.

The word for "the senses" is related to the name of this deity, suggesting an understanding of the senses as powerful. They can be used for good but should be treated as potential gateways into troubles. Like Indra, the senses can create disturbing storms, become intoxicated with overuse, misuse, or abuse, or they can be powerful allies in perceiving and learning the lessons that life provides.

In Buddhism, *indriya* also refers to twenty-two psychological and physical faculties.

ātmakaṃ = consists

consisting or composed of, belonging to, having the nature or character of, loving one's self, desire for the Self, desirous of emancipation, loving the supreme spirit, possessed of, self-conceit

from **ātma** = self + **ka** = a possessive suffix, or from **kam** = to desire

Traditionally, *kama* (pleasure) is one of the four accepted values – goals of life – regulated by *dharma* and eventually superseded by the highest desire: *moksha*, liberation.[60]

[60] The four goals are *artha* (material needs), *kama* (pleasure), *dharma* (righteousness), and *moksha* (liberation). We can easily imagine how the first two goals can get out of hand when ruled by self-interest and ignorance. The last two goals help regulate and direct the first two.

Patanjali's *Sutras* presents *prakriti* in a materially-based way, as gross and subtle elements. Using this model, *prakriti* is described by most commentators much like the way scientists describe matter – as the building blocks of objects, devoid of life. This approach captures much of the nature of *prakriti*, but could there be another dimension? Let's break it down.

Look at the list of definitions for *atmakam*, or what *prakriti* consists of. Going deeper into that list, we find words that have undertones of what appear to be emotions. These words all come from the root, *kam* (to desire). *Kam* is the root of *kama*, as in the *Kama Sutra*. That is why the translation for *atmakam* includes *desire for the Self* or *liberation* and *loving the supreme Spirit*.

The notion of *prakriti* having an element of love may seem a bit odd. But it may not seem odd once we add the second sentence of this sutra, which presents the purpose of *prakriti*. We can see a picture of *prakriti* emerging that reveals a profound understanding of nature. If the purpose of the seen (*prakriti*) is to give us experiences that bring liberation, why couldn't the relationship between Seer and seen be regarded as love, a quality innate in any healthy relationship?

Need further indications of this understanding of *prakriti*? Look to sutra 4.2 which, along with sutra 4.3, describes the nature of *prakriti's* manifestations. The acts of creation result from an *abundance, an overflowing, of prakriti*. Here, we have a picture of *prakriti* as if it is intent on flowing and filling the universe. Why? To provide experiences and liberation for the individual.

There's still more that supports this intimate relationship between *Purusha* and *prakriti*. For this, we'll look to Samkhya philosophy upon which much of the *Sutras* rests.

Prakriti has been described as a woman dancing to get the attention of the *Purusha*.[61] But once *Purusha's* attention fully turns to *prakriti's* dance, she vanishes. Isn't this just a metaphorical way of saying that

[61] The *Purusha* thinks, "'*She has been seen by me and therefore loses all interest.*' *Prakriti* thinks, '*I have been seen,*' and ceases her dance. Therefore, even if there is still connection, there is no motive for further evolution." –*Samkhya Karika*, verse 66

prakriti gives us experiences that lead to liberation? *Kaivalya* is Patanjali's term to describe enlightenment. *Kaivalya* means *independence, liberation, isolation*. It is the vanishing of *prakriti* as the only reality, allowing the Seer, the *Purusha*, to stand apart – to be experienced – in its True Nature as *citi shakti*, the power of pure consciousness (See 4.34).

The message here is profound: this universe, with all its tumult, unexpected hardships, and confounding human behaviors, is a benevolent place. The universe is on our side. Teachings and practices, such as those in the *Yoga Sutras,* help us to see this truth by peeling away the layers of ignorance that obscure our True Nature and the True Nature of the universe in which we live. (See 2.21 to expand on the subject matter of this sutra.)

Also see the comments on *bhoga* and on *artham* that follows.

bhoga = experiences

enjoyment, any winding or curve, feasting, feeding on, use, application, fruition, sexual enjoyment, enjoyment of the earth or of a country, perception of pleasure or pain, utility, advantage, delight, any object of enjoyment, property, wealth, revenue (See 2.13)

Look at the list of definitions for *bhoga*. Note that most of them express some sort of joy or delight. Especially pertinent is *enjoyment of the earth*.

Are we to understand that nature is not an enemy to be overcome, but a gift to be enjoyed? And, that it is the perfect arena of challenges, as well as for spiritual growth and enlightenment?

apavarga = liberation

emancipation, completion, end, final beatitude, gift, donation

from ***apa*** = away, off + ***varga*** = a division, class, set, multitude of similar things, group, company, family, everything comprehended under any department or head, everything included under a category, province or sphere of, from ***vrj*** = twist, bend, turn, crooked, enclosed, tangled

arthaṃ = purpose (See 1.28, 1.32, 1.42–1.43, 2.2, 2.18, 2.21–2.22, 3.3, 3.17, 3.36, 4.23–4.24, 4.32, 4.34)

This sutra affirms that the purpose of the seen is to provide experiences and liberation for the individual. The entire universe is a university that exists for the benefit of our liberation. Yet, what about the countless manifestations of the seen that no human ever sees? Science tells us, for example, that two-thirds of all living beings exist in the ocean, still undiscovered. Why would the seen express in ways, and in beings, that no human has ever seen and may never see?

The answer may be that this sutra can have another, expanded meaning. Reflect on this alternate translation, using the same original Sanskrit as the source:

The seen consists of the elements and sense organs and has the qualities of illumination, activity, and inertia. Its purpose is delight and freedom.

The three words: *bhoga, apavarga, and artha* form a compound in the original Sanskrit: delight, freedom, and purpose or experience. This leaves room for the discovery of layers of meaning.

The seen exists for the Seer, but the Seer is not just the Self of all beings. It is the essential Self of all objects in the universe. The Seer delights in the seen and this delight exists in a free-flowing state of freedom. This description of delight may be the best way we can understand or describe what is essentially beyond the grasp of the mind. The Seer delights in the seen and this leads to a state of complete freedom. Freedom from what? The categorizations, motives, and emotions the human mind projects onto creation.

When the Seer and seen get mixed together, their true essences are obscured by an overlay of our notions, philosophies, aspirations, fears, and desires. From the unenlightened mind's limited perspective, neither the Seer nor seen is free to exist according to its essential nature.

From the perspective of the Seer, freedom is the unrestrained delight in the "show" put on by the seen. This delight is innate in the witnessing of the play of the universe: the drama, comedy, romance, adventure, and horror. The seen exists for the delight of the Seer.[62] The Seer and seen, in

[62] And the Seer is our True Self, True Nature – our source and essence.

Patanjali's Yoga, coexist eternally together. And freedom is a hallmark of that relationship.

When we say that the Seer *delights*, it's a human-centric way of expressing the state of harmony of purpose. This is what has been experienced and revealed to the great sages and saints and is waiting for us to discover for ourselves.

My spiritual master was once asked to describe enlightenment. He said: ***"You're in the light. You feel light. And you take delight in everything."*** The fully enlightened being is someone who has become an embodiment of the dance of delight of the Seer and seen. It sounds like love, doesn't it?

This truth is not limited to Yoga. It is found in all faith traditions. Here's an example from *Psalm 148* (an excerpt from the *Berean Study Bible*):

Praise the Lord from the earth,
All great sea creatures and ocean depths,
Lightning and hail, snow and clouds,
Powerful wind fulfilling His word,

Mountains and all hills,
Fruit trees and all cedars,
Wild animals and all cattle,
Crawling creatures and flying birds,

Kings of the earth and all peoples,
Princes and all rulers of the earth,
Young men and maidens,
Old and young together.
Let them praise the name of the Lord.

dṛśyam = the seen

the seeable, what is to be seen

2.19 There are four different stages of the evolution of the seen. They are, from gross to subtle:

- **Discernible by the senses: gross elements**
- **Not discernible by the senses: subtle elements**
- **The discriminative faculty (*buddhi*), the first product of *prakriti***
- **Undifferentiated matter, the *gunas* in equilibrium without any form**

viśeṣa-aviśeṣa-liṅga-mātra-aliṅgāni guṇa-parvāṇi

viśeṣa = discernible by the senses

specific, distinction, difference, peculiarity, characteristic difference, special property, a kind, species, individual, choice, distinguished, individual essence

from ***vi*** = asunder, away + ***śeṣa*** = remainder, from ***śis*** = to leave (See 1.22)

aviśeṣa = not discernible by the senses

nonspecific, indistinct, no distinction, no difference, no peculiarity, no sectarian mark (See above and 1.22)

from ***a*** = not + ***viśeṣa*** = distinct

Avisesa, in this sutra, refers to the inability of the senses to discern – or perceive – the subtle elements. It's not that the elements do not have discernible characteristics.

liṅga = the purest product of prakṛti

designator, signifier, indicator, mark, spot, sign, badge, emblem, symptom, a proof, evidence, the sign of gender, the image of a God

from ***liṅg*** = paint, mark

Linga can be understood as the invariable or constant mark that proves the existence of anything. For example, smoke is an invariable mark or sign *(linga)* of fire. In this sutra, it refers to *buddhi*, the first and most subtle evolute of *prakriti.*

The existence, and our experience of our intelligence (*buddhi*), stands as a sign, symptom, or evidence of the existence and nature of the *Purusha*. This is due to the *buddhi's* closeness to the *Purusha*.

Buddhi, as the intellect and discriminative faculty, helps us decide on courses of action in life.

mātra = suffix designating measure or quantity

entirely, only, elementary matter, element

from ***mā*** = measure

Linga (See page 169) + *matra* becomes *lingamatra*. This refers to the state of matter prior to emergence of specific objects. It can also be understood as *mahat* or *buddhi.*

aliṅgāni = the *gunas* in equilibrium, undifferentiated matter

undefinable, literally, without mark, unmanifest

from ***a*** = not + ***liṅga*** = mark = formless, undifferentiated, equilibrium of the *gunas*

guṇa = left translated

qualities, constituent of nature, literally, strand or thread

Refer to 1.16 for more on *guna*.

parvāṇi = stages

division, level, limb, step of a staircase, member of a compound

from ***pṛ*** = fill

2.20 The Seer is nothing but the sheer power of seeing – pure consciousness. Although it is pure and unchanging, it appears to have the qualities and contents of the mind.

draṣtā dṛśi-matrah śuddho'pi pratyaya-anupaśyaḥ

draṣṭā = the Seer (See 1.3)

witness

dṛśi = the power of seeing

seeing, consciousness, perceiving, behold, look at, consider, to wait on, visit, to see with the mind, learn, understand, to notice, to care for, examine, try, to see by divine intuition, think of, find out, compose, contrive, become visible, appear, to be shown or manifested

from ***dṛś*** = to see

matrah = nothing but

the totality, simply, sheer, the full measure, only, alone, being nothing but

This word is often used to express emphasis.

śuddha = sheer[63]

pure, correct, cleansed, pure spirit, bright, white, acquitted, free from error, faultless, blameless, accurate, exact, according to rule, complete, entire, unmitigated, tried, examined, sharp as an arrow

from ***śudh*** = purify, clean, to become pure, to become clear or free from doubts, to be excused or cleared from blame

We can see from the list of definitions of *suddha*, that "pure" represents only one dimension of this term. The sense of this word includes: *bright* and *white*, *accurate, complete,* and *sharp as an arrow*. When combined with *matrah (nothing but)*, a powerful three-dimensional image arises that offers a hint of the nature of pure consciousness.

api = although

also, even, too, reaching to, proximity, moreover, besides, surely

pratyaya = content of the mind (at any given moment)

through the mind, intention, thoughts, firm conviction, basis, proof, ascertainment, to acquire confidence, assumption, notion, idea, the motive or cause of anything, the concurrent occasion of an event as distinguished from its proximate cause. (See 1.10, 1.18–1.19, 2.20, 3.2, 4.27)

[63] The word "sheer" suggests, *nothing other than; without limitation.*

anupaśyaḥ = appears

to be looked upon, to be taken as, perceiving, keeping in view, seeing

from ***anu*** = after, alongside, near to, under subordinate to, after, with + ***paś*** = to perceive, see, behold

2.21 The seen is worthwhile, beautiful, and pleasing since it has meaning – its nature and essence is truly for the purpose of experience and liberation.

tad-artha eva dṛśyasya-ātmā

Refer to 2.18 for more on the seen.

tad = (*refers to the Seer*)

that, this

artha = purpose

meaning, aim, cause, motive, reason, advantage, use, utility, relating to a thing or object, material, means of life, object of the senses, matter, profit, for the sake of (See 1.28, 1.32, 1.42–1.43, 2.2, 2.18, 2.21–2.22, 3.3, 3.17, 3.36, 4.23–4.24, 4.32, 4.34)

Refer to 1.28 for more on *artha*.

eva = truly

indeed, only, so, just so, exactly so, really

The several definitions of *eva* suggest that this simple word carries a sense of emphasis. The relationship between *Purusha* and *prakriti* is close, intimate, and eternal.

dṛśyasya = the seen, worth seeing or looking at, beautiful (See 2.17)

the state of being visible, worth seeing or looking at, beautiful, or pleasing

ātmā = exists

essence, self, the principle of life and sensation, the individual self, soul, nature, character, peculiarity, the person or whole body considered as one as opposed to the separate members of the body, the body, living entity, a person, one's soul, Supreme Soul, consciousness, heart, the understanding, intellect or mind, the highest personal principle of life, effort, firmness, the sun, fire, a son (See 2.5, 2.21, 2.41, 4.13, 4.25)

from ***at*** – to breathe or ***ap*** = to pervade, reach up to

Refer to 2.5 for more on *Atma*.

2.22 For the liberated, the purpose of the seen – providing experiences and liberation – is fulfilled. It's as if it disappears, although it doesn't really vanish since the experience of its reality and its relevance is common to others.[64]

kṛita-arthaṃ prati naṣṭa api anaṣṭam tad anya-sādhāraṇatvāt

kṛita= fulfilled

done, accomplished, completed

arthaṃ = purpose

Refer to 1.28 for more on *artha*.

prati = for

with regard to, toward

naṣṭa = seems to disappear

disappeared, lost, destroyed, expelled, wasted, lost sight of, invisible, damaged, corrupted, spoiled, fruitless, in vain, deprived of, spoiled, in vain

from ***naś*** = perish, remove, drive away, expel, to lose from memory, to reach, attain, meet with, find

Of all the definitions listed for this word, *fruitless* and *to lose from memory* provide keys to unlocking the meaning of this sutra. The seen – the universe – doesn't really disappear, but for the Self-realized individual, it loses its relevance for the purpose of liberation. (Refer to 1.10 for more on *pratyaya*.)

[64] See the commentary for 2.27 for further clarification of this concept.

Nature's highest purpose has been fulfilled for the realized being and its relevance for attaining happiness is radically changed. There are no more spiritual fruits to be harvested from the seen. And although the seen is not literally gone from memory or memories – thoughts and desires – of the world of matter lose their power to draw the mind away from realization of the Self as one's True Nature.

The enlightened can still enjoy life in the world of matter. In fact, the enlightened enjoy it much more. There is a profound freedom that comes from the disappearance of fruitless hopes, fears, and cravings.

See the definitions of *api* and *anastam* below and sutras 4.31 and 4.32 for more on this subject.

api = although

even, also, too, moreover, besides, surely, and, uniting or annexing, reaching to, proximity, placing near or over

Since *api* has the sense of proximity, it emphasizes that the seen does not actually disappear: it *nearly* disappears.

anaṣṭam = it doesn't really vanish

not destroyed (See *nasta*, above)

tad = (*refers to the Self-realized*)

that

anya = others

different, other than, opposed to, one of a number

sādhāraṇatvāt = common

universality, community

from ***sadharana*** = having or resting on the same support or basis, belonging or applicable to all, from ***sā*** = with + ***dhāraṇa*** = holding, from ***dhṛ*** = to hold + ***tvat*** = having the quality of

2.23 Confusing the natures and powers of the Owner (Seer) and owned (seen) creates the condition for perceiving them as one.

sva-svāmi-śaktyoḥ svarūpa-upalabdhi-hetuḥ samyogaḥ

sva = owned

own, one's own

svāmi = owner

proprietor, chief, commander, a husband, learned pundit, one who has achieved self-mastery

The *Sutras* refer to the relationship between *Purusha* and *prakriti* as Seer and seen and Owner and owned. In Hindu philosophy, that which is experienced *(prakriti)* must logically exist for the one that experiences *(Purusha)*. This is why *Purusha* is referred to in terms that seem to indicate a kind of superiority. In fact, *Purusha* and *prakriti* are two coexistent eternal realities. In the *Sutras* and in Samkhya philosophy, they need each other. Their relationship is intimate. The Seer needs something to see, or why would it be called the Seer. The seen would not be referred to as seen if there were no Seer. Finally, the seen exists to give experiences and liberation to the Seer (2.18).

This might seem counter to much of what is taught and written about Yoga being all about oneness, that there is only one truth or reality and that the creation we see around us is just a manifestation of *maya*, illusion. There is only one essence and source. This is not, at least overtly, what Patanjali espouses. That vision of oneness migrated from Advaita Vedanta.[65]

We need to keep in mind that all of these theories, theologies, and teachings are the attempts that highly spiritually evolved human beings made to describe what is indescribable. They are based on personal subjective experiences of subtle truths filtered through culture, capacity, and beliefs. Even the highest philosophy is transmitted by words and words are fingers that point to the truth, not the truth itself.

Becoming attached to whatever approach speaks most clearly to us can lead to "only my way" or "only one way" thinking, an attitude that has wreaked a lot of havoc on our planet.

[65] Although Advaita Vedanta is often described as the philosophy based on the oneness of all creation, it is more about there not being any duality in creation. Advaita literally means, *not two*. In other words, Advaita is not about what creation is, but what it is not. What creation is, is left up to personal experience.

śaktyoḥ = powers

ability, strength, effort, energy, capability

In Sanskrit, *shaktyoh* is in the dual case, meaning it is specifically referring to two, in this case, the Seer and the seen.

***svarūpa* = nature of**

one's own form or shape, one's own condition, character or distinct nature, peculiarity (See 1.3, 1.43, 2.23, 2.54, 3.3, 3.45, 3.48, 4.34)

Refer to 1.3 for more on *svarupa*.

upalabdhi = perceive

recognition, apprehension, acquisition, gain, observation, understanding, knowledge, becoming aware, knowledge, appearance, perceptibility, the condition of faculty of perceiving

from ***upa*** = to, unto + ***labdh***, from ***labh*** = obtain, gain, acquisition

In the presence of the *Purusha* (Seer), the nature of *prakriti* is revealed, including its latent powers and qualities. The perceptive abilities of the yogi, steadily increasing through dedicated practice, gradually reveal more and more of the character of the seen. These increasingly subtle insights lead to being able to discern the distinction of the natures and capabilities of the *Purusha* and *prakriti*, which leads to liberation.[66] (See 3.54)

hetuḥ = cause

reason (See 2.17)

samyogaḥ = apparent conjunction due to confusion

joining, conjunction, union (See 2.17, 2.23, 2.25)

from ***sam*** = together, with, completely, absolutely + ***yoga*** = union, junction, addition, total, partaking of, putting on, application or concentration of thoughts, wealth, team, lucky conjuncture, diligence, strategy, disposition, device, any act conducive to concentrating the mind, combination, application, work,

[66] The final and most subtle differentiation to be made is the difference between the pure, *sattvic* mind and the *Purusha*.

discipline, attaching, devotion, vehicle, original meaning of a word, contact with from ***yuj*** = yoke

Refer to 2.17 for more on *samyoga*.

2.24 Ignorance is the cause of confusing the Seer and seen as one.

tasya hetur avidyā

tasya = of this

its

hetuḥ = cause

reason (See 2.17)

***avidyā* = ignorance**

delusion (See 2.3–2.5, 2.24)

Refer to 2.3 for more on *avidya*.

2.25 Without ignorance, this confusion ceases to exist. The Seer stands apart from the seen as the Self. This is liberation (*kaivalya*).

tad-abhāvāt samyoga-abhāvo hānam tad-dṛśeh kaivalyam

tad = (*refers to ignorance*)

that

abhāvāt = without

absence, nonexistence, negation, removal, to nullify, non-entity

from ***a*** = not + ***bhāva*** = being, from ***bhụ*** = to be (See 1.10)

Abhavat, in the world of philosophy, is also the presentation of a proof of something based on the non-existence of something else. For example, if there are no mice, there must be cats. If there is liberation, there must be no confusion.

samyoga = correlation (See 2.17)

abhāvaḥ = no such

absent, nonexistent (See above and 1.10)

hānam = stands apart

removal, absence, escape, giving up, relinquishing, abandoning, cessation, stand apart, getting rid of, want, lack

from ***hā*** = depart

To stand apart indicates distinctive qualities that mark something as different from other things.

tat = (*refers to the Seer*)

that

dṛśeh = the seen (See 2.20)

kaivalyam = pure, free

liberation, independence, isolation, aloneness, single, unitary, uncompounded, release, total separation, transcendent aloneness (See 2.25, 3.51, 3.56, 4.26. 4.34)

from ***kevala*** = alone, not connected to anything

Kaivalya is often translated as *isolation or aloneness*. The idea here is that *kaivalya* results from isolating – discriminating the difference between – the ego-based self that seems to have consciousness as a property, and the pure consciousness that is the *Purusha*. In this sense, *kaivalya* is liberation or release from ignorance and the suffering it brings.

Kaivalya is also described by Patanjali (4.34) as the return to the origin (*pratiprasava*) of the *gunas*. The same sutra goes on to say *kaivalya* is the establishment of the nature and power of higher awareness (*citi-shakti*). The mind is no longer limited to being the holder of ignorance and the center of self-identity.

Kaivalya can also refer to pure seeing, the experience of the *Purusha's* innate capacity for unconditioned, unlimited, unchanging knowing of the contents of the mind.

In sutra 3.56, *kaivalya* is said to be experienced when the *sattva* of individual mind reaches a state of purity analogous to that of the *Purusha*.

2.26 The remedy that removes ignorance is an unwavering flow of discriminative discernment (*viveka*) that perceives the difference between the Seer and seen. (See 4.25–4.26, 4.29–4.30)

viveka-khyātir aviplavā hāna-upāyaḥ

viveka = unwavering discriminative discernment

discernment, consideration, discussion, investigation, true knowledge, right judgment, the faculty of distinguishing and classifying things according to their real properties, (in Vedanta) the power of separating the invisible Spirit from the visible world (or spirit from matter, truth from untruth, reality from mere semblance or illusion) (See 2.15, 2.26, 2.28, 3.53, 3.55, 4.26, 4.29)

from ***vic*** = to sift, to separate, deprive of, to discriminate, discern, judge

The nature of *viveka* is *sattva*: clear, luminous, tranquil. Refer to 2.15 for more on *viveka*.

khyātir = discernment

perception, knowledge, view, idea, being well-known, fame (See 1.16)

from ***khyā*** = to see, to be named, to be known, to relate, tell, declare

In addition to discernment, *khyatir* means *fame* or *to be well-known*. This suggests a degree of discernment that stands out from what is common. It's not just being able to tell the difference between red and blue, one shade of red from another, or olive oil from France from that produced in Italy. It is discernment of a much higher order than that, and its purpose is different. *Khyatir*, paired with *viveka*, refers to the most highly refined, intuitive state of discernment that is ultimately able to perceive the difference between Seer and seen, mind and Self (See 4.25–4.26).

aviplavā = unwavering, flow

unfaltering, unbroken, uncorrupted, chaste, to swim, slope toward, be inclined to

from ***a*** = not + ***vi*** = as (asunder, away) + plava, from plu = float

hāna = removal

escape (See 2.25) absence, escape, giving up, relinquishing, abandoning, cessation, gone, departed, the act of abandoning, relinquishing, giving up, getting rid of

from ***ha*** = depart

upāyaḥ = remedy

goal, means, method, that by which one reaches a goal, coming near, approach, arrival, strategy, joining in or accompanying (in singing)

from ***upa*** = to, unto + ***aya***, from ***i*** = go

In Hindu astrology, an *upaya* is a remedy for difficult situations and karma. These remedies can include mantras, meditation, prayer, *pujas* and ritual sacrifices, fasting, charity, and the use of gemstones.

If ignorance is the disorder, then the remedy needs to be able to remove ignorance. *Viveka* is the remedy and is composed of the yogic lifestyle,[67] and practices such as meditation, devotion to *Ishvara*, and nonattachment.

2.27 For the yogi who attains this unwavering discernment (*viveka*), seven insights arise that lead to the final stage – liberation.

tasya saptadhā prānta-bhūmiḥ prajñā

tasya = (*refers to the yogi*)

his (or her)

from ***tad*** = he, she, it, that, this, these, in that place, then, at that time, in that case, in this manner, for that reason

saptadhā = sevenfold

in seven parts, seven times

[67] The yogic lifestyle consists of, and is based on, attitudes and practices such as the *yamas* and *niyamas*, the Four Locks and Four Keys (1.33), *Kriya Yoga* (2.1), *asana, pranayama, pratyahara, pratipaksha bhavana* (2.33), and *Ishvara pranidhanam* (1.23).

from ***sapta*** = seven + ***dhā***, suffix = fold, that which expresses location: here, there, with

prānta = final

edge, boundary, margin, verge, extremity, end, a point or tip, dwelling near the boundaries, the back part of a carriage, brought forward to completion, going beyond the existing boundaries, breaking of old boundaries, finding a new edge

from ***pra*** = before, forward + ***anta*** = end, limit

This refers to an insight that precedes the liberating *samadhi*. This insight is *pranta-bhumih*, unerring wisdom that goes beyond old boundaries of scriptural texts, ritual, tenets, and teachings. It is direct perception, without the mediation of logic, past conceptions, desires, and habit.

From this insight, the yogi finds a *new edge* (suggested by one of the definitions of *pranta*). Hence, the seven insights that lead to liberation arise, one leading to the next. The inner pilgrimage taken by yogis leads them beyond boundaries of what the ego could perceive as conceivable. To directly experience what was once inconceivable is innate to the experience of Yoga.

bhūmiḥ = stage

place the earth, soil, ground, territory, country, district, a place, situation, position, posture, attitude, floor of a house, stage of Yoga (See 1.14, 1.27, 3.6)

In metaphysics, *bhumih* refers to a step, a degree, or a stage of attainment.

In Buddhism, *bhumi* refers to the ten stages Buddhists must go through to attain buddhahood.

prajñā = insight

wisdom, intuitive insight (See 1.20, 1.48–1.49, 2.27, 3.5)

In Buddhism, *prajna* is understood as true or transcendental wisdom.

Refer to 1.20 for more on *prajna*.

Reflection

From the practice of unwavering discriminative discernment, the spirit of deep inquiry is ignited and seven insights arise that strengthen the yogi's resolve and expand the boundaries of consciousness. This prepares the individual for intuitive insight, which leads to liberation.

Patanjali offers no details on the seven insights he is referring to, but a commonly accepted list follows:

1. Through *viveka*, the causes of suffering are recognized. Therefore, there is nothing more to be known on this subject.
2. The causes of suffering, having been identified, are progressively weakened.
3. Through *samadhi*, the causes of suffering are eliminated. There is nothing more to be gained in this area.
4. Mastery in *viveka* having been reached, there is nothing else self-effort can accomplish.
5. *Sattva* dominates the functioning of the mind-stuff.
6. The *gunas*, having fulfilled their purpose, lose their foothold like stones falling from a mountain peak and incline toward reabsorption into *prakriti*.
7. The *Purusha* is realized as independent from the *gunas*. Liberation is attained.

2.28 By integrating the limbs of Yoga into daily life, impurities – all born from the root causes of suffering (*klesas*) – dwindle away. The mind becomes illumined with the light of wisdom, culminating in unwavering discriminative discernment (*viveka*).

yoga-aṅga-anuṣṭhānāt aśuddhi-kṣaye jñāna-dīptir ā viveka-khāyteh

yoga = left untranslated

union (See 1.1–1.2, 2.1, 2.28)

Refer to 1.2 for more on Yoga.

aṅga = limb

member, division, body (See 1.31)

anuṣṭhānāt = integrating

following, carrying out, devotion to, undertaking, doing, to attend to, religious practice or observance, a long and stipulated period of time, repeating a mantra for a set number of times over a given period of time, acting in conformity to, to stand alongside, to stand together, to stand near or with, to govern, rule, appoint

from ***anu*** = alongside, with, after, together, every, each + ***sthā*** = to stand, ***sthanā*** = position, proximity

aśuddhi = impurity

sullied (See 2.20)

from ***a*** = not + ***śudh*** = purity, authorized, faultless, free from error, unequalled, unmixed, free from misperception, free from the obscuring effects of the *tamas* and *raja gunas*

kṣaye = dwindling

destruction, wearing away, loss

from ***kṣi*** = to destroy, to remain, be quiet, going, moving, corrupt, ruin, make an end of, kill, injure, to diminish, decrease, wane, waste away, perish, to pass (said of the night)

jñāna = wisdom

knowledge (See 1.9, 1.38, 1.42, 2.28, 3.16–3.19, 3.22, 3.26–3.29, 3.36, 3.53, 3.55, 4.31)

Refer to 1.9 for more on *jnana*.

dīptir = light

from ***dīp*** = to blaze, flare, shine, be luminous

ā = leads to,

up to, as far as

viveka = discrimination

(See 2.15, 2.26, 2.28, 3.53, 3.55, 4.26, 4.29)

Refer to 2.15 for more on *viveka*.

khyāteh = discernment

perception, knowledge, declaration, opinion, view, idea, assertion, glory, celebrated, discovered, point of view, glory (See 1.16)

from ***khyā*** = to see, to be named, to be known, to relate, tell, declare

In the *Sutras, khyati* is a degree of discernment that is only possible when the individual's *buddhi* is purified. In this sutra, it is compounded with *viveka*, strengthening and elevating it.

The sense of this word is the discernment, discovery, perception of something special. This is evidenced by the definitions of *glory, celebrated, to be known* and *declared.*

Khyati in Hindu mythology is the daughter of Daksha, a son of Brahma, the creator. Daksha is one of seven divine beings that personify the laws that rule the universe and society. Daksha represents skill, sacrifice, and the rules for performing ritual sacrifice. This suggests that *khyati* is a capacity born of skill and sacrifice, and that it has a relationship to creative power.

In practical terms, *khyati* manifests as cultivating skill in our spiritual practices and making ourselves – our time and energy – available for those practices and lifestyle changes.

Khyati then has the aura of the divine. *Khyati* is a refined capacity for insight and discernment (*viveka*) capable of penetrating the veils of ignorance.

2.29 The eight limbs of Yoga are:

1. *Yama* = universal resolves that foster harmonious relationships to self, others, and life
2. *Niyama* = additional resolves taken on by yogis to encourage spiritual growth
3. *Asana* = posture

4. *Pranayama* = regulation of breath

5. *Pratyahara* = management and withdrawal of the senses

6. *Dharana* = concentration

7. *Dhyana* = meditation

8. *Samadhi* = absorption

yama-niyama-āsana-prāṇāyāma-pratyāhāra-dhāraṇā-dhyāna-samādhayo' stāv-aṅgāni

yama = universal governing principles

govern, self-control, holding back, moral duty, any rule, rein, curb, bridle, a driver, suppression

from ***yam*** = hold, support, reach, restrain, to establish, to be firm, not budge, to give one's self up to, be faithful, obey, to sustain, to raise, wield (a weapon), to stretch out, expand, spread, display, govern, subdue, to offer

The *yamas* are classified as universal because they apply to all social divisions and categories of people, and because they are to be applied regardless of the era we live in or situations we are experiencing.

However, it is important not to equate their universality as meaning that they are morals to which we blindly or unthinkingly cling. That would lead to rigidity. Instead, the *yamas* are more like guides that nudge us toward the awakening of our innate inner guidance system, our inner light. Through study, contemplation, practice, mindfulness, and guidance, we uncover the spirit that animates the *yamas*. Though we necessarily begin with the letter of the "law," it is the spirit that we ultimately follow by applying these resolves faithfully and intelligently in daily life.

Using the *yamas* as guiding lights helps us learn how to make wise decisions and take life paths that bring growth and benefit. When our inner guidance system awakens, we find that memorized morals are not needed. Our vision will naturally express virtue itself.

Wise or virtuous decisions are those that bring the highest good for the most people.

niyama = additional resolves taken by yogis

any fixed rule or law, obligation, a minor or lesser vow or observance dependent on external conditions and not as obligatory as *yama*, any act of voluntary penance or meritorious piety, to stop, hold back, detain, to stay, remain, to fasten, tie to, to bring near, govern, regulate

from ***ni*** = down, into + ***yam*** = restrain, reach

Although by strict word definition *niyama* is not regarded as being as obligatory as *yama*, for the yogi, the *niyamas* are regarded as being equally vital as the *yamas*.

Yamas represent universal moral codes of behavior. They cross over all religious, cultural, and temporal lines. The *niyamas* represent the ethics or morals applied to a specific group that helps guide behavior. Within the group, the ethics are regarded and treated the same as morals.

āsana = posture

position, sitting down, to be present, exist, sitting in a particular posture, a seat, couch, place, stool, abiding, dwelling, maintaining a post against an enemy

from ***ās*** = sit, be, dwell, abide, remain, continue, continue doing anything, to cease, to have an end, solemnize, celebrate, do anything without interruption, to last

Here, this word refers to the posture assumed for meditation. The fact that the definitions include to *exist, abide, to be present,* suggests that the posture adopted by the practitioner should be comfortable enough to be maintained for prolonged periods of meditation without discomfort.

prāṇāyāma = regulation of breath

from ***prana***, from ***pra*** = before, forward + ***an*** = breathe + ***yāma*** = restrain

pratyāhāra = management and withdrawal

retreat, holding back (especially of the senses), drawing back (troops from battle)

from ***prati*** = against, back + ***a*** = unto + ***hara***, from ***hr*** = take, hold

Both *management* and *withdrawal* are used to indicate that *pratyahara* can refer to the wise use of the senses as well as the necessary withdrawal of sense input. This is a necessary stage for the practices of *dharana*, *dhyana*, and *samadhi*.

Since it is the initial turning of attention within, *pratyahara* begins, in earnest, the journey from belief to self-transformation for most seekers.

dhāraṇā = concentration

act of holding, retaining, wearing, supporting, protecting, preserving, maintaining, understanding, intellect, firmness, steadfastness, certainty, the two female breasts (See 2.29, 2.53, 3.1)

from ***dhṛ*** (or ***dhā***) = hold, maintain, to put, place, lay on or in, bestowing, have, cause, name of Brahma (the Creator in Hinduism or Brahma as the Supreme Absolute Reality)

If we review the different translations of *dharana*, we will find a correlation between the ability to hold attention, the intellect, and understanding. A focused mind can come to understand anything since it has a natural - an innate - ability to probe whatever it holds its steady focus on.[68]

A noteworthy definition is the two female breasts. Combining this with definitions such as holding and protecting, we can reframe the practice of concentration as one of nurturing rather than a forced practice that can veer into bullying the mind.

dhyāna = meditation (See 1.39, 3.2, 3.11, 3.30, 4.6)

Possible derivations:

1. ***dhā*** = placing, putting, holding, possessing, having, bestowing, granting, causing, virtue, merit, wealth, property + ***ya*** = to go forward, moving or going, support, meditation, arrive at, approach, vagina, restrain, attain, to find out, behave, withdraw
2. ***dhi*** = religious thought, mind, meditation, splendor, light, prayer, devotion, receptacle + ***ya*** = to go forward, moving or going, support, meditation,

[68] Steady is not the same as still. Stillness may be the ultimate state of mind that brings enlightenment, but steadiness is the path the mind takes. There is movement, but it is focused, directed, tranquil, and undisturbed.

arrive at, approach, vagina, restrain, attain, to find out, behave, withdraw ***dhi*** and ***dha*** are related terms. ***Dhi*** may have derived from ***dha***, a stronger term

3. ***dhyai*** = meditate, think of, contemplate

Historically, *dhih*, a Vedic term, precedes *dhyana*. In *dhih*, a specific deity is visualized. Often translated as "thought," *dhih* means *visionary insight*, or *a thought-provoking vision*. These insights are said to have often inspired songs, poems, prayers, and hymns.

As with *dharana*, we find what seems to be an odd or out of place definition for *dhyana*: *vagina (womb)*. With *dharana*, we found evidence of nurturance: *breastfeeding*. With *dhyana*, a deeper practice, we go deeper, to the womb, a place of perfect nurturance, the ideal environment for the beginning of life.

This reinforces the idea that meditation practice requires an inner environment of gentility, kindness, and nurturance. It also suggests that self-discipline is not just a matter of willpower, but of heart power. Any practice or lifestyle change needs to be motivated and fed by love for what it is and what it will bring.

samādhi = absorption

joining or combining with, contemplation, intense concentration, unified state of awareness, bringing into harmony, joining with, attention, whole, accomplishment, conclusion, union, concentration of thoughts, profound meditation, enstasy (joy from within), super-conscious state, bringing into harmony, completion (See 1.20, 1.46, 1.51, 2.2, 2.29, 2.45, 3.3, 3.11, 3.38, 4.1, 4.29)

Although *samadhi* without any qualifiers (such as *nirvitarka*, etc.) usually refers to the highest state of enlightenment, here and in other sutras, it may refer to a number of states of mental absorption. These deep meditation experiences bring profound intuitive insights into the object of contemplation, or in higher states, the meditators themselves.

Patanjali uses the term, *nirbija samadhi,* or *kaivalya,* to refer to the highest states. We can also add the word "Yoga" to this list, referring to the experience of realizing a state of unity of Seer and seen.[69]

Refer to 1.20 for more on *samadhi.*

aṣtau = **eight**

aṅgāni = **limbs** (See 2.28)

2.30 *Yama* – the universal resolves – consists of:

- ***Ahimsa*** = **harmlessness**
- ***Satya*** = **truthfulness**
- ***Asteya*** = **nonstealing**
- ***Brahmacharya*** = **a life dedicated to self-mastery and liberation**
- ***Aparigraha*** = **freedom from craving to possess sense objects**

ahimsā-satya-asteya-brahmacarya-aparigrahāḥ yamāḥ

ahimsā = **harmlessness** (See 2.35)

absence of the desire to kill or injure

from ***a*** = not + ***himsā*** = injury, harm, hurt, hostile, mischief, the three wrongs: hatred, abusive language, and acts of violence, from ***han*** = strike, kill

Ahimsa is the highest of the *yamas* because the impulse to engage in violent thoughts, words, and deeds arises from feelings of fear – from real, exaggerated, or imagined threats. Competition for resources, lust for power and wealth, uncertainty and change, all played against the

[69] Strictly speaking, the union of Seer and seen is not how Patanjali presents the highest state. Instead, he emphasizes independence from, or the isolation of, of the pure consciousness of the Seer from all objects of perception *(prakriti)*. The union of Seer and seen, in Patanjali's Yoga, is a philosophical overlay from the perspective of Vedanta. That said, if we look carefully at how the *Sutras* describe the final realization (4.34), we see that all of nature resolves back to its source. The Seer stands free and is experienced as the power of pure consciousness. This is a state of supernormal harmony. Anyone who experiences this state could describe it as one completely devoid of doubt or fear – a state or experience of connectedness, of a common unifying purpose of all of creation. With this in mind, it is appropriate to include oneness or unity as a description of the goal of Yoga.

underlying background of *duhkha*,[70] creates a fertile ground for violence. Note that the other *yamas* all help create and support *ahimsa*.

On a personal level, the impulse to do harm, to dislike, and even hate others has to be pacified and transcended in order to progress spiritually. Certainly all of the Yoga practices and principles help accomplish this, but perhaps faith (see *Ishvara pranidhanam*, 2.23) and the four locks and four keys (*Brahma Viharas*), sutra 1.33, stand out as the foremost.

On a societal level, no real progress can be made in communal ideals – peace, harmony, prosperity, opportunity – until a way of reducing and controlling violence is devised. In fact, legal systems (a major advancement in human history) were developed not primarily to find truth in disputes, but to end cycles of violence and retaliation – tragic situations that we can still see today. While the military, police forces, judges, lawyers, and juries are all essential components of managing and preventing violence, cultivating, teaching, and living *ahimsa* is more beneficial as it gets to the root of the problem.

We can regard the rest of the *yamas* from both individual and societal levels – even *brahmacharya* (as constructive sexual relationships), whose societal benefits include helping to cultivate and maintain clear, honest, and fruitful relationships that form the basis of societies.

satya = truthfulness

authenticity, sincerity, veracity, genuine, sincere, honest, pure, virtuous, good, successful, reality, speaking the truth, effectual, valid

from ***sat*** = being, existing, occurring, happening, being present, abiding in, belonging to, living, lasting, enduring, real, actual, as any one or anything ought to be, right, beautiful, wise, venerable, a being, beings, creatures, that which really is, existence, essence, the true being or real existence, that which is good or true, reality + suffix, ***ya*** = meaning to have the quality of the word it is attached to. In this case, it means to have the quality of existence or reality

Sat is from the root, *as* = to be, exist.

[70] *Duhkha* = the innate persistent pervasive feeling of precariousness common to all human beings. Refer to 2.15.

asteya = nonstealing (See 2.37)

from ***a*** = not + ***steya***, theft, robbery, larceny, anything stolen or liable to be stolen, anything clandestine or private, from ***stai*** = to steal

brahmacarya = a life dedicated to self-mastery and liberation (See 2.38)

continence, celibacy, chastity, behavior, conduct, the due observance of all rites and customs, a religious mendicant's life, practice, dwelling in brahma, the path that leads to brahma (the Absolute Reality)

from **brahma** = relating to sacred knowledge, prescribed by the *Vedas*, scriptural, relating to the brahmins or the priest class, belonging to an inhabitant of brahma's world of man, one versed in sacred knowledge, from **brh** = greater than the greatest + ***charya*** = engaged in, to be practiced or performed, driving in a carriage, proceeding

In this text, *brahmacharya* is given a broader meaning than the usual translations of *continence* or *celibacy*. While these are valid translations, we can consider a wider context of the word, where it means to regulate all aspects of life in order to create and conserve energy and then apply that energy to the goal of liberation.

The roots of the word mean to behave in a way that leads to *Brahman*, the Absolute. *Brahmacharya*, then, may be best understood as a moral, ethical life dedicated to liberation through self-mastery, one-pointedness of mind, and dedication (selfless service, devotion to *Ishvara*).

When considering *brahmacharya* as sexual restraint, it can also include not using sex for manipulation or to work out psychological problems. *Brahmacharya,* within a relationship, can be defined as physical intimacy for expressing love, caring, fidelity, generosity, and devotion to another. In this context, *brahmacharya* is also about learning to discriminate between lust and love.

aparigrahāḥ = freedom from craving for sense objects (See 2.39)

nongreed, nonpossession, renunciation of nonessentials, poverty, deprivation, freedom from clinging, nonacceptance, non-possessiveness, renouncing, grasping for what is beyond one's needs, a desire that takes over the entire person

from ***a*** = not + ***parigraha*** = laying hold of on all sides surrounding, enclosing, fencing around (especially the sacrificial altar by means of three lines or furrows), wrapping around, assuming a form, comprehending, summing up, totality, taking, accepting, receiving or anything received, a gift or present, acquisition, possession, property, household, family, attendants, a house, abode, root, origin, hospitable reception, taking a wife, choice, selection, understanding, conception, undertaking, beginning, performance of, homage, reverence, grace, favor, help, dominion, control, force, constraint, punishment, claim on, relation to, concern with, a curse, oath, an eclipse of the sun, the reserve of an army.

from ***pari*** = toward, against, away from, around, about (in reference to space and time), fully, beyond, away, outside of + ***graha*** = holding, seizing, obtaining, perceiving, recognizing, any state which proceeds from magical influences and takes possession of the whole person, the part of the bow that is grasped by the hand, receiving, accepting gifts, from ***grah*** = to grasp, seizing, holding, obtaining, name of a group of demons or spirits who seize or exercise a bad influence on the body and mind of humans (causing insanity), any state which proceeds from magical influences and takes possession of the human being, the five sense organs + ***manas***, the beginning of any piece of music, keeping back, obstructing, imprisoning, effort

Literally, *to not grasp beyond, around, or away, parigraha* indicates a state of mind so overtaken by a passionate desire for something that one is tempted to break moral and ethical precepts in order to grasp, hold onto, or obtain material possession or status. Therefore, greed is not just wanting something or more of something. Greed drives us to actions that harm others or ourselves in some way. It's when our desire for material advantage allows us to disregard the welfare of others.

Parigraha, a root of the word, has the sense of dallying or wasting time. It suggests an ethically, morally, and spiritually fruitless mindset that takes possession of the individual. In other words, greed crowds out or diminishes most other beneficial and selfless thoughts, goals, and objectives.

The fact that one of the roots of the word, *graha*, also means, *a state that precedes from magical influence and takes possession of the whole person*, shows that self-centered desire overpowers our authentic self, our innate humane nature.

Aparigraha has also been translated as *not having possessions*. One way of practicing it is to contemplate the fact that we need not ever feel that we possess anything. It is the feeling of ownership that causes many of our problems. Instead, think of all of the objects as having been provided for your service or to provide opportunities for learning and growth.

Hoarding, grasping, and harboring the unrealistic expectation that any *thing* can bring happiness is a manifestation of ignorance. Happiness always comes from within, not from any object or situation. Enjoy things when they come, for as long as they remain, and send them off in peace when they go.

yamāḥ = left untranslated

precepts of self-control

2.31 The *yamas* are universal resolves for proper behavior in society. They are bright lights that reveal the way to a life of virtue and joy. Because they hold the capacity to bring peace and harmony, they apply to every being, regardless of social status, time, or circumstance.

jāti-deśa-kāla-samaya-anavacchināḥ sārva-bhaumā mahā-vratam

jāti = social status

class, birth, production, rebirth, the form of existence (as man, animal, etc.) determined by birth, position assigned by caste, family, rank, lineage, or race, natural disposition, genuine or true state of anything (See 2.13)

deśa = place

region, location

from ***diś*** = point out

kāla = time

a fixed or right point of time, a period of time, the time of the world (*yuga*), time as leading to events, the causes of which are imperceptible to the mind, destiny, fate, time as destroyer of all things (personified as Yama, the Lord of Death) (See 1.14, 1.26)

from the root, ***kāl***, to calculate or enumerate

samaya = circumstance

coming together, agreement, occasion

from ***sam*** = together + ***aya***, from ***i*** = to go

anavacchināḥ = regardless

not limited, unbounded

from ***an*** = not + ***ava*** = down + ***chinna***, from ***chid*** = cut

sārva = every

all

bhaumāḥ = global

anything related to or dedicated to the world or earth, produced or coming from the earth, spheres, earthly, terrestrial

Sarva + *bhaumah* form a compound translated here as universal.

Note that the first "a" of *sarva* is long, signifying a strengthened form of its meaning. *Bhaumih* is a strengthened form of *bhumi*, earth. This emphasizes that these resolves apply to every single human being regardless of status, place, time, and circumstance – no exceptions.

mahā = bright lights

great, large, extensive, mighty, strong, abundant, light, luster, brilliance, to become full, extensive, numerous, considerable

from ***mah*** = great, might, strong, powerful, light, brilliance, luster, to magnify, excite, gladden, esteem, highly honor, to rejoice or delight in, a festival of Spring

vratam = resolves

vow, conduct, decision, mode or manner of life, law, ordinance, sphere of action, religious vow, and spiritual practice or pious observance, meritorious act, act of devotion or austerity, firm purpose

from ***vṛ*** = choose, decide, to cover

To make a resolve is to decide firmly on a course of action. The roots of the word, *re* + *solver* suggest to definitely set free or untie. A resolve allows us to be free from other undesirable options.

We could say that the *yamas* represent Yoga's fundamental morals while the *niyamas*, its ethics. Morals are the more universal principals of right and wrong. They are guidelines that help create and maintain proper behavior in society, as well as build the necessary foundation for spiritual growth of the individual.

Ethics are codes of conduct that pertain to a particular category of people. For example, everyone should follow truthfulness (a moral principle), but it would be unethical for a baker to charge a fee for counseling someone in need.

In Yoga, morals and ethics are based on emulating the behavior of the wise.

2.32 *Niyama* – additional resolves yogis observe – consists of:

- *Saucha* = purity
- *Santosha* = contentment
- *Tapas* = accepting challenge, struggle, discomfort, and self-discipline as a help for purification
- *Svadhyaya* = regular repeated study and integration of sacred wisdom into one's life
- *Ishvara pranidhanam* = wholehearted devotion and dedication to *Ishvara* (See 1.24)

śauca-santoṣa-tapaḥ-svādhyāya-īśvara-praṇidhānani niyamāh

śauca = purity

shining, glowing, gleaming, radiant, bright, white, clear, clean, pure, honest, virtuous, holy, a true friend, the condition of a religious student (See 2.5, 2.32, 2.40)

from ***śuci*** = clear, bright, luminous

Sauca is a strengthened form of *suci*. Purity for the yogi means overcoming the influence of ignorance, karma, subconscious impressions (*samskaras*), the *klesas*, and the *gunas*. It includes purity of body, mind, and intention. From this, we can deduce that an impurity – physical or mental – is anything that inhibits or obstructs the innate harmony among the various facets of the individual and the individual's relationship to society and nature.

In the Hindu tradition, purity comprises physical, mental, moral, and ritual purification. In Yoga, we don't see ritual emphasized, although we can regard regular practice as taking the place of ritual.

santoṣa = contentment

pleasure, satisfaction, delight, joy, connectedness, to be joined or connected to (See 2.32, 2.42)

from ***sam*** = with, together, completely, absolutely + ***tuṣ*** = to be satisfied

Santosha is not about creating contentment by collecting as many pleasant objects and experiences as possible. The word carries a sense of being connected to something. To what?

A clue to understanding *santosha* can be found in Hindu mythology in which *santosha* is personified as a son of the god Dharma and the goddess Tushti.

Dharma, literally defined as *that which holds together*, is defined as duty, spiritual teachings, and living according to the way of wisdom. *Tushti* means contentment.

Santosha, then, is not just feeling good about the way things are going in your life. It is experienced when contentment is wedded to, or arises from, wisdom. It is not based on material attainments.

Since wisdom is by nature stable, *santosha* is a stable happiness that exceeds pleasure based on the accumulation of possessions or accomplishments, or on the satisfaction of any sense desire.

Those who experience *santosha* know the deep satisfaction that results from being fully integrated into the flow of life.

tapaḥ = accepting challenge, struggle, discomfort, and self-discipline as a help for purification austerity, self-discipline, creative heat, consuming by heat, causing pain or trouble, distressing, tormented by, warmth, an attendant of Siva (See 2.1, 2.15, 2.32, 2.43, 4.1)

from ***tap*** = to burn, to make hot

Refer to 2.1 for more on *tapas*.

svādhyāya = regular, repeated study, study of sacred texts

self-study, reciting, repeating or rehearsing to one's self, repetition or recitation of the *Veda* in a low voice to one's self, recitation or study of any sacred text (See 2.1, 2.32, 2.44)

from ***svā*** = self + ***adhi*** = to go over or on + ***a*** = hither, unto + ***ya*** = from ***i*** = to go

Refer to 2.1 for more on *svadhyaya*.

īśvara = God

Lord, king, master, able to do, capable (See 1.23–1.24, 2.1, 2.32, 2.45)

Refer to 1.23 for more on *Ishvara*.

praṇidhānani = wholehearted devotion and dedication

to hold within and in front of, laying on, fixing, applying, dedication, access, entrance, exertion, endeavor, respectful conduct, attention paid to, profound religious meditation, abstract contemplation of, vehement desire, vow, threefold prayer (*Dharmas*) (See 1.23)

***Ishvara* + *pranidhanam* = wholehearted devotion and dedication to *Ishvara*.**

niyamāh = additional resolves yogis adhere to

observances, internal disciplines (See 2.29, 2.32)

Refer to 2.29 for more on the *niyamas*.

2.33 When doubt or wayward thoughts disturb the cultivation of the *yamas* and *niyamas*, generate the opposite: a counterforce of thoughts, images, or feelings that have the power to uplift, invigorate, inspire, and steady the mind. This is *pratipaksha bhavana*.

vitarka-bādhane pratipakṣa-bhāvanam

vitarka = doubt, wayward thoughts

a dubious or questionable matter, discursive thoughts, thoughts, conjecture, supposition, guess, fancy, imagination, opinion, uncertainty, reasoning, deliberation, consideration, purpose, intention, a teacher, instructor in divine knowledge (See 1.17)

from ***vi*** = asunder, away + ***tark*** = conjecture, reason, reflect, speculation

Vitarka, as discursive thought, refers to knowledge obtained by reason and argument rather than intuition. Discursive thought is a mental function that is also marked by digressing from subject to subject.

The word *wayward* was chosen because it means *thoughts that are difficult to control* or to *predict* because of behavior that is unusual, unreasonable, or that occurs in spite of the consequences. Synonyms for *wayward* include *erratic, undisciplined, rebellious,* and *defiant.*

bādhane = disturb

oppressing, harassing, opposing, refuting, opposition, resistance, oppression, molestation, affliction, removing

from ***bādh*** = harass, oppress, trouble, to force or drive away, repel, remove

pratipakṣa = the opposite

the opposite side, hostile party, adversary, opponent, match for, equal, a respondent (especially in an appeals or divorce case), the opposite side, defendant (in law) from ***prati*** = against, back, in opposition to, in comparison, in reversed direction, about, to, in the presence of, on account of, near, upon, in return, foe, in reversed direction + ***pakṣa*** = wing of a bird, flank, side, any opinion, deductive reasoning, the feathers on both sides of an arrow, the fin of a fish, partisan, adherent, an alternative, half of anything

The most effective remedy for wayward thoughts are those that generate a powerful counterforce, that opens your heart, compelling thoughts or images that uplift and inspire.

bhāvanam = cultivation

reflection, meditation, causing to be, affecting, producing, displaying, manifesting, promoting or affecting anyone's welfare, imagining, forming in the mind, conception, apprehension, imagination, supposition, fancy, thought, direct one's thoughts to (See 1.28, 2.2, 2.33–2.34, 4.25)

from ***bhu*** = to be, to exist, arise, come into being, live, stay, abide, to cherish, to foster, animate, to present to the mind, think about, devote oneself to

Refer to 1.28 for more on *bhavanam*.

Reflection

If we look deeply at the implications of *pratipaksha bhavanam*, we find that it can expand to a very powerful and beneficial dimension. This practice is not just for momentary first aid when the mind is disturbed. It is also a blueprint for transformation – a chance for new beginnings, a practice that can help us turn our lives around, opening new horizons and providing a clear path for a spiritually prosperous future.

Pratipaksha bhavanam works because it reflects back to us what is true, deep, and abiding. It provides opportunities to transcend an ego hampered by desires for limits, boundaries, the need to always be in control, and to be right (rather than in right, as in productive, relationship with truth).

2.34 Dubious reasoning and wayward thoughts such as causing harm, etc., whether done, incited, or approved of; whether arising from lust, anger, or delusion; and regardless of being mild, medium, or extreme in intensity, have ignorance and endless dissatisfaction and suffering (*duhkha*) as their fruits. Reflecting on this is also *pratipaksha bhavana*.[71]

vitarkāḥ himsā-ādayah kṛta-kārita-anumoditāḥ lobha-krodha-moha-pūrvakāḥ mṛdu-madhya-adimātrāḥ duḥkha-ajñāna-ananta-phalā iti pratipakṣa-bhāvanam

vitarkāḥ = doubt, wayward thoughts

doubt, discursive thought, questionable matter, deliberation, conjecture, supposition, guess, fancy, imagination, opinion, doubt, uncertainty, a dubious or questionable matter

Refer to 1.17 for more on *vitarkah*.

himsā = harm

hurt, injury, hostile, mischief, the three "wrongs"– bearing malice, hatred, evil, spite, or cruelty, abusive language, acts of violence, mean-spirited behavior, to damage

The breadth of definitions for *himsa* (*causing harm*) is worth noting. It reminds us of how many ways we can cause harm to others. It includes motive, behavior that is mean in spirit, and abusive language (one of the main ways we hurt others).

Refer to 2.30 for more on the importance and wide-reaching impact of violence and its remedy, *ahimsa*, harmlessness.

ādayah = etcetera

beginning with, and the rest

[71] Jainism holds true: opposite is also true: any positive acts – ones that foster peace, truth, generosity and other virtues – whether engaged in, incited, or approved of, bring spiritual growth. This is based on the spiritual principle: As you think, so you become.

kṛta = done

make, cultivated, obtained, acquired, accomplished, prepared

from ***kṛ*** = to do

kārita = incited

caused to be done, brought about

from ***kṛ*** = to do

anumoditāḥ = approved

permitted, pleased, delighted, applauded, agreeable, acceptable, sanctioned, allowed

from ***anu*** = along, after + ***modita***, from mud = rejoice, celebrate

The word also has the suggestion of acquiescence – to accept reluctantly but without protest. For the yogi, feeling bad, unhappy, uncomfortable, or guilty over the unfortunate plight of others does not absolve them from violating the *yamas*.

lobha = lust

greed

from ***lubh*** = entice, allure

krodha = anger

wrath, passion

from ***krudh*** = to be angry

moha = delusion

bewilderment, perplexity

from ***muh*** = be stupefied or deluded

Moha means to be bewildered, perplexed, deluded, to go astray. It is infatuation or anything that leads to error. For Buddhists, it is equivalent to ignorance.

pūrvakāḥ = arising from

consisting of, preceded by, connected with

from ***pūrva*** = prior

mṛdu = mild (See 1.22)

madhya = medium (See 1.22)

adimātrāḥ = extreme

intense, extreme, above measure, excessive (See 1.22)

from ***adhi*** = over, on + ***mātra*** = measure, quantity, from ***mā*** = measure + ***tva***, a suffix meaning to have the quality of

duḥkha = dissatisfaction, suffering

distress, discontent, anxiety, stress, pain, uneasiness, difficulty, sorrow, trouble, to cause or feel pain, unpleasant (See 1.31, 1.33, 2.5, 3.15–3.16, 3.35)

from ***duś*** = difficult, wicked, bad, inferior + ***kha*** = axle hole, cavity, hollow, cave discursive thought, deliberation, conjecture, supposition, guess, fancy, imagination, opinion, doubt (YS[72]), uncertainty (YS), a dubious or questionable matter

Refer to 1.31 for more on *duhkha*.

ajñāna = ignorance

from ***a*** = not + ***jñāna*** = knowledge

Refer to 1.9 for more on *jnana*.

ananta = endless

boundless, eternal, infinite, number one, silken cord, sky, atmosphere

from ***a*** = not + ***anta*** = end

phalāh = fruit (See 2.14)

iti = on this

thus, so

[72] YS means that the definition is particularly associated with the *Yoga Sutras*.

pratipakṣa = left untranslated:

the opposite side, match for, equal, opposition (See 2.33)

bhāvanam = reflecting

cultivate, meditation, causing to be, affecting, producing, displaying, manifesting, promoting or affecting anyone's welfare, imagining, forming in the mind, conception, apprehension, imagination, supposition, fancy, thought, direct one's thoughts to (See 1.28, 2.2, 2.33–2.34, 4.25)

Refer to 1.28 for more on *bhavanam*.

2.35 In the presence of one who is firmly established in nonviolence, hostility recedes.

ahimsā-pratiṣthāyām tat-sannidhau vaira-tyāgaḥ

This is the unusual thing about nonviolence – nobody is defeated, everybody shares in the victory.
– Martin Luther King Jr.

ahimsā = nonviolence (See 2.30)

pratiṣthāyām = established

abiding, standing firmly, steadfast, leading to, famous, center or base of anything

from ***prati*** = against, back, in opposition to, again, in return, upon, toward, in the vicinity of, near, beside, at, on, on account of + ***ṣthāyam***, from ***sthā*** = to stand, to stand firmly, station one's self, stand upon, to take up a position on, to stay, remain, continue in any condition or action, to remain occupied or engaged in, be intent on, make a practice of, keep on, persevere in any act, to continue to be or exist, endure, to be, exist, be present, be obtainable or at hand, to be with or at the disposal of, belong to, abide by, be near to, be on the side of, adhere or submit to, acquiesce in, serve, obey, stop, halt, wait, tarry, linger, hesitate, to behave or conduct oneself, to be directed to or fixed in, to be founded or rest or depend on, to rely on, confide in, resort to, arise from, to remain unnoticed, be left alone, to affirm, settle, determine, direct or turn toward (See 1.8, 1.13, 1.35, 1.41, 2.18, 2.35–2.39, 2.46, 3.52, 4.34)

The word translated as *firmly established, pratishthayam*, is feminine in gender (as is *ahimsa*). In Eastern metaphysics, the feminine represents power, *shakti*. But *shakti* is power that is not limited to aggressive strength, which has its vital uses, but is one-dimensional.

Aggressive strength seeks to create and then defend boundaries, to amass and hold onto power. *Shakti* encompasses the power to generate, innovate, and to create. In short, it is the kind of power needed to create the possibilities for poking holes in the walls that hostility creates.

All this means is that our recourses for ending violence should not be limited to force, but through finding points of unity, harmony, and creative solutions to our conflicts.

tat = (*refers to ahmsā*)

that

sannidhau = presence

nearness, proximity

from ***sam*** = with, together + ***ni*** = down, back, in, into, within + ***dhi***, from ***dha*** = put, place

vaira = hostility

animosity, enmity, detrimental, revengeful, grudge, quarrel or feud with, a hostile host

from **vīra** = vehemence, hostility, animosity, enmity, passion, ardor, violence, urging, enthusiasm, strength, vigor, intensity, fully, zeal, hero, brave or eminent person, chief, son

It will be helpful to consider the meanings of *hostile*. Hostility is from the Latin word *hostilis,* meaning stranger, enemy. Although empathy is innate in us, unfortunately, we can learn to be suspicious of people who are different from us. In more egregious cases, those outside our group are devalued, even hated.

Fear and ignorance create an isolating bubble of comfort and security within our group. We need to be mindful that there is a short road that can lead from being a loyal group member to someone who has allowed fear, stereotypes, negative opinions, and mistrust to creep into the heart. In such cases, while we can be loyal, generous, and empathetic to members of our group, we tend to create barriers (born of ignorance) between us and those we consider outsiders.This unbalanced mindset can readily bloom into harmful prejudicial, even violent behaviors directed toward those outside our group.

Minds that react to (withdraw, are suspicious of) superficialities such as skin color, political affiliations, faith traditions, sexual preferences, and nationality are vulnerable to fear-based hostility that can manifest as unfriendliness, lack of sympathy, conflict, anger, opposition, resistance, hatred, spite, antagonism, confrontational words or acts, unwarranted aggression, the intent or desire to do harm, or violence (harm to another that is planned or that arises spontaneously).

All of these attitudes and behaviors start with a mindset of intense ill will.

Let's now look to the Sanskrit to complete this analysis: One definition of the root, *vira*, is especially interesting in the context of this sutra: *vehemence, a display of strong feelings, to urge, to be enthusiastic*. This suggests that the hostile person's anger gives rise to feelings of greater strength (most often we overestimate our anger-enhanced strength) and righteous anger (refer to *vira's* definitions of *hero, brave, eminent*).

The combination of self-perceived greater strength and righteous anger (against others perceived as threats) gives license to do violence that the individual or individuals misperceives as altruistic acts. A prime example is a terrorist who sanctions acts of violence against innocents as holy or virtuous.

It is noteworthy that those who engage in hostile acts often do not arrive at that state through clear, objective reason, but by strong feelings often manipulated by those with authority, or through propaganda, or other influences. This being so, reasoning is often not a viable counterforce to inflamed hostility. In fact, reason can lead such people to cling to their misperceptions and hostilities more strongly. Such individuals actively seek arguments that support their views, a mindset known as confirmation bias.

Especially in such cases, people resist abandoning a false belief unless they have a compelling alternative.

Yoga offers such an alternative: to become one firmly established in harmlessness; an understanding of humanity's common struggles and pain; the power, peace and joy of faith; and the freedom of knowing that we are all one in Spirit.

Understanding this sutra as if it were describing a miracle – someone established in *ahimsa* walking into the middle of a violent confrontation and causing everyone to spontaneously drop their weapons – is tempting, and based on deep wishes for peace and harmony. History clearly tells a different story. Great sages and saints have not always been able to quell violence or hatred. Some have been murdered or executed. So, what is this sutra really saying?

The practical and very real and powerful message of this sutra is that the mere presence – demeanor, words, and actions – of one firmly established in *ahimsa* generates a space for entrenched feelings and misperceptions to recede. This is no small feat.

Keep in mind that nearly 95 percent of communication is nonverbal. The masters of harmlessness radiate compassion, harmony, and hope in countless subtle and powerful ways. Yet, the minds of those in their presence need to be open – at least a little – to receive that vibration in order to abandon, change, or modify strongly held beliefs. But given even a tiny opening, the presence of the enlightened peacemakers can work wonders.

Blessed are the peacemakers for they shall be called children of God.

– Matthew 5:9

The quote above indicates that peace is the master plan of the universe, even though so often it does not seem to be so. Those who seek peace within and without, and who become radiators of peace, are aligning themselves with the deepest, subtlest forces of the universe.

tyāgaḥ = recedes

withdraw, abandonment, leaving behind, giving up, resigning, to offer, sacrificing one's life

from ***tyaj*** = renounce, to leave, abandon, quit, go away, to let go, dismiss, discharge, to give up, surrender, resign, part from, get rid of, to free oneself from (any passion), to give away, distribute, offer, to set aside, to leave unnoticed, disregard, to cause anyone to quit

While, in the Sanskrit, *tyaga* is not presented as an action (it's in the nominative case), we can still benefit from considering the breadth of meanings of the roots of this word. We can visualize hostility moving away, being transcended, or being distributed – scattered – implying that the factors that formed the foundation of the hostility have begun to unravel.

2.36 On being firmly grounded in truthfulness, every thought, word, and deed will be an expression of the nature of *sat*: truth, existence; that which is good, real, authentic, wise, venerable and is in harmony with the essential nature of a being.

satya-pratiṣṭhāyām kriyā-phala-āśrayatvam

satya = truthfulness

authenticity, sincerity, veracity, genuine, sincere, honest, pure, virtuous, good, successful, reality, speaking the truth, effectual, valid (See 2.30)

from ***sat*** = truth, being, existing, occurring, happening, being present, abiding in, belonging to, living, lasting, enduring, real, actual, as any one or anything ought to be, right, beautiful, wise, venerable, a being, beings, creatures, existence, essence, the true being or existence, that which is good, reality + ***ya*** = from

You will know the truth and the truth will set you free.

– John 8:32

If you review the sutra, you'll see that adhering to *satya* is essentially about being in harmony with what's real, true, authentic, and what fosters harmony. Being established in *satya* is the ultimate "going with the flow." It is being in a clear, unselfish relationship with the ways and wisdom of life. This is why the truth will set you free – free from biases, misperceptions, and anxiety. The mind no longer has to carry the burden of ignorance.

To be established in *satya* requires experiencing a deep transformation of self based on the study of sacred wisdom, contemplation, and profound, honest introspection. In other words, it requires living the Yoga life.

Such a person's thoughts, words, and deeds will naturally arise from *sat*. The results of those thoughts, words, and deeds will also naturally be of the nature of *sat*.

In Hindu tradition and mythology, there is a great emphasis on the importance of keeping one's word. This is not just about being a good person. Before there were courts and legal systems - before there was the written word and contracts - there was one's word. What you said and who you are were one. Break your word and you became someone that could not be trusted. This could lead to serious disagreements, conflict, and violence (we can see the connection between truthfulness and harmlessness/nonviolence).

This sutra takes this principle and applies it to those who are firmly established in truthfulness. They become the embodiment of *sat*, of truth.

pratiṣṭhāyām = established

abiding, standing firmly, steadfast, leading to, famous, center or base of anything

from ***sthā*** = to stand, to stand firmly, station one's self, stand upon, to take up a position on, to stay, remain, continue in any condition or action, to remain occupied or engaged in, be intent on, make a practice of, keep on, persevere in any act, to continue to be or exist, endure, to be, exist, be present, be obtainable or at hand, to be with or at the disposal of, belong to, abide by, be near to, be on the side of, adhere or submit to, acquiesce in, serve, obey, stop, halt, wait, tarry, linger, hesitate, to behave or conduct oneself, to be directed to or fixed in, to be founded or rest or depend on, to rely on, confide in, resort to, arise from, to remain unnoticed, be left alone, to affirm, settle, determine, direct or turn toward (See 1.8, 1.13, 1.35, 1.41, 2.18, 2.35–2.39, 2.46, 3.52, 4.34)

kriyā = action

doing, performing, occupation with, act, undertaking, work, bodily action, exercise of the limbs, medical treatment or practice, applying a remedy, cure, a religious rite or ceremony, sacrificial act, sacrifice, rites performed immediately after death, purificatory rites, religious action, worship, study (See 2.1)

phala = result

fruit, consequence (See 2.14)

āśrayatvam = be in harmony

conform to, correspond, dwelling in, depending on, following, as a consequence of the proximity, essence of the dependable, that to which anything is annexed or with which anything is closely connected or on which anything depends or rests, seat, resting place, shelter, protection, help, authority, attaching to, choosing, joining, vicinity of, relation, an appropriate act that is consistent with the character of the actor

from ***asraya*** = protection, refuge, that upon which something depends + ***tva*** = suffix, denoting having the quality of

2.37 On being firmly grounded in nonstealing, all that is truly valuable comeṣ near.

asteya-pratiṣṭhāyām sarva-ratna-upasthānam

asteya = nonstealing (See 2.30)

from ***a*** = not + ***steya*** = theft, robbery, larceny, anything clandestine or private, anything liable to be stolen

Reflecting on some of the definitions of *steya*, we get the sense of not having anything private, or hidden to ourselves. We rob others and ourselves when we fail to live as our authentic self, without embarrassment, pretense, or self-centered intents.

pratiṣthāyām = established (See 2.34)

from ***sthā*** = to stand, to stand firmly, station one's self, stand upon, to take up a position on, to stay, remain, continue in any condition or action, to remain occupied or engaged in, be intent on, make a practice of, keep on, persevere in any act, to continue to be or exist, endure, to be, exist, be present, be obtainable or at hand, to be with or at the disposal of, belong to, abide by, be near to, be on the side of, adhere or submit to, acquiesce in, serve, obey, stop, halt, wait, tarry, linger, hesitate, to behave or conduct oneself, to be directed to or fixed in, to be founded or rest or depend on, to rely on, confide in, resort to, arise from, to remain unnoticed, be left alone, to affirm, settle, determine, direct or turn toward (See 1.8, 1.13, 1.35, 1.41, 2.18, 2.35–2.39, 2.46, 3.52, 4.34)

sarva = all

every, whole, entire, every one

possibly from ***sara*** = core; solid interior; firmness; strength; essence, marrow, heart, or essential part of anything; best part

ratna = truly valuable

wealth, jewel, gems, treasure, gift, anything valuable, the best of its kind, something excellent, present, goods, riches, precious stone, anything of value or the best of its kind, a magnet, loadstone, water

from ***ra*** = brightness, splendor, acquiring, possessing, fire, heat, desire, speed + ***tana*** = offspring, posterity

Gems are more than valuable objects, they are symbols of highly valued spiritual realities that radiate special energies.

Gems, born in the womb of the earth, symbolize the manifestation of the unfathomable collective unconscious. Incorporating a gem into jewelry gives a stone additional value by virtue of human creativity and handiwork. Both the vast collective unconscious, as well as the essence and effort of human beings, come together in a partnership that brings beauty and benefit.

In Hinduism, it is taught that gems have gone through all the possible phases of the refinement of matter. Gems symbolize the *Atma*, Self. One famous jewel that illustrates this symbolism is the gem, *Kaustubha*, The Jewel Treasure of the Ocean of Immortality. Worn on the chest of Lord Narayana, the preserver deity, it represents the sum total of all consciousness,[73] the witness and enjoyer of all creation, and the light that illumines all things: sun, moon, fire, speech.

From the *Bhagavata Purana* 10.238:

> *The flowers and pearls and precious stones (which are angels, saints, and sages) ever cling to Hari (Narayana), the Remover of Sorrow.*

In Buddhism, *triratna*, is the triple gem of The Buddha (teacher), *dharma* (teachings), and *sangha* (community of followers).

[73] Including the consciousness of the *Atma*, the individual soul.

In Islam, the jewel beyond price (*al-jawhar alfard*) is the incorruptible essence of being.

In ancient Judaism, the jewels on the High Priest's breastplate symbolize truth.

All the above makes an argument for not taking this sutra literally, but symbolically. Certainly, there have been many great yogis, renunciates, and sages, who were firmly established in *asteya* but lived without great material wealth. They may have rejected offers of wealth, but that just proves this point: material wealth is not the point of this sutra. It is about coming to a deep realization of what real wealth is. It is truth, connection/communion with Spirit, essence, Source and through that communion, knowing unshakable peace and joy.

upasthānam = comes near

the act of being near to, going near, appearance, approaches, comes, coming into the presence of, going near to in order to worship, waiting on, standing near, a sanctuary, abode, a place of abiding, any object approached with respect, at hand, readily accessible when needed, about to happen, to remain in readiness

from **upa** = to, unto, toward, by the side of + **ṣṭāna**, from **sthā** = stand

Upa (the same root as in *Upanishad*[74]) implies being in direct contact with something great, powerful, or holy, but it also implies not having a sense of inferiority. In this sutra, we can surmise that although wealth does bring power, it is not somehow better or above our innate humanity and especially, our true spiritual Self.

2.38 On being firmly grounded in a life of self-mastery and liberation (*brahmacharya*), one gains the power to endure, persevere, and succeed.

brahmacarya-pratiṣthāyām vīrya-lābhaḥ jāti

[74] *Upanishads* (literally, sitting near devotedly) are central scriptures of Advaita Vedanta, the philosophy of nondualism.

It does not matter how slowly you go as long as you do not stop.
– Confucius

brahmacarya = life of self-mastery and liberation (See 2.30)

Brahmacharya is usually translated as continence, chastity or celibacy. But *brahmacharya* is not just about sexual matters. It literally translates as path to Brahma.[75] That is why the word has been translated here with a phrase: to live a life of self-mastery and liberation.

A life without physical intimacy is not only outside the desire of most sincere seekers, it does not reflect the deeper intent of the practice of *brahmacharya*.

The reason that *brahmacharya* is so closely associated with the sex act is because the sex act is one of the single greatest expenditures of the subtle energy necessary for spiritual progress. However, it should also be kept in mind that extreme anger, greed, and lust may waste even more energy.

The good news is that living the Yoga life and engaging in regular Yoga practices helps attain and maintain the vital subtle energy we need for self-transformation.

To deepen our understanding of *brahmacharya*, let's look at the tradition from which it is born:

Brahmacharya is one of the four *ashramas*, or stages of life in traditional Hinduism. *Ashrama* is defined as: *a place of refuge, a halting place, level, hermitage, a place of striving, a place of nonwandering, a place that removes the fatigue of worldliness*. The four stages are:

- Student (*brahmacharya*)
- Householder (*grihasta*)
- Retiree (*vanaprasta*, literally, forest dweller)
- Renunciate (*sannyas*, renunciation of all worldly responsibilities)

---

[75] Brahma = the Absolute, Spirit, holy, sacred, relating to sacred knowledge, prescribed by the *Vedas*, the supreme, the great, the creator deity.

Each stage has specific duties and disciplines. By refraining from behavior that is nonproductive or nonconducive to the responsibilities (*dharma*) of one's stage of life, cultivates energy, focus, and the power of pure intention.

From adhering to the responsibilities and lifestyle of one's *ashrama,* there arises an effortless flow of thought, word, and deed that supports the ideals of that *ashrama*.

For a student, a youngster in school, the focus is on study and learning the ways of the world. Physical intimacy can distract from this and cause entanglements in relationships for which the young student is not ready.

For an adult student of Yoga, *brahmacharya*, as moderation of physical intimacy, becomes important. It doesn't mean that a yogi needs to be celibate. But excessive or self-centered sex wastes energy and can lead to confused, troublesome relationships and large expenditures of energy. On the other hand, a loving, giving, caring physical exchange between committed partners does not waste energy. For a yogi, the best sex takes place within a loving, committed partnership where the act becomes an expression of the depth of the relationship.

In its broadest sense, *brahmacharya* is about not wasting energy. Energy is wasted when thoughts, words, or actions strengthen – or give rise to – ignorance. Behavior that only brings fleeting excitement, but not fulfillment or joy, or when it leads one away from their spiritual goals – that is a waste of effort and energy.

Brahmacharya invites us to examine how we spend our days, to assess every facet of our lives – including our speech, thought processes, goals, recreation, diet, and habits – to identify how what we do takes us closer or further from our spiritual intentions.

The efficient use of attention, time, and energy is moderation – and the essence of *brahmacharya*. Following this path enhances the depth, breadth, and speed of learning and growth.

Refer to 2.30 for more on *brahmacharya*.

pratiṣṭhāyām = established

steadfast (See 2.34)

from ***sthā*** = to stand, to stand firmly, station one's self, stand upon, to take up a position on, to stay, remain, continue in any condition or action, to remain occupied or engaged in, be intent on, make a practice of, keep on, persevere in any act, to continue to be or exist, endure, to be, exist, be present, be obtainable or at hand, to be with or at the disposal of, belong to, abide by, be near to, be on the side of, adhere or submit to, acquiesce in, serve, obey, stop, halt, wait, tarry, linger, hesitate, to behave or conduct oneself, to be directed to or fixed in, to be founded or rest or depend on, to rely on, confide in, resort to, arise from, to remain unnoticed, be left alone, to affirm, settle, determine, direct or turn toward (See 1.8, 1.13, 1.35, 1.41, 2.18, 2.35–2.39, 2.46, 3.52, 4.34)

vīrya = power to endure, persevere, succeed

vigor, virility, energy, power, heroism, luster, semen, efficacy, dignity, valor, bravery, strength

from ***vīr*** = to be powerful

Refer to 1.20 for more on *virya*.

lābhaḥ = gains

obtained

from ***labh*** = to obtain

jāti = life

station in life, class, birth, production, rebirth, the form of existence (as man, animal, etc.) determined by birth, position assigned by caste, family, rank, lineage, or race, natural disposition, genuine or true state of anything

2.39 The meaning of life awakens when freedom from sense craving is unwavering.

aparigraha-sthairye janma-kathaṃtā saṃbodhaḥ

aparigraha = freedom from sense cravings

nongreed, nonpossession, renunciation of nonessentials, nonacceptance, poverty, deprivation, freedom from clinging, non-possessiveness, renouncing, grasping for what is beyond one's needs, a desire that takes over the entire person, not including, non-acceptance, renunciation of any possession besides the necessary utensils of ascetics, deprivation, destitution, destitute of attendants or a wife (See 2.30)

from ***a*** = not + ***pari*** = toward, against, away from, around, about, fully, beyond, away + ***graha*** = holding, seizing, obtaining, perceiving, recognizing, any state which proceeds from magical influences and takes possession of the whole person, the part of the bow that is grasped by the hand, receiving, accepting gifts, from ***grah*** = to grasp

Refer to 2.30 for more on *aparigraha*.

sthairye = unwavering

confirmed, steadfastness, firmness, steadiness, stability, immobility, solidity, hardness, fixedness, calmness, constancy, patience, firm attachment to, constant delight in

from ***sthā*** = to stand, to stand firmly, station one's self, stand upon, to take up a position on, to stay, remain, continue in any condition or action, to remain occupied or engaged in, be intent on, make a practice of, keep on, persevere in any act, to continue to be or exist, endure, to be, exist, be present, be obtainable or at hand, to be with or at the disposal of, belong to, abide by, be near to, be on the side of, adhere or submit to, acquiesce in, serve, obey, stop, halt, wait, tarry, linger, hesitate, to behave or conduct oneself, to be directed to or fixed in, to be founded or rest or depend on, to rely on, confide in, resort to, arise from, to remain unnoticed, be left alone, to affirm, settle, determine, direct or turn toward (See 1.8, 1.13, 1.35, 1.41, 2.18, 2.35–2.39, 2.46, 3.52, 4.34)

Patanjali uses *sthairye* instead of *pratisthayam,* as in the previous four sutras, but they share the same root, *stha* (to stand).

Sthairye does seem to strike the additional notes of tranquility and immobility (a stronger, more serene, established state than the steadiness of *pratisthayam*).

The end goal of *aparigraha* is to awaken the meaning of life. This includes the meaning of our own lives, the significance of events that come our way, and more incredibly, the meaning of existence itself. Such an attainment requires an absolutely firm, unwavering state of freedom from craving that has no hint of self-denial, but is instead rooted in a mind saturated with the requisite *patience, openness, and delight.* (Refer to the definitions for *sthairye*, above).

janma = life

existence, birth, origin (See 2.12)

kathaṃtā = the meaning of life

the why, how, or what of something

from ***katham*** = How? In what manner? From where? How is that? Why? What is to be done now? + ***ta*** = feminine suffix denoting the quality of something

Sometimes, *katham* merely introduces an interrogation, or the word can imply *amazement, surprise, pleasure,* or *abuse*. The word *katham*, as used in this sutra, suggests that the sutra's benefit lies in an answer to a question shared by all human beings: What is the purpose of life?

Craving – a state of deep longing to satisfy the changing whims of the senses – obscures the gifts, dimensions, timelessness, and meaning of life that is found in the present moment.

saṃbodhaḥ = awakens

knowledge, understanding, awaking, arousing, recognizing, perceiving, reminding

from ***sam*** = together, along, with, conjunction, union, thoroughness, intensity, completeness, to join together + ***bodha*** = awareness, from ***budh*** = to awaken

Bodha is awareness. The prefix *sam* tells us that this is an intense awakening. The image is like the story of a lion, who from a cub was raised by sheep. The lion never knew its True Nature as king of beasts, until it sees its reflection in the waters of a still pond. *Sambodha* is an awakening that precipitates transformation.

2.40 From purity, one's instinctive protective intelligence awakens. Infatuation with one's own body, as well as sensual contact with others that is incompatible with the goal of Yoga, is naturally avoided.

śaucāt svaṅga-jugupsā parair asaṃsargaḥ

śaucāt = purity (See 2.5, 2.32, 2.40)

Refer to 2.32 for more on *sauca*.

svaṅga = one's body

limb, good or handsome limb

from ***sva*** = one's own, his or her own, their own, , one's own self or *Atma*, the ego, a kinsman, sometimes loosely used for my, thy, his, our + ***aṅga*** = limb, member, the body, any subdivision, anything inferior or secondary, anything immaterial or unessential, an expedient,[76] the mind

jugupsā = instinctive protective intelligence

dislike, disgust, distanced from, drawn away from

from ***jū***[77] = quick, speedy, inciting, driving, the atmosphere + ***gup*** = to guard, defend, protect, preserve, defend oneself from, to hide, conceal, to be on one's guard, to be aware of, shun, avoid, detest, to feel offended or hurt + ***sa*** (as a suffix) = wanting to

This sutra is mostly about our relationship to our bodies.

It is interesting to note that *svanga-jugupsa* (often translated as *disgust for one's own body*) is a term Patanjali seems to have coined. It does not appear in scripture prior to this.

Most translations render this sutra as a version of:

[76] An expedient is a means of attaining a goal, especially one that is convenient but improper or immoral.

[77] In the sutra, *jugupsa* does not have the long "u" (ū). It seems likely that this does not change the definition very much, since variations of meanings with other words are fairly consistent throughout with such differences.

From purity arises dislike (or disgust or indifference) for one's own body and for noncontact (or disgust, desire for non-contamination, or *disinterest) with others.*

Questions regarding this sutra are common among students. This arises from the idea of *disgust* or *dislike* for the body. It seems out of place with Patanjali's message, which has been, up to this point, positive. Nonattachment is one thing, but disgust? It strikes many students as being puritanical and out of touch with today's understanding of the benefits of physical contact (not just sexual contact). Refraining from physical contact is an appropriate teaching for a celibate monastic, but what about the rest of us? Let's unpack *svanga-jugupsa* to see where it might lead us.

First, look at the root of *svanga*. *Anga*, while it means *body*, also refers to anything inferior or less important. Since the subtle is the cause of the gross, what is subtle is considered more powerful. The closer we come to the source of something, the closer we come to knowing its nature. The body has been called "solidified mind." In this light, the body – being grosser than the mind – is seen as less vital and, in some way, further from the Self.

But that's not how we usually treat the body. We identify ourselves strongly – even primarily – as the body. The body is the self we present to the world. It is the main way we are identified. We infuse how we look, dress, and accessorize with a lot of meaning and importance. The media showcases idealized role models that present physical standards few attain. It's an easy slide from taking care of the body to spending an inordinate amount of time, effort, and expense on physical appearance and the status it can offer. We want to be accepted by others and physical appearance is a primary condition for acceptance, among many.

While cleanliness and good grooming make sense and are appropriate, the idolization of cultural standards of beauty are not. We too often judge others and ourselves by physical characteristics: facial features, hair or lack of it, skin color, weight, wrinkles, etc. In addition, we strive to erase the natural, physical signs of aging. Not only are they counter to standards of beauty, but they are reminders of our own mortality. The result is that we develop a superficial vision of who we, and others, are.

Through purification, we come to intimately know the nature of the body. We discover that it can never be free of toxins, waste products, and the effects of disease and aging. Valuable as it is as our vehicle in this life, we find that our infatuation with it has been misplaced. We find ourselves disillusioned and maybe a little embarrassed at our former attitude. *Jugupsa* is the facing of the discomfort and contradictory feelings that we have toward others and ourselves that are rooted in cultural standards of physical beauty. The disgust (literally, *to taste bad*) we discover is not over the body, but over our former attitude toward it.

In Jainism, the word *jugupsa* refers to the self-disgust that comes from hiding (*gup*) one's own shortcomings while finding fault or gossiping about the shortcomings of others.[78] *Jugupsa* is a state of conflict, self-contradiction, or hypocrisy. We could well feel disappointed with ourselves when the practice of purity reveals how our opinion of others and ourselves has often been formed from physical traits.

Purity brings other changes. The deep-seated urge to possess others, to have contact and intimacy with them, diminishes, and for some, may evaporate. But physical intimacy could very well remain a part of the yogi's life. What changes is the impetus toward intimacy. It shifts to a subtler level: love and caring for the other's character – the delight we find in being with another human being rather than their physical attributes. Sex becomes an expression of selfless love and giving.

Surprisingly, the sutra on disgust has led to loving acceptance of the physical nature of ourselves and others.

This interpretation may or may not push the limits of this sutra. It might not have been part of Patanjali's intention, yet, it does present interesting and important viewpoints.

We can go one step further in our study of *jugupsa*, this time seeing how it can pertain to our body's protective instincts.

---

[78] Jain references can be illuminating when studying the *Sutras*. Scholars state that Patanjali includes Jain influences in his text. The *yamas* and *niyamas* are prime examples.

Examine the roots of *jugupsa*. *Ju* is *quick* and *speedy*. *Gup* suggests protection: *to guard, preserve,* or *defend.* Put these together and we get an interesting definition, something like: *wishing to quickly protect, to guard, defend,* or *preserve*. It could be referring to our immune system functioning at its utmost. A body that has been polluted by toxins loses much of its natural protective impulses.

Ayurveda, the ancient Indian system of health and healing, holds that purity naturally leads to nonattachment and to balance and harmony, which causes unnatural, unhelpful cravings to diminish and innate protective instincts to arise.

When the body and mind are well-purified, there arises a natural reluctance to engage in physical relations that are devoid of care and love or that can hurt another.

A mind purified of self-centered attachments can sense activities, people, and relationships that are risky to our happiness and welfare. Such a mind can also sense falsehoods, deceptive behavior, and speech. As the nature of a pure mind arises, it becomes increasingly easy to spot inauthenticity. This keeps us away from toxic relationships.

parair = others

far, distant, remote, farther than, beyond, extreme, former, another, different from, other than, distant, past, strange, on the other or far side, past, future, best or worse

The term is from the Tamil, *paraiyar*, from which we get the English word, *pariah*. It is used to refer to what were considered lower castes and outcasts. We can take the general sense of this word into this sutra where it can then be applied, not to certain classes or castes, but to sexual behavior with others that is foreign – contrary or not beneficial – to yogis.

asaṃsargaḥ = infatuation with sensual contact is naturally avoided

cessation of contact, nonassociation, not combining, not commingling, not mixing or having union together, not blending, no sexual intercourse with, no confusion, not indulging or partaking, no sensual attachment, nonfamiliarity, nonacquaintance from ***a*** = not + ***sam*** = together, come together, to let go, discharge, cast, throw + ***sarga***, from ***sṛj*** = emit, quit, leave, abandon, to emit from one's self, procreate, produce

It is interesting that the roots of *asamsargah* can be combined to mean: *To not come together to procreate or produce*. Can we be seeing an ancient warning against sex outside of a stable relationship? Having a child outside a stable relationship or before the couple is ready, or as the result of infidelity, can cause great grief. Purity of body and mind can help minimize the problems that arise from unwise sexual behavior.

2.41 Furthermore, when the mind is purified, it becomes clear and steady (*sattvic*). From this arises cheerfulness, one-pointedness, mastery of the senses, and fitness for Self-realization.

sattva-śuddhi-saumanasya-eka-agrya-indriya-jaya-ātma-darśana-yogyatvāni ca

sattva = clear and steady

being, existence, entity, true essence, nature, disposition of mind, character, spiritual essence, mind, consciousness, energy, strength, resolution, courage, good sense, self-mastery, wisdom, pure, steady, goodness, illuminating, cheerful, joy, lightness, being-ness, one of the primary constituents (*guna*) of nature, as a state of mind, it is lucidity itself without any taint of influence of conceptions or biases (See 2.41, 3.36, 3.50, 3.56)

from ***sat*** = existence + ***tva*** = indicating quality of

Sattva literally translates as *having the quality of sat*: the state of pure being or existence, the true essence of anything, and spiritual essence. *Sattva* is illumination, peace, balance, and harmony. The entire science of Patanjali's Yoga can be understood as having the objective of cultivating a pure *sattvic* state of mind. This is as far as self-effort can take us. The rest is grace (See 4.25–4.26).

In the context of the sutras, *sattva* generally refers to the quality of purity of mind (without the influence of the *klesas* or karmic residue). *Sattva* is developed in order to overcome these obstacles and to neutralize the limiting effects of *rajas* and *tamas*. A *sattvic* mind is one that is honest, wise, clear, peaceful, and loving.

Sattva **is one of the three *gunas* (constituents of nature):**

- ***Sattva*** **= balance**
- ***Rajas*** **= activity**
- ***Tamas*** **= inertia**

śuddhi = purified

cleansing, holiness, freedom from defilement, purificatory rite, setting free from danger, rendering secure, innocence (established by ordeal or trial), making true, genuineness, accurate knowledge regarding, to ascertain for certain (See 2.20, 2.31, 3.56)

from ***śudh*** = to purify

Looking at the roots of the word, we find several meanings that convey the sense of being freed. Through purity, the mind is freed from any mental states or functions that block *sattva*. This seems to give this part of the sutra an added sense of joy – the joy of release, spiritual freedom.

Ceasing to do evil, purifying the heart: This is the teaching of the Buddhas.

– Dhammapada, 1.83

saumanasya = cheerfulness

gladness, satisfaction of mind, causing gladness or cheerfulness of mind, coming from or consisting of flowers, flowery, pleasing, enjoyment, comfort

from ***sau***, a strengthened form of ***su*** = goodness, virtuous, excellent + ***manasya*** = to have in mind

eka = one

agrya = (refers to eka)

intent, closely attentive

from ***agra*** = foremost

Agrya **+ *eka* (above) indicate one-pointedness of attention.**

indriya = sense organs (See 2.18)

jaya = mastery

conquering, triumph, surpassing, excelling, winning, being victorious in battle, dice, or a lawsuit, victory over or complete capacity to manage the senses, the sun, a gatekeeper of the palace of Lord Vishnu (the preserver deity) (See 2.41, 3.5, 3.40, 3.45, 3.48)

from ***ji*** = conquer, to acquire by conquest, defeat, excel, surpass, to conquer passions, overcome or remove selfish desires, difficulties or disease, to expel

Note the last definition of *jaya*: a gatekeeper in the palace of Lord Vishnu. In this sutra, we can see an analogy between Jaya, a mythological demigod and the senses as gatekeepers of what is allowed into the mind.

In one myth, Jaya and his brother Vijaya refused to let sages into the celestial palace to see the Lord. The sages, who had traveled a long distance, were insulted. They cursed the brothers to lose their divinity and be born as normal beings, bound to roam the earth forever.

The brothers appealed to Lord Vishnu to remove the curse. He did not, but offered them a choice: to be reborn many times as his devotees or only a few times as his enemy. They chose the latter, thinking that the sooner they could serve their sentence, the better.

If we take Jaya and Vijaya as representing the senses, we can see that they made a grave error when they turned away the sages. This symbolizes turning away from the wisdom that leads to the Absolute. In doing so, they alienated themselves from the Lord they loved and were committed to serve.

Mastery of nature is vainly believed to be an adequate substitute for self mastery.

– Reinhold Niebuhr

If people knew how hard I worked to get my mastery, it wouldn't seem so wonderful at all.

– Michelangelo

ātma = self (See 2.5)

darśana = realization

vision, view, seeing, looking at, perception, examination, meeting with, experiencing, contemplating, understanding, doctrine, philosophical system, becoming visible (See 1.30, 2.6, 2.41, 3.32)

Refer to 1.30 and 3.32 for more on *darsana*.

yogyatvāni = fitness

readiness, suitability, ability

from ***yogya*** = suited for use, fit, fitting, fit for the yoke, useful, perceptible, from ***yuj*** = join + ***tva*** = indicating to have the quality of

The roots of the word suggest a state that has the quality of union. In other words, purity brings a state in which union is virtually inevitable. Such an elevated level of purity brings with it a high degree of discriminative discernment, the capacity needed to remove *avidya*, ignorance.

ca = and

both, as well as

In Sanskrit, putting "and" at the end of a long list, suggests that all items on the list are equally important.

2.42 By contentment, the swift, easy flow of supreme joy is attained.

samtoṣāt anuttamaḥ sukha lābhaḥ

samtoṣāt = contentment (See 2.32, 2.42)

from ***sam*** = with, together, completely, absolutely + ***tuṣ*** = to be satisfied

Refer to 2.32 for more on *santosha*.

anuttamaḥ = supreme

highest, unsurpassed, excellent

from ***an*** = not + ***ud*** = up + ***tama*** = suffix forming the superlative

Anuttamah samtosa is happiness that arises from an inner state of contentment, not from satisfying the senses or any material or worldly desire. It is uncreated joy, a joy that is not the result of effort, but of realization of its eternal presence within.

sukha = moving swiftly or easily (applied to cars or chariot), happiness

happiness, easy, pleasant (rarely with this meaning in the *Vedas*), agreeable, gentle, mild, comfortable, happy, prosperous, virtuous, pious, the sky, heaven (See 1.33. 2.5, 2.7, 2.42, 2.46)

from ***su*** = well, good + ***kha*** = axle hole

Sukha (literally, *good axle hole*) is translated as a *swift, easy flow of joy*. This is to capture the spirit of the root meaning.

A good (centered) axle-hole provides a comfortable, secure, trustworthy ride. *Sukha* also implies that contentment is inherent in us – a swift, *easy* joy – that flows forth since obstructions, such as ignorance, are removed.

Sukha, as a sense of the inherent rightness of life, is the opposite of *duhkha*, a persistent feeling of unease and dissatisfaction.

Refer to 1.33 for more on *sukha*.

lābhaḥ = attained

gained, meeting with, finding, profit, capture, conquest, perception, apprehension, knowledge, enjoying (See 2.38)

2.43 From the fire of self-discipline and the acceptance of life's inevitable hardships – and the lessons that can be learned from them – impurities evaporate and the full manifestation of the powers of the body and senses arise.

kāya-indriya-siddhi aśuddhi-kṣayāt tapasaḥ

kāya = body

assemblage, trunk of a tree, the body of a lute (except the wires), house, habitation, natural temperament

from ***ci*** = to gather

indriya = sense organs (See 2.18)

siddhi = full manifestation

perfection, accomplishment, attainment, occult powers, modes of success, any effort to attain one's objective, become perfect, to attain bliss or grace, to be valid, to be set right, to be healed or cured, to be well cooked, to yield to, arise, cause, unusual skill or faculty, efficacy, efficiency, fulfillment, complete attainment, hitting the mark, solution to a problem, maturing, success (See 2.43, 2.45, 3.38, 4.1)

from ***sidh*** = accomplish, to go, move, turning out well + ***dha*** = to hold, place, solution to a problem, maturing, success

In the Yoga world, *siddhi* is most often associated with the various extraordinary powers found in the third section of Patanjali's *Sutras*. But, we can see that the word holds several noteworthy nuances: *modes of success, to attain bliss or grace, to be healed* or *cured, to be well cooked*. Let's take a look at the implications.

- *Modes of success*: This includes any philosophical school and practices that help overcome suffering and foster wisdom.
- *To attain bliss or grace*: This accompanies the attainment of success in matters of Spirit. Bliss is the twin of grace. Grace is ever present, but to make full use of it requires yielding to (accepting with tranquility) the ebb and flow of life – trusting the inherent wisdom of life.
- *To be well-cooked*: This definition seems particularly appropriate to this sutra. In India, when making curries, it is important to make sure that the various spices are cooked in order to remove the raw flavor. This can be a great metaphor for the seeker who comes to maturity, with the aid of *tapas*. My spiritual master used another analogy: *bhajis* (fritters). When the cook first ladles the batter into the hot oil, they sputter, giving off excess moisture. Oil spatters and they hiss (complain). The cook's response is to take the ladle and submerge them deeper under the oil until all of the moisture cooks

out. Then these same fritters seem to enjoy floating serenely in the hot oil. Hardships in life are like these examples. When accepted with faith, tranquility and wisdom, the moisture of ignorance gets cooked out.

In this sutra, some translate the word *siddhi* as occult power. This definition is supported by sutra 4.1, which states that the supernormal powers listed in Chapter 3 can be attained by *tapasya (tapas)*. Yet, at this point in Patanjali's presentation of his vision of the yogic path, the definition of *siddhi* as *full manifestation*, nicely fits into this present section, which is about practice. Therefore, in this sutra, we can understand *tapasya*, to mean creating an ideal state of body and mind for realizing the goal of Yoga.

aśuddhi = impurities (See 2.28)

from ***a*** = not + ***śuddha*** = purity = cleansing, purification, purity, holiness, freedom from defilement, purificatory rite, freeing from danger, making secure, innocence, acquittal, making true, genuineness, clarity, certainty, accurate knowledge

kṣayāt = evaporate

diminish, weaken, be the master of, have power over (See 2.28)

tapasaḥ = fires of self-discipline, acceptance of hardships

austerities (See 2.1, 2.15, 2.32, 2.43, 4.1)

from ***tap*** = to burn

Refer to 2.1 for more on *tapas*.

2.44 By the repeated study and integration of sacred wisdom, and the repetition of mantras, seekers create the condition for experiencing communion with their *Ishta Devata* – the symbol, image, or enlightened being that is their most cherished connection with divinity.

svādhyāyā iṣṭa-devatā-saṃprayogaḥ

svādhyāyā = repeated study, integration of sacred wisdom and repetition of mantras

study, self-study, repeated study, study of sacred wisdom

from ***sva*** = self + ***adhi-i*** = to go over, to turn something over in the mind repeatedly, to recite until memorized and absorbed (See 2.1, 2.32, 2.44)

Svadhyaya **is a term rich with meaning. This translation presents two of its most important meanings in order to avoid slipping back into a limited understanding of study as book learning or simply acquiring information.**

Svadhyaya **does include obtaining reliable knowledge (See 1.6), but the heart of study in Yoga is self-transformation through repeated effort and self-discipline.**

Adhi-i **(repeated recitation), suggests that** ***japa*** **is the main practice referred to in this sutra. The tradition of study in Yoga and Hinduism also places a great deal of value in the efficacy of mantra repetition. For example, repetition of the mantra OM is considered equivalent to the study of the entire** ***Vedic*** **scriptures.**

Refer to 2.1 for more on ***svadhyaya*****.**

iṣṭa = most cherished connection with divinity

intended, sought, desired, liked, cherished, beloved, revered, valid, lover or spouse

from ***iṣ*** = wish, to seek, search, to endeavor to attain, to strive to attain

devatā = divinity

god, deity

from ***deva*** = god, divine (also said of human beings of unusually high spiritual attainment: the great sages, saints, and Gurus), heavenly, image of a god, luminous being + ***tā*** feminine suffix denoting to have the quality of

If the Absolute is like the sun, one's ***Ishta Devata*** **is like a ray of sunlight, inherently united with the sun, yet expressing as a specific name and form.**

Ishta Devata **is the best, highest, holiest, all-pervading image the seeker has encountered, can imagine, or has fervently hoped to realize. One's** ***Ishta Devata*** **can be any name and form of the Divine or one's Guru.**

For devotees, the *Ishta Devata* is the nearest, dearest expression of God who is their support and protector, guide, and their most trusted source of wisdom. The *Ishta Devata* also serves as a role model, inspiring the seeker to cultivate the divine qualities they perceive in their *Ishta Devata*.

The name and form of one's *Ishta Devata* are a way to grasp a bit of the Absolute. It is like greeting someone by their shaking hand. We greet and establish a relationship with the entire person even though we only grasp their hand.

Devotion to one's *Ishta Devata* naturally cultivates nonattachment. Sense satisfactions are found lacking in comparison.

Through study, the seeker is able to pierce the name and form of their divine beloved to perceive the Light that is the essence and source of all names and forms, the Absolute.

saṃprayogaḥ = connection

union, joining together, fastening, conjunction, all of the necessary connections, contact with, matrimonial or sexual union with, correct or proper cognition, direct contact, establishing a connection, correct functioning

from ***sam*** = together, completely, with, intensity, completely + ***prayoga*** = joining together, connection, offering, presenting, commencement, device, application, employment, practice, experiment, utterance, recitation, cause, motive, coming to a meal

It is noteworthy that the definitions of *samprayogah* include *proper cognition*. This resonates with the Buddhist meaning of the word and brings us back to direct perception as the basis of reliable knowledge (See 1.7, 3.33 – yogic vision, *pratyaksa*).

Look again at the components of *svadhyaya*. Study in Yoga is not just accumulating information. Information needs to be interpreted and integrated into one's daily life. This takes clear, objective, repeated study of spiritual principles, and very importantly, the insights of an adept or master teacher.

Masterful interpretation provides a kind of checks and balances system preventing us from projecting our own hopes, perceptions, misperceptions, and habitual thought-patterns on truths. We might be tempted to reshape truths to forcefit them into our preconceived notions. Instead, we need to expand and reshape our perceptions to know the truth.

2.45 By wholehearted dedication to *Ishvara*, *samadhi* can be perfected or attained.

samādhi-siddhir īśvara-pranidhānā

samādhi = *left untranslated*

contemplation, bringing into harmony, settlement, joining with, intense absorption, attention, whole, accomplishment, conclusion, concentration of mind, union, concentration of thoughts, profound meditation (See 1.20, 1.46, 1.51, 2.2, 2.29, 2.45, 3.3, 3.38, 4.1, 4.29)

Refer to 1.20 for more on *samadhi.*

siddhir = perfected, attained

attainment, accomplishment, occult powers (See 2.43, 2.45, 3.38, 4.1)

It is appropriate to use both *perfected* and *attained* in this context. That is because both wholehearted devotion and faith are enough alone to attain, as well as perfect, *samadhi*. The path of *Bhakti Yoga* (devotion) is complete, in and of itself.

In the context of a holistic practice – such as that presented in the *Sutras* – devotion is not only a central facet, but serves to sweep away the last vestiges of egoism, so difficult to overcome. The natural emptying of one's self-centered thinking, and a fervent wish for union with the beloved, is inherent to loving devotion.

Not all Yoga practitioners are drawn to participate in devotional practices, especially in the beginning. The path of love and devotion, to a form of the Divine requires a good measure of faith. For those not inclined to a path of devotion, meditation, knowledge, wisdom, study, self-analysis, and selfless service take them to the same goal.

It should be noted that faith may arise naturally and spontaneously through the study of Yoga theory and application of the practices or through contact with great spiritual masters.

Refer to 2.43 for more on *siddhi.*

īśvara = left untranslated

Lord, king, master, able to do, capable (See 1.23–1.24, 2.1, 2.32, 2.45)

from ***iś*** = to rule, to own, to command + ***vara*** = valuable, eminent, choicest, from ***vṛ*** = to choose

Refer to 1.23 for more on *Ishvara*.

pranidhānā = wholehearted dedication

devotion, surrender, alignment to, laying on, fixing, applying, access, entrance, exertion, endeavor, respectful conduct, attention paid to, profound religious meditation, abstract contemplation of, vehement desire, vow

Refer to 1.23 for more on *pranidhana*.

Devotion complete culminates in knowledge supreme.
– Sri Ramana Maharshi

2.46 *Asana* should be steady and easeful.

sthira-sukhaṃ āsanam

sthira = steady

firm

from ***sthā*** = to stand

A steady seated posture prepares the individual for the practice of meditation and allows the meditator to begin the practice of *pratyahara* (See 2.29), the drawing of attention away from the senses.

Refer to 1.8 for more on *stha*, the root of *sthira*.

sukhaṃ = easeful

joy, happiness, running swiftly or easily (applied only to cars or chariot), pleasant, agreeable, gentle, mild, comfortable, happy, prosperous, virtuous, pious, the sky, heaven, pleasant (See 1.33, 2.5, 2.7, 2.42, 2.46)

Refer to 1.33 for more on *sukha*.

āsanam = *left untranslated*

posture, to be present, sitting in a particular posture, a seat, couch, place, stool, abiding, dwelling, maintaining a post against an enemy

from ***as*** = sit, be (See 2.29)

Refer to 2.29 for more on *asana*.

2.47 *Asana* naturally becomes steady and easeful by relaxing physical effort and contemplating one's connection with the infinite. The yogi rests like the cosmic serpent Ananta, floating on the primordial waters, on whom rests Vishnu, the Lord of the Universe.

prayatna-śaithilya-ananta-samāpattibhyām

prayatna = (physical) effort

striving, great care, volitions, exertion, endeavor, continued effort (to go forward being active – see below)

from ***pra*** = before, forward + ***yatna***, from ***yat*** = strive, be active, effective

śaithilya = relaxing

relaxation of a rule or connection, looseness, flaccidity, not rigid, decrease, diminution, smallness, weakness, remission

from ***sratu*** = untie, loosen

ananta = infinite

boundless, eternal, endless, number one, silken cord, sky, atmosphere (See 2.34)

from ***a*** = not + ***anta*** = end

The word *ananta* is also the name of the Hindu cosmic snake deity,

upon whom the god, Vishnu (the preserver) reclines between cycles of creation. Ananta is the guardian of sacred wisdom. Ananta, ever alert, forms a canopy to protect the Lord during his rest.

This image suggests that we can relax our effort because we too are protected by wisdom and mindfulness. This mythic image also suggests great power, stillness, and rejuvenating rest – the model for the stressless, easy posture adopted for meditation.

samāpattibhyām = contemplation

meditating on (See 1.41–1.42, 2.47, 3.43)

from ***samapatti*** = ***samadhi***, balanced state, complete engrossment, attainment, state of becoming one, coincidence + ***bhyam*** = with

Refer to 1.20 for more on *samadhi*, a synonym for *samapatti.*

2.48 From this, one is undisturbed by dualities.

tato dvandva-anabhighātāh

tato = from this

thereafter, thus

dvanḍva = dualities

pairs of opposites, literally "two-two"

from ***dva*** = two

anabhighātāh = undisturbed

assault, attacking, assailing

from ***an*** = not + ***abhi*** = to, unto + ***ghāta***, from ***hand*** = strike, kill

2.49 When a steady, easeful asana is achieved, *pranayama* can be practiced by regulating the movements of inhalation and exhalation.

tasmin sati śvāsa-praśvasyoḥ gati-vicchedah prāṇāyāma

tasmin = when,

in that, in this, upon this

sati = achieved

in (as in being in), being, existing, occurring (See 2.13)

śvāsa = inhalation

from ***śvas*** = breathe

praśvasyoḥ = exhalation

from ***pra*** = before, forward + ***śvasa*** = breathe

gati = movements

flow, notion, procession

from ***gam*** = to go

vicchedah = regulating

control, interrupted, intercepted, cutting off, breaking, division, separation, cessation, space, interval (See 2.4)

from ***vi*** = away, asunder + ***cheda***, from ***chid*** = cut

prāṇāyāma = *left untranslated*

regulation of the breath (See 2.29)

from ***prāna*** = vital force, vital energy, breath, life force, spirit, respiration, vitality, from ***prāṇ*** = breathing, inhalation, breathe + ***yāma*** = a rein, curb, a driver, the act of checking or curbing, suppression, restraint

2.50 The movements of the breath – inhalation, exhalation, and retention – are regulated according to the:

- **Area of focus during practice**
- **Length of time of inhalation, exhalation, and retention**
- **Number of repetitions**
- **Perception that the breath, with practice, becomes subtle and penetrates deeply.**

bāhya-abhyayantara-stambha-vṛittir deśa-kāla-samkhyābhiḥ paridhṛṣṭaḥ dīrgha-sūkṣmaḥ

bāhya = exhalation

external, outer

from ***bahis*** = outside

abhyayantara = inhalation

internal, inside

from ***abhi*** = to, unto + ***antar*** = interior, inside

stambha = retention

stationary, suppressed, stopped, obstructed

from ***stamb*** = to stop, hold up

vṛittir = movements

modification, fluctuation (See 1.2)

deśa = area of attention

place, space (See 2.31)

kāla = duration

time (See 1.14)

samkhyābhiḥ = number

observation, calculation, summing up, numeration, deliberation, reasoning, reflection, intellect

from ***sam*** = together + ***khyā*** = count

paridhṛṣṭaḥ = perceived

beheld, seen

from ***pari*** = around + ***dṛṣṭa***, from ***dṛṣ*** = to see

dīrgha = penetrates deeply

lofty, tall, to lengthen, to be able to stretch, to exert one's self, to roam, to tire, to be long or slow (See 1.14)

sūkṣmaḥ = subtle

short, minute, small, fine, thin, narrow, insignificant, intangible (See 1.44)

2.51 There is a fourth *pranayama* that transcends efforts to regulate the internal and external movements of the breath. It is a natural spontaneous suspension of breathing that occurs when the mind is steady.

bahya-abhyantara-vishaya-ākṣepī caturthaḥ

The wording of this sutra makes its meaning very difficult to decipher. Here, it is understood as referring to a natural suspension of breathing that happens when the mind's attention is deeply absorbed, as in profound states of meditation.

bahya = external (See 2.50)

abhyantara = internal (See 2.50)

vishaya = movements

conditions, sphere of activity or concern, that which is experienced through the senses (See 1.11)

Here, the "movements" referred to are the two basic conditions of the breath: external and internal. Since this is a practice that regulates the rhythm and flow of the breath, "movement" was chosen over "condition" since it is more descriptive of the practice that leads to the spontaneous suspension of the breath.

ākṣepī = transcends

surpasses, goes beyond, drawing together, applying, cast, send, beyond, withdrawal, convulsion, palpitation, giving up, removing, charming, transporting, hinting, challenge, of a man, movement of the hands in reciting prayers

from ***a*** = hither, unto + ***kṣepin***, from ***kṣip*** = to throw

caturthaḥ = fourth

from ***catur*** = four

The importance of the breath/mind connection is affirmed in the *Hatha Yoga Pradipika*:

Pranayama without meditation can make the mind more restless. When the prana moves, the mind moves. When the prana is without movement, the mind is without movement.

2.52 Then the veil that obscures the inner light (*sattva*) dissipates.[79]

tataḥ kṣīyate prakāśa-avaraṇam

tataḥ = then

from that

kṣīyate = dissipates

destroyed, dissolved, diminished

from ***kṣi*** = to decrease, destroy

prakāśa = inner light

light, clearness, brightness, splendor

from ***pra*** = before, forward + ***kāśa*** = to shine, be brilliant, to be visible

avaraṇam = veil

covering, concealing

from ***a*** = not + ***vṛ*** = to cover

Vyasa, the great classic *Yoga Sutra* commentator, states that the "veil" refers to karma and the resulting subconscious impressions (*samskaras*) that are created. *Pranayama* helps diminish the veiling power of the misperception of self-identity that is supported by actions, their reactions, and subconscious impressions.

[79] Dissipate means to disperse, scatter, disappear. All these words provide good images of what the practitioner is experiencing at this stage of *pranayama*.

2.53 And the mind attains *dharana*, the ability to hold focused attention. (See 1.34, 1.40)

dhāraṇāsu ca yogyatā manasaḥ

dhāraṇāsu = focused attention

bearing, holding, keeping in remembrance, preserving, protecting, maintaining, having, enduring, concentration (See 2.29)

from ***dharana*** = holding, concentration, maintaining, protecting + ***su*** = permitting, possessing power or supremacy. ***Su*** always qualifies the meaning of a verb.

Dharanasu **is the plural of the word "concentration." This suggests that when the veil covering the inner light is dissipated, the mind gains the ability to both focus and hold attention on any object.**

ca = and

yogyatā = fit

suitability, ability

from ***yogya***, from ***yuj*** = join + ***tva*** = indicating quality of (See 2.41)

Yogaya **also refers to the straps with which horses are attached to the yoke of a carriage. It gives the driver the ability to control or regulate the movement of the horses, according to his or her will.**

manasaḥ = mind

of the mind, organ of cognition and perception

from ***man*** = think, believe, conjecture (See 1.35, 2.53, 3.49)

Refer to 1.35 for more on *manas*.

2.54 When the mind is indrawn the senses follow, withdrawing from sense objects. This is *pratyahara*, sense management.

sva-viṣaya-asaṃprayoga cittasyah svarūpa-anukāra iva
indriyāṇām pratyāhāra

Pratyahara can be considered as the beginning of the journey of self-mastery. Many seekers – for this reason – find that *pratyahara* is often the first step that leads from belief (conditional faith) to faith (certain knowledge) and to self-transformation.

sva = (*refers to the sense objects*)

their, own, self

viṣaya = objects

circumstance (See 1.11)

asaṃprayoga = withdrawal

disengagement, separating, unattaching, disconnecting, ceasing contact with, not applying, not employing

from ***a*** = not + ***sampra*** = enter into completely + ***yoga*** = union

cittasyah = of mind (See 1.2, 1.30, 1.33, 1.37, 2.54, 3.1, 3.9, 3.11–3.12, 3.19, 3.35, 3.39, 4.4–4.5, 4.15–4.18, 4.21, 4.23, 4.26)

Refer to 1.2 for more on *citta*.

svarūpa = (refers to the nature of the indrawn mind, which the senses are emulating or following)

own form or shape, own condition, peculiarity, character, nature, having a like nature or character, similar, identically (See 1.3, 1.43, 2.23, 2.54, 3.3, 3.45, 3.48, 4.34)

Refer to 1.3 for more on *svarupa*.

anukāra = follow

emulate, imitate, resemble

from ***anu*** = along, after + ***kṛ*** = to do

iva = (*refers to the action of the senses imitating the condition of an indrawn mind*)

as if, as it were, just as

indriyāṇām = the senses (See 2.18)

pratyāhāra = sense management

sense withdrawal, abstraction (See 2.29)

from ***prati*** = against or away + ***ā*** = unto + ***hāra***, from ***hṛ*** = to take, hold

or

prati = against, away + ***ahāra*** = food

Sense management was chosen to translate *pratyahara* since it suggests the broader scope of the practice. It is not just reining in unruly senses, but gaining the ability to use them wisely.

2.55 From this practice, the highest mastery of the senses arises.

tataḥ paramā vaśyatā indriyāṇām

tataḥ = from this

then

paramā = highest

utmost, best, superlative form of ***para*** = far, distant, remote (in space), opposite, farther than, extreme, more than, final, superior to, exceptional, in high degree, completely

vaśyatā = mastery

command, control, being subdued or subjected

from ***vaśyā***, from ***vaś*** = will, command + ***tā*** = suffix meaning to have the quality of

indriyāṇām = senses (See 2.18)

Chapter Three

Vibhuti Pada

The Chapter on Accomplishments

What is *Vibhuti*?

The strength of an elephant, the ability to fly or become invisible... this section is well known for its listing of a number of supernormal powers that can be cultivated by the advanced yogi. But we should not overlook its function as a detailed, practical exposition on advancing in meditation.

Before going forward, we pause to note that the word *vibhuti* does not appear in any of the sutras in any chapters. Curious, since this section is entitled, *Vibhuti Pada*. What is *vibhuti*?

Definitions include: *penetrating, pervading, mighty, powerful, presiding over, development, multiplication, expansion, abundance, prosperity, manifestation of might, great power, successful sacrifice, splendor, glory, fortune, holy ash made from cow dung,* and *divine manifestation*

Let's break down the word into its roots to get a better sense of what it implies:

From *vi*, which means *divided* and *bhuti*, which means *power, ornament, ground, decoration, wellbeing, fortune, holy ash, thriving, welfare personified, existence, earth*.

The root (*bhuti*) carries most of the meaning of the word. What does the prefix (*vi*) add? The prefix vi suggests that these powers or attributes are apart from – different, above, beyond – any of the skills, powers, or attainment we find in even accomplished individuals. In short, *vibhuti* refers to the manifestations of what are considered Divine attributes in a human being.

In Hinduism, these supernormal powers are typically connected with various Hindu deities. For example, eight supernormal powers (*vibhuti*) are associated with the Lord Siva: the capacity to become as small as an atom, extreme lightness, the ability to attain or reach anything, irresistible will, unlimited bulk, supreme dominion, the ability to subjugate by supernatural means, and the transcendence of all desires. These eight powers can be attained by wholehearted devotion to Lord Siva. For many, *vibhutis* are seen as the unfolding of divine qualities in a human being – a divinization of the individual.

Many of these supernormal powers are found in the *Yoga Sutras* and can be intentionally sought by the yogi, or they may appear as a by-product of their practices, or through divine grace. Patanjali – and most masters – don't place much value on attaining supernormal powers. They are seen as obstacles, distractions, or temptations for ego attachments.

A wise old adage from India is appropriate here:

You can spend ten years in deep meditation gaining the ability to walk on water to cross the river, or you can pay the boatman ten cents.

Why?

Students often wonder why Patanjali would include a listing of supernormal powers, only to discourage the seeker from attaining them in sutra 3.38.

Supernormal powers were so strongly associated with yogis that any treatise on Yoga would need to include some mention of these powers to be considered legitimate. But there may also be other reasons why Patanjali included them.

First, not all of the powers are superhero or science fiction in scope (See 3.24 and 3.53). The same essential technique that leads to becoming invisible[80] can also lead to deeply enhanced virtues such as friendliness, and selfless joy, and to heightened discriminative discernment,[81] a requirement for liberation.

There is another important theme that flows through this section: a caution to avoid temptation. Whether it is attaining the ability to become invisible or gaining the capacity for extraordinary discriminative discernment, the yogi should be careful not to allow these accomplishments to generate attachment. The admiration or awe directed toward one who has these capabilities are powerful traps that can ensnare the yogi and can lead to undesirable consequences (See 3.52).

[80] The technique or practice of *samyama* – directing concentrated awareness, meditative focus, and contemplative absorption to one object of attention. Refer to 3.1 – 3.4.

[81] *Viveka*, (see 2.26).

That said, this chapter has a number of deeply profound and inspirational sutras that are meant to guide the yogi beyond matter, space, time, and toward liberation.

3.1 The practice of nurturing and holding a flow of attention toward one chosen object, place, or idea is *dharana*, concentration.

deśa-bandhaś cittasya dhāraṇā

deśa = object, place, idea

region, location, spot, institute, ordinance, to settle in a place (See 2.31)

from ***diś*** = to point out, show, exhibit, to produce, bring forward, to promote, grant, assign, to order, command, teach, communicate, inform, a region pointed at, direction, place, country, foreign country, precept

Though *desa* is most frequently used to indicate location, other possibilities – such as a region, precept, and direction – suggest that *dharana* can be practiced on a large variety of objects.

bandhaḥ = holding

binding, a bond, damming up (a river), connection with, putting together, uniting, combining, forming, producing, a mode of sexual union, fixing or directing the mind, cherishing, a border, framework, receptacle

from **bandh** = bind, fix, fasten, tie, put on, to catch, take or hold captive, direct, rivet (eyes, ears, or mind) on, to hold back, arrest, to bind a sacrificial victim, offer, sacrifice, to join, unite, put together or produce anything in this way, construct, compose, to form or produce in any way, to take up one's abode

cittasya = attention

mind, consciousness, reasoning, heart, imagination (See 1.2, 1.30, 1.33, 1.37, 2.54, 3.1, 3.9, 3.11–3.12, 3.19, 3.35, 3.39, 4.4–4.5, 4.15–4.18, 4.21, 4.23, 4.26)

Refer to 1.2 for more on *citta*.

dhāraṇā = concentration of the mind

bearing, holding, supporting, maintaining, retaining, keeping (in remembrance), a good memory, preserving, protecting, understanding, intellect assuming the shape of, resembling, the two female breasts, immovable concentration on (See 2.29)

from ***dhṛ*** = to hold, maintain

One surprising definition of *dharana* is the *two female breasts*. What does this have to do with meditation? Reflect on the image of an infant at the mother's breast, cradled in her loving arms: warm, safe, contented, and at peace. Food comes without hunting or gathering, a gift offered and received. Could this be the ideal image of the practice of *dharana*, the feeling of a focused mind? It is a far cry from the more muscular images of self-mastery to which we are accustomed.

One of the biggest obstacles to success in *dharana* is the tendency to struggle to attain a tight-fisted grip on the mind. This is grounded in the feeling that distracting thoughts are like bombs that we desperately need to avoid. In this context, every wandering of the mind is seen as a defeat. Who could persist with such a practice?

Generating and maintaining an inner environment that is gentle, loving, and accepting of our efforts is by far the most effective inner environment for success in *dharana*.

Practice meditation regularly. Meditation leads to eternal bliss.
Therefore, meditate. Meditate.
– Sri Swami Sivananda

3.2 When the mind achieves an effortless unbroken flow of attention toward that one object, that is *dhyana* (meditation).

tatra pratyaya-eka-tānatā dhyānam

tatra = when

in that case, on that occasion, of these, there, in that place, to that place, under those circumstances, then, therefore (See 1.13)

pratyaya = mind

the content of consciousness at any given moment, cognition, thoughts, the image of an object on the mind, firm conviction, intention, basis (See 1.10, 1.18–1.19, 2.20, 3.2, 4.27)

from ***prati*** = against + ***i*** = to go forth)

Pratyaya is a tricky word to translate. Since it has many meanings, we must look to the context to determine what best fits the intention of the sutra. Here, it is translated as *mind*, but *pratyaya* can also imply a *flow of attention*. In this second sense, it refers to the seamless stream of awareness directed toward the object of meditation.

Note that the word *vritti* does not appear in this sutra. In a state of true meditation, *vritti* activity – the forming of concepts based on sense input, reasoning, and subconscious impressions – has ceased.

Refer to 1.10 for more on *pratyaya*.

eka = one (See 1.10)

tānatā = continuous

extend, stretch

from ***tan*** = uninterrupted succession, continuation, to extend, spread, shine, reach to, weave, offspring, posterity, propagation + ***tā*** = having the quality of

dhyānam = meditation

thought, reflection (especially profound and abstract religious meditation) (See 1.39)

from ***dhyai*** = to meditate, think of, contemplate, imagine, call to mind, recollect, brood mischief against, to be thoughtful, to let the head hang down (pertaining to an animal) + ***yāna*** = leading, conducting to or in, way, path, teaching

related to ***dhi*** = to perceive, think, reflect, to hold, receptacle, wish, desire, religious thought, devotion, prayer, understanding, intelligence, wisdom, science, art, disposition, intention, splendor or ***dhā*** = to put, place, set, lay in or on, to take or bring help to, to direct or fix the mind on, think of, resolve to, establish, make, produce, generate, create, take hold of, perform, hold, support, to accept, obtain, conceive (especially in a womb), to take pleasure or delight in

A number of the root definitions of *dhyana* suggest that meditation, like concentration (*dharana*), is a practice performed with vigilance and delight, but without force.

The roots also suggest that meditation is a pathway (*yana*) to wisdom and understanding. But, the most interesting possibility is found in the root meaning, *to conceive, especially in a womb* – a safe, nurturing place to prepare for birth.

In sutra 3.1, we considered the fascinating possibility that relates *dharana* to two female breasts. Reflecting on these two seemingly far-fetched definitions reveals subtle truths. Both *dharana* and *dhyana* imply nurturing, safety, and growth. They also reflect the principle of *pratiprasava* (returning to the origin – see 4.34). *Dharana* and *dhyana* are pathways that carry us closer to our origin, the Self.

3.3 By continuing in this manner, the flow of attention becomes prolonged until *samadhi* – a state of mental integration and absorption – certainly arises. In this state, it's as if the mind gives up its own form so that the essence of the object alone shines forth.

tad eva-artha-mātra-nirbhāsaṃ svarūpa-śūnyam iva samādhi

tad = continuing in this manner

in this manner, with regard to that, that, it, this, there, in that place, to that spot, at that time, in that case, thus, on that account, for that reason, therefore, consequently, so also, just so

eva = certainly

indeed, without a doubt, truly, just so, exactly so, really (often at the beginning of a verse)

probably from **evā**, moving, going, speedy, quick, way, a way or manner of acting, conduct, custom

The word *eva* strengthens or intensifies the word to which it is attached. In this sutra, it appears in a four word phrase, *eva-artha-matra-nirbhasam*. Therefore, it is intensifying the fact that the object alone shines forth.

Patanjali is emphasizing the amazing state in which the individual's mind gives up its own form/self-identity – notions, memories, knowledge, and hopes regarding the object of contemplation – in favor of the revelation of the object of contemplation as it truly is.

artha = object

meaning, aim, purpose, cause, motive, reason, advantage, use, utility, relating to a thing or object, material, means of life (See 1.28, 1.32, 1.42–1.43, 2.2, 2.18, 2.21–2.22, 3.3, 3.17, 3.36, 4.23–4.24, 4.32, 4.34)

Refer to 1.28 for more on *artha*.

mātra = alone

only, simply, merely, amounting to, sheer, being nothing but, possessing as much as or no more than, an element, elementary matter, measure, quantity, sum, size, duration, measure of any kind, the whole or totality, the one thing and no more, nothing but (See 1.43)

from ***mā*** = to measure

nirbhāsaṃ = shines forth

apparent or illumined

from ***nir*** = outward, away, without, out, forth + ***bhāsa*** = to be bright, light, luster, brightness, impression made on the mind

svarūpa = essence

own form, innate form (See 1.3, 1.43, 2.23, 2.40, 2.54, 3.3, 3.45, 3.48, 4.34)

Refer to 1.3 for more on *svarupa*.

śūnyam = gives up

naturally loses, void, empty, barren, destitute of (See 1.9)[82]

iva = as if

samādhi = absorption

bringing into harmony, settlement, joining with, attention, joining or combining with, whole, accomplishment, conclusion, concentration of mind, union, concentration of thoughts, profound meditation (See 1.20, 1.46, 1.51, 2.2, 2.29, 2.45, 3.3, 3.11, 3.38, 4.1, 4.29)

Refer to 1.20 for more on *samadhi*.

3.4 When these three (*dharana*, *dhyana*, and *samadhi*) are all directed toward one object, it is called *samyama*.

trayam ekatra samyama

trayam = these three

threesome

ekatra = together

in one, one and the same, in one place, in a single spot, on the one side, all together

from ***eka*** = one

samyama = left untranslated

binding together, holding together, restraint, control (See 3.4, 3.16–3.17, 3.21–3.22, 3.27, 3.36, 3.42–3.43, 3.45, 3.48, 3.53)

from ***sam*** = together, perfect, well done, proper + ***yama*** = from ***yam*** = restraint, to sustain, hold up, support, to stretch out, expand, spread, show, obey, to be faithful to, to be firm, unwavering

***Samyama* will be mentioned eleven more times in this chapter as the yogic tool that can cultivate the supernormal powers.**

[82] In the *Yogacara* of Buddhism, *sunyam* considers that all objects are empty (devoid of intrinsic reality) because they arise from the mind (*citta*).

It would be reasonable to think that if we can attain *samadhi*, that we would also automatically pass through *dharana* (concentration) and *dhyana* (meditation). However, that is not always the case. One can attain *samadhi* by a sudden profound absorption of the mind due to extraordinary external or internal stimuli. One could also attain *samadhi* through grace, an unexpected launch into absorptive consciousness.

Samyama is a process of progressive absorption that gives rise to knowledge, insight, and supernormal attainments. The three stages of contemplative depth help reveal all facets of the object of contemplation.

The word root, *yam*, can mean expansion. It is noteworthy that as the mind becomes absorbed into the object of contemplation, individual consciousness expands, not necessarily encompassing more and more separate objects, but discovering deeper and more subtle realities. These realities are the inner essences of all objects in nature. See the definition of *alokah* in the following sutra.

3.5 With mastery of *samyama*, the penetrating[83] light of intuitive insight arises.

taj-jayāt prajñā alokaḥ

tat = (*refers to samyama*)

that, this, it

jayāt = mastery

having victorious armies (See 2.41, 3.5, 3.40–3.41, 3.45, 3.48–3.49)

from ***ji*** = to conquer, or ***ji*** = to renew or rouse to life, especially life that has been inert or suspended, conquering, winning, victory, triumph, the sun

Refer to 2.41 for more on *jaya*.

prajñā = intuitive insight (See 1.20, 1.48–1.49, 2.27, 3.5)

Refer to 1.20 for more on *prajna*.

[83] Penetrate = to succeed in entering into a thing; to succeed in gaining understanding or insight.

ālokaḥ = penetrating light

sight, aspect, vision, looking, seeing, beholding, luster, splendor, glimmer, praise, flattery

from ***ā*** = hither, unto + ***lokaḥ*** = wide space, world, the universe or any division of it, the earth, the world of human beings, the inhabitants of the world, ordinary life, the faculty of sight, from ***lok*** = see, behold

Alokah implies being able to perceive an entire world – a dimension of knowledge – that, up to this moment, was unseen. This suggests that the drama and power inherent in entirely new levels of existence is able to be perceived.

The word's roots invite interpretation. *A* means "not" and *lokah* means "world" (referring to our current vision/understanding of the world we live in). Therefore, it can also be translated as *not this world,* or *the end limit of this world.*

Another understanding of *alokah* is that it is light that is not tied to the material plane.

Considering all of this, *alokah* suggests the attainment of insights that are transcendent and, therefore, transformative.

This sutra puts the supernormal attainments, that are about to be listed, into context.

3.6 Mastery of *samyama* progresses in stages.

tasya bhūmiṣu viniyogaḥ

tasya = (refers to *samyama*)

its, of it

bhūmiṣu = stage

ground, earth, a place, site

from ***bhūmih*** = the earth, soil, ground, territory, country, district, a place, situation, position, posture, attitude, floor of a house, stage of Yoga (See 1.14)

As a metaphor, *bhumisu* refers to a step, degree, or stage.

The great sage, Shankaracharya states that if something has stages it must also possess degrees of accomplishment or perfection. *Samyama*, then, is not a static all or nothing state, but a fluid, flowing, deepening of the powers of a concentrated mind.

viniyogaḥ = progression

application, distribution, division, appointment to, duty, task, relation, correlation, separation, impediment

from ***vi*** = asunder, away + ***ni*** = down, into + ***yoga*** = act of yoking, attaching, harnessing, vehicle, use, application, performance, a means, way, manner, method, strategy, undertaking, work, acquisition, partaking of, possessing exertion, endeavor, diligence, care, attention, application or concentration of thoughts, abstract contemplation, meditation

3.7 Compared to the preceding five limbs, *dharana*, *dhyana*, and *samadhi* are more inwardly directed.

trayam-antar-aṅgaṃ pūrvebyaḥ

trayam = three (See 3.4)

antar = internal

interior, inside (See 2.50 and 2.51)

aṅgaṃ = limb (See 1.31)

pūrvebyaḥ = preceding

previous (See 1.18)

from ***purvam*** = before, formerly, hitherto, previously, former

3.8 But even these three are external compared to the seedless (*nirbija*) *samadhi*, which transcends ignorance and brings liberation. (See 1.51)

tad api bahir-aṅgaṃ nirbījasya

tad = that

api = actually

indeed, in truth, also

Api is often used to express emphasis in the sense of *even, also,* or *very.* It can also mean *uniting* or *placing near.* This suggests that *nirbija samadhi* is on a continuum with concentration, meditation, and *samadhi.*

bahir = external

outer

aṅgaṃ = limb (See 1.31)

nirbījasya = seedless (See 1.51)

The clause "external compared to the seedless *samadhi,*" indicates that the practice of *samyama* does not include *nirbija samadhi,* the state of liberation from ignorance and the suffering it brings.

We can see that *samyama,* although having the capacity to endow the practitioner with extraordinary abilities and experiences, does not confer liberation.

3.9 This is how *nirodha* develops until it permeates the mind. Practice and nonattachment generate subconscious impressions of *nirodha.* As each moment of *nirodha* appears, it subdues the impressions that perpetuate the fluctuating, externalized states of mind.

vyutthāna-nirodha-sāmskārayor abhibhava-prādurbhāvau nirodha-kṣaṇa-citta anvayo nirodha-pariṇāmaḥ

This sutra can be thought of as describing an encounter of opposing *samskaras* (subconscious impressions). It describes the gradual tilting of the influence of *samskaras* away from externalization toward those of *nirodha.* A subtle, profound change is taking place through transforming the *samskaras.*

The power of *nirodha* is emphasized by the fact that progress is made by the force of moments of *nirodha.* A moment is the shortest unit of time.

vyutthāna = externalization

emergence, state of being turned outward, outgoing, arising, emergence

from ***vyutthā*** = to get up, to go astray, oppose, contradict, grow strong, resist, instigate, rouse, disagree, win over, remove, obstruction, following one's own bent of mind, from ***vi*** = in two parts + ***ud*** = implies separation or disjunction + ***sthā*** = to stand

Vyutthana is an externally oriented mindset, which through repetition, creates subconscious impressions (*samskaras*) that predispose the mind to continue its externally-oriented thought patterns and that resists introspection and contemplation.

More than a matter of the mind wandering off its intended object of attention or being distracted, *vyutthana* is the mind's collection of values that are based on priorities such as social status, possessions, physical beauty, acknowledgment, and the need for the approval of others to validate our self worth.

Vyutthana is the predominant characteristic of ordinary consciousness in which the ego sense is strengthened. It is also the relentless desire and search for satisfaction or permanent happiness from sense objects and experiences.

Vyutthana is based on cognitions and experiences that arise from *avidya*. It leads to repeatedly misperceiving self-identity as the limited body-mind-ego complex.

As we see in this sutra, *nirodha* is the polar opposite of *vyutthana*.

nirodha = *left untranslated*

obstruct, restrict, arrest, avert, support, confinement, locking up, imprisonment, investment, siege, enclosing, covering up, restraint, check, control, suppression, destruction (See 1.2, 1.12, 1.51, 3.9)

from ***ni*** = down, into, leading, guiding, within, back + ***rodha*** = sprouting, growing, moving, upwards, ascending, stopping, checking, obstructing, impeding, suppressing, preventing, confining, surrounding, investing, besieging, blockading, from ***rudh*** = obstruct, arrest, avert

Looking at the roots of *nirodha*: *down, back, into, within + sprouting, growing, moving*, we can see a suggestion of at least one intent of the word: a change in direction. The word *nirodha* suggests not just a state of mind in meditation, but a profound change in lifestyle and the usual habits and movements of the mind.

Refer to 1.2 for more on *nirodha*.

sāmskārayoḥ = subconscious impressions

from ***sam*** + ***kṛ*** = to do, make, or cause (See 1.18, 1.50, 2.15, 3.9–3.10, 3.18, 4.9, 4.27)

Refer to 1.18 for more on *samskara*.

abhibhava = subdued

overpowered, powerful, submerge, subjugate, prevailing, defeat, predominance

from ***abhi*** = to, into, toward + ***bhava*** = state of existence, coming into existence, birth, production, origin, turning into, worldly existence, from ***bhu*** = becoming, being, existing, produced

In Hinduism, *bhava* (the root of *abhibhava*) also refers to a deity who serves the Lord Rudra. Rudra is known for two opposite natures: he is the god of storms and fire who brings disease, but is also benevolent and brings healing.

Using this as food for an analogy, we can regard an uncontrolled, externalized state of mind (*vyutthana*) as the disruptive, fierce Rudra, and a mind that cultivates *nirodha* as the benevolent, caring, healing Rudra.

prādurbhāvau = appear

manifest

from ***prā*** = before + ***dur*** = door + ***bhu*** = to become

nirodha = *see above*

kṣaṇa = moment

instant, any instantaneous point of time, a fit or suitable moment, opportunity, center, middle

Ksana refers to the smallest unit of time. Even a moment of *nirodha* helps one move forward in mastering the mind.

citta = mind (See 1.2, 1.30, 1.33, 1.37, 2.54, 3.1, 3.9, 3.11–3.12, 3.19, 3.35, 3.39, 4.4–4.5, 4.15–4.18, 4.21, 4.23, 4.26)

Refer to 1.2 for more on *citta*.

anvayoḥ = permeate

following, succession, connection, associated, being linked or connected with, logical connection of cause and effect, conclusion, end product, as a result

from ***anu*** = along, after + ***aya***, from ***i*** = to go

The word "permeate" was chosen to emphasize that this is a dynamic process. The moments when the mind "connects" with impressions of *nirodha* form a succession – a flow or current – of thoughts that gradually pervade the mind, transforming it.

nirodha = *see above*

pariṇāmaḥ = development

transformation, modification, engagement, change, evolution, ripeness, maturity, result, consequence (See 2.15, 3.9, 3.11, 3.13, 3.15–3.16, 4.2, 4.14, 4.32–4.33)

from ***pari*** = around, fully, abundantly + ***nam*** = to bend or bow

Parinama is that which brings about transformation, development, or changes. In this sutra, it describes how one and the same mind transforms from a many-pointed and distracted to a state of the calm flow of attention. The mind's attention, gradually redirected to the object of contemplation, attains a calm flow of awareness toward that object (See 3.10).

Refer to sutra 2.15 for more on *parinama*.

3.10 When impressions of *nirodha* become strong and pervasive, a calm flow of *nirodha* is attained.

tasya praśānta vāhitā samskārāt

tasya = when

its, of this

praśānta = calm

pacified, quiet, composed, extinguished, ceased, removed

from ***pra*** = before, to go forth + ***śanta*** = tranquil, calm, free from passion, peaceful, quiet, calmness of mind, undisturbed, appeased, pacified, from ***sam*** = to stop, finish, come to an end, rest, be calm

The root "*sam*" is the same as the familiar mantra "*shanti*" chanted by many yogis the world over. Note that *prasanta* is more than just the absence of anxiety. It is a higher degree of peace that includes the qualities of freedom (*free from passion*) and strength (*undisturbed*).

The yogi whose mind is truly peaceful (prasanta), who has subdued their passions
and is free from the darkness of nonvirtue,
attains ultimate happiness in Self-realization.
– Bhagavad Gita (6.27)

vāhitā = flow

exertion, endeavor

from ***vah*** = bearing or carrying

Let's reflect on these two key words: calm (*prasanta*) and flow (*vahita*).

The arc of progress in meditation, from beginner to master, is marked by calmness and flow. Even when describing one-pointedness of mind, Patanjali describes it as a state in which arising and subsiding thoughts are identical – an unbroken flow of attention.

This reminds us that the forceful crushing of the mind's activities does not lead to advancement (or use: progress) in meditation. Instead, it is the guided redirection of attention that achieves the goal.

Only in the highest meditative state, *nirbija samadhi*, does the mind attain stillness (the mind is transcended, or better yet, unplugged from the process of self-identification). But stillness is not the goal, but the means to the goal of ending (*nirodha*) the misperception of the body-mind as Self.

samskārāt = impressions (See 1.18, 1.50, 2.15, 3.9–3.10, 3.18, 4.9, 4.27)

Refer to sutra 1.18 for more on *samskara*.

3.11 As all of the various distractions to *nirodha* dwindle,[84] the one-pointed awareness that cultivates *samadhi* arises.

sarva-arthatā-ekāgratayoḥ kṣaya-udayau
cittasya samādhi-pariṇāmah

sarva = all the various

whole, entire, every, everything, of all sorts, various, different

arthatā = distractions

sense object or intention, thingness, objectness, objectivity (See 1.28)

from ***artha*** = possession, wealth, cause, motive, reason, advantage, use, utility, thing, object, object of the senses + ***tā*** = feminine suffix denoting having the quality of

***ekāgratayoḥ* = one-pointedness** (See 2.41)

***kṣaya* = dwindle**

destruction, dwelling, abode, seat, house, house of Lord Yama, loss, waste, wane, diminution, decay, wearing away (See 2.28)

from ***ksi*** = to destroy

udayau = arises

going up, swelling up, rising up, the Eastern Mountain behind which the sun rises, going out, becoming visible, appearance, development, creation, production, conclusion, consequence, result, that which follows, reaching one's aim, success, good fortune, advantage, income

from ***ud*** = up + ***aya***, from ***i*** = to go

cittasya = awareness

mind, consciousness (See 1.2, 1.30, 1.33, 1.37, 2.54, 3.1, 3.9, 3.11–3.12, 3.19, 3.35, 3.39, 4.4–4.5, 4.15–4.18, 4.21, 4.23, 4.26)

Refer to 1.2 for more on *citta*.

---

[84] Dwindle means to diminish gradually in size, amount, strength, and importance.

samādhi = *left untranslated*

absorption (See 1.20, 1.46, 1.51, 2.2, 2.29, 2.45, 3.3, 3.11, 3.38, 4.1, 4.29)

Refer to 1.20 for more on *samadhi.*

pariṇāmah = cultivates

transformation, engagement, change, alteration, evolution, development, ripeness, maturity, digestion, consequence, result

from ***pari*** = around, fully, abundantly + ***nam*** = to bend or bow (See 2.15, 3.9, 3.11–3.13, 3.15–3.16, 4.2, 4.14, 4.32–4.33)

When *nirodha parinama* (3.9) becomes increasingly stable and extended, it naturally leads to *samadhi parinama*. It is the result of the appearance of one-pointed attention.

When the mind attains one-pointedness, it naturally unites to, or is absorbed in, the object of contemplation and *samadhi* arises, but the state is still not steady. At first, the mind slips into and out of *samadhi*.

The following sutra describes the next higher attainment that arises when one-pointedness of mind is sustained.

Refer to 2.15 for more on *parinama*.

3.12 From repeated practice, the subsiding and arising thoughts become identical. Sustaining this one-pointed awareness develops *samadhi.*

tataḥ punaḥ śānta-udita tulya-pratyayau
cittasya-ekāgrata-parinamah

tataḥ = from

that, hence, due to that, therefore, from that time, resulting from that, then, from there

punaḥ = repeated

again, moreover, besides, in turn, but, further, anew, on the other hand from ***punar*** = back, home, in an opposite direction, to go back or away

Looking at the root *punar* reminds us that all of our efforts, repeated practices, resolves, and lifestyle changes combine to nudge us away from a life that is ego-centered and rooted in ignorance, and to return to our home – to our Self.

śānta = subsiding

quieted, appeased, pacified, calm, undisturbed

from ***sam*** = be quiet

udita = rising

apparent, visible

from *ud* = up + ***ita*** = from ***i*** = to go

tulya = identical

same, equal, similar, comparable, of the same kind or class or number or value

from ***tul***= weigh

pratyaya = thought

firm conviction, basis, intention, the image of an object imprinted on the mind – cognition, the content of individual consciousness (See 1.10, 1.18–1.19, 2.20, 3.2, 4.27)

from ***prati*** = against, back + ***aya*** = going, from ***i*** = to go

Pratyaya is an integral part of the process of perception:

- The powers behind the five senses (*jnanendriyas*) flow out through the sense organs to perceive sense objects
- The mind, the internal organ (*antahkarana*), grasps these objects (*pratyaya* = *prati* + *i* = to go forth)
- These images are imprinted on the mind, which presents them to *Purusha* (See 1.10)

Refer to 1.10 for more on *pratyaya*.

cittasya = awareness

mind (See 1.2, 1.30, 1.33, 1.37, 2.54, 3.1, 3.9, 3.11–3.12, 3.19, 3.35, 3.39, 4.4–4.5, 4.15–4.18, 4.21, 4.23, 4.26)

Refer to 1.2 for more on *citta*.

ekāgrata = one-pointed, sustained (See 2.41)

eka = one + ***agrya*** = closely attentive

The roots of *ekagrata* (*eka*, meaning "one" and *agrya* meaning "intent, closely attentive"), can be understood as unbroken intention or attention.

parinamah = development

transformation, engagement, change, alteration, evolution, ripeness, maturity, digestion, consequence, result (See 2.15, 3.9, 3.11–3.13, 3.15–3.16, 4.2, 4.14, 4.32–4.33)

from ***pari*** = around, fully, abundantly + ***nam*** = to bend or bow

Refer to 2.15 for more on *parinama*.

3.13 By understanding the transformations of mind, we can also understand the transformations of the form, characteristics, and condition of the elements of nature and the senses.

etena bhūta-indriyeṣu dharma-lakṣaṇa-avasthā-parinamāḥ vyākhyātāh

etena = (refers to the transformations of consciousness of the previous four sutras)

thus, by this, through this

bhūta = the elements (See 2.18)

indriyeṣu = the sense organs (See 2.18)

dharma = form

nature, character, essential quality, that which is established or held, virtue, religion, visible characteristics (See 3.13–3.14, 4.12)

from ***dhṛ*** = to hold, uphold, establish, support

Dharma literally translates as *that which holds together. Dharma* is the basis of order – whether physical, social, moral, or spiritual. As a moral or ethical principle, it is instrumental for the attainment of liberation (*moksha* or *kaivalya*).

When describing the principles of *prakriti, dharma* can refer to specific and distinct forms or functions of matter.

Dharma is also used to mean *mark, sign, token, essential attributes, nature's properties*.

In Jainism, the word is used to refer to the medium of motion that pervades the entire universe. It is one and eternal. It provides the capacity for movement, even though it does not move itself.

In Buddhism, it is used to refer to scriptural texts, quality, cause, spiritual teachings, cosmic order, natural law, the teachings of The Buddha, norms of conduct, ideas, and factors of existence.

lakṣaṇah = characteristics

mark, sign, symbol, definition, characteristic, attribute, quality, symptom

from ***lakṣ*** = to recognize, perceive, observe, to indicate or express indirectly

Laksanah is a secondary meaning or characteristic of an object that is revealed over time. For example, the oak tree is a *laksanah* of the acorn.

Laksanah refers not only to the unfolding of physical characteristics that are revealed over time, but to the characteristics, which are the symbols or spirits of those objects that carry pertinence and power. This may be the power that shamans call forth in their rites.

avasthā = condition

stability, state, to abide in a state or condition, to stay, to enter

from ***ava*** = down + ***stha*** = stand

parinamāḥ = transformation

development, engagement, change, alteration, evolution, ripeness, maturity, digestion, consequence, result

from ***pari*** = around, fully, abundantly + ***nam*** = to bend or bow (See 2.15, 3.9, 3.11–3.13, 3.15–3.16, 4.2, 4.14, 4.32–4.33)

In this sutra, *parinamah* refers to the transformations that manifest as changes in the external forms of objects or in the characteristics that appear in objects over time.

Refer to 2.15 for more on *parinama*.

vyākhyātāh = understand

explained, fully detailed, related, told, fully dealt with

from ***khyā*** = to be named or announced, to make known, proclaim, to relate, tell, say, declare, betray, denounce, from ***kāś*** = to be visible, appear, to shine, be brilliant, have an agreeable appearance (See 1.44)

The definitions of *vyakhyatah* suggest a depth of understanding that is more than merely intellectual. It is knowledge that is deep, detailed, and clear and is in a category and degree of knowledge only revealed in a contemplative mind.

3.14 *Prakriti* is the substratum of the changes of form and characteristics that objects exhibit as they go through the succession of stages:

- **Subsiding (past)**
- **Arising (present)**
- **Unmanifest (future)**

śānta-udita-avyapadeśya-dharma-anupattī-dharmī

śānta = subsiding

quieted, appeased, pacified, calm, undisturbed, past

from ***sam*** = be quiet (See 3.12)

udita = arising

apparent, visible

from ***ud*** = up + ***ita*** = from ***i*** = to go (See 3.12)

avyapadeśya = unmanifest

undetermined, undefined, indistinguishable

from ***a*** = not + ***vi*** = asunder, away + ***apa*** = away + ***deśya*** = from ***diś*** = point out

dharma = characteristic, form

nature, character, essential quality, that which is established or held, virtue, religion, visible characteristics (See 3.13–3.14, 4.12)

from ***dhṛ*** = to hold, uphold, establish, support

Refer to 3.13 for more on *dharma*.

anupattī = following

goes through, conforming, corresponds to

dharmī = substratum

holder of *dharma*, the essential characteristic, knowing or obeying the law, faithful to duty, virtuous, pious, endowing with any characteristic marks, or peculiar property, subject to any state or condition, the bearer of any characteristic mark or attribute, object, thing (See *dharma*, 3.13)

from ***dharma*** + ***in*** = suffix indicating possession

In this sutra, *dharmi* refers to *prakriti*.

"Subsiding," "arising," and "unmanifest" correspond to past, present, and future forms of objects. What we discover here is that *prakriti* is the underlying medium – the stuff – out of which all objects are created. We are reminded that there is one ground and essence of all things created, of matter. The changes we see are simply the unfolding of the forms and characteristics that are latent in all objects.

The classic example of the changes referred to in this sutra is a clay jar. It begins as a lump of clay. Through time, and the efforts of the potter, it is transformed into a jar. But this change of form doesn't change its essential nature: clay. The clay as a jar now exists in the present and is for our use. At some point, either through breaking or over the centuries, the clay no longer exists as a jar. It returns to clay dust.

Gradually learning to perceive the changeless essence behind the names and forms is a vital practice in Patanjali's Yoga. It is essential to the all-important process that brings liberation, the discerning of the difference between *prakriti* (always changing) and *Purusha* (changeless).

The mind, as one aspect of *prakriti*, also changes due to the passage of time and the effects of stimuli arising externally (events in life) or from within (such as memories). One of the latent characteristics of our minds is *sattva*: tranquility, happiness, balance, and luminosity. Strictly speaking, since it is latent in every mind, it need not be developed, but is revealed in a mind that is peaceful, clear, and one-pointed.

The most important capacity brought by pure *sattva* is the ability to discern the difference between the mind and the *Atma* (higher Self, spirit).[85] (See 4.25 and 4.26)

3.15 The transformation of characteristics that manifest in objects is caused by the succession of these three phases. (However, there is only one underlying substance.)

krama-anyatvam pariṇāma-anyatve hetuḥ

krama = succession

series, sequence, uninterrupted or regular progress, step, system, proceeding, course, going, way, power, strength, custom, according to rank, order, regular arrangement, method, manner, in drama: the attainment of the desired object, a rule sanctioned by tradition, a position taken by an animal prior to attacking,

---

[85] This distinction is the ultimate knowledge. It overcomes ignorance. It is considered that which is to be known.

uninterrupted progress, progressing step-by-step (See 3.53, 4.32–4.33)

from ***kram*** = to approach, realistic, to gain a footing, to step, to proceed well, to take possession of, to walk, to stride, to go across, to go, to undertake, to succeed

We might undervalue this word, only imagining it as a sort of parade of changes marching by as we watch. But, looking closely, we see elements that suggest that this passing parade also has the power to create illusions.

One example is a movie. The illusion of movement is created by a succession of images, each only slightly different from the next. A succession of thoughts also creates illusions. A series of repeated or related thoughts creates habits and beliefs. Habits and beliefs create character. Character determines how we understand and respond to the objects and events of life. This understanding is why repetition is central to Yoga practice. It creates new beneficial habits and clear, expansive ways of perceiving and experiencing life and self.

anyatvam = different

change, otherness

from ***anya*** = other, different, opposed to, one of a number + ***tvam***, denoting having the quality of

pariṇāma = transformations

phases, evolution, changes (See 2.15, 3.9, 3.11–3.13, 3.15–3.16, 4.2, 4.14, 4.32–4.33)

Refer to 2.15 for more on *parinama*.

anyatve = (*refers to the transformation of objects*)

differences in, change, the otherness

hetuḥ = cause

impulse, motive, reason for, primary cause (Buddhism), the external world and the senses, mode, manner, condition (See 2.17)

3.16 By *samyama* on these three phases of transformation, knowledge of past and future can be known.

pariṇāma-traya-saṃyamād atīta-anāgata-jñānam

pariṇāma = transformation

change, evolution (See 2.15, 3.9, 3.11–3.13, 3.15–3.16, 4.2, 4.14, 4.32–4.33)

Refer to 2.15 for more on *parinama*.

traya = three

threefold

saṃyamād* = by *samyama

binding together (See 3.4, 3.16–3.17, 3.21, 3.27, 3.36, 3.42, 3.45, 3.48, 3.53)

Refer to 3.4 for more on *samyama*.

atīta = past

gone by, dead, one who has gone through or got over or beyond, one who has passed by or neglected, negligent

from ***ati*** = over, beyond, hither, derived from ***i*** = to go

anāgata = future

yet to happen, not arrived, belonging to the future

from ***an*** = not + ***ā*** = hither, unto + ***gata*** = gone, departed, departed from the world, the past, come forth from, arrived at, contained in, approached, having walked (a path), gone to any state or condition, relating to, referring to, connected with, visited, going, manner of going, motion, the place where anyone has gone, anything past or done, belonging to the future, from ***gam*** = to go

jñānam = knowledge

knowing, becoming acquainted with, higher knowledge derived from meditation, conscience (See 1.9, 1.38, 1.42, 2.28, 3.16–3.19, 3.26–3.27, 3.29, 3.36, 3.53, 3.55, 4.31)

Refer to 1.9 for more on *jnanam*.

3.17 A word, the object it refers to, and the ideas associated with that object are normally superimposed on one another, creating one unified impression in the mind. By *samyama* on the distinction between these three factors, knowledge of the meaning of the sounds produced by all beings is attained.

śabda-artha-pratyayānām itara-itara adhyāsāt saṃkaraḥ tat pravibhāga-saṃyamāt sarva-bhūta-rūta-jñānam

śabda = word

language, sound, noise, voice, speech

artha = object

thing, meaning, aim, purpose (See 1.28)

pratyayānām = ideas

thought, intention (See 1.10)

itara-itara = on one another

one upon the other

adhyāsāt = superimposed

imposition, overlapping

from ***adhi*** = over, on + ***asa***, from ***as*** = to be

saṃkaraḥ = unified

confused, mixed together, commingled

from ***sam*** = together + ***kara***, from ***kr*** = scatter

tat = (*refers to word, object, and ideas*) that

pravibhāga = distinction

separation, division,

from ***pra*** = before + ***vi*** = asunder + ***bhaga***, from ***bhaj*** = divide

saṃyamāt = *left untranslated*

concentration, meditation, and *samadhi* performed together (See 3.4, 3.16–3.17, 3.21–3.22, 3.27, 3.36, 3.42–3.43, 3.45, 3.48, 3.53)

Refer to 3.4 for more on *samyama*.

sarva = all (See 1.25)

bhūta = beings (See 2.8)

creature, created being, occurrence, fact, present, existing, a child, a great devotee or ascetic, related to a priest of the gods, any living being (divine, human, animal, vegetable), become, past, a reality, that which has come into being, the world, a good or evil spirit

We will consider *bhuta* and *ruta* together (below).

rūta = sound

utterance, cry, noise, yell, hum, song, the neigh of horses, the notes of birdsongs, the hum of bees

from ***ru*** = roar

One practical ability that can be gained from this *samyama* is that we can perceive the truth that is sometimes hidden behind words. Intent can be revealed through the sounds – intonation, inflection, pitch, volume, rhythm – of the words themselves.

The ability presented here can be a boon in relationships and for discerning the motive behind salespeople and politicians, for example. We all have experienced this ability but on a more basic, less subtle and complete level than is suggested in this sutra. Now, let's stretch out this sutra...

Bhuta – beings – includes more than humans. It includes animals – anything that is alive, including vegetables! Really. See the list of definitions above and the explanation below. Next, we add the word, *ruta*...

Ruta's meanings include *song*, the *notes of birdsongs,* and the *hum of bees.* Can we allow ourselves to imagine that the yogi who has attained this *siddhi* (supernormal[86] power) can "hear" and draw meaning from the songs and sounds "sung" by nature – including birds, bees, spinach, tomatoes, and onions! Why not? The universe was created by and through sound:

In the beginning was Brahman with whom was the Word
and the Word was the Supreme Brahman.
– Rig Veda

In the beginning was the word and the word was with God
and the word was God.
– John 1:1

Everything in the universe continues to come into being, evolve, and dissolve. In this, we can perceive its undercurrents of deep harmony. This is embodied in the most important of all mantras, OM, whose three letters A-U-M represent creation, evolution, and dissolution.

Read in this light, this sutra treats us to a wondrous and powerful image of a universe alive with song and enjoyed by a human being so in harmony with creation that they can discern it.

Did Patanjali mean to include this interpretation? Maybe. Maybe not. But this image does point to, and hold, profound truth.

jñānam = knowledge (See 1.9, 1.38, 1.42, 2.28, 3.16–3.19, 3.26–3.27, 3.29, 3.36, 3.53, 3.55, 4.31)

Refer to 1.9 for more on *jnanam*.

3.18 By *samyama* on the subconscious impressions that form the mind's deep-rooted tendencies comes direct perception of them. From this, knowledge of previous births is obtained.[87]

[86] Supernormal is a more accurate word than supernatural to translate *siddhi*. Supernatural suggests beyond nature. The *siddhis* are decidedly not that. While amazing and rare, they are part of nature, deriving from union with the subtle currents of nature's power. Supernormal suggests that the powers are not normally encountered.

[87] Refer back to sutra 2.39, in which perfecting nongreed leads to knowledge of past lifetimes, though in this book it is translated as "awakening to the meaning of life." Both translations are suitable. The reason I chose this translation for 2.39 is that the "line" between nongreed and finding deeper meaning in life is more direct than the "line" between nongreed and knowledge of past lifetimes.

saṃskāra-sākṣāt karaṇāt pūrva-jāti-jñānam

saṃskāra = subconscious impressions

from ***sam*** = together + ***kṛ*** = to do, make, or cause (See 1.18, 1.50, 2.15, 3.9–3.10, 3.18, 4.9, 4.27)

Refer to 1.18 for more on *samskara*.

sākṣāt = direct perception

perceived by the eyes, evident to the senses, clearly, evidently, visibly, immediately, directly

from ***sa*** = with + ***akṣa*** = eye

karaṇāt = by making

doing, affecting, from some cause or reason, for the sake of, on account of

from ***kr*** = made, do

pūrva = previous (See 1.18)

jāti = births (See 2.13)

jñānam = knowledge (See 1.9, 1.38, 1.42, 2.28, 3.16–3.19, 3.26–3.27, 3.29, 3.36, 3.53, 3.55, 4.31)

Refer to 1.9 for more on *jnanam*.

3.19 By *samyama* on the ideas and intentions of others arises the ability to know their minds.

pratyayasya para-citta-jñānam

pratyayasya = ideas, intentions

thoughts

This sutra could be referring to either the contents or the nature of someone's mind.

***Pratyayasya* is in the genitive case, indicating a close association. In this instance, it refers to the close association between the nature of**

an individual's mind that is rooted in the subconscious, and the ideas and intentions that rise to the surface.

This sutra could also be suggesting a relationship between the attainment of sutra 3.18, the direct perception of one's own subconscious impressions, and through this self-understanding, the ability to know the minds of others.

The same ability could be said of one's own mind. Knowing the deep contents - subconscious impressions - of one's own mind, reveals its full nature.

Refer to 1.10 for more on *pratyaya*.

para = others

another, different from

from ***pṛ*** = rescue, protect

citta = mind

thought, individual consciousness, heart (See 1.2, 1.30, 1.33, 1.37, 2.54, 3.1, 3.9, 3.11–3.12, 3.19, 3.35, 3.39, 4.4–4.5, 4.15–4.18, 4.21, 4.23, 4.26)

Refer to 1.2 for more on *citta*.

jñānam = know

knowledge (See 1.9, 1.38, 1.42, 2.28, 3.16–3.19, 3.26–3.27, 3.29, 3.36, 3.53, 3.55, 4.31)

Refer to 1.9 for more on *jnanam*.

3.20 But this knowledge does not include the object on which the thoughts are based since it is not the purpose of this perception.

na ca tat sālambanam tasya aviṣayībhūvatatvāt

na = not

ca = but

tat = its

that (See 1.12)

sālambanam = with basis

with support (See 1.10)

from ***sa*** = with + ***ālambana*** = support, depending on, based on, resting on (See 1.10)

tasya = *(refers to samyama)*

of it, its

aviṣayībhūvatatvāt = it is not the purpose

because it is not the object

from ***aviṣayī*** = which has no object, without having an object or condition, from ***a*** = not + ***viṣai*** = condition, that which is experienced through the senses (See 1.11) + ***in*** = possessive suffix + ***bhūvatatvāt*** = element, constituent of the manifest world, nature or object of being, from ***bhūta*** = elements: earth, water, fire, air, space, constituents of the manifest universe (See 2.18) + ***tva*** = suffix denoting having the quality of

3.21 By *samyama* on the visible form of the body comes the understanding that vision is the ability to perceive the light that is reflected off of objects. Arising from this is the capacity to intercept the light from the eyes of observers, making one's body invisible to them.

kāya-rūpa-saṃyamāt tat grāhya-śakti-stambe
cakṣuh prakāśa-asaṃyoge antardhānam

kāya = body (See 2.43)

rūpa = form

outward appearance, phenomenon or color, shape, one of the subtle elements, dreamy or phantom shapes, nature, character, peculiarity, feature, mark, sign, symptom, likeness, image, reflection, mode, manner, way, a single specimen or example, a show, play or drama, the quality of color, material form or body (Buddhism)

saṃyamāt = from *samyama* (See 3.4, 3.16–3.17, 3.21–3.22, 3.27, 3.36, 3.42–3.43, 3.45, 3.48, 3.53)

Refer to 3.4 for more on *samyama*.

tat = *(refers to the body)*

its, that

grāhya = perceive, perception

grasped (See 1.41)

śakti = capacity

power (See 2.6)

stambe = intercept

checked, suspension, suppression, stoppage, a post, pillar, column, stem of a tree, support, strengthening, inflation, pretentiousness, arrogance, stiffness, rigidity, becoming hard, or solid (See 2.50)

cakṣuh = eye

from ***cakṣ*** = to see

prakāśa = light

illumination, splendor, brightness, pure consciousness, visible, shining out, expanded, universally noted, having the appearance of, before the eyes of all, clear, manifest, open, public, expanded, universally noted, appearance, display, manifestation, diffusion, laughter, it is the principle by which everything else is known, the principle of self-revelation. Self-shining conscious light and its ability to hold a reflection of itself (See 2.18, 2.52, 3.21, 3.44)

from ***pra*** = before, forward, in front, on, forth, very much, great + ***kāś*** = to be visible, to appear, to shine, be brilliant, to have an agreeable experience

Refer to 2.18 for more on *prakasa*.

asaṃyoge = *not directly included in the translation*

disconnect, disunion, disjunction

from ***a*** = not + ***saṃyoga*** = union

Although this word is not directly translated, it is implied as one element of a two-part process. The light is first disconnected from the eye of others and then held in check, making the yogi invisible to their eyes. Intercept (*stambe*, see page 275) carries the sense of both words combined.

antardhānam = invisible

hidden concealed, hidden or inner treasure, placed within

from ***antar*** = internal, within, between + ***dhāna*** = prize, contest, booty, any valued object, wealth, property, from ***dhā*** = to put, place, lay in or onto put one's foot in another's footstep, imitate, to bring to, take to, help to, to direct or fix the mind or attention, resolve on, impart to, take hold of, hold, bear, support, accept, obtain, conceive (especially in the womb), get, take, to assume, have, show, exhibit, undergo, to wish to give or present, to strive for

3.22 In the same way, the disappearance of sound, touch, taste, smell, etc. is explained.[88]

etena śābhadi antardhānam utkam

etena = by the same way

śābhadi = sound, etc. (See 3.17)

antardhānam = disappearance (See 3.21)

utkam = is explained

3.23 There are two categories of karma: karmas that are active during the present lifetime and karmas that are deferred for future births. From *samyama* on the distinction between these two, or on omens found in natural phenomena, knowledge of the time of death arises. (See 2.12 - 2.14, 3.18)

sopakramaṃ nirupakramaṃ ca karman tad saṃyamāt
aparānta-jñānam ariṣṭebhyaḥ va

[88] This sutra is not included in some translations, which is why the total number of sutras varies and can be either 196 or 195.

sopakramaṃ = active

set in motion, undertaken

from ***sa*** = with + ***pa*** = to unto + ***krama***, from ***kram*** = step

Refers to *prarabdha* karma, the karmas experienced in the present lifetime.

nirupakramaṃ = deferred

not in motion, not taken up, not pursued

from ***nir*** = away from + ***pa*** = to, unto + ***krama***, from ***kram*** = to step

Refers to *sancita* karma, the storehouse of karmas.

ca = and

karman = left untranslated

action, reaction (See 1.24, 2.12, 3.22, 4.7, 4.30)

Refer to 1.24 for more on *karman*.

tad = (refers to *samyama*)

from, that

saṃyamāt = *samyama* (See 3.4, 3.16–3.17, 3.21–3.22, 3.27, 3.36, 3.42–3.43, 3.45, 3.48, 3.53)

Refer to 3.4 for more on *samyama*.

aparānta = time of death

literally, the Western extremity the latter end, conclusion, death

from ***a*** + ***para*** = on the farther side of + ***anta*** = end

jñānam = knowledge (See 1.9, 1.38, 1.42, 2.28, 3.16–3.19, 3.26–3.27, 3.29, 3.36, 3.53, 3.55, 4.31)

Refer to 1.9 for more on *jnanam*.

***ariṣṭebhyaḥ* = natural phenomena**

boding misfortune, ill omens, signs of approaching death

from ***ariṣṭa*** = unhurt, proof against injury or damage, secure, safe, boding misfortune (as birds of misfortune, such as a heron or crow), ill-luck, misfortune, good fortune, happiness, a woman's apartment, the lying-in chamber (where women give birth), a natural phenomenon boding approaching death + ***bhyo*** = from

va = or

3.24 By *samyama* on friendliness, compassion, selfless joy, equanimity, and other such virtues, their full powers manifest.

maitrī ādiṣu balāṇi

maitrī = friendliness (See 1.33)

ādiṣu = and other

etc., and so forth

balāṇi = powers

strengths, force, stamina, strength, vigor, validity, by means of, on the strength of, military force, semen, virile, a young shoot

from ***bal*** = to live, breathe, to hoard grain, to hurt, to give, to nourish, rear, to explain, describe

3.25 By *samyama* on the strength of elephants and other such animals, their strength is attained.[89]

baleṣu hasti-bala-ādīni

baleṣu = on the strength

in powers (See 3.23)

hasti = elephant

bala = strength

[89] A note of caution. Be careful!

power (See 3.23)

ādīni = other such

and so forth, others

3.26 By *samyama* on the inner light (*sattva*) that illumines sense perception, one gains knowledge of objects that are subtle, hidden from view, or distant. (See 1.36, 3.5)

pravṛitti-āloka-nyāsāt sūkṣma-vyavahita-viprakkṛṣṭa-jñānam

pravṛitti = perception

activity, moving onward, cognition, engagement, self-identity based on tangible factors (See 1.35)

from ***pra*** = before, forward, in front of, forth + ***vritti*** = a commentary, comment, gloss, explanation (especially of a sutra), being, existing, occurring or existing in, common practice, rule, mode of being, nature, kind, character, disposition, mode of conduct, mood of the mind, devotion or addiction to, working, activity, function, rolling, rolling down, business, practice, behavior, course of action, moving onward, advance, progress, coming forth, appearance, manifestation, rise, source, origin, activity, exertion, efficacy, function, active contemplative devotion (defined as consisting of the wish to act, knowledge of the means, and accomplishment of the object), conduct, continuance, fate, lot, destiny, news, tidings, cognition, from ***vṛt*** = to turn

Pravritti can refer to the self-identity that was developed and influenced by engagement in worldly experiences.

Nivritti – its opposite – means disengagement from self-identity based on worldly experiences.

Yoga teaches a balance between these two apparently conflicting orientations: being *in* the world but not *of* the world.

āloka = light

sight, aspect, vision, luster, splendor, glimmer, praise, flattery, a public speech or text in praise of someone or something, respect (See 3.5) from ***ā*** = hither, unto + ***lokaḥ*** = world, from ***lok*** = see, behold

Definition 1: not the world, end of the world

Definition 2: looking, seeing, beholding, sight, aspect, vision, light, luster, splendor, glimmer, flattery, praise, complimentary language

In Jainism, *aloka* refers to the immaterial or spiritual world, or the transcendent world of liberated souls. It can also refer to infinite empty space.

nyāsāt = a synonym for *samyama*

directing, placing or setting down, applying, cast down, project, to throw upon

from ***ni*** = down, back, into, in + ***ās*** = to sit

***Nyasa* (a synonym for *samyama*) can also refer to a ritual process used to strengthen the experience of micro/macro-cosmic relationships. By meditating on light within (the microcosm), subtle, hidden, and remote aspects of the macrocosm are revealed.**

sūkṣma = subtle

minute, small, fine, thin, narrow, short, insignificant, unimportant, acute, keen, exact, precise, atomic, intangible matter, subtle all-pervading spirit, Supreme Soul, marrow, the Vedanta philosophy (See 1.44)

vyavahita = hidden

concealed, obstructed

vi = asunder, away + ***ava*** = off, away, down, down from + ***hita*** = sent, impelled, urged on, set in motion, going, running, anything useful or suitable or proper, friend, benefactor, prepared, made ready

hita, derived from ***dhā*** = put, placed, laid, laid upon, imposed, contained in

What is concealed is not just a static hidden object that we work hard to find. It is a reality that our minds have moved away from. We can't perceive – perceive accurately or completely – that which is obstructed by ignorance.

viprakkṛṣṭa = distant

remote, a long way off

from ***vi*** = asunder, away + ***pra*** = before + ***kṛṣṭa***, from drawn or dragged apart, plough, cultivated ground, lengthened

jñānam = knowledge (See 1.9, 1.38, 1.42, 2.28, 3.16–3.19, 3.26–3.27, 3.29, 3.36, 3.53, 3.55, 4.31)

Refer to 1.9 for more on *jnanam*.

3.27 By *samyama* on the sun, knowledge of all planes of existence in the universe is attained.

bhuvana-jñānam surye saṃyamāt

bhuvana = all planes of existence

cosmos, world, region, a being, living creature, humankind, the earth, place of being, abode, residence

from ***bhū*** = to be, become, earth

jñānam = knowledge (See 1.9, 1.38, 1.42, 2.28, 3.16–3.19, 3.26–3.27, 3.29, 3.36, 3.53, 3.55, 4.31)

Refer to 1.9 for more on *jnanam*.

surye = sun

the sun itself or its deity, later identified with the twelve months of the year

from ***svar*** = heaven

saṃyamāt = *samyama* (See 3.4, 3.16–3.17, 3.21–3.22, 3.27, 3.36, 3.42–3.43, 3.45, 3.48, 3.53)

Refer to 3.4 for more on *samyama*.

3.28 By *samyama* on the moon, knowledge of the stars' alignment is attained.

candre tārā-vyūha-jñānam

candre = on the moon

the personified deity of the moon, glittering, shining (as gold), having the brilliancy of light, a lovely or agreeable phenomenon of any kind

from ***cand*** = shine

tārā = of the stars

prominent grouping or pattern of stars (smaller than a constellation), a fixed star, the pupil of the eye, a kind of meteor

from ***tṛ*** = pass beyond

vyūha = alignment

arrangement, distribution, placing apart, orderly arrangement of the parts of a whole, shifting, transposition, displacement, detailed explanation or description, a section, division, form, manifestation, formation, structure

from ***vi*** = asunder, away + *vūh* = remove

jñānam = knowledge (See 1.9, 1.38, 1.42, 2.28, 3.16–3.19, 3.26–3.27, 3.29, 3.36, 3.53, 3.55, 4.31)

Refer to 1.9 for more on *jnanam*.

3.29 By *samyama* on the pole star, knowledge of the stars' movements is attained.

dhruve tat gati-jñānam

dhruve = on the polestar

from *dhruv* = firm, fixed, certain, unchanging

tat = (*refers to the stars mentioned in the prior sutra*)

that

gati = movements

motion (See 2.49)

jñānam = knowledge (See 1.9, 1.38, 1.42, 2.28, 3.16–3.19, 3.26–3.27, 3.29, 3.36, 3.53, 3.55, 4.31)

Refer to 1.9 for more on *jnanam.*

3.30 By *samyama* on the navel plexus, knowledge of the body's constitution is attained.

nābhi-cakre kāya-vyūha-jñānam

nābhi = navel

central point, the hub of a wheel, point of junction or of departure, home, origin, affinity, relationship, a chief

from ***nābh*** = fissure, spring, opening, to be torn asunder, burst, hurt, to cause to burst, tear open

cakre = plexus

center of energy in the body, wheel, orb, circle, multitude, army, circuit, district, province, domain, plexus, discus, a mystical circle or diagram, a cycle, troop, multitude, a number of villages, the wheel of a monarch's chariot rolling over his dominions or realm, the winding of a river, a whirlpool

from ***kṛ*** = to do

During Patanjali's time, the now familiar representation of a human being having seven *chakras* was not prevalent. The seven *chakras* came into more general use later, with the rise of popularity in the Tantra Yoga movement.

Patanjali doesn't offer information on *chakras*. One reason may be that *chakras,* and the *kundalini* energy that rises through them, need not be a central focus. By a virtuous life, a clear, one-pointed mind, and a nonattached mindset, we enable the *chakras* to be purified and the *kundalini* to rise naturally – without any further special effort or practices.

kāya = body

assemblage, trunk of a tree, the body of a lute (except the wires), house, habitation, natural temperament (See 2.43)

vyūha = constitution

arrangement, distribution, placing apart, orderly arrangement of the parts of a whole, shifting, transposition, displacement, detailed explanation or description, a section, division, form, manifestation, formation, structure (See 3.28)

jñānam = knowledge (See 1.9, 1.38, 1.42, 2.28, 3.16–3.19, 3.26–3.27, 3.29, 3.36, 3.53, 3.55, 4.31)

Refer to 1.9 for more on *jnanam*.

3.31 By *samyama* on the pit of the throat, cessation of hunger and thirst is attained.

kaṇṭha-kupe kṣudh-pipāsā-nivṛittiḥ

kaṇṭha = throat

neck

kupe = pit

hollow, cavity, well

kṣudh = hunger

pipāsā = thirst

desire to drink

from ***pā*** = drink

nivṛittiḥ = cessation

disappearance

from ***ni*** = down, into, not + ***vritti*** = to whirl (See 1.2)

3.32 By *samyama* on the tortoise-shaped channel located in the chest, one's body and mind become steady.

kūrma-nādyāṃ sthairyam

kūrma = tortoise

turtle; one of the *pranas*, which causes the closing of the eyes

nādyāṃ = channel

conduit, tube, vein, artery, flow of *prana* along pathways

from ***nādi*** = any pipe or tube, the pulse, any hole or crevice + ***ya*** = go

There are different opinions regarding the exact location of the *kurma nadi*. Many locate it in the center of the chest; others at (or near) the navel plexus.

The *kurma nadi's* function is to stabilize the body and mind. It could be thought of as the body-mind's innate impulse toward balance or homeostasis (a dynamic process whereby the body-mind strives to keep its functions within the parameters necessary to sustain life).[90]

The symbolism of the tortoise is significant in Hinduism. In Hindu mythology, an enormous tortoise carries a giant elephant on its back which, in turn, supports the entire universe – a fit image of strength and stability. In this image, the elephant represents the masculine principle and the tortoise the feminine, giving it a similar connotation as the well-known Tai Chi (yin-yang) symbol.

The lower or bottom shell of the tortoise is symbolic of the earth, while its upper shell is the heavens.

The tortoise also symbolizes the waters, the moon, Earth Mother, the beginning of creation, the first living creature, time, immortality, fertility, and regeneration.

Significantly, the tortoise is one of the ten avatars (incarnations) of Lord Vishnu, the Preserver deity. There is a tale in which Lord Vishnu took the form of a giant tortoise to save the world from destruction. As the story goes, through the negligence of Indra, the king of the gods (*devas*), the gods were losing their power. Malevolent spirits (*asuras*) were threatening to take over. Lord Vishnu directed that the ocean of milk needed to be

[90] The sphere of influence of the *nadis* would also include the mind, therefore, the *kurma nadi* would also be responsible for maintaining balance of mind.

churned in order to attain the nectar of immortality. To churn this large ocean, they needed to use a mountain as a churning stick, but it was so heavy it began to sink. That is when Lord Vishnu took the form of the giant tortoise to support the mountain on his back so the churning could continue.

sthairyam = steady

stability, motionless, steadfastness (See 2.39)

from ***sthā*** = stand (See 1.13)

Refer back to the sutras on *parinama*, transformation (3.9–3.12), to review how development in stability is key to advancement in meditation.

3.33 By *samyama* on the light just below the crown of the head, *darshan* (vision) of the *siddhas* (perfected beings) can be attained.

mūrdha-jyothiṣi siddha-darśanam

There are two possible meanings of this sutra: to see perfected beings and to attain the same vision as perfected beings.

In this context, *siddhas* most likely refers to those who have attained and have displayed miraculous powers. Note that although we can attain insight equal to that of that class of *siddhas*, the following sutra describes a higher state, one that makes omniscience possible.

"The light just below the crown of the head," is likely referring to the *brahmarandhra chakra*, also known as the *Guru chakra*, or *jnana chakra*. It is located above the third eye *chakra* (*ajna chakra*) and below the crown *chakra* (*sahasrara chakra*).

The *brahmarandhra chakra* is also considered to be a transmitting and receiving center for communication with one's Guru. If this is the function that Patanjali has in mind, he may not be referring to *siddhas* of supernormal abilities, but to one's Guru (living or having left the body) and his or her lineage, or other of the Guru's assemblage[91] (as described in the *Guru Gita*).

mūrdha = crown of the head

jyothiṣi = on the light

light, brightness

from ***jyut*** = to shine

siddha = masters and perfected beings

accomplished, fulfilled, affected, gained, acquired, one who has attained the object of desire, successful, one who has attained the highest goal, thoroughly skilled, perfected, endowed with supernatural faculties, holy, divine, sacred, effective, powerful, subdued, those who are considered as immortals, although they live only to the end of a *kalpa* (a world cycle of immense duration), any inspired sage or great saint

from ***sidh*** = to succeed, to attain, to be accomplished, fulfilled, to become perfect, perfected ones

Synonyms for *siddha* include: perfected being, an accomplished one, a seer, an adept, a perfected yogi, or those who have attained oneness with the highest Reality. The term often refers to those who have attained miraculous powers (*siddhis*).

In some schools of thought, a *siddha's* blessings were indispensable for the successful practice of Jnana Yoga, the path of knowledge and self-analysis.

darśanam = vision

seeing, being seen, audience with, meeting, showing, looking at, vision, exhibiting, teaching, perception, examination, contemplating, apprehension, intention, doctrine, philosophical system, understanding, view, presence, becoming visible or known, semblance, a mirror, a sacrifice (See 1.30)

[91] The *Guru Gita* describes the Guru as being surrounded by a multitude of heavenly beings, ascended masters, and demigods and goddesses. This is to emphasize that the guru can lead a sincere disciple to all "heavenly" attainments and assistance.

Darshanam, translated as "vision," although conveying the gist of the word, misses much of its beauty, strength and depth. *Darshanam* has been a vital aspect of spiritual life in India for millennia. Its centrality is found in all of India's spiritual traditions.

Darshanam is not possible without light. There is no vision of physical objects without physical light. And, there is no vision of emotions, inner images, or the contents of the mind without inner light (awareness).

Light, as a symbol for consciousness, truth, divinity, insight, and righteousness has held a central place in Yoga from ancient times. Some of these principles include:

- The Self is the inner light that shines through the eyes and illumines the objective world. The same light enlightens all of the senses and all states of mind.
- There is a link between the eyes and the heart (the heart was considered the seat of the mind and has the power to see what is invisible to the physical eyes).
- A luminous channel (*nadi*) runs from the *brahmachandra chakra* (such as the Guru *chakra*) to the center of the heart. This is the *chakra* that is central to this sutra.
- The *Purusha* (Seer, Self) is simultaneously present in the sun, the eyes, and the heart.
- *Dharana* and *dhyana*, which are integral to *samyama*, are both rooted in *dhi* (knowledge, vision, luminosity). We see the connection between light, vision, and a clear, one-pointed mind. This leads to a central innate capacity, without which there is no valid Yoga theory of self and life: *yoga pratyaksha*, yogic perception.
- *Yoga pratyaksha* is unmediated perception that transcends sense perception. The knowledge gained from these perceptions is the basis of the wisdom of *Vedic* sages, yogis, and *siddhas* (See *siddha* in this sutra). All other forms of cognition, although valid, are inferior to *yoga pratyaksha*.
- *Yoga pratyaksha* is what enables seers to apprehend the truths of Self and existence – it transcends the distortion caused by the

senses, ignorance, and ingrained mindsets and beliefs.

We can understand why *darshanam* is a central practice in Hinduism that cuts across all sects.

Darshanam is also the act of seeing and being seen by the image of a deity or spiritual master. Most of us wouldn't consider seeing or being seen as actual physical contact, but it is. Visual contact (especially when amplified by faith, love, and reverence) is a way of absorbing something of the nature, virtues, and powers of the deity or spiritual master.[92]

It should be kept in mind that the ultimate goal is not the image being beheld. It is the ultimate Reality, Truth, or Absolute Divine Consciousness that is behind and beyond it.

Darshanam is like a window into the experience of the Absolute (windows can both let light out as well as in). Through this contact, the devotee can gain insight, inspiration, energy (*shakti*), and discernment. *Darshanam* is a way of cultivating an intimate relationship with the Absolute through a form the devotee reveres and loves.

Central to understanding *darshanam* is the principle that light is not only a symbol of wisdom, but is wisdom itself. We can only see when there is light. A dark room may house many treasures and dangers, but they remain unknown unless we stumble on them, or better yet, if light reveals them to us. The relationship between *darshanam*, light, seeing, and wisdom is intimate.

When a seeker does experience the richness and power of *darshanam*, it increases their faith and provides inspiration.

Darshanam provides another, vital facet to spiritual life: the confirmation of belief through a noncognitive process. The rational mind, along with its limitations, is transcended. Being noncognitive, it brings the devotee in touch with realities beyond space and time.

[92] Ancient texts refer to this mutual seeing and being seen as a form of eating!

3.34 Or, any or all of the accomplishments listed in the previous seventeen sutras, can come spontaneously – without *samyama* – when the light of intuitive insight bursts forth in a pure, clear, steady mind. (See 3.53–3.55)

prātibhād vā sarvam

prātibhād = intuitive insight

vividness, divination, intuitive knowledge, gift, endowment, talent, genius, brilliance, ability, power, creativity, success

from ***pra*** = before, forward, in front, forth, very, much, excessively, + ***ati*** = over, beyond, surpassing, exceedingly, very + ***bha*** = shine, a light or beam of light, luster, splendor, appearance, resemblance, likeness, to shine bright, to be beautiful or eminent, to be, exist, manifest

Pratibhad **implies perception that is more than our usual abilities allow. The roots of the word include: *bha* (light), *pra* (forward), and *ati* (surpassing, very). This describes a powerful moving forward – a breaking through – of light (wisdom) – a powerful, transformative insight.**

vā = or

sarvam = everything

all

3.35 By *samyama* on the heart, the center of an individual's consciousness, there arises full knowledge of the mind and its source.

hridaye citta-saṃvit

hridaye = heart (as the seat of emotions and sensations)

soul, mind (as the seat of mental operations), the center or core or essence or best or dearest or most secret part of anything (from the *Atharva Veda*), abode of the *Atma* (Self), true or divine knowledge, the *Veda*, science

citta = mind (See 1.2, 1.30, 1.33, 1.37, 2.54, 3.1, 3.9, 3.11–3.12, 3.19, 3.35, 3.39, 4.4–4.5, 4.15–4.18, 4.21, 4.23, 4.26)

Refer to 1.2 for more on *citta*.

saṃvit = full knowledge

full understanding, to perceive, to know together, know thoroughly, recognize, feel, taste, consciousness, Supreme Consciousness, an appointment or rendezvous, treaty, convention

from ***sam*** = together, along with, completely, absolutely + ***vid*** = to know

The heart is the root and seat of the mind. It is meditated on as the source and abode of the *Atma*, the Self within.

Translating *samvid* as "full knowledge" is meant to indicate a thorough, direct insight into the nature of the workings of the mind: its strengths, weaknesses, subconscious influences, and contents.

Now, look at some of the definitions of *samvid*. They include two words that seem out of place: *rendezvous, treaty*. The implication is that full knowledge is not only concerned with the depth of awareness, but integrating – bringing together – the various fluctuating facets of individual consciousness into a harmonious functioning whole. Going even further, there is an integration of the purified and integrated mind with the heart, the mind's source and anchor.

3.36 *Sattva* (the pure, luminous intellect) and the *Purusha* (the power of awareness) are distinct realities. The intellect exists for the *Purusha*. The *Purusha*, beyond the limit of the intellect, exists to express its own inherent and true meaning. Failure to perceive the distinction between the two is the cause of all experiences of pleasure and pain. By *samyama* on this distinction, knowledge of the *Purusha* is attained.

sattva-puruṣayor atyanta-asaṃkīrṇayoh pratyaya-aviśeṣaḥ bhogaḥ para-arthātva svartha-samyamāt-jñānam

sattva = intellect

clarity of mind, discernment, beingness, existence, true essence, nature, character, spiritual essence, spirit, mind, consciousness, strength, firmness, energy, resolution, courage, self-command, good sense, wisdom, magnanimity, the quality of purity and goodness (*sattva* renders the person true, honest, and wise and an object pure and clean), a living or sentient being, embryo, fetus, rudiment of life (See 2.41, 3.36, 3.50, 3.56)

Refer to 2.41 for more on *sattva*.

puruṣayoh = *Purusha* (See 1.16, 1.24, 3.36, 3.50, 3.56, 4.18, 4.34)

Refer to 1.16 for more on *Purusha*.

atyanta = pure

perfect, totally, absolute, endless, unbroken, perpetual, very great, beyond the proper end or limit, very strong

from ***ati*** = over, beyond, exceedingly, very + ***anta*** = end

asaṃkīrṇayoh = distinct

different, unmixed, not unclean, not confused, pure

from ***a*** = not + ***saṃkīrṇa*** = scattered, thrown (See 1.42)

pratyaya = perceive

cognition, intention, arising thought (See 1.10, 1.18–1.19, 2.20, 3.2, 4.27)

Refer to 1.10 for more on *pratyaya*.

aviśeṣaḥ = failure to perceive this distinction

indistinct, no difference (See 1.22, 2.19)

bhogaḥ = experience

worldly experience, enjoyment, eating (See 2.13)

from ***bhuj*** = to enjoy

para = (*refers to Purusha*)

another, other, different from (See 3.19)

arthātva = exists for

purpose, interest, due to the purpose, distinct from the purpose, due to the nature of its purpose, because of its aim, suitable to the object, fitting, full of reality, real, significant, according to a purpose from ***artha*** = purpose, utility, aim, as its object + ***tva*** = having the quality of (See 1.49)

svārtha = expressing its own inherent or true meaning

for its own sake, own purpose self, personal matter or advantage, having a natural or literal meaning, having similar merits, one's own affair, original meaning, adapted to its purpose (See 1.28)

from ***sva*** = self + ***artha*** = purpose, utility, aim

Philosophically, it is taught that anything that is a compound made up of several factors, does not exist for its own sake. For example, Phil builds a house (a composite of materials and forms). The house does not exist for itself, but for Phil. In the same way, the eye does not exist for its own purpose, but to serve the brain in order to attain vision, and the vision exists for the individual. The mind is made up of several functions (*manas, buddhi, ahamkara*), which are formed from the fundamental constituents of nature (*gunas*). As a composite, the mind also does not exist for itself, but for another: the *Purusha*, unchanging, non-composite consciousness.

Furthermore, if we look at two of the definitions of *svartha*, we can discover more hints regarding the mystery of *Purusha's* purpose...

It is a personal matter:

The reason that the *Purusha* exists is ultimately *Purusha's* private business. We say that *Purusha* exists to experience the seen and to express its nature, but *Purusha's* full nature is unknowable by the intellect. What we can know is that when our misperception regarding our own True Nature is removed, we experience an end to suffering (*duhkha*). See sutra 2.16.

It has similar merits:

This could suggest that *prakriti* (the seen) is as worthy as *Purusha*. This is a matter of equating the means with the goal. For example, we do this when we say, "I flew to Rome last week." The plane flew, we were passengers. We equate a necessary factor with the goal. This is an aspect found in Hindu philosophy. For example, we regard a Guru, a great sage, or saint as Divine (or divinely inspired) since a Guru shows the way to enlightenment.

Refer to sutra 2.21: The seen exists only for the purpose of the Seer.

samyamāt = by *samyama* (See 3.4, 3.16–3.17, 3.21–3.22, 3.27, 3.36, 3.42–3.43, 3.45, 3.48, 3.53)

Refer to 3.4 for more on *samyama*.

puruṣa = *left untranslated*

the Self, the power of seeing or awareness (See 1.16)

jñānam = knowledge (See 1.9, 1.38, 1.42, 2.28, 3.16–3.19, 3.26–3.27, 3.29, 3.36, 3.53, 3.55, 4.31)

Reflection

This sutra presents a central principle in Patanjali's Yoga. There are two fundamental aspects to life and our experience of it:

- Objects and sensations to experience that have no inherent consciousness
- The Seer – the pure, unbounded, eternal consciousness that experiences everything

In Yoga, the importance of discerning the difference between Seer and seen is made clear by the fact that there are 12 sutras in the final three chapters of the *Sutras* that deal with this topic. There is no Yoga practice, lifestyle, or attainment without making this fundamental distinction. Following are the twelve sutras:

2.18 The seen consists of the five elements and sense organs and has the qualities of translucence, activity, and inertia. Its purpose is to provide experiences and liberation.

2.20 The Seer is nothing but the sheer power of seeing, pure consciousness. Although it is pure and unchanging, it appears to have the qualities and contents of the mind.

2.21 The seen is worthwhile, beautiful, and pleasing since it has meaning – its nature and essence is truly for the purpose of experience and liberation.

2.22 For the liberated, the purpose of the seen – providing experiences and liberation – is fulfilled. It's as if it disappears, although it doesn't really vanish, since the experience of its reality and its relevance is common to others.[93]

2.23 Confusing the natures and powers of the Owner (Seer) and owned (seen) creates the condition for perceiving them as one.

2.24 Ignorance is the cause of confusing the Seer and seen as one.

2.25 Without ignorance, this confusion ceases to exist. The Seer stands apart from the seen as the Self. This is liberation (*kaivalya*).

2.26 The remedy that removes ignorance is an unwavering flow of discriminative discernment (*viveka*) that perceives the difference between the Seer and seen.

3.36 *Sattva*, the pure, luminous intellect, and the *Purusha*, the power of awareness, are distinct realities. The intellect exists for the *Purusha*. The *Purusha*, beyond the limit of the intellect, exists to express its own inherent and true meaning. Failure to perceive the distinction between the two is the cause of all experiences of pleasure and pain. By *samyama* on this distinction, knowledge of the *Purusha* is attained.

3.50 One who attains the capacity to discern the distinction between the clear, luminous state of *sattva* and the *Purusha,* without confusing the nature of each, attains supremacy over all states of being and becoming (omnipotence) and knowledge of all (omniscience).

4.25 For one who discerns the distinction between the mind and the *Atma* (Self), false or limited notions of self-identity cease forever.

[93] The idea here is that when something is no longer central to your life, it's as if it doesn't exist. For example, a long time vegetarian may not even notice the new burger restaurant that opened in their neighborhood. It's not that the restaurant is irrelevant. It provides food and employment for others. In that sense, it does have a certain limited relevance, even to a vegetarian. It just doesn't take up much mental space. It is peripheral to their life.

4.26 Then, the mind naturally inclines toward discriminative discernment and, not being far from liberation, gravitates[94] toward it.

We end this section by noting that the required discernment needed to distinguish Seer from seen, according to Patanajli, is *viveka* (2.26) and *viveka* can be attained by the practice of the eight limbs (2.29).

3.37 From this knowledge, the powers of intuitive hearing, touch, sight, taste, and smell are born spontaneously, without the practice of *samyama*.

tataḥ prātibha-śrāvana-vedana-ādarśa-āsvāda-vārtāḥ jāyante

tataḥ = from this

thence, hence

prātibha = intuitive

supernormal, vividness, divination, intuitive knowledge, to come into sight, to offer one's self, to appear to the mind, become clear or manifest, occur to (See 3.34)

from ***pra*** = before, forward, in front, forth, very, much, excessively + ***ati*** = over, beyond, surpassing, exceedingly, very + ***bha*** = shine, a light or beam of light, luster, splendor, appearance, resemblance, likeness, to shine bright, to be beautiful or eminent, to be, exist, manifest

śrāvana = hearing

relating to or perceived by the ear, audible, taught in the *Vedas*, causing to be heard, announcing, proclaiming, knowledge derived from hearing, clairaudience

from ***śru*** = to hear

vedana = touch

sensation, feeling, announcing, proclaiming, perception, knowledge, making known, finding, procuring, act of marrying, property, goods, higher touch

from ***vid*** = to know

[94] Gravitate, as understood in physics, nicely expresses the sense of grace suggested in this sutra. Gravitate means to move toward a center of gravity or other attractive force.

ādarśa = sight

seeing, act of perceiving by the eyes, clairvoyance, supersensory seeing

from ***a*** = hither + ***darśa***, from ***dṛś*** = to see

āsvāda = tasting

enjoying, eating, eating with relish, flavor, higher taste

from ***ā*** = hither + ***svād*** = eat, to taste well, be sweet or pleasant to, to taste with pleasure, relish, enjoy, delight in, to make palatable, season, to be wholesome

vārtāḥ = smell

from ***vṛt*** = to stir

jāyante = arises

from ***jan*** = to beget, to be born, produce, create, generate

3.38 Although these powers may be considered as great accomplishments to an outwardly directed mindset, they obstruct the highest *samadhi.*

te samādhau upasargā vyutthāne siddhayaḥ

te = these, they (refers to the *siddhis* or supernormal abilities)

samādhau = highest *samadhi* (See 1.20)

Since the supernormal powers are the result of *samyama*, which includes the practice of *samadhi*, this sutra is specifically referring to the highest *samadhi, nirbija samadhi.*

vupasargā = obstruct

obstacles, impediment, trouble, misfortune, a natural phenomenon considered as boding evil, eclipse of the sun or a star or the moon, a fit from being possessed by a demon, change occasioned by a disease, symptom of death

from ***upa*** = to unto + ***sarga***, from ***sṛj*** = create

vyutthāne = outwardly directed mindset

externalized state, in emergence, rising up, awakening, yielding, swerving from the right course, neglect of duties, independent action, a kind of dancing or gesticulation (See 3.9)

from ***vi*** = in two parts + ***ud*** = implies separation or disjunction + ***sthā*** = to stand

Refer to 3.9 for more on *vyutthana*.

siddhayaḥ = abilities

powers, accomplishments, perfections (See 2.43, 2.45, 3.38, 4.1)

Refer to 2.43 for more on *siddhi*.

3.39 When the subconscious impressions that bind the mind to the body are loosened, and the mind's pathway into and out of the body is perceived, one can join with (and function through) another's body.

bandha-kāraṇa-śaithilyāt pracāra-saṃvedanāt
ca cittasya para-śarīra-āveśaḥ

bandha = bind

bondage, holding, tying, fetter, damming (a river), capture, arrest, connection or intercourse with, uniting, combining, forming, producing, any configuration or position of the body (especially of the hands and feet), a mode of sexual union, bridging over the sea, obtainment of a body, conceiving, cherishing, feeling, a border, framework, enclosure, receptacle, the body, attachment to this world (See 3.1)

kāraṇa = (*refers to the subconscious impressions*)

cause, reason, the cause of anything, instrument, means, motive origin, principle, an element, elementary matter, an action, an organ of sense, agency, condition, the cause of being, cause of creation, the body

from ***kṛ*** = to do

śaithilyāt = loosened

relaxing (See 2.47)

pracāra = pathway into and out of

coming forth, showing oneself, manifestation, appearance, roaming, wandering, occurrence, application, employment, conduct, behavior, a playground, a place of exercise, pasture

from ***pra*** = before, forward, forth + ***cāra***, from ***cār*** = to move

saṃvedanāt = is perceived

consciousness, sensation, the act of perceiving or feeling, making known, communication, announcement, information

from ***sam*** = thorough, complete, together + ***vedana***, from ***vid*** = knowledge

ca = and

cittasya = the mind

consciousness, thinking, reflecting, imagining, thought, intention, aim, wish, the heart, memory, intelligence, reason

from *citta* (See 1.2, 1.30, 1.33, 1.37, 2.54, 3.1, 3.9, 3.11–3.12, 3.19, 3.35, 3.39, 4.4–4.5, 4.15–4.18, 4.21, 4.23, 4.26)

Refer to 1.2 for more on *citta*.

para = another

far, distant, remote (in space), opposite, beyond, on the other side of, extreme, former, future, past, next, following, subsequent, final, more than, highest, supreme, strange, foreign, alien, adverse, different from (See 3.19)

śarīra = body

support, supporter, that which is easily destroyed or dissolved, solid parts of the body, dead body

from ***śri*** = support or supporter, or from ***śṛ*** = that which is easily destroyed or dissolved, the body, frame, solid parts of the body, one's own person, a dead body

A word that is related to *sarira* is *sara*: the core, pith, or solid interior of anything; the chief component of the body.

āveśaḥ = join with

enter into, take possession of, entrance, penetrating, empowered, absorption of the faculties in one wish or idea, being intent, devotion to an object, frenzy, anger, indistinctness of an idea

from ***ā*** = hither, unto + ***veśa*** = a settler, small farmer, tenant, neighbor, a dependent, vassal, entrance, ingress, a house, dwelling, trade, business, house of prostitution, from ***viś*** = enter

Avesh is a name for Lord Vishnu and holds the meaning of intervening compassion. In Patanjali's Yoga, this suggests that the phenomenon of inhabiting another's body is a benevolent act.

A yogi entering another's body is not necessarily an invasion or a subjugation. It can be an act of subtle, but powerful, wordless communication, or of blessing or guidance directed to a sincere devotee or seeker. For those on the receiving end, many have benefited as a result of experiencing guidance or comfort from a benevolent consciousness—like one's *Ishta Devata*, for example (2.44).

Another example would be a Guru blessing the disciple through the transference of subtle spiritual energy. Such an act is based on mutual love, respect, and devotion between the Guru and disciple.[95] It is something like the influence asserted by loving parents, friends, and teachers. This aspect of the Guru-disciple relationship is powerful and transformative. Yet, within it lies the possibility of the abuse of that power – or the craving on the disciple's part – to have spiritual growth and enlightenment "gifted" to them, without their having to do the necessary inner work themselves.

There are two other important and valid views on the subject matter of this sutra. There was a time in India when yogis were feared. Some, calling themselves yogis, developed extraordinary powers (sometimes they were really magic tricks) but were criminals, kidnappers, and abusers of power. One of the powers that was most feared was their ability to take over someone's body. In the context of the *Yoga Sutras*, we can safely

[95] Love always includes a kind of union between lover and beloved. The lover yearns to, in some way, inhabit the beloved. It is an act of giving or joining, not of invasion. It only works when the beloved allows it to happen. Both give of and to each other. Although we can't say that this sutra is about this, it is not altogether separate from this reality. There are many stories, however, that tell of abuse of this power, when motivated by greed, lust, or power.

assume that Patanjali wouldn't approve. Though they were considered yogis, we would never agree.[96] See sutra 3.52 for Patanjali's warning about abusing powers.

The other take on this sutra is that if a seeker is to realize the Self as Cosmic Consciousness - as more than body and mind - they need to understand how the mind enters into and leaves the body. This could possibly be the reason why it was once widely held that unless a yogi could enter and leave a body at will, they would not succeed in Yoga.

3.40 Two versions are possible for this sutra. The first is more literal and is the one found in virtually every translation of the *Yoga Sutras*. The second seems more in harmony with the overall intent of the *Yoga Sutras*.

1) By mastery over *udana* (the upward moving current of *prana*) one moves, without obstruction, over the water, swamps, and thorns and there is a rising above them.

2) By mastery over *udana*, one moves through the world free from nonvirtuous acts, moral impurity, and confusion. This uplifting of consciousness brings transformation.

udāna-jayāt jala-paṅka-kaṇṭaka-adiṣhu asaṅgaḥ utkrāntiś ca

udāna = upward moving *prana*

from ***an*** = to breathe + ***ud*** = up + ***ā*** = toward

Udana is one of the five primary *pranas* (vital energies) in each individual. It directs the vital currents upward. It circulates in all of the limbs and joints and is associated with digestion. In states of meditation absorption (*samadhi*) *udana* also brings *prana* upward to the head. It is seated in the throat or palate. *Udana* is a stimulator of acupoints (*marma*).

jayāt = by mastery (See 2.41, 3.5, 3.40–3.41, 3.45, 3.48–3.49)

Refer to 2.41 for more on *jaya*.

[96] Yogis - for good or bad – have always been associated with great powers.

jala = water, stupid (translated as nonvirtuous acts)

a stupid man, of a man, any fluid

from ***jal*** = to be rich, to cover, to be sharp, to be stiff or dull

paṅka = swamp, moral impurity

mud, dirt, clay, ointment, sin, a kind of beard grass, fourth mansion

from ***pac*** = to spread

kaṇṭaka = thorn, an annoyance or source of confusion

anything pointed, the point of a pin, sting, a fish bone, horripilation, unevenness or roughness, a troublesome seditious person, a sharp stinging pain, fault or defect, detection of error, symptom of a disease, vexing or injurious speech, obstacle, impediment, name of makara (a marine monster, symbol of Kamadeva, the god of love in Hindusim – similar to cupid)

adiṣhu = etc.

and others, and so forth

asaṅgaḥ = free from

unattached, independent, moving without obstacles, having no attachment or inclination for or interest in

from **a** = not + ***saṅg***, from ***sañj*** = cling

utkrāntiḥ = rising, uplifting

power to levitate, stepping up, passing away, dying

from ***ud*** = up, upward + ***krānti*** = going, proceeding, step, overcoming, surpassing, attacking, the sun's course, from ***kram*** = to go across, go over, to climb, to stretch over, project over, tower above, to take possession of, to strive after, make effort for, to proceed well, advance, make progress, gain a footing, succeed, to have an effect, to step to and fro, to wander about, stride

ca = and

3.41 *Samana prana* is the vital energy that governs physical and mental transformation. By mastering it, one gains radiance of body and mind.

samāna-jayāt jvalanam

samāna = left untranslated

alike, similar, equal, same, holding the middle between two extremes, common, general, universal, virtuous, good, a friend

from ***sam*** = together + ***ana***, from ***an*** = to breathe

Samana prana is centered around the navel and is responsible for transformation. Its primary role is to collect and assimilate the *prana* obtained by breathing, eating, and mental activities. It harmonizes the *prana* and distributes it throughout the individual's system thereby empowering all aspects of life. When mastered, *samana prana* activates the *susumna nadi*, the main *pranic* channel that is associated with the higher states of consciousness.

Our vital energy (*prana*), when purified and increased through yogic practices and lifestyle, creates a special radiance of body. It emanates subtle currents of energy and can be seen in the eyes as increased happiness, focus, serenity, compassion, and kindness.

Peace, joy, and love are never private affairs. These great virtues will always seek to spread – and they do.

jayāt = mastery (See 2.41, 3.5, 3.40–3.41, 3.45, 3.48–3.49)

Refer to 2.41 for more on *jaya*.

jvalanam = radiance

effulgence, shining, fire, blazing

from ***jval*** = to blaze, burn, flame

The *Bhagavad Gita* (11.28–29) presents a powerful, almost violent image of *jvalanam* as the power of the Absolute to dissolve (destroy) all created beings and objects in order to return them to their source.

All the worlds rush into your mouths, like moths swiftly entering a blazing (jvalanam) fire to be destroyed.[97]

[97] Arjuna, the disciple, sees this as he gazes at Lord Krishna's cosmic form.

Jvalanam is not just a bright, shining light, it is a fire that wields the power of transformation. It can destroy darkness.

3.42 By *samyama* on the relationship between hearing and *akasha*, one can perceive sounds (such as the *pranava*, OM) through which divine knowledge is gained. (See 3.37)

śrotra-ākaśayoḥ sambandha-samyamāt-divyam śrotram

śrotra = hearing

ear, the act of hearing or listening to, familiarity with the *Vedas* or sacred knowledge in general

from ***sru*** = to hear, listen, attend on anything, to learn about or from anything, study, to hear from a teacher

ākaśayoḥ = ether

the subtle element of space, the first and most subtle of the elements, inner sky, sky, the ether, the atmosphere, a free or open space, the vehicle of life and sound that pervades the universe, the creator god Brahma

from ***ā*** = not, change of direction, but also: near, near to, toward + ***kāś*** = visible

Akasha (ether[98]) is the subtlest of the five physical elements and gives rise to the other four: earth, water, air, fire.[99] *Akasha* is all-pervasive and is outside time and three-dimensional space.

The word is also used to indicate the consciousness of the individual.

Akasha can be regarded as the organizing principle of the created universe. It is like a glue that binds aspects of creation together. It provides a handy way to describe the order we see in creation. Day and night follow each other in the same pattern: apple seeds always produce apple trees, etc. In this sense then, it is also a way of describing relationships in nature.

[98] *Akasha*, ether, is the subtlest of the five gross elements (*mahabhuta*): ether, air, fire, water, and earth that make up the material universe.

[99] In Jainism, the five elements are considered living beings.

sambandha = relationship

connection, union, association, to be attentive, to be obedient

from ***sam*** = with, together + ***bandh*** = to bind

samyamāt = by *samyama* (See 3.4, 3.16–3.17, 3.21–3.22, 3.27, 3.36, 3.42–3.43, 3.45, 3.48, 3.53)

Refer to 3.4 for more on *samyama*

divyam = divine

heavenly, wonderful, of divine nature, supernatural, magical, celestial, charming, beautiful, agreeable, the divine world or anything divine, celestial regions, sky

from ***div*** = to radiate

***Divyam* can be understood as perception arising from the grace of God, independent of the functioning of the senses.**

śrotram = perceive

hearing, ear (See above)

3.43 By *samyama* on the connection between the body and ether and from contemplative absorption (*samadhi*) on the lightness of cotton fiber, one can move unrestricted through space.

kāya-ākaśayoḥ sambandha-samyamāt-laghu-
tūla-samapātteh-ca ākaśa-gamanam

kāya = body

assemblage, trunk of a tree, the body of a lute (except the wires), house, habitation, natural temperament (See 2.43)

ākaśayoḥ = ether (See 3.42)

sambandha = relationship

connection, union, association (See 3.42)

from ***sam*** = with, together + ***bandh*** = to bind

samyamāt = by *samyama* (See 3.4, 3.16–3.17, 3.21–3.22, 3.27, 3.36, 3.42–3.43, 3.45, 3.48, 3.53)

Refer to 3.4 for more on *samyama*.

laghu = light

easy, not difficult

Because the movement is light and easy, it is translated here as *unrestricted.*

tūla = cotton fiber

tuft of grass or reeds, a loose, branching cluster of flowers

samapātteh = contemplative absorption

attainment, coming together, meeting, encountering, accident, chance, falling into any state or condition, getting, becoming, assuming an original form, completion, conclusion, yielding, giving way, state of becoming one (See 1.41–1.42, 2.47, 3.43)

Samapatteh is a synonym for *samadhi* (See 1.20)

ca = and

ākaśa = ether (See 3.42)

gamanam = moving

traveling, going, manner of going, departure, sexual intercourse, undergoing, attaining, going away, departure

from ***gam*** = to go, to go toward, to go to any state or condition

3.44 When the mind's activities are genuinely experienced as external – not limited – to the body, it is called the great bodiless awareness. From this experience, the veil that obscures the light of the pure *sattvic* mind is completely removed. (See 1.19, 2.52, 3.39)

bahir akalpitā vṛitter mahā-videhā tataḥ prakāśa-āvaraṇa-kṣayaḥ

bahir = external

outer, not essential, the external part, the preliminary part of a religious ceremony (See 3.8)

from ***bah*** = to bear down, endeavor, make effort, try + ***is*** = to move quickly, throw, let fly, send out, pour out

Looking at the roots of *bahir* suggests an experience of freedom and expansion that a simple translation such as "external" does not convey.

akalpitā = genuinely

not manufactured, not artificial, not pretended, natural, actual

from ***a*** = not + ***kalpitā*** = made, fabricated, artificial, invented, inferred, assumed, composed, from ***kḷp*** = be adapted

vṛitter = activity

the fluctuating, whirling excursions of the mind (See 1.2, 1.4–1.5, 1.10, 1.41, 2.11, 3.44, 4.18)

Refer to 1.2 for more on *vritti.*

mahā = great (See 2.31)

from ***maha*** = great, mighty, strong, abundant, the festival of spring, light, luster, brilliance, great deeds

videhā = bodilessness

out-of-body

from ***vi*** = divided, asunder, apart, different + ***dehā*** = form, shape, mass, bulk, person, individual, appearance (See 1.19)

tataḥ = from this

by that

prakāśa = light of pure sattvic mind

illumination, splendor, brightness, pure consciousness, visible, clear, manifest, open, public, expanded, universally noted, before the eyes of all, appearance, display, manifestation, diffusion, laughter, it is the principle by which everything else is known, the principle of self-revelation, self-shining conscious light and its ability to hold a reflection of itself (See 2.18, 2.52, 3.21, 3.44)

In this sutra, *prakasha* refers to the pure light of the *sattvic buddhi* (the discriminative faculty of the mind), the first evolute of *prakriti.*

āvaraṇa = veil

covering, concealing (See 2.52)

from ***ā*** = not + ***vṛ*** = to cover

Sage Vyasa states that *avarana* refers to karmic residue, the *samskaras, rajas,* and *tamas.*

kṣayaḥ = completely removed

destruction or dwindling, wearing away, loss

from ***kṣi*** = to destroy, to remain, be quiet, going, moving, corrupt, ruin, make an end of, kill, injure, to diminish, decrease, wane, waste away, perish, to pass (said of the night), destruction (See 2.28)

3.45 Mastery over the elements is gained by *samyama* on their:

- **Gross form – that which can be perceived by the senses**
- **Essential character – the special features that distinguish one element from another[100]**
- **Subtle form – the essence or potential that gives rise to the material elements[101]**
- **Relationship to the *gunas* – which are common to all objects**
- **Purpose for being – which is to bring experience and liberation to the *Purusha* (See 2.18)**

sthūla-svarūpa-sūkṣma-anvaya-arthavattva-samyamat bhūta-jayaḥ

sthūla = gross form

[100] These are qualities such as the solidity of rock, the heat of fire, and liquidity of water.

[100] This refers to the *tanmatras*: sound, touch, sight, taste, and smell. These are the smallest elements from which the grosser ones are formed. They cannot be directly perceived by the senses. They take up no space and are perceived in the domain of time as experience and change. *Tanmatra*, from *tad* (that) and *ma* (to measure).

coarse, solid, material

svarūpa = essential character

one's own peculiar form or shape or nature or, the form or shape of, own condition, peculiarity, similar, like (in Samkhya philosophy), having a like nature, pleasing, handsome, wise, learned (See 1.3, 1.43, 2.23, 2.54, 3.3, 3.45, 3.48, 4.34)

The essential character of the elements is subtler than the subtle elements themselves. It is the essence of a thing: solidity of a rock, liquidity of water, etc.

Refer to 1.3 for more on *svarupa*.

sūkṣma = subtle form (See 1.44)

anvaya = relationship

correlative, connection, following, succession, association, being linked to or concerned with, logical connection of cause and effect (See 3.9)

This refers to the relationship of the elements to the *gunas,* which are common to all objects.

arthavattva = purpose

significance, importance

from ***artha*** = purpose + ***vat*** = suffix indicating possession + ***tva*** = suffix indicating having the quality of

Purpose refers to the *why* of matter, which is for the sake of the Seer. (See 2.18)

samyamāt = by *samyama* (See 3.4, 3.16–3.17, 3.21–3.22, 3.27, 3.36, 3.42–3.43, 3.45, 3.48, 3.53)

Refer to 3.4 for more on *samyama*.

bhūta = elements (See 2.18)

jayaḥ = mastery (See 2.41, 3.5, 3.40–3.41, 3.45, 3.48–3.49)

Refer to 2.41 for more on *jaya*.

3.46 From that *samyama* arises powers such as the ability to become minute, perfection of the body, and freedom from the limitations of the elements that form it.

tataḥ-anima-ādi-prādurbhāvah kāya-sampad
tad-dharma anabhighātaś-ca

The perfection referred to in this sutra is not a theoretical ideal, but a practical reality. Several of the definitions of *sampad* imply this: *condition for success, accomplishment, fulfillment, wealth.*

Perfection of the body is not attaining a model's or athlete's physique. It is a state of physical resilience, stamina, and harmony that becomes the support for spiritual progress. The next sutra expands on this.

tataḥ = from that

from that, hence, as a result of this

anima = minuteness

small as an atom, fineness, thinness, atomic nature, the smallest particle

from ***anu*** = atom

ādi = as well as

etc., so forth

prādurbhāvah = manifest

appearance, that which is visible (See 3.9)

kāya = body (See 2.43)

sampad = perfection

to happen well, succeed, prosper, accrue to, amount to, to become full or complete (as a number), to meet or unite with, obtain, get into, partake of, be absorbed in, be born, arise, to be produced, to be conducive to, to transform, to make or turn into, to provide or furnish with, to procure for, to ponder on, deliberate, to agree, completion, fulfillment, a condition of success, agreement, stipulation, equalization of similar things, blessing, right condition or method, correctness, excellence, glory, splendor, beauty, abundance, high degree, fate, riches, wealth, success, accomplishment

from ***sam*** = together + ***pad*** = go

tat = that

dharma = form

nature, character, essential quality, that which is established or held, virtue, religion, visible characteristics, functions (See 3.13–3.14, 4.12)

from ***dhr*** = to hold, uphold, establish, support

Dharma literally translates as *that which holds together. Dharma* is the basis of order, whether physical, social, moral, or spiritual. The word is also used to mean: mark, sign, token, essential attributes, nature's properties.

Refer to 3.13 for more on *dharma*.

anabhighātaḥ = freedom from

undisturbed, not assaulted, not attacking, not assailing, absence of limitations, nonaffliction (See 2.48)

from ***an*** = not + ***abhi*** = to, unto + ***ghata***, from ***han*** = strike, kill

ca = and

3.47 Perfection of the body is to have (or, you can use: means to have) a physical form that is solid, well-proportioned, and stable. Such a body possesses potent strength and radiates gracefulness.

rūpa-lāvanya-bala-vajra-saṃhananatvāni kāya-sampad

rūpa = form

appearance, figure, likeness, shape, feature, any outward appearance, phenomenon, or color (See 1.8)

lāvanya = gracefulness

salt, the taste or property of salt, beauty, loveliness, charm, agility, poise, balance, grace

"Grace," one of the definitions of *lavanya*, is worthy to reflect upon. Grace is from the Latin, *gratus*, which means "pleasing." It relates to posture and movement that has no appearance of difficulty. It is the easy flow of subtle matter expressing through the grosser matter of the body.

Another definition of *lavanya* is *salt*. Salt is fire born of water (through evaporation), so salt is both an essence and opposite of water. In Tantra, a grain of salt dissolved in water symbolized the reintegration of the ego into the Self. Salt preserves food (making it a symbol for incorruptability), but it is corrosive to many materials. Since it can either preserve or destroy, salt can refer to the laws of physical, moral, and spiritual transformation. Salt can also symbolize infertility because when it is poured over land it can no longer produce crops.

bala = potent strength

vigor, force, power, semen, virile, military force, an army, expertise in

from ***bal*** = to breathe, live

Bala is potent strength, not just blind power. It is the strength to attain spiritual goals and to accomplish good for others.

Bala is traditionally one of the six glorious features of *Ishvara,* along with *jnana* (wisdom), *shakti* (potency), *aisvarya* (Lordship), *virya* (valor), and *tejas* (splendor).

vajra = stable

thunderbolt, hard, mighty, adamantine (unbreakable)

from ***vaj*** = be strong

Vajra as *thunderbolt*, can mean any thunderbolt, but it is especially associated with the thunderbolt weapon of the god Indra. It is said to have been formed out of the bones of sages. This thunderbolt is depicted in the form of a discus, or in later times as having the form of two transverse bolts in an "x" shape. From this concept, *vajra* evolved as a term that refers to any mythical weapon that destroys spells or charms.

Vajra can also refer to a diamond, which was thought to be of the same substance as a thunderbolt.

Other meanings for *vajra* include: a kind of talc, a form of penance (one month of eating barley prepared with cow's urine[102]), sour gruel, a kind of column or pillar, hard mortar or cement.

In Buddhism, both the thunderbolt and diamond refer to the indivisible and imperishable nature of enlightenment.

saṃhananatvāni = solid

compact, robustness, firmness, steadfastness, robustness, agreement, harmony

from ***sam*** = together + ***hanana***, from ***han*** = strike + ***tva*** = suffix denoting having the quality of

kāya = body (See 2.43)

sampad = perfection

to happen well, succeed, prosper, accrue to, amount to, to become full or complete (as a number), to meet or unite with, obtain, get into, partake of, be absorbed in, be born, arise, to be produced, to be conducive to, to transform, to make or turn into, to provide or furnish with, to procure for, to ponder on, deliberate, to agree, completion, fulfillment, a condition of success, agreement, stipulation, equalization of similar things, blessing, right condition or method, correctness, excellence, glory, splendor, beauty, abundance, high degree, fate, riches, wealth, success, accomplishment (See 3.46)

from ***sam*** = together + ***pad*** = go

3.48 By *samyama* on the essential nature of the senses – the factors that work together to create sense perception – mastery over the sense organs is gained. These factors are:

- **Reception of input: the mind (*manas*) responds to stimuli through the sense organs**
- **Illumination: *sattva*,[103] the precursor and essential nature of the sense organs. It illumines the process of perception with the light of consciousness.**

[102] This is a recipe that doesn't appeal.

[103] *Sattva* is the basis of the principle of perception.

- **Ego sense: identification of sense experiences as self**
- **Interconnected relationship: as products of the *gunas*, the above three aspects work together**
- **Purpose: to give experiences and liberation to the *Purusha* (See 2.18)**

grahaṇa-svarūpa-asmitā anvaya-arthavattva
vsamyamad indriya-jayaḥ

One of the key words of this sutra is *svarupa* (essential nature), which refers to the essential nature – the mechanics – of perception.

The senses too often drag around our minds, carrying with them our good intentions and better judgment. The question being answered here is, How, or where, can we intervene in this sense process to attain mastery over them? The answer is, Not at the sense organ level, although that is where we usually begin. The ultimate remedy for uncontrolled senses is not on the physical organ level. Mastery lies in understanding the subtle aspect of senses, that part of the senses that continues to operate in our imagination or in dreams. In our mind's eye, we can see a sweet apple pie – we can even taste it. The inner recesses of the mind are where the root and power of sense perception lies. Sense management is cultivated on that deep level of consciousness. (See 3.49)

While meditation is the prescription given here, we can also cultivate mastery through other yogic practices, including devotional practices, selfless service, deep introspection, and study.

grahaṇa = reception

grasping, power of perception (See 1.41)

svarūpa = essential nature

own-form (See 1.3, 1.43, 2.23, 2.54, 3.3, 3.45, 3.48, 4.34)

Refer to 1.3 for more on *svarupa*.

asmitā = ego sense (See 1.17)

anvaya = interconnected relationship

following, succession, connection, associated, being linked or connected with, logical connection of cause and effect, conclusion, end product (See 3.9)

from ***anu*** = along, after + ***aya***, from ***i*** = to go

arthavattva = purpose

significance (See 3.44)

samyamat = by *samyama* (See 3.4, 3.16–3.17, 3.21–3.22, 3.27, 3.36, 3.42–3.43, 3.45, 3.48, 3.53)

Refer to 3.4 for more on *samyama*.

indriya = sense organs

senses (See 2.18)

jayaḥ = mastery (See 2.41, 3.5, 3.40–3.41, 3.45, 3.48–3.49)

Refer to 2.41 for more on *jaya*.

3.49 From mastery over the senses, one gains swiftness of mind. This is a state with, the capacity for sense perception, without the aid of the sense organs – and mastery over primordial matter (*prakriti*).

tataḥ mano-javitvaṁ vikaraṇa-bhāvaḥ pradhāna-jayaś ca

The sense organs ultimately limit the extent and reach of consciousness and mastery over undifferentiated *prakriti*.

tataḥ = from

thence, as a result

mano = mind (See 1.35, 2.53, 3.49)

Refer to 1.35 for more on *manas*.

javitvaṁ = swiftness

fast movement, speed, having the quality or condition of moving swiftly

from ***jā*** = speedy, swift, victorious, eaten, enjoyment, light, luster + ***i*** = to go, walk, flow, to blow, to advance, spread, get about, to go to or toward, to go away, escape, pass, retire, to arise from, to return, to succeed, reach, obtain, come to, approach with prayers, gain by asking, to undertake anything, go on with, to appear, to go quickly or repeatedly, to ask, request + ***tva*** = the quality of

Javitvam **is another indication of the theme of light that pervades the *Sutras*. Its secondary meaning (from *jav*) is *luster, light*. In the context of the *Sutras*, it indicates the quality of awareness: clear, quick, observant.**

The mind can attain the speed of light!

vikaraṇa = without the aid of sense organs

deprived of organs of sense, independence, change, modification, a disturbing influence

from ***vi*** = asunder, away + ***karana*** = organ of senses, change, scribe, helper, companion, making, affecting, doing, from ***kṛ*** = to do

Looking at the root *(karana)*, we can see that this state of mastery enables perception, without the sense organs as mediators. As constant companions all through our lives, we have assumed that without these organs, we would be deprived of the input of the outside world. Not so, declares Patanjali.

bhāvaḥ = state

becoming, being, existing, true state or condition, temperament, nature, way of thinking, disposition

from ***bhū*** = to be

pradhāna = primordial matter

primary cause, originator, original source of what is manifest, *prakriti*

from ***pra*** = before, forward + ***dhāna***, from ***dhā*** = put

jaya = mastery (See 2.41, 3.5, 3.40–3.41, 3.45, 3.48–3.49)

Refer to 2.41 for more on *jaya*.

ca = and

3.50 One who attains the capacity to discern the distinction between the clear, luminous state of *sattva* and the *Purusha,* without confusing the nature of each, attains supremacy over all states of being and becoming (omnipotence) and knowledge of all (omniscience).[104] (See 4.25)

sattva-puruṣa-anyatā-khyāti-mātrasya sarva-bhāva adhiṣṭhāṛtitvaṃ-jñatṛitvaṃ ca

sattva = clear, luminous

lightness, being-ness, existence, pure intellect, the basis of the process of perception (See 2.41, 3.36, 3.50, 3.56)

from ***sat*** = existence + ***tva*** = indicating having the quality of

Refer to 2.41 for more on *sattva*.

puruṣa = *left untranslated*

Self (See 1.16, 1.24, 3.36, 3.50, 3.56, 4.18, 4.34)

Refer to 1.16 for more on *Purusha*.

anyatā = distinction

difference

from ***anya*** = other + ***tā*** = feminine suffix meaning "having the power of"

khyāti = discernment

knowledge, vision (See 1.16)

from ***khyā*** = to be known, to be named, to make known, promulgate, proclaim, to relate, tell, say, declare, betray, denounce, from ***kyā*** = to see

[104] Omniscience is not knowledge of everything in the usual sense. Enlightenment does not bring knowledge of how to build a satellite, for example. In a spiritual context, omniscience means both knowing what needs to be known to ensure unshakable peace and freedom from suffering, and knowing the source and essence of all creation.

mātrasya = without

only, of only, merely, being nothing but (See 1.43)

from ***mātra*** = an element, measure, quantity, sum size, duration, measure of any kind, a finger's breadth, the whole or totality, the one thing and no more, nothing but, entirely, only, possessing only as much as or no more than, amounting only to, being nothing but, simply or merely

sarva = all (See 1.25)

bhāva = state of being and becoming (See 1.28, 2.2, 2.33–2.34, 3.49–3.50, 4.25)

Refer to 1.28 for more on *bhava*.

adhiṣṭhāṛtitvaṃ = supremacy

sovereignty, rulership, supremacy over

from ***adhi*** = over, on + ***ṣṭhāṛ***, from ***sthā*** = to stand + ***tṛ*** = a suffix indicating the cause of an action + ***tvam*** = suffix meaning, "having the quality of"

sarva = all (See 1.25)

jñatṛitvaṃ = knowledge

literally, the quality stemming from being a knower

from ***jñā*** = to know + ***tṛ*** = suffix indicating the cause of an action + ***tvam*** = suffix meaning, "having the quality of"

Refer to 1.9 for more on *jnana*.

ca = and

3.51 By nonattachment to even omnipotence and omniscience, ignorance (the seed of all the root obstructions, *klesas*) is destroyed and liberation is experienced.

tad-vairāgyāt api doṣa-bīja-kṣaye kaivalyaṃ

tad = this

vairāgyāt = nonattachment (See 1.12)

api = even

doṣa = obstruction

impediment, detriment, fault, defects, evening, darkness, vice, deficiency, want, disadvantage, sinfulness, wickedness, transgression, guilt, damage, harm, detrimental effect, disease, morbid element

from ***duṣ*** = to be impaired, spoil, to become corrupted or impure, be wrong, to spoil or corrupt the mind

Dosa is another way of referring to the root causes of suffering, the *klesas*.

bīja = seed (of plants)

semen, any primary cause or principle, source, origin, truth (as the seed or cause of being), anything serving as a receptacle or support (See 1.25)

Bija is of uncertain origin.

kṣaye = destroyed

dwindling, wearing away, loss (See 2.28)

from ***kṣi*** = to destroy, to remain, be quiet, going, moving, corrupt, ruin, make an end of, kill, injure, to diminish, decrease, wane, waste away, perish, to pass (said of the night)

Looking at the last definition (to pass like the night) we can see that *ksaye* can imply that the passing of ignorance is inevitable. The night always gives way to daylight.

kaivalyaṃ = liberation

independence, isolation (See 2.25, 3.51, 3.56, 4.26, 4.34)

Refer to 2.25 for more on *kaivalya*.

3.52 Invitations to display supernormal accomplishments (*siddhis*) should be rejected, whether extended by those of high social status, those in authority, or by celestial beings who promise the joys of heaven. Fostered by adulation and flattery, such associations could generate undesirable consequences: renewed worldly attachment, arrogance, and pride.

sthāni-upanimantraṇe saṅga-smaya-akaraṇam punah aniṣṭa-prasaṅgāt

sthāni = celestial, well-established, having a place, those in authority

being in the right place, well-placed

from ***sthā*** = to stand

Several of the possible definitions of *sthani* have been included in this translation. This reflects the historical fact that yogis (or those who were referred to as yogis) were often sought out and tempted by royalty to use – or misuse – their extraordinary abilities to increase royal wealth, fame, and power.

upanimantraṇe = invitation

admiration, offer

from ***upa*** = to unto + ***ni*** = inward, within, down, back + ***mantraṇa*** = consultation, a summons, calling, from ***mantra*** = sacred speech, from ***man*** = to think

saṅga = attachment

sticking, clinging to, touch, contact with, relation to, association with, addiction to, devotion to, propensity for, especially worldly or selfish attachment or affection, desire, wish

smaya = pride, arrogance

smile

from ***smi*** = to smile

akaraṇam = rejecting

not doing, not accepting, absence of cause (See 3.37)

from ***a*** = not + ***kṛ*** = to make, to do

punah = renew

again, indulge

aniṣṭa = undesirable

unwanted, not wished for, disadvantageous, unfavorable, bad, wrong, evil, ominous

from ***an*** = not + ***iṣṭa***, from ***iṣ*** = to wish

prasaṅgāt = contact

association, devotion to, attachment, adherence, inclination to, indulgence in, fondness for, occupation with, evil inclination, connection, all that is connected with or results from anything, occurrence of a possibility, an occasion, when the occasion presents itself, a secondary or subsidiary incident

from ***pra*** = before, forward + ***sanga***, from ***sanj*** = to adhere to, to cling

3.53 By *samyama* on the present moment and on the moments that follow, intuitive knowledge born of discriminative discernment (*viveka*) arises.

kṣaṇa-tat-kramayoḥ saṃayamāt viveka-jaṃ jñānam

This sutra can be considered one on mindfulness – an attentive state of mind/awareness that resists getting sidetracked or lost in distractions, memories, daydreams, or fears. An inattentive state of mind can bring regrets for opportunities missed or fumbled, a longing for past pleasures, or obsessing over a future that can never be controlled. It's not so much that the past and future are enemies of peace of mind, instead they can obstruct the loss of lessons, insights, peace, and harmony that the present moment offers.

Because the knowledge arises from *viveka*, it is unlike that gained through study of sacred wisdom. One experiences direct contact with truths, and intuitive insights born of a superconscious state. This is a key accomplishment, as we will see in the next sutra. It is the door to liberation.

kṣaṇa = moment

an instantaneous point of time, instant, a leisure moment, vacant time, leisure, wait patiently for, a fit or suitable moment, opportunity, dependence, the center or middle (See 3.9)

tad = its (*refers to the sequential flow of changes*)

kramayoḥ = sequence

succession, a step, going, proceeding, course, the way, a position taken by an animal before springing, uninterrupted or regular progress, order, series, method, manner, rule sanctioned by tradition, power, strength, according to order to rank (See 3.15)

saṃayamāt = by *samyama* (See 3.4, 3.16–3.17, 3.21–3.22, 3.27, 3.36, 3.42–3.43, 3.45, 3.53)

Refer to 3.4 for more on *samyama*.

viveka = discrimination

discernment, distinguishing, separated, kept apart, examining, investigating, judicious, prudent (See 2.15, 2.26, 2.28, 3.53, 3.55, 4.26, 4.29)

from ***vi*** = apart + ***vekin***, from ***vic*** = divide, distinguish, sift + ***in*** = possessive suffix

Refer to 2.15 for more on *viveka*.

jaṃ = gained

born of (See 1.50)

jñānam = knowledge (See 1.9, 1.38, 1.42, 2.28, 3.16–3.19, 3.26–3.27, 3.29, 3.36, 3.53, 3.55, 4.31)

Refer to 1.9. for more on *jnanam*.

3.54 This intuitive knowledge gives rise to the ability to discern the difference between *sattva* and *Purusha*: two things that are almost identical, that cannot be distinguished by origin, characteristics, and location.

jāti-lakṣaṇa-deśair anyatā anavaccedāt tulayoḥ tataḥ pratipattiḥ

Those that know others are clever.
Those that know themselves have discernment.
– Tao Te Ching

In Patanjali's teachings, the number two holds special significance since it reminds us of one of the Sutras' central teachings: the distinction between pure consciousness (*Purusha*) and *sattva* (pure mind).

This is a titanic task, especially when considering that *sattva* - subjectively and insistently - appears to have consciousness as its nature. We can therefore infer that this sutra is about having developed the height of intuitive insight, *yoga pratyaksha*, yogic vision.

This necessary insight is the reason yogis meditate daily. Each day of practice may not seem up to the task, but each meditation session contributes to a brook that becomes a rivulet, eventually becoming a mighty river of focused light-filled awareness - and it all begins with a trickle.

Patanjali mentions that there are three indistinguishable factors shared by the *sattvic* (pure) mind and the Self (*Purusha*). He states that they *cannot* be distinguished by origin, characteristics, and location. Let's look at the three:

- Origin: the source of both the *sattvic* mind and *Purusha* are either the same or so close in nature as to be without any difference
- Characteristics: for both the *sattvic* mind and *Purusha*, the shared characteristic is consciousness, the light of awareness (as essence or as reflected on the mind), the experience of pure existence
- Location: as far as we - as individuals - are concerned, both seem to be located within

This emphasizes that the intuitive knowledge born of *viveka* (See 3.53) is not an ordinary knowledge, the result of a thought process, but is a transcendent intuitive knowledge utterly without the influence of ego. It is the highest degree of discernment wedded to the highest degree of nonattachment.[105]

jāti = origin

birth, production, rebirth, the form of existence (human, animal, etc.) determined by birth, position assigned by caste, family, rank, lineage, or race, natural disposition, genuine or true state of anything, generic properties (See 2.13)

[105] Refer to 1.15, 1.16, and 3.51 for nonattachment, and 2.26 and 2.29 for *viveka*.

from ***jam*** = to beget, to be born

lakṣaṇa = characteristics

mark, sign, symbol, definition, designation (See 3.13)

from ***lakṣ*** = to recognize, perceive, observe, to indicate or express indirectly

***Laksana* is the secondary meaning or characteristic of an object that is revealed over time.**

deśair = location

position, place

from ***diś*** = direction, quarter or region pointed at, direction, place, to point out, show exhibit, to produce, bring forward, promote, communicate

anyatā = difference

distinction (See 3.50)

from ***anya*** = other + ***tā*** = feminine suffix meaning "having the power of"

anavaccedāt = cannot be distinguished by

not being cut or limited or separated, unconditioned (See 1.26)

from ***an*** = not + ***ava*** = down, from, away, favor, off + ***cheda*** = cutting off, interrupting, from chid = cut, amputate

tulayoḥ = similar

identical, same, equal (See 3.12)

from ***tul***= weigh

tataḥ = from that

hence, thus (See 1.22)

pratipattiḥ = discern

perceive, distinguishable, observation, ascertainment, acknowledgment

from ***prati*** = against, back + ***patti***, from ***pad*** = go

3.55 Knowledge born of intuitive discernment (*viveka*) is transcendent and liberating. Free from the bonds of time, it encompasses all objects in all conditions simultaneously. (See 4.25–4.26, 4.33)

tārakam sarva-viṣayam sarvathā viṣayam
akramaṃ ca iti viveka-jaṃ jñānam

tārakam = transcendent and liberating

enabling one to cross over, rescuing, saving, a float, a raft

from ***tāra*** = protector, from ***vṛ*** = to pass

Tarakam is sometimes translated or referred to as the *deliverer*, a term that resonates with the Judeo-Christian faith traditions (Moses as the Deliverer and Jesus as the Savior) and has the sense of *being rescued* or *to be set free from.*

For the yogi, knowledge born of intuitive discernment is the deliverer. The essence of this principle is that all human beings need grace in some form to help lift them out of ignorance. *Viveka* is not grace, but prepares the yogi to receive grace (See 4.25 and 4.26). But before it manifests in its most subtle forms, grace is found in the form of the great spiritual masters (*Ishvara* is the Guru of even the most ancient Gurus. See 1.26).

sarva = all (See 1.25)

viṣayam = object

condition (See 1.11)

sarvathā = free from bonds of time (past, present, future)

at all times, in all (ways, conditions), in every way or respect

from ***sarva*** = all + ***thā*** = temporal suffix

viṣayam = condition

objects (See 1.11)

akrama = in the present moment

at the same moment, without succession, simultaneous

from ***a*** = not + ***kram*** = succession, series, order, happening at once

ca = and

iti = this

thus

viveka = discriminative discernment (See 2.15, 2.26, 2.28, 3.53, 3.55, 4.26, 4.29)

Refer to 2.15 for more on *viveka.*

jaṃ = born (See 1.50)

jñānam = intuitive knowledge (See 1.9, 1.38, 1.42, 2.28, 3.16–3.19, 3.26–3.27, 3.29, 3.36, 3.53, 3.55, 4.31)

The word "*intuitive*" is added to indicate that this knowledge is not the result of gaining information through sacred wisdom sources or from a logical progression of thought. It is the result of the supra-rational insight experienced in *samadhi.*

Refer to 1.9 for more on *jnanam.*

3.56 When the mind attains purity of *sattva* that is equal to the purity of the *Purusha* (Self), liberation (*kaivalya*) dawns.

sattva-puruṣayoḥ śuddhi-sāmye kaivalyaṃ

sattva = left untranslated

being, existence, entity, true essence, nature, disposition of mind, character, spiritual essence, mind, consciousness, energy, strength, resolution, courage, good sense, self-mastery, wisdom, pure, steady, goodness, illuminating, cheerful, joy, lightness, being-ness, existence, one of the primary constituents (*guna*) of nature, as a state of mind, it is lucidity itself without any taint of influence of conceptions or biases (See 2.41, 3.36, 3.50, 3.56) from ***sat*** = existence + ***tva*** = indicates having the quality of

Refer to 2.41 for more on *sattva*.

puruṣayoḥ = of the *Purusha*

true Self, Spirit, animating principle, pure consciousness, the Self (See 1.16, 1.24, 3.36, 3.50, 3.56, 4.18, 4.34)

may be from ***puru*** = a being connected with the sun

Refer to 1.16 for more on *Purusha*.

śuddhi = pure

correct, cleansed, purification, holiness, rendering secure, innocence (established by trial or ordeal), truth, clearness, certainty (See 2.20, 2.31, 3.56)

from ***śudh*** = purify, clean, to become clear or free from doubts, to be excused or free from blame

In this sutra, Patanjali gives us the ultimate requirement to attain *kaivalya* (liberation). So, it makes sense to pay close attention to it.

The key phrase is, "*When sattva* (the foundation of the mind) *attains purity equal to the purity of the Purusha*." We need to have a good grasp of what is meant by purity since it is what we need in order to attain liberation.

Key definitions of *suddhi* include:

- Clear
- Correct
- Without doubt

Patanjali has been teaching us about meditation and nonattachment as ways to attain clarity of mind. He has also taught us how to develop *viveka*, so that our vision of life and self is correct. Doubt is removed by intuitive insight and by faith and devotion (*Ishvara pranidhanam*).

We should address one more, very important requirement found among the definitions of *suddhi*: *to be free from blame*. We can take this on two different levels.

- To live a life firmly established in the *yamas* and *niyamas*.
- To have experienced the power of forgiveness: the forgiveness we direct to others, the forgiveness that is a matter of grace from our Source and Essence, and self-forgiveness.

It is an extraordinary person who fulfills all of the above – but that's what yogis are.

sāmye = equal

sameness, evenness

from ***sama*** = same

kaivalya = liberation

independence, isolation, aloneness, single, unitary, uncompounded, absolute freedom, total separation, transcendent aloneness (See 2.25, 3.51, 3.56, 4.26, 4.34)

from ***kevala*** = alone, not connected to anything

Refer to 2.25 for more on *kaivalya*.

Chapter Four

Kaivalya Pada

The Chapter on Liberation

4.1 Supernormal powers (*siddhis*) may also be born from practices performed in previous births, by herbs, mantra repetition, asceticism, or as a side-effect of contemplative absorption (*samadhi*).

janma-auṣadhi-mantra-tapaḥ-samādhi-jāḥ siddhayaḥ

janma = births

existence, life (See 2.12)

from ***jan*** = to beget, to be born, come into existence

auṣadhi = herbs

remedy, drug, plant

mantra = not translated

instrument of thought, sacred sound formula, speech, prayer, song of praise, mystical verse, sacred text, pious thoughts, magic formula, incantation, charm, spell (often used to attain supernormal powers), advice, resolution, secret, plan, design, messages, intimate discussions, initiation, the teachings of seers, *Vedic* hymns

from ***man*** = to think, evoke, call up or ***mnā*** = to utter + ***tra*** = faculty, save, rescue, protect, instrument of action, names of instruments of actions or sometimes names of places

The only instance that the word "mantra" appears in the *Sutras* is here, although in the first chapter, sutras 1.27 – 1.29, the practice of mantra repetition (*japa*) is presented. Since mantra repetition is also associated with study, refer to sutras 2.1, 2.32, 2.44.

A basic definition of mantra could be: sound syllables that resonate and tap into innate divine potentials and powers.

Mantras were received in deep meditation by inspired seers. Used in a focused, nonattached manner, they are vehicles to create, convey, and concentrate subtle forces and for communion with the essence of the aspect of divinity that is connected to the mantra. All sacred teachings, sacred texts, and the words of great spiritual masters hold the place of mantras in Yoga.

When we examine the roots of the word "mantra," we can see the associations it has with power, mystery, and divinity: *spell, song of praise, incantation, charm,* and *pious thought*.

We also find meanings of *advice, counsel,* and *design*. These definitions help explain mantra repetition's association with study in classic Yoga. Mantras open up areas of the mind and vistas of life that expand knowledge and wisdom.

Repetition of sounds, words, or texts are found in the practices of most faith traditions. Such repetition helps focus the mind, and can prepare it for deeper contemplative practices and to understand the subtle essence of spiritual teachings.

In Buddhism, mantras are sound syllables – sometimes including the name of a Buddha – that manifest certain cosmic forces and aspects of the Buddhas. In Vajrayana Buddhism, mantra is defined as that which protects the mind. It is also believed that repetition of mantras purifies one of the faults caused by speech. The repetition of mantras is usually accompanied by visualizations and bodily postures (*mudras*).

Mantras are also a central practice of Jainism. The most important of Jain mantras is the *Namokar Mantra* (also known as *Navkar*, or *Namaskar Mantra*). It is a series of five praises to great seers, teachers, and seekers everywhere and serves as a reminder of liberation from the delusion of ignorance.

Islam places great emphasis on mantra repetition, including the recitation of the ninety-nine names of Allah. Mantras are used to bring peace and prosperity.

tapaḥ = asceticism

austerity, self-discipline, creative heat, consuming by heat, causing pain or trouble, distressing, tormented by, warmth, an attendant of Lord Siva

(See 2.1, 2.15, 2.32, 2.43, 4.1)

from ***tap*** = to burn, to make hot

Refer to 2.1 for more on *tapas*.

samādhi = *left untranslated*

bringing into harmony, settlement, joining with, intense absorption, attention, joining or whole, accomplishment, conclusion, concentration of mind, union, concentration of thoughts, profound meditation, combining, intense application or fixing the mind on, attention (See 1.20, 1.46, 1.51, 2.2, 2.29, 2.45, 3.3, 3.11, 3.38, 4.1, 4.29)

Refer to 1.20 for more on *samadhi.*

jāḥ = arise

born, sprung from (See 1.50)

siddhayaḥ = supernormal powers

perfections, accomplishments, attainments, modes of success, supernormal powers (See 2.43, 2.45, 3.38, 4.1)

Refer to 2.43 for more on *siddhi.*

4.2 The transformations and attributes that manifest at each birth are the result of the inflow of the vast, innate potentials of *prakriti* under the influence of the individual's subconscious impressions (*samskaras*).

jāti-antara-pariṇāmah prakṛti-āpūrāt

jāti = birth

production, rebirth, the form of existence (as human, animal, etc.) determined by birth, position assigned by caste, family, rank, lineage, or race, natural disposition, genuine or true state of anything (See 2.13)

antara = each

other, another, interior, near, proximate, related, intimate, lying adjacent to, distant, different from, exterior, a hole, opening, the contents, soul, heart, supreme soul, interval, intermediate space or time, period, term, opportunity, occasion, place, remainder, peculiarity, weakness, weak side, representation, guarantee, respect, regard

pariṇāmah = transformation

change, alteration, evolution, development, ripeness, maturity, digestion, consequence, result, product, fullness (See 2.15, 3.9–3.13, 3.15–3.16, 4.2, 4.14, 4.32–4.33)

from ***pari*** = around, fully, before, abundantly + ***nam*** = to bend or bow

Refer to the notes on *apurat* (below) and to sutra 2.15 for more on *parinamah*.

prakṛti = *left untranslated*

making or placing before or at first, the original or natural form or condition of anything, original or primary substance, origin, nature, character, disposition, pattern, model. In Samkhya philosophy, *prakriti* is the original producer of the material world (consisting of the three *gunas*, it is also considered as the passive power of creating) (See 1.19, 4.2, 4.3)

from ***pra*** = before, forward + ***kṛiti*** = act of doing or creating, from ***kṛ*** = to do or make (this is also the root for karma)

Refer to 1.19. for more on *prakriti*.

āpūrāt = inflow, vast

overflow, excess, abundance, flooding, literally, to fill from into

from ***ā*** = to unto + ***pūra*** = filling, making full, fulfilling, satisfying, the swelling or rising of a river or of the sea, a large quantity of water, flood, a cake, a kind of breathing practice (*puraka*), the cleansing of a wound, a kind of incense, from ***pṛ*** = to fill

All objects are formed from *prakriti*. It is the substratum of all creation. The changes we observe in nature occur according to the innate potentialities of the object. Innate in the acorn is the oak tree.

In addition to the transformations we associate with the passage of time, changes are also brought about by environmental and external forces. The oak tree, in an unfavorable environment, may not grow as tall, or be as full and green, as one in a more supportive environment. We also can find change resulting from such external forces as drought, storms, lightning, insects, bacteria, and the impact of human activity.

Change, location, and external forces serve as instigators for manifestations of *prakriti*, which is ready to overflow into the changes (perceivable or not) and new forms that are being created. It is because of the effects of time, location, and other external factors that not all of the essential characteristics of an object manifest at once.

The essential orderliness of change is not to be overlooked. Gravity pulls objects toward the earth, fire burns (destroys or purifies), wind chills and blows objects over, acorns always produce oaks, never tomatoes. The order we see in *prakriti* is the reason it can be said that although *prakriti* has no consciousness of its own, it does display intelligence.

This transforming property of *prakriti* extends to the mind, also a part of material nature. Our innate potentials will arise given the proper internal and external environments. Hence, the centrality of the Yoga lifestyle and practice, supportive relationships, and conducive environments are essential to advancement in Yoga.

4.3 Efforts don't directly initiate this inflow. Effort, like a farmer removing obstacles to the flow of water, removes obstacles to the evolutionary streams of nature (*prakriti*).

nimittam aprayokakam prakṛtīnām varaṇa-bhedas
tu tataḥ kṣetrikavat

nimittam = not directly

incidental cause, motive, ground, reason, instrumental cause, because of, on account of

from ***ni*** = down, into + ***mitta***, from ***mā*** = to measure

aprayokakam = not initiated

not due to, not causing an effect, not prompting, or instigating

from ***a*** = not + ***pra*** = before + ***yojaka***, from ***yuj*** = to yoke

prakṛtīnām = left untranslated

prakriti, nature, manifestations, process of evolution, material forces (See 1.9, 4.2–4.3)

Prakriti is in the plural form in this sutra, which is why in this translation, "streams" is plural. This reflects the various primary and secondary evolutes and differentiations of primordial matter. More specifically, it refers to the five elements that form the body (the *prakritis* of the body)[106] and the ego sense (the *prakriti* of the senses). These *prakritis* follow the individual from birth to birth.

Prakriti's nature is to manifest its potentials. The way of creation is that potentials manifest as obstacles are removed. The shell of the acorn protects it, but is also an obstacle to unfolding its potential as the oak tree. Water, the minerals of earth, and the warmth of the sun remove those obstacles.

Our efforts don't cause the potentialities of *prakriti* to manifest and express itself as change. Effort is not the initiator of manifestations, but serves as channels for them.

Refer to 1.19 for more on *prakriti*.

varaṇa = obstacles

surrounding, enclosing so as to limit, wall, choice, covering, possibility, embankment, to keep off, prohibit, bridge

from ***vṛ*** = to cover, to choose, restrain, prevent, hidden, keep back

bhedaḥ = remove

separation, division, distinction, breaking, tearing, breaking open

from ***bhid*** = to split, distinguish, discriminate, to be opened (as in hands or eyes)

Obstacles are factors that veil or obstruct the experience of higher truths, which are not realities to be gained, just uncovered. They are eternally present. That's why much of the Yoga life and practices revolve around removing obstacles. Our True Nature is already in us as *us*. We don't create unshakable serenity and joy. We unveil it by removing obstacles.

---

106 The five elements are: ether, air, water, fire, and earth. They represent essential qualities of the one *prakriti*. They can also be understood as a further elaboration of the theory of the three *gunas*: *sattva* (balance), *rajas* (activity), *tamas* (inertia).

This sutra reminds us not to get caught in the trap of reducing Yoga to its practices. If we do that, we are in danger of becoming more focused on satisfying the ego's need to do the right thing. Consuming yourself with doing the right thing is most often the mind trying to control nature. "If I do the right thing, then I can control and determine the outcome of my efforts." Instead, we should be in right relationship, which is based on knowledge, effort, and acceptance. Life is more like a dance we need to learn to enjoy than a court case we need to win.

Our ultimate worth is not rooted in performance. Our worth is divine in nature and is already fully present within. My Guru summarized spiritual life in a beautiful and simple, but powerful way:

Peace is your nature, do not disturb it.
–Sri Swami Satchidananda

tu = but

tataḥ = instead

from that, hence

kṣetrikavat = like a farmer

like the owner of a field

from ***ksetra*** = field + ***ika*** = possessive suffix + ***vat*** = suffix indicating likeness

Now, a little history of irrigation in Patanjali's time. It will illumine a subtlety of this sutra.

Most farmers constructed earthen reservoirs for irrigating their fields. These earthen canals were not stable. They needed to be continuously maintained in order to control weed growth and to repair damage done by animals and from erosion. Why mention this?

Patanjali's students would have been very familiar with how farmers had to toil to maintain their irrigation systems. Although this sutra might conjure an image of a farmer simply lifting up a sluice gate (device that controls flow of water) when irrigation was needed, it was not so. Irrigation required the vigilant attention of the farmer.

The need for vigilance is something farming and spiritual life have in common. The seeker needs to always be mindful of the presence or emergence of obstacles, such as those listed in sutras 1.30 and 2.3.

Faithfully following the eight limbs of Yoga (2.29) forms the core for good yogic maintenance.

4.4 Individual minds are created from the primary ego sense (*asmita matrat*) – the principle of individuation.

nirmāna-cittani asmitā-mātrāt

nirmāna = individual

creating, making, forming, fabricating, measuring, reach, extent, transformation, the best of anything, structure, free from pride, work, the act of building

from ***nir*** = out, away from + ***māna***, from ***mā*** = to measure, allocate, apportion, making, creating

The word *individual* was chosen since when combined with *citta* (the mind), and *asmita* (ego sense), we can infer that the subject of this sutra is the individual mind. In other words, the individual mind is created (*nirmana*) from the cosmic or primary ego sense (*asmita matrat*).

In Buddhism, *nirmana* refers to transformation. If we insert this translation of the word, we can see a relationship between this sutra and the preceding one. Individual minds can be understood as transformations in *asmita matrat*.

cittani (pl.) = mind

consciousness (See 1.2, 1.30, 1.33, 1.37, 2.54, 3.1, 3.9, 3.11–3.12, 3.19, 3.35, 3.39, 4.4–4.5, 4.15–4.18, 4.21, 4.23, 4.26)

from ***cit*** = to know

Refer to 1.2 for more on *citta*.

asmitā = ego sense

I-am-ness (See 1.17, 2.3, 2.6, 4.4)

from ***as*** = to be + ***tā*** = suffix suggesting to have the quality of

For those that have studied the *Sutras*, there may be a question regarding the difference between *asmita* and *ahamkara*, since both words are usually defined as ego sense. They refer to the experience of the sense of individuality.

- *Asmita* = the essence or quality of being or existence
- *Ahamkara*, literally, the "I-maker"

Ahamkara is the term used in Samkhya philosophy to refer to the individual self. The word (I-maker) suggests an ongoing activity. *Ahamkara* constantly claims all experience as its own and, from this, creates and maintains a sense of unique individuality.

Asmita leans a bit toward referring to the potential for individuality. (See next sutra for more).

Knowing this may be interesting, but it doesn't really bring any great benefit to spiritual life. Still, if it settles the matter for the mind, it's nice.

mātrāt = primary

only, no more or less than anything, from that one thing and no more, alone, individuality, amount, degree, sheer, being nothing but, mode, quantity, size (See 1.43)

Asmita matrat refers to the potential for individualization. It is the beginning of the differentiation between a distinct, limited subject (ego sense) and object (the seen).

4.5 Although the activities of the many minds are diverse, the one primary ego sense is the origin of them all.

pravṛitti-bhede prayojakaṃ cittam ekam anekeṣām

pravṛitti = activity

perception, moving onward, cognition, advance, progress, coming forth, appearance, manifestation, rise, source, origin, exertion, efficacy, function, active contemplative devotion (defined as consisting of the wish to act, knowledge of the means, and accomplishment of the object), conduct, behavior, practice, continuance, fate, lot, destiny, news, tidings (See 1.35)

bhede = diverse

differ, distinction, separation, remove (See 4.3)

prayojakaṃ = origin

initiator, cause, prompter, instigator, driver, composer, author, leading to, what is essential, anointer (See 4.3)

cittam = mind

consciousness (See 1.2, 1.30, 1.33, 1.37, 2.54, 3.1, 3.9, 3.11–3.12, 3.19, 3.35, 3.39, 4.4–4.5, 4.15–4.18, 4.21, 4.23, 4.26)

Refer to 1.2 for more on *citta*.

ekam = one

anekeṣām = many

from ***an***= not + ***eka*** = one

4.6 Of these activities, those born of meditation leave no subconscious karmic residue.

tatra dhyāna-jam anāśayam

tatra = of these

there, here, therein

dhyāna = meditation

thought, reflection (especially profound and abstract religious meditation), dullness, the mental exemplification of the personal attributes of a deity (See 1.39, 3.2, 3.11, 3.30, 4.6) from ***dhyai*** = to meditate, think of, contemplate, imagine, call to mind, recollect

Here, *dhyana* (which, literally can be translated as "the act of placing") may not only refer to formal, seated meditation. *Dhyana* also has the meanings of *thought, reflection,* and *the manifestation of the attributes of a deity in one's mind.*

This suggests that for the purposes of this sutra, we can consider meditation to include any spiritually-oriented mental activity, engaged in with full focus, faith, and devotion.

jam = born (See 1.50)

anāśayam = leave no residue

nonaccumulation (See 1.24)

from **an** = not + ***āśaya*** = residue, resting place, bed, seat, place, abode, retreat, a receptacle, any recipient, any vessel of the body, the stomach, the seat of feelings and of thinking. In Yoga, it is the balance of the fruits of previous works which lie stored as *samskaras* in the subconscious mind which ripen into the individual's experience of rank, lifespan, and enjoyment, the will, pleasure, virtue, vice, fate, fortune, property

Karmic residue, the subconscious seeds created by the law of cause and effect, requires the ego to bind the experience to itself (*ahamkara*, the I-maker). A meditative mindset gradually, but surely, neutralizes the grasping function of the ego.

The nature of a mind engaged in a meditative activity, leaves no karmic residue – at least in part – because such a mind seeks to expand its boundaries and even look outside itself for truth and wisdom. It is curious about life, self, and the universe. It remains inspired, knowing that more profound discoveries lie ahead to be enjoyed. It is a mind increasingly not motivated by self-interest, and therefore is not a good resting place for karmas.

A central teaching of Jainism is purging of the bonds of karma. This faith tradition influenced Patanjali's Yoga. For example, the *yamas* appeared in Jainism before Patanjali's time.

4.7 The actions of the yogi are neither white (good) nor black (bad); the actions of others are of three kinds: white, black, and mixed.

karma-aśukla-akṛṣṇam yoginas trividham itaresham

karma = actions (See 1.24, 2.12, 3.22, 4.7, 4.30)

Refer to 1.24 for more on *karma*.

aśukla = neither white

from ***a*** = not + ***śukla*** = white, pure, stainless, from ***śuc*** = gleam, to be bright

akṛṣṇam = not black

from ***a*** = not + ***kṛṣṇa*** = black, dark

We see the word "krishna" in this sutra. It literally translates as *dark* or *black*. Spiritually, this symbolizes that the essence of Krishna (the name of an avatar, or divine incarnation) is beyond our usual abilities of perception.

yoginas = of the yogi

one who has Yoga (See 1.1)

trividham = three kinds

threefold

from ***tri*** = three + ***vidha*** = division, part + ***dhā*** = put

itaresham = for others (See 1.20)

4.8 From the three categories of karma – white, black, mixed – only those subliminal[107] traits (*vasanas*) that are suitable to this birth manifest.

tatas tad-vipāka-anuguṇānām eva abhivyaktir vāsanānāṃ

tataḥ = from that

due to that, therefore, from that time, from that, then, from there

[107] "Subliminal" means: a stimulus or mental process that is below the threshold of the senses or consciousness; something that affects the mind but is outside the conscious awareness of the individual.

tat = (*refers to the three types of karma*)

that, it, their

vipāka = manifest

fruition, consequence (of actions performed in the present or former births), ripe, mature, effect, result, any change of form or shape, cooking (See 1.24)

from ***vi*** = away + ***paka***, from ***pac*** = to cook, cooking

anuguṇānām = suitable to

correspond to, according to one's merits, having similar qualities, congenial to

from ***anu*** = along, after + ***guna*** = quality of nature (See 1.16)

eva = only

specific

abhivyaktiḥ = manifest

distinction

from ***abhi*** = to unto + ***vyakti***, from ***vi*** = asunder + ***akti***, from ***anj*** = anoint, display

vāsanānāṃ = subliminal trait

habit pattern, desires, tendencies, memory traces, personality traits, current awareness of past perceptions, knowledge derived from memory, fancy, imagination, idea, notion, false notion, mistake, thinking of, longing for, expectation, desire, inclination, liking, respectful regard, trust, confidence, proof, demonstration (See 4.8, 4.24)

from ***vas*** = to abide, stay, dwell

Vasanas are a subset of the storehouse of subconscious impressions until conditions are ripe for their fruition. They form the deep habit patterns and personality traits of the individual. It is primarily the *vasanas* that determine how we react and respond to the experiences of life. The *vasanas*, along with the rest of the *samskaras* (subconscious impressions), are stored in the *karmasaya*, the womb or receptacle of karmic residue.

Vasanas lie dormant in the subconscious mind until conditions are present for their fruition. For example, until taking a trip to Las Vegas, one may not realize that they have *vasanas* of gambling stored in the subconscious from previous births. The environment – being conducive to risky games of chance – causes *vasanas,* specific to gambling, to become active. If these *vasanas* are strong enough, gambling can become a regular feature of life. The same is true for *vasanas* of Yoga and spirituality. At a Yoga center or ashram, *vasanas* arise that inspire and fuel spiritual progress.

4.9 Although the creation of the subliminal traits (*vasanas*) that manifest as an individual's present characteristics may be separated from each other by birth, place, and time, there is continuity of selfhood because the memories that form one's present traits are taken from the mind's storehouse of subconscious impressions (*samskaras*).

jāti-deśa-kāla-vyavahitānām api āntaryam
smṛiti-samskārayoḥ eka rūpatvāt

jāti = birth

life, state (See 2.13)

deśa = place (See 2.31)

kāla = time (See 1.14)

vyavahitānām = separated

concealed, to be laced apart, not contiguous or immediately connected, interrupted, obstructed, disturbed, screened from view, covered, remote, distant (See 3.26)

api = although

even

āntaryam = continuity

uninterrupted relationship, unbroken relationship, noninterruption, causal relationship, link, immediate sequence or succession from ***an*** = not + ***antar*** = different (See 4.2)

smṛiti = memories

remembrance, reminiscence, thinking of or upon, calling to mind, memory as one of the *vyabhichari bhavas* = a transitory state of mind or body, having a secondary meaning or several meanings, the entire body of sacred wisdom remembered by teachers, desire, wish (See 1.6 and 1.11)

samskārayoḥ = subconscious impressions

subliminal activators (See 1.18, 1.50, 2.15, 3.9–3.10, 3.18, 4.9, 4.27)

Refer to 1.18 for more on *samskara*.

eka = one (See 1.32)

rūpatvāt = formness, having form

from ***rūpa*** = form (See 1.3) + ***tva*** = suffix indicating the possession of a quality

Eka **and** ***rupatvat*** **together indicate uniformity, one nature, one form, one essence, or identical. In the sutra, this refers to the fact that memories and** ***samskaras*** **are essentially the same.**

4.10 And these subliminal traits (*vasanas*) have no beginning since the desire for continued existence that sustains them is also without beginning. (See 1.19 and 2.9)

tāsām anāditvaṃ ca āśiṣo nityavāt

tāsām = (*refers to the vasanas*)

they, of these

anāditvaṃ = having no beginning

beginningless

from ***an*** = not + ***ādi*** = and so forth + ***tvam*** = suffix denoting a quality possessed

ca = and

āśiṣaḥ = desire

hope, asking for, prayer, wish, blessing, a particular medication, a serpent's fang, wishing for any other, primordial will, the will to live

from ***ā*** = hither, unto + ***śis,*** from ***śās*** = order, the long "a," denotes a stronger form of *sas*

The root of this word is the same as for *asha*: hope, wish, desire, expectation, prospect.

nityavāt = without beginning

eternal, continuance (See 2.15)

from ***nitya*** = eternal + ***tva*** = denoting quality possessed

4.11 The *vasanas* are held together by the interdependence of:

- **Cause and effect (karma), which leaves subconscious memories and desires**
- **The foundation (ignorance), the root of suffering and the major impediments to progress (*klesas*), as well as being the root of karma**
- **Support (sense experiences) that sustains desires through attachment and aversion**

When these factors are absent, the *vasanas* disappear.

hetu-phala-āśraya ālambanaiḥ-saṇgrihītatvāt
eṣām abhāve tad abhāvaḥ

hetu = cause

impulse, motive, reason for (See 2.17)

from ***hetu***, from hi = impel, incite

phala = effect

fruit, consequence, result, retribution (good or bad), gain or loss, reward or punishment, advantage or disadvantage, benefit, enjoyment, compensation, the end of an action, a gaming board, a blade of a sword or knife, the point of an arrow, a shield, a point or spot on a die (See 2.14)

from ***phal*** = to produce fruits, to ripen

āśraya = foundation

correspondence, dwelling in, depending on, following, as a consequence of the proximity, essence of the dependable, basis, correspondence (See 2.36)

from ***ā*** = hither, unto + ***śraya*** = protection, refuge, from ***śri*** = rest on

ālambanaiḥ = support

based on, depending on, resting on (See 1.10)

saṇgrihītatvāt = held together

sustained, that which is grasped, seized, caught, gathered

from ***sam*** = together + ***gṛhīta***, from ***grabh*** = grasp + ***tva*** = suffix indicating possession of a quality

eṣām = (*refers to the three factors listed above*)

of these

abhāve = absent

cease, with the disappearance, non-becoming, absence (See 1.10 and below)

tad = (*refers to the vasanas*)

that, those

abhāvaḥ = cease

disappear, non-becoming, absence, non-existence, annihilation, non-entity (See 1.10)

from ***a*** = not + ***bhāva*** = being, becoming, from ***bhū*** = to be become, exist

In Buddhism, *bhava* is a process of becoming, creating, and sustaining individuality. It is produced by identifying with the characteristics of individuality. It is related to craving; to crave something is to sustain the false sense of individuality and self-identity. To begin to drop cravings is thought of as a process of non-becoming.

4.12 The past and future characteristics of an object that manifest during the course of its existence are innate to its nature.

atīta-anāgatam svarūpapato asti adhva-bhedāt dharmāṇām

atīta = past

gone by, dead, negligent, left behind (See (3.16)

from ***ati*** = over, beyond + ***ita*** = past perfect participle of ***i*** = to go

anāgatam = future

not come, not arrived, not learned, unknown (See 2.16)

from ***an*** = not + ***ā*** = unto + ***gam*** = to go

svarūpapataḥ = innate

essential nature, essentially, in one's own form, according to one's own form, analogously, similarly, identically, by nature, in reality, by itself

asti = exist

existent, present, it exists

adhva = course

path, road, way

from ***dhav*** = to flow along

bhedāt = changes

modification, alteration, distinction, remove, separation, division (See 4.3)

dharmāṇām = characteristics

form, nature, character, essential quality, that which is established or held, virtue, religion (See 3.13 – 3.14, 4.12)

from ***dhṛ*** = to hold, uphold, establish, support

Dharma **literally translates as** ***that which holds (something) together.*** ***Dharma*** **is the basis of order, whether physical, social, moral, or spiritual.**

The word is also used to mean *mark, sign, token, essential attributes, nature's properties*.

Refer to 3.13 for more on *dharma*.

4.13 These characteristics, whether manifest or intangible, have the three fundamental components of nature (*gunas*) as their essence.

te vyakta-sūkṣmāḥ guṇa-ātmānaḥ

te = these

they

vyakta = manifest

apparent, visible, developed, evolved, distinction

from ***vi*** = asunder + **akta**, from ***añj*** = to anoint (See 4.8)

sūkṣmāḥ = intangible (See 1.44)

subtle

guṇa = ***left untranslated***

primary constituent of nature (See 1.16, 2.15, 2.19, 4.13, 4.32, 4.34)

Refer to 1.16 for more on the *gunas*.

ātmānaḥ = essence

essence, self, the principle of life and sensation, the individual self, soul, nature, character, peculiarity, the person or whole body considered as one as opposed to the separate members of the body, the body, living entity, a person, one's soul, Supreme Soul, consciousness, heart, the understanding, intellect or mind, the highest personal principle of life, effort, firmness, the sun, fire, a son (See 2.5, 2.21, 2.41, 4.13, 4.25)

from ***at*** = to breathe or ***ap*** = to pervade, reach up to

Refer to 2.21 for more on *Atma*.

4.14 The transformations of these three fundamental components (*gunas*) are unique to the nature of an object. This is why the essential nature of an object remains consistent throughout all of its changes.

pariṇāma-ekatvāt vastu-tattvaṃ

pariṇāma = transformation

change, alteration, evolution, development, ripeness, maturity, digestion, consequence, result (See 2.15, 3.9, 3.11–3.13, 3.15–3.16, 4.2, 4.14, 4.32–4.33)

Refer to 2.15 for more on *parinama*.

ekatvāt = unique

oneness, uniformity, unity, union, coincidence, identity, singleness, soleness

from ***eka*** = one + ***tva*** = suffix denoting having the quality of

vastu = object

item, natural disposition, house, becoming dawn, morning, seat or place of, the real, the right thing, a valuable or worthy object, subject matter, the pith or substance of anything (See 1.9)

tattvam = essential nature

essence or substance of anything, essential nature, that-ness, subject, true or real state, truth, reality, principle, an elementary property (See 1.32, 4.14)

4.15 Each mind perceives the same object differently. Even though the object is the same, perception of it is influenced by each mind's unique viewpoints, priorities, and experiences.

vastu-sāmye citta-bhedāt tayoḥ vibhaktaḥ panthāḥ

Our viewpoints, biases, aspirations, and priorities shape and guide our experiences in life, and are the reasons why the same object is perceived differently by different minds.

vastu = object (See 1.9, 4.14)

sāmye = same

evenness, equal, equilibrium, equipoise, normal state, likeness, identity with, equality of rank or position, measure, time, impartiality, indifference, to act justly toward (See 3.56)

citta = mind (See 1.2, 1.30, 1.33, 1.37, 2.54, 3.1, 3.9, 3.11–3.12, 3.19, 3.35, 3.39, 4.4–4.5, 4.15–4.18, 4.21, 4.23, 4.26)

Refer to 1.2 for more on *citta*.

bhedāt = difference

remove, separation, division, distinction, (See 4.3)

tayoḥ = their

vibhaktaḥ = unique

separated, distinct

from ***bhaj*** = to allot

panthāḥ = viewpoints, priorities, experiences

path, way, road, course, a wanderer, traveller, the sun (wanderer in the sky)

from ***path*** = to go, move

4.16 An object's existence doesn't depend on a single mind's perception of it. If it did, what would become of that object when it is not being perceived by that mind?

na ca eka-citta-tantram vastu tad-apramāṇakaṃ tadā kiṃ syāt

na = not

ca = and (connects the subject matter of this to the previous sutra)

eka = single

one

citta = mind

consciousness, heart, to know, to be aware (See 1.2, 1.30, 1.33, 1.37, 2.54, 3.1, 3.9, 3.11 – 3.12, 3.19, 3.35, 3.39, 4.4–4.5, 4.15–4.18, 4.21, 4.23, 4.26)

from ***cit*** = to know, observe, perceive, think, be aware

Refer to 1.2 for more on *citta*.

tantraṃ = dependent

characteristic feature, thread, essential part, main point, system, framework, teaching, doctrine, theory, scripture, crosswise threads on a loom (the making of cloth is dependent on the crosswise threads which weave above and below the vertical threads), context, continuum

from ***tan*** = extend, to do in detail + ***tra*** = object that facilitates action

vastu = object (See 1.9)

tad = that

apramāṇakaṃ = not perceived

not provable, not demonstrated

from ***a*** = not + ***pra*** = before + ***māṇaka***, from ***mā*** = to measure

tadā = if it did

in that case, then

kiṃ = what

a pronoun indicating a question

syāt = become

could be

from ***as*** = to be

4.17 An object is known or unknown depending on whether it colors the mind.

tat-uparāga-apekṣitvāc-cittasya vastu jñāta-ajñātam

tat = that *(refers to the object)*

uparāga = coloring

dyeing, darkening, influence, eclipse of the sun and moon, affecting, misbehavior, bad conduct

from ***upa*** = to, near to, by the side of, with, together with, under, down, approach + ***rañj*** = to be excited, tint, red color, inflammation, to be affected or moved, charmed or delighted by, to be attracted by, enamored of, to fall in love with, feeling of passion, the act of coloring or dyeing

One of the meanings of *uparaga* is *eclipse of the sun and moon*, the two sources of light for our world. This sutra, which uses light as a symbol for awareness, suggests that the coloring process enabling perception has, as one consequence, a dimming of the inner light. This dimming could be due to the influences that the *klesas,* karma, or *samskaras* have on the act of perception.

apekṣitvāt = dependency

due to the need, anticipation, expectation, wished, looked for, consideration, required, referred to

from ***apa*** = away, off, back, down + ***īkṣitva***, from ***īkṣ*** = to see + ***tva***, suffix denoting possession of a quality

The fact that this word also carries meanings of *anticipation* and *looked for* suggests that the object that is perceived is not necessarily known as it is, but can be colored by the attachments or aversions of the perceiver.

cittasya = the mind (See 1.2, 1.30, 1.33, 1.37, 2.54, 3.1, 3.9–3.12, 3.19, 3.35, 3.39, 4.4–4.5, 4.15–4.18, 4.21, 4.23, 4.26)

Refer to 1.2 for more on *citta*.

vastu = object (See 1.9)

jñāta = perceived

known, ascertained, comprehended, understood, meant, taken for, known as

from ***jan*** = to know

ajñātam = not perceived

not known

from ***a*** = not + ***jñā*** = to know

4.18 All of the mind's seesaw whirling excursions (*vrittis*) – all its changes and fluctuations – are always known to the mind's transcendent sovereign, the eternal changeless consciousness (Seer, Self, *Purusha*).

sadā jñātā citta-vṛittayas tat-prabhoḥ puruṣaya apariṇāmitvāt

sadā = always

from ***sa*** = with + ***dā*** = indicates time

jñātā = witness

known (See 4.17)

citta = mind (See 1.2, 1.30, 1.33, 1.37, 2.54, 3.1, 3.9–3.12, 3.19, 3.35, 3.39, 4.4–4.5, 4.15–4.18, 4.21, 4.23, 4.26)

Refer to 1.2 for more on *citta*.

vṛittayaḥ = seesaw whirling excursions of the mind

fluctuations or modifications of the mind (See 1.2, 1.4–1.5, 1.10, 1.41, 2.11, 3.44, 4.18)

Refer to 1.2 for more on *vritti*.

tat = (refers to the *vrittis*)

its, that, of those

prabhoḥ = transcendent sovereign[108]

literally, to come forth; Lord, excelling, mighty, powerful, rich, abundant, more powerful than, having power to, able, capable, to come forth, spring up, appear, become visible, constant, eternal, king, referring to the gods, master, chief or leader

[108] *Transcendent* sovereign was chosen here since it keeps the sense of Lordship, but adds a sense of above and beyond. Transcend, meaning "beyond" and the root of sovereign being "above."

from **pra** = before, forth, forward + **bhu** = to become, caused, to come into being, exist, arise, belong to, be on the side of, serve for, tend to, be occupied with, devote oneself to, thrive or prosper in, to be useful

The *Purusha*, though distinct from mind (an aspect of the seen, *prakriti*) is not in opposition to it.

In this sutra, *Purusha* is described as *prabhu*, master or ruler of the mind. This is not meant to portray the mind as being in a slave–master relationship to the *Purusha*. The mind is not a conquered enemy.[109] Instead, like a father, *prabhu* is the source, enlightener, friend, and refuge of the mind. The *Purusha* is depicted as master because it perceives all of the mind's activities.

The *Purusha* and all of *prakriti*, including the mind, have a part to play in the cosmic drama of life. In this sutra, Patanjali is affirming that, not only are we *not* the body, we are *not* the mind. The conscious Self (*Purusha*) is our true, enduring Self.

The roots of *prabhu*, can be translated as: causing to come forth or appear.[110] This reminds us of sutras 1.3 and 2.25:

When that (nirodha) is accomplished, the Seer
(pure, unchanging, eternal consciousness) stands free.

Without ignorance, this confusion ceases to exist. The Seer stands apart
from the seen as the Self. This is liberation (kaivalya).

In Hinduism, *prabhu* is used as an epithet, a descriptive word or phrase for someone or something. *Prabhu* is an epithet for the gods Surya (sun god) and Agni (god of fire). Both gods have the essence of light, a symbol of awareness.

[109] Note that *praboh* is in the genitive case. Here, this suggests a close association between the mind and *Purusha*. A mind free from ignorance is not in opposition to the *Purusha*. From the *Bhagavad Gita*, 6.6: "As you gain control of your mind, with the help of your higher self, then your mind and ego become your allies. But the uncontrolled mind behaves as an enemy."

[110] Hence, we can think of *prabhu* as carrying the qualities of a good, caring father.

The following verse (9.18) from the *Bhagavad Gita* expands on the meaning of *prabhu*:

I am the goal. I uphold everything; I am the Lord (prabhu), the witness, the abode, the refuge, the friend, the beginning and the end. I am the foundation, the infinite treasure house and indestructible seed of creation.

puruṣaya = to the *Purusha*

true Self, Spirit, animating principle, pure consciousness (See 1.16, 1.24, 3.36, 3.50, 3.56, 4.18, 4.34)

Refer to 1.16 for more on *Purusha*.

apariṇāmitvāt = changeless

without transformation, not changing

from ***a*** = not + ***parinama*** = transformations, evolution, changes + ***tva***, suffix meaning to have the quality of

4.19 The mind, like everything in nature, is an object of perception. Therefore, it is not self-illuminating; awareness is not its essential nature.

na tat-svābhāsam dṛiśtyatvāt

na = not

tat = that, its

svābhāsam = self-luminous

own light

from ***sva*** = self + ***ā*** = to + ***bhāsa*** = to shine

dṛiśtyatvāt = object of perception

seeable nature, because it can be perceived (See 2.17)

from ***dṛṣya*** = to see + ***tva***, indicating the possession of a quality

4.20 A further proof that the mind is not self-illuminating is that it cannot perceive both itself and an object at the same time.

eka-samaye ca ubhaya-anavadhāraṇam

eka = same

one, single, one and the same

samaye = at the same time

at the appointed time, circumstance, coming together, agreement, occasion (See 2.31)

from ***sam*** = together + ***aya***, from ***i*** = to go

ca = and

ubhaya = both

anavadhāraṇam = cannot perceive

non discernment, not ascertaining

an = not + ***ava*** = down + ***dharana***, from ***dhr*** = to hold

4.21 If it is thought that each mind has a second that illumines the first, it would suggest that there is an endless series of intellects, each perceiving another. The result would be confusion of memory.

citta-antara-dṛśye buddhi-buddher
atiprasaṅgaḥ smṛiti-saṃkaraś ca

Let's follow the logic of this argument. There is a "first mind," which perceives an object. How do we know this? Is there a second mind that perceives the first that is perceiving the object? If this is so, if we know that the second mind is perceiving the first, then there must be a third mind to perceive the second that is perceiving the first that is perceiving the object. If this is so, there would be an endless procession of minds causing a mental mess.

citta = mind (See 1.2, 1.30, 1.33, 1.37, 2.54, 3.1, 3.9, 3.11–3.12, 3.19, 3.35, 3.39, 4.4–4.5, 4.15–4.18, 4.21, 4.23, 4.26)

Refer to 1.2 for more on *citta*.

antara = another (See 4.2)

dṛśye = perceive

seen (See 2.17)

buddhi = intellect

reason, the inner organ of discrimination, discernment, judgment, comprehension, understanding, the power of forming and retaining concepts and general notions, mind, perception (See 4.21–4.22)

from ***budh*** = awaken, to be aware

In Samkhya philosophy, *buddhi*[111] is the first principle to emerge from *prakriti. Buddhi* is the purest and most basic form of *prakriti* and as such gives rise to its grosser forms. The *buddhi* is also the discerning faculty of the mind, its highest function.

The word can be used in the sense of wisdom or cognition (the mental process of acquiring information and understanding through the senses and experiences).

Buddhi is also known as *mahat* (the great one). Its nature is pure *sattva*.

buddheḥ = intellect

The two forms of the word *buddhi* in this sutra (here and above), combine to mean something like, *perceiver of perceiver.*

atiprasaṅgaḥ = endless

excessive attachment, too diffused

from ***ati*** = beyond + ***pra*** = before + ***saṅga***, from ***sañj*** = to adhere

---

[111] *Buddhi* is the feminine form of *buddha.*

This word is used to express an unwarranted stretching of a rule of logic.

smṛiti = memory (See 1.6)

saṃkaraḥ = confused

mixed together, commingled, anything that is defiled by an unclean thing (See 3.17)

from ***sam*** = together + ***kara***, from ***kṛ*** = scatter

ca = and

4.22 Transcendent unchanging consciousness (*Purusha*) reflects on the mind making it seem as if the mind possesses awareness of its own. (See 1.4, 2.17)

citer apratisaṁkramāyās tat-ākāra-āpattau
svabuddhi-samvedanam

citeḥ = transcendent consciousness

higher awareness, awareness

Citeh is not the same as *citta*, though both words can be translated as consciousness. *Citta's* meaning is more general: the ability to know.

Citeh derives from *citi*, not *citta* (mind) and refers to the power of changeless consciousness, the Seer, the *Purusha*. (See 1.2, 2.6, 4.34)

apratisaṁkramāyāh = unchanging

nonsequential, no intermixture, nondissolution

from ***a*** = not + ***prati*** = against + ***sam*** = together + ***krama***, from ***kram*** = step

tat = *(refers to the individual mind, citta)*

it, that

ākāra = making it seem or appear

essential nature, form, figure, shape, features, stature, external gesture or aspect of the body, expression of the face (as furnishing a clue to the disposition of the mind)

from ***kṛ*** = to do

āpattau = reflects

assumes, upon the appearance, occurrence, arising, entering into a state or condition, changing into, entering into a relationship with, happening, occurring, fault, transgression, calamity, misfortune

from ***pat*** = to fall, to partake of, the share in, flying

svabuddhi = consciousness of its own

self-cognition, one's own intellect

from ***sva*** = own + ***buddhi*** = intellect, reason, discernment, judgment, comprehension, understanding (See 4.21)

samvedanam = awareness

the act of perceiving or feeling, consciousness, knowing, perception, sensation, making known, communication, announcement, information (See 3.39)

from ***sam*** = thorough, complete, together + ***vedana***, from ***vid*** = knowledge

4.23 The mind, colored by both the Seer and the seen, can perceive all objects. (See 2.17–2.18)

draṣṭṛ-dṛśya-uparaktaṃ cittaṃ sarva-arthaṃ

In sutra 1.18, we learned that the purpose of nature (*prakriti*) is to give experiences and liberation to the *Purusha*. Some experiences are painful, some are not. But all experiences are caused by the mind being colored – impacted, affected – by the seen (*prakriti*, nature). Though they are different, there is a relationship between Seer and seen. The mind seems to have consciousness while the *Purusha* is consciousness. Liberation is the direct experience of this difference.

Refer to sutras 3.54–3.56, which present liberation as the result of being able to discriminate between *sattva* in its most refined state (pure mind) and *Purusha*, which seem identical.

draṣṭṛ = Seer (See 1.3)

dṛśya = seen (See 2.17)

uparaktaṃ = colored

tinted, affected

from ***upa*** = to, unto + ***rakta***, from ***rañj*** = to be colored

cittaṃ = mind (See 1.2, 1.30, 1.33, 1.37, 2.54, 3.1, 3.9, 3.11–3.12, 3.19, 3.35, 3.39, 4.4–4.5, 4.15–4.18, 4.21, 4.23, 4.26)

Refer to 1.2 for more on *citta*.

sarva = all

every, everything, altogether, wholly, completely

arthaṃ = object

meaning, purpose (See 1.28, 1.32, 1.42, 2.2, 2.18, 2.21–2.22, 3.3, 3.17, 3.36, 4.23–4.24, 4.32, 4.34)

Refer to 1.28 for more on *artha*.

A review of the last six sutras will be helpful before going forward:

4.18: The *Purusha* knows all of the changes and activities of the mind.

4.19: The mind, like any component of *prakriti*, is an object of perception.

4.20: Although the mind can be aware of itself (but not all of its mental activities – that ability is reserved for the *Purusha*), it cannot be aware of itself and perceive an object at the same time.

4.21: Patanjali reduces the relationship between the mind and consciousness to its most basic: there is the mind and there is the *Purusha*. *Purusha* is the sole possessor of awareness.

4.22: The mind seems to be conscious, but it is only a "borrowed" consciousness, a reflection of the *Purusha's* light of awareness on the mind.

4.23: Perception happens because the mind is impacted by objects and illumined by the light of the *Purusha*.

4.24 The mind, a composite made up of several elements and streaked[112] with countless subconscious impressions, desires, and tendencies, acts for the purpose of another (the *Purusha*). (See 3.36)

tat-asaṅkhyeya-vāsanābhiś-citraṃ api para-arthaṃ saṃhatya kāritvāt

tat = (*refers to the citta*)

that

asaṅkhyeya = countless

innumerable, multitude

from ***a*** = not + ***saṃkhyeya*** = a form of ***saṃkhyā***, from ***sam*** = together + khyā = to see

vāsanābhiḥ = tendencies, subliminal traits, desires

habit patterns (See 4.8, 4.24)

Refer to 4.8 for more on *vasana*.

citraṃ = streaked

conspicuous, variegated, spotted, speckled, various, manifold, excellent, distinguished, bright, clear, strange, wonderful

from ***cit*** = to perceive

Look at the definitions above. Can there be better words to describe the mind: *various, excellent, bright, strange, and wonderful*?

---

[112] The word "streaked" is chosen here to give a vivid picture of the mind's usual state. Streak means to: cover with streaks, to move quickly in a direction, to smear, smudge or cover with flecks.

api = although

also

para = another

other (See 1.28)

arthaṃ = purpose

object (See 1.28, 1.32, 1.42–1.43, 2.2, 2.18, 2.21–2.22, 3.3, 3.17, 3.36, 4.23–4.24, 4.32, 4.34)

Refer to 1.28 for more on *artha*.

saṃhatya = for the purpose

in association, stuck together, compound, put together, joined, combined

from ***sam*** = together + ***uhati***, from ***han*** = to strike

kāritvāt = acting

from ***kāri***, from ***kṛ*** = to do + ***tva*** = a suffix meaning a possession of a quality

4.25 For one who discerns the distinction between the mind and the *Atma* (Self), false or limited notions of self-identity cease forever.

viśeṣa-darśina ātma-bhāva-bhāvanā-vinivṛittiḥ

viśeṣa = distinction (See 1.22)

The distinction mentioned here refers to the mind and the *Purusha*, a subject that has appeared several times in the *Sutras*.

Note that, in this context, *Atma* and *Purusha* are essentially the same thing. We can say that use of the word "*Atma*", places an emphasis on the subjective experience of the *Purusha* as the ground of being – or Self – of the individual.

darśina = discerns

the one seeing, the one who has sight, seer, *Purusha*

from ***darśa***, from ***dṛś*** = to see + ***in*** = a possessive suffix + ***a*** = suffix denoting coming from

ātma = left untranslated

Self, the soul, the person or whole body considered as one and opposed to the separate members of the body, the principle of life and sensation, the individual soul, self, abstract individual, essence, nature, peculiarity, the body, understanding, intellect, mind, the highest personal principle of life, the sun (See 2.5, 2.21, 2.41, 4.13, 4.25)

from ***an*** = to breathe, ***at*** = to move, to breathe, or from the verb root ***ap*** = to pervade, reach up to

Refer to 2.5 for more on *Atma*.

bhāva = identity

proper or peculiar nature, becoming, existing, condition, intention (See 3.9)

Atma **(above) +** ***bhava*****, could be translated as sense of self or self-identity, the nature or sense (*bhava*) of Self (*Atma*).**

bhāvanā = notions

thoughts, produced by imagination or meditation, coming to be, producing or cultivating, consideration, mental discipline. It can also refer to a memory arising from direct perception and is used as a synonym for meditation.

In Jainism, *bhavana* is a class of knowledge that represents an insight in which the nature of a familiar phenomenon is revealed so that a new phenomenon, related to it, can be known. In this sutra, the insight that is gained is that self-identity, rooted in the mind, is nothing other than a reflection of the *Atma*.

vinivṛittiḥ = cease

turned back, withdrawn, abandoned, cessation, coming to an end, discontinued

4.26 Then, the mind naturally inclines toward discriminative discernment and, not being far from liberation, gravitates[113] toward it.

tadā viveka-nimnaṃ kaivalya-prāgbhāraṃ cittaṃ

God is more anxious to bestow His blessings on us
than we are to receive them.

– Augustine of Hippo

tadā = then

in that case, at that time

viveka = discriminative discernment (See 2.26, 2.28, 3.53, 3.55, 4.26, 4.29)

Refer to 2.26 for more on *viveka*.

nimnaṃ = incline toward

bending into

from ***ni*** = down, into + ***na***, from ***nam*** = to bend

kaivalya = liberation

absoluteness, independence, isolation (See 2.25, 3.51, 3.56, 4.26, 4.34)

Refer to 2.25 for more on *kaivalya.*

prāgbhāraṃ = gravitates toward

inclination, propensity, being not far from, the slope of a mountain, bending, a subsiding mass, multitude, heap or quantity, a shelter-roof

from **prāk** = turned toward the front, directed toward + **bhāra** = mass, weight, burden, load, pressure, from **bhṛ** = to bear

cittaṃ = mind (See 1.2, 1.10, 1.33, 1.37, 2.54, 3.1, 3.9, 3.11–3.12, 3.19, 3.35, 3.39, 4.4–4.5, 4.15–4.18, 4.21, 4.23, 4.26)

Refer to 1.2 for more on *citta*.

[113] "Gravitate," as understood in physics, nicely expresses the sense of grace suggested in this sutra. Gravitate means: to move toward a center of gravity or other attractive force.

4.27 The flow of discriminative discernment may be interrupted now and then by the force of subconscious impressions (*samskaras*), which cause distracting thoughts to arise.

tac-chidreṣu pratyaya-antarāṇi samskārebhyaḥ

tad = that (*refers to the flow of discriminative discernment*)

chidreṣu = interrupted

in between, torn asunder, containing holes, pierced, defect, fault

from ***chid*** = to cut

pratyaya = thought

intention (See 1.10, 1.18–1.19, 2.20, 3.2, 4.27)

Refer to 1.10 for more on *pratyaya*.

antarāṇi = now and then (refers to distracting thoughts that interrupt discriminative discernment)

other, in the middle, inside, within, between, near, distant, almost, in the meantime, now and then, for some time, during, another, proximate, related, intimate, lying adjacent to, distant, different from, exterior, a hole, opening, the contents, interval, intermediate space or time, period, term, opportunity, occasion, place, remainder, peculiarity, weakness, weak side, representation, guaranty, respect, regard (See 4.2)

Antarani has a number of meanings, some that contradict each other, such as *near* and *distant*. The main idea, in this context, is that despite the flow of discriminative discernment, until full liberation is attained, there will be periods in which focused discernment is disrupted. We see this in such defintions as: *in the middle, within, now and then, interval, for some time*. Other definitions of *antarani* give us a more complete picture of what the word conveys: *lying adjacent to, almost,* and *near.*

The suggestion is that even if the flow of discernment is interrupted at this stage of spiritual maturity, the seeker is not far from returning to it. Liberation is still not automatic, but it is near.

This same sutra could form the basis for self-forgiveness. Slipping back a step from our growth is not necessarily caused by a moral defect or lack of capacity for enlightenment. The mind, as part of nature, goes through changes (See 2.15). Patience, perseverance, and faith inevitably lead to a transcendent state of mind in which no setbacks occur.

The state of being permanently established in discriminative discernment is given in sutra 4.29 – *dharmamegha samadhi.*

samskārebhyaḥ = from *samskaras*

past impressions (See 1.18, 1.50, 2.15, 3.9–3.10, 3.18, 4.9, 4.27)

Refer to 1.18 for more on *samskaras.*

4.28 These subconscious impressions (*samskaras*) can be removed in the same way as was described for the root causes of suffering (*klesas*):

- Meditation (2.11)
- Tracing them back to their cause (2.10)
- Uninterrupted discriminative discernment (2.26)

hānaṃ eṣāṃ kleśavat uktaṃ

hānaṃ = removal

ending, cessation, relinquish, give up, gone, depart, gotten rid of, to lose (See 2.26)

eṣāṃ = of these (*refers to old samskaras*)

kleśavat = in the same way as for the *klesas*

the major impediments to progress and the root cause of persistent uneasiness, anxiety, and suffering (See 1.24, 2.2–2.3, 2.12–2.13, 4.28, 4.30)

from ***kleśa*** = root causes of suffering + ***vat*** = a suffix indicating analogy

Refer to 1.24 for more on the *klesas.*

uktaṃ = described

from ***vac*** = to speak

For a refresher on the *klesas*, see sutra 2.3. Also examine 2.10 and 2.11, which describe the method to overcome and remove them, and 2.26 which presents *viveka* (discriminative discernment) as the means to end them.

4.29 One who does not seek personal gain from even the highest insights, remains in a state of discriminative discernment under all circumstances. From this, arises the cloud of *dharma samadhi* (*dharmamegha samadhi*). (See 1.16)

prasaṃkhyāne'pi akusīdasya sarvathā vivekakhyāteḥ
dharma-meghaḥ samādhiḥ

prasaṃkhyāne = highest insights

payment, liquidation, enumeration, reflection, consideration, total number, sum, meditation, elevation, the highest rewards

from ***pra*** = before, forward + ***sam*** = together + ***khyāna***, from ***khyā*** = to see, appear

Prasamkhyane has been translated as *omniscience, the highest samadhi, the highest elevation,* and *the highest kind of intellectual knowledge.* At this point, the yogi is now established in faith, self-surrender, and grace. Self-interest and reliance solely on self-effort are permanently left behind.

Samkhyana, a root of *prasamkhyane*, is translated as: *enumeration, reckoning up, becoming seen, number, appearance, multitude, and measurement*. The suggestion is that even when the individual has accumulated a large number of insights – enough to be seen or obvious to them and to others – they still have not reached the highest goal. The seeker ultimely needs to let go of all self-interest and egoism.

api = even

indeed, placing near or over, uniting to, annexing, reaching to, proximity, also, moreover, besides, surely, assuredly, as well as

Api is often used to express emphasis in the sense of *even, also, very.*

akusīdasya = no interest for gain

without gain, without usury

from ***a*** = not + ***kusīda*** = loan to be repaid with interest

sarvathā = constant, under all circumstances

in every way, always, at all times, in whatever way, however, altogether, entirely, in the highest degree, exceedingly (See 3.55)

vivekakhyāteḥ = discriminative discernment, right knowledge (See 2.26, 2.28, 3.53, 3.55, 4.26, 4.29)

from ***viveka*** = discernment + ***khyā*** = to see (See 1.16)

Ignorance, the fundamental misperception of self-identity, is the root cause of all of our suffering. *Vivekakhyateh* is correct, direct vision or seeing. It unveils the highest truths, bestows omniscience, and flings the door to liberation wide open. Such is the state of *dharmamegha samadhi* (See 4.30 – 4.32). It is the highest degree of direct perception and transcends all other forms and depths of direct perception.

Patanjali refers to this lofty state as "the deliverer," the state that delivers us from ignorance (See 3.55).

Recall that in a related sutra (2.26), unwavering discriminative discernment is given as the means to remove ignorance and the pain (*duhkha*) it brings. Also, recall that *viveka* is cultivated through the practice of the eight limbs of Yoga (2.29).

dharma = left untranslated

virtue, form, nature, righteousness, character, essential quality, that which is held (See 3.13 – 3.14, 4.12, 4.29)

from ***dhṛ*** = to hold

Refer to 3.13 for more on *dharma*.

meghaḥ = cloud

sprinkler, a mass, multitude

from ***mih*** = sprinkle

Traditionally, these are some ways clouds are symbolized:

- White clouds are considered as messengers of peace, hope, and love.
- Dark clouds represent impurities that cover the intellect (*buddhi*).
- Clouds also symbolize connection and communication that we have with each other, nature, and higher realms of existence.
- They are also used to symbolize the transitory nature of life.

We could see how the above symbols for clouds might apply to *dharmamegha samadhi.*

samādhiḥ = left untranslated

(See 1.20, 1.46, 1.51, 2.2, 2.29, 2.45, 3.3, 3.11, 4.1, 4.29)

Refer to 1.20 for more on *samadhi.*

4.30 This *samadhi* ends the influences of the root causes of suffering (*klesas*) and past actions (karma).

tataḥ kleśa-karma-nivṛittiḥ

tataḥ = from this (*refers to dharmamegha samadhi*)

kleśa = root causes of suffering

affliction, fundamental impediments to enlightenment (See 1.24, 2.2–2.3, 2.12–2.13, 4.28, 4.30)

Refer to 1.24 for more on *klesa*.

karma = past actions

cause and effect (See 1.24, 2.12, 3.22, 4.7, 4.30)

Refer to 1.24 for more on karma.

nivṛittiḥ = ends the influences

cessation, disappearance, escaping from, ceasing from worldly acts, rest, repose, inactivity, ceasing to be valued, destruction, abolition, prevention

from ***ni*** = inward, down, within, back + ***vṛt*** = to whirl, the root of ***vritti*** (whirling excursions of mind (See 1.2)

The roots of the word can form a charming image. As the result of *dharmamegha samadhi*, the mind whirls and twirls within, effortlessly floating down within, traveling back to its source. This return to the source is called *pratiprasava* (See 4.34). This sweet, gentle state leads to an ultra-dramatic transformation of self and the release from ignorance.

4.31 At that time, knowledge that is boundless and eternal arises and all impurities and obstructions withdraw. Compared to this knowledge, what remains to be known is of no consequence to the attainment of liberation.

tadā sarva-āvaraṇa-mala-apetasya jñānasya
ānantayāt jñeyam alpam

tadā = at that time

then, in that case

from ***taḍ*** = to beat strike, knock, strike with arrows, wound, punish, to strike a musical instrument, to speak or to shine

The root of this simple word suggest a powerful poetic image: the moment in which ignorance is wounded, allowing wisdom and light pour forth.

It is a moment in which delusion is permanently shattered.

sarva = all

āvaraṇa = obscure

covering (See 2.52, which describes the veil over the inner light being destroyed by *pranayama*)

mala = impurities (can refer to both physical and moral)

dirt, filth, dust, any bodily excretions or secretions, original sin, natural impurity, the tip of a scorpion's tail, unbelieving, godless

apetasya = withdraw

departed, gone, free from

from ***apa*** = away, off + ***ita***, from ***i*** = to go

jñānasya = knowledge (See 1.9, 1.38, 1.42, 2.28, 3.16–3.19, 3.22, 3.26, 3.28–3.29, 3.36, 3.53, 3.55, 4.31)

Refer to 1.9 for more on *jnana*.

ānantayāt = eternal, without bounds

endless, infinite

from **a** = not + ***anta*** = end (See 2.34 in the context of *pratipaksha bhavanam*)

jñeyam = to be known (See 1.9, 1.38, 1.42, 2.28, 3.16–3.19, 3.22, 3.26, 3.28–3.29, 3.36, 3.53, 3.55, 4.31)

from ***jñā*** = to know

Refer to 1.9 for more on *jnana*.

alpam = is of no consequence

little, small, unimportant, trivial, minute, easily

Alpam is usually translated as "little," and when considered with *jneyam*, this sutra reads something like, "*What is left to be known is very little.*" Of course, this brings up the question: "*What is it that is left to be known?*"

Other definitions of *alpam – unimportant, trivial, minute* – offer a different understanding this sutra.

Defining *alpam* as, "of little consequence" uncovers an important facet of any contemplative spiritual tradition. What we are considering here is a product of one-pointed focus and fervor. There are still many things to be known, but they are of little consequence – they have little effect, if any.

on the state of liberation. For example, for a longtime vegetarian, a new local hamburger restaurant would be very peripheral to their life. It might barely impact their awareness. Its presence and impact is so weak that it's almost as if it didn't exist at all. It still has relevance to hamburger lovers and to the workers it employs. Like the hamburger restaurant for the vegetarian, worldly material objects and experiences, while they can still be enjoyed, are not relevant to the liberation from ignorance.

This state of mind is the product of a gradual process in which priorities and aspirations begin to shift toward those that encourage spiritual growth. This is one way of describing the cultivation of nonattachment (See 1.15 and 1.16). The seeker naturally searches for values (experiences, mindsets) that lie beyond the influences of ignorance and egoism.

4.32 From this knowledge, the purpose of the *gunas* and their succession of transformations is fulfilled.[114]

tataḥ kṛta-arthānām pariṇāma-krama-samāpatiḥ guṇānāṃ

tataḥ = this

then, from that

kṛta = fulfilled

done, achieved, performed, prepared, made ready, obtained, gained, acquired, placed at hand, well done, good, proper, cultivated, appointed (as a duty), deed, work, action (See 2.22)

arthānām = purpose (See 1.28, 1.32, 1.42–1.43, 2.2, 2.18, 2.21–2.22, 3.3, 3.17, 3.36, 4.23–4.24, 4.32, 4.34)

Refer to 1.28 for more on *artha*.

pariṇāma = transformations

changes, evolution (See 2.15, 3.9, 3.11–3.13, 3.15–3.16, 4.2, 4.14, 4.32–4.33)

Refer to 2.15 for more on *parinama*.

[114] Recall that in sutra 2.18, the purpose of the *gunas* (constituents and qualities of nature) is given as providing experiences and liberation.

krama = succession

series, sequence, uninterrupted or regular progress, step, system, proceeding, course, going, way, power, strength, custom, according to rank, order, regular arrangement, method, manner, in drama: the attainment of the desired object, a rule sanctioned by tradition, a position taken by an animal prior to attacking, uninterrupted progress, regular arrangement, progressing step-by-step (See 3.15, 3.53, 4.32–4.33)

from ***kram*** = to approach, realistic, to gain a footing, to step, to proceed well, to take possession of, to walk, to stride, to go across, to go, to undertake, to succeed

samāpatiḥ = fulfilled

completes, conclude, terminate, accomplishment, complete acquisition (as in knowledge), perfection, reconciling differences

from ***sam*** = together + ***āpti***, from ***āp*** = obtain

guṇānām = the *gunas* (See 1.16)

4.33 The series of transformations correlates to moments (time) which are transcended when the transformations end.

kṣaṇa-pratyogi pariṇāma-aparānta-nigrāhyaḥ kramaḥ

kṣaṇa = moments (See 3.9, 3.53, 4.33)

second, any instantaneous points of time, center, middle, instant, twinkling of an eye, dependence, phase, leisure

In Samkhya, according to sage Vyasa, the time it takes for an atom to move its own measure of space is called a "moment" (*ksana*).

If we substitute another of the definitions of *ksana,* "center", we find a noteworthy facet of the word:

"Time is a series of individual centers..."

What this implies is that each moment, although passing in a flash, is a center. Even that fleeting moment creates a sense of stability in the mind.

Time is not a flowing continuum, but a blazingly fast procession of centers of matter and experience.

pratyogi = correlates

corresponds, counterpart, match

from ***prati*** = against, back + ***yogin***, from ***yuj*** = to join

pariṇāma = transformations

change, evolution (See 2.15, 3.9, 3.11–3.13, 3.15–3.16, 4.2, 4.14, 4.32–4.33)

Refer to 2.15 for more on *parinama*.

aparānta = end

at the utmost limit, at the other end

nigrāhyaḥ = transcended

defeat, overthrow, boundary, limit, to hold down, lower, depress, to keep or hold back, draw near, attract, to seize, catch, apprehensible, terminated, recognized, to be suppressed

from ***ni*** = down, into + ***grāhya***, a form of ***grabh*** = grasp

kramaḥ = series

series, sequence, uninterrupted or regular progress, step, system, proceeding, course, going, way, power, strength, custom, according to rank, order, regular arrangement, method, manner, in drama: the attainment of the desired object, a rule sanctioned by tradition, a position taken by an animal prior to attacking, uninterrupted progress, regular arrangement, progressing step-by-step (See 3.15, 3.53, 4.32–4.33)

from ***kram*** = to approach, realistic, to gain a footing, to step, to proceed well, to take possession of, to walk, to stride, to go across, to go, to undertake, to succeed

Refer to 3.15 for more on *kramah*.

. . . for we physicists believe the separation between past, present, and future is only an illusion, although a convincing one.

– Albert Einstein

Modern physics offers several theories of the nature of time. In general, it is agreed that time is part of space-time continuum and that time cannot exist independent of the universe. Both space and time began with the Big Bang. Every event occurs in both space and time.

For advanced yogis, when the *gunas* resolve back to their source, so does time. In the highest *samadhi*, the yogi transcends space and time. All limitations – space, time, the material universe – are transcended.

4.34 The three qualities of nature (*gunas*), having concluded their purpose for the *Purusha*, return to their original state of equilibrium. In other words, the power of pure consciousness stands steadfast and unchanging in its essential nature as the Self. This is liberation. (See 1.2 – 1.4)

puruṣa-artha-śunyānāṃ gunanāṃ pratiprasavaḥ
kaivalyaṃ svarūpa-pratisha vā citi-śaktir iti

puruṣa = left untranslated

Self (See 1.16, 1.24, 3.36. 3.50, 3.56, 4.18)

Refer to 1.16 for more on *Purusha*.

artha = purpose (See 1.28, 1.32, 1.42–1.43, 2.2, 2.18, 2.21–2.22, 3.3, 3.17, 3.36, 4.23–4.24, 4.32)

Refer to 1.28 for more on *artha*

śūnyānām = having concluded

empty, devoid, possessing nothing (See 1.9)

from ***śu***= to swell

guṇānām = the *gunas* (See 1.16, 2.15, 2.19, 4.13, 4.32)

Refer to 1.16 for more on *gunas*.

pratiprasavaḥ = return to a state of equilibrium

reabsorb, return to the origin, disassociation from the creation process, counter-order, return to the original state, inverse propagation (See 2.10)

from ***prati*** = against, back + ***prasava*** = creation, begetting, from ***pra*** = before forward + ***sava*** = pressing out, from ***su*** = generate, impel

Returning to a state of equilibrium could be referring to the subjective experience of the movements, purpose, and relevance of *prakriti* coming to an end. It is complete freedom from the craving for sense experiences, harmful emotions, and subconscious impressions (*samskaras*) born of ignorance, karma, and rebirth. The mind, freed of all these entanglements, now naturally, lives, delights, and remains in – and is guided by – the light of pure awareness, *Purusha*.

Pratiprasava is a key principle in Yoga, but not one so easily grasped. We can get a peek into its meaning by seeing how it applies to the practice of meditation. When we meditate, we don't speak. We could say that speech has resolved into its source, the mind. The quieting of the gross leads to its subtle cause. The same can be said of the stoppage of other senses: smell, sound, sight, and touch. The senses return to their origin, the mind. The mind, when it quiets, reveals its source, *sattva* – its origin. The pure, stable state of *sattva*, having been attained, allows for the experience of the Self.[115]

Let the wise merge their speech into the mind, the mind into the intellect (buddhi), and the intellect into the Great Self (Atma), and the Great Self into the Peaceful Self.
– Katha Upanishad 1.3.13

Beyond the senses is the mind, higher than the mind is the intellect, higher than the intellect is the Great Self, higher than the Great Self is the unmanifested (undifferentiated prakriti, called maya by adherents of Vedanta).

Beyond the unmanifested is the Purusha, all-pervading and devoid of identifying marks. Those who know this are liberated and obtain immortality.
– Katha Upanishad 2.3.7-8

[115] This logic is in keeping with the evolution of *prakriti* according to Samkhya philosophy, upon which much of Patanjali's Yoga is based.

kaivalyam = liberation

absoluteness, independence, isolation (See 2.25, 3.51, 3.56, 4.26)

Refer to 2.25 for more on *kaivalyam*.

svarūpa = True Nature

own form, own nature (See 1.3, 1.43, 2.23, 2.54, 3.3, 3.45, 3.48)

Refer to 1.3 for more on *svarupa*.

pratiṣṭhā = steadfast and unchanging

settles in, firm, unwavering, perseverance, standing firmly, ending with, leading to, famous, preeminence, point of support, the center or base of anything

from ***prati*** = against, back + ***stha*** = stand (See 1.8)

vā = in other words

or, and

citi = absolute consciousness

higher awareness (See 4.22)

***Citi* is not to be confused with *citta*, the individual mind. This is a higher state of consciousness which only arises when extraordinary one-pointedness, tranquility, clarity, and nonattachment occur.**

śaktiḥ = power (See 2.6, 2.23, 2.34, 3.21)

***Citi* plus *shakti* translates as "the power of pure consciousness." *Citi* is pure, unbounded consciousness – consciousness that transcends, and is the source of, the mind's reflected consciousness (See 4.22). It is the power of the *Purusha*, the power of seeing.**

In a normal state of consciousness, we have the power *(shakti)* of the mind *(citta)*. It allows us to be aware of gross and subtle objects and interactions in the physical universe. With the arising of *citi shakti*, the mind, having attained the power of pure, unbridled awareness – unhindered by ignorance – gains the power to discern the *Purusha* as Self.

Refer to 2.6 for more on *shakti*.

This final sutra restates the realization of the goal that Patanjali set out in sutras 1.2 and 1.3.

It is thus.

iti = (refers to the end of Patanjali's teachings)

it is thus

The destination has been reached. Patanjali ends his exposition in a wonderfully clear, simple, and powerful way. The message here is direct: What is contained in the *Sutras* is true. It is real. We can rely on the guidance given.

Can there be a better way of ending this journey to enlightenment?

If we only would look within, we would see the Light
as if we were seeing our own image in a mirror.
– Sri Swami Satchidananda

Continuous Translation With Narrative

This section provides a sense of the flow and interconnectedness of the major themes that form the foundation of the *Yoga Sutras*. It presupposes a basic familiarity with the major teachings and practices of the *Yoga Sutras* – at least the major teachings found in the first and second chapters. Use it for a review and as a reference for deeper study and understanding. It is also a handy tool to help teachers gather and organize information for their classes.

Notice that key topics appear in several sections of the text. It might be tempting to think that the *Yoga Sutras* is a slightly disorganized or mysteriously ordered collection of teachings. Instead, repetition is a powerful technique that serves to solidify our grasp of the fundamental teachings by presenting additional perspectives and nuances each time a particular principle appears.

The Major Theme: *Nirodha*

The first and foremost tenet to examine is *nirodha*. It's not an exaggeration to state that the entirety of the *Yoga Sutras* revolves around what this one tenet implies.[1]

The pinnacle of *nirodha* is the complete quieting of the whirling excursions of thought that make up the conscious and subconscious mind. If we limit our understanding of *nirodha* to mind control through contemplative practices, we run the risk of missing *nirodha's* full power to transform lives on every level. While it is true that the *Sutras* place an emphasis on contemplative practices that directly help still the fluctuations of the mind, a deeper look at the *Sutras* reveals that *nirodha* – and therefore all of Yoga – embodies a truly holistic approach that includes moral and ethical guidelines, physical practices, nonattachment, study, and devotion to the Absolute. In its broadest sense, *nirodha* is about the process of individual spiritual evolution, of self-transformation. It is pivoting away from ignorance and suffering and moving toward the Light of truth, peace, joy, and wisdom. (See 1.2, 1.12, 1.51, 3.9).

[1] Recall that *nirodha* is not just about gaining mastery over the fluctuations of thought, but is the ending of misperception that the mind-body is the Self. A complete overview of the breadth and depth of *nirodha* is found in the extended notes of sutra 1.2.

As you read through the *Sutras*, note the central role played by the following principles and practices. They are powerful catalysts for self-transformation and enlightenment.

- *Dharana*: concentration. The first stage in the practice of meditation, it is the repeated redirection of attention on the chosen object of contemplation when our attention has wandered.[2]

- *Dhyana*: meditation proper. The mind rests in a meditative state when attention is sustained longer than *dharana*. The meditative state provides the first tastes of stable, deep, clear, focused attention.

- *Samadhi*: contemplative absorption. It is experienced when the state of meditation (*dhyana*) is prolonged. A state of absorption or oneness with the object of contemplation arises. (See 1.20, 1.46, 1.51, 2.2, 2.29, 2.45, 3.3, 3.11, 3.37, 4.1, 4.29)

- *Prajna*: intuitive insight. Usually arising from the states of *samadhi*, *prajna* becomes the major tool used to delve into the inner workings of self and the universe. *Prajna* is the highly refined direct perception of subtle truths. In some faith traditions, these direct perceptions are referred to as revelations. (See 1.20, 1.47–1.51, 2.27, 3.5)

- *Vairagya*: the state of nonattachment, self-mastery, and absence of ego-driven desires. (See 1.12, 1.15, 3.50)

- *Ishvara pranidhanam*: whole-hearted devotion to God. This is mentioned four times in the *Sutras* suggesting its importance to the yogic path to liberation. (See 1.23, 2.1, 2.32, 2.45)

[2] See sutras 1.34–1.39 for a listing of some objects suitable for contemplation. But note that the undisturbed calmness of mind that is the goal of meditation is first mentioned in sutra 1.33 – the Four Locks and the Four Keys, again emphasizing the holistic nature of Yoga.

- *Viveka*: the ability to discern the difference between: the Real and the unreal, the permanent and the impermanent, the painful and the pleasurable, the Self and the non-Self. Unwavering *viveka* is needed to attain liberation. It is cultivated through the practice of the eight limbs. (See 2.5, 2.26, 2.28–2.29, 3.52, 3.54, 4.26, 4.29)

- *Pratiprasava*: returning to the source and essence. *Pratiprasava* is the natural outcome of a clear, peaceful, one-pointed mind free from selfish attachment. *Pratiprasava* can be regarded as an apt overall description of the yogic path and goal. All theories and practices, all lifestyle observances and resolves, help usher the yogi's return to his or her source and essence. (See 2.10, 4.3)

Chapter One
Samadhi Pada: The Chapter on Absorption

The first four sutras provide the fundamental definition and premise of Yoga. You might think of these sutras as the Core Four. If you widen your attention to include the next twelve sutras, you will discover the unifying theme upon which all of the principles and practices found in the Yoga *Sutras* are based. These sixteen sutras - the "Sweet Sixteen" - offer a clear, precise description of what Yoga theory and practice is truly about.

A call to action:

1.1 Now is the time for Yoga[3]. (See sutra 2.15)

Yoga is defined:

1.2 Yoga ends the misperception that the Seer/Self is the same as the mind's usual tangle of whirling excursions of thought (*vrittis*).

1.3 When this mistaken perception ends, the Seer (pure, unchanging, eternal consciousness) stands free as the true Self.

1.4 Otherwise, the mind continues to mistake the whirling excursions of thought (*vrittis*) as the Self.

The five categories of whirling excursions of mind (*vrittis*) that obscure the experience of the Self/Seer are presented:

1.5 There are five types of *vrittis*. Those that are afflicted by ignorance of one's True Self bring pain. Without the influence of ignorance, they are painless.

1.6 The five types are:

- Reliable knowledge
- Unreliable knowledge

[3] This opening sutra implies a sense of urgency. Patanjali seems intent on igniting curiosity and resolve regarding the path of Yoga and the Yoga life. The very last word in the *Sutras* – *iti* – tells us that Patanjali has satisfied the curiosity and needs of even the most ardent seeker.

- Knowledge based on words without substance
- Sleep
- Remembering

1.7 *Vrittis* bring reliable knowledge – knowledge that is trustworthy and useful – through:
- Information obtained from the senses' direct contact with sense objects
- Inference properly applied
- Authoritative testimony

1.8 Knowledge is unreliable when based on errors in perception, which result in false information regarding the True Nature of an object or event.

1.9 Words without substance refers to knowledge that is based on words alone without any tangible reality to verify it.

1.10 Deep sleep occurs when the waking and dreaming states (*vrittis*) are naturally overcome by inertia. There is only awareness of the thought of non-existence.

1.11 Remembering is the recollecting of objects and occurrences that have been experienced.

Nonattachment and practice – the fundamental two-pronged approach to self-transformation and Self-realization – is defined:

1.12 The ingrained habit of mistaking the *vrittis* as the Self ceases by practice and nonattachment.

1.13 Of these, practice is the regular repeated effort to break free from this misidentification by cultivating steady resolve and a tranquil focused flow of awareness.

1.14 Practice becomes fully integrated into one's life when it is carefully nurtured for a long time and engaged in faithfully, with inner reflection and fervor.

1.15 Nonattachment is self-mastery and freedom from craving. It manifests when love of liberation (from ignorance and the suffering craving brings) awakens due to the recognition of the beguiling and captivating nature of craving for objects seen, heard, or described.

1.16 The highest nonattachment arises when the *Purusha* is correctly discerned as the True Self. This realization ends all craving, the compulsive urge to find lasting satisfaction from any sense experience that can be provided by nature (*gunas*, the constituents of nature).

With regular practice of Yoga's techniques, in tandem with the cultivation of nonattachment, the mind becomes clearer, steadier, and more able to pierce deeper levels of creation and self. *Samadhi* (sometimes also referred to as *samapatti*) is the name for various levels of meditative absorption. In *samadhi*, intuitive insights arise, unearthing profound, life-altering truths. *Samadhi* serves as yogis' primary investigative tool on his or her spiritual journey.

1.17 When practice and nonattachment strengthen, intuitive insight (*samprajnata*) arises. As this insight deepens, it reveals four increasingly subtle levels of nature (*prakriti*), bringing complete and accurate knowledge of the object of contemplation.

The four levels are:

- *Vitarka (investigation into the gross form of objects)*: The mind investigates and gains knowledge of the gross aspect of an object.
- *Vichara (knowledge of subtle essences)*: The factors that brought the object into existence are revealed.
- *Ananda (bliss of a sattvic mind)*: At this level, attention naturally turns to awareness itself. Devoid of a gross or subtle object (*manas*) the part of the mind that constantly seeks objects to grasp becomes clear and tranquil, resulting in the experience of joy.
- *Asmita (ego sense)*: The direct experience of the ego sense, pure I-amness.

The duality of mind and object remains in all these states.

1.18 Another, deeper insight manifests with the sustained practice of quieting all conscious thoughts, intentions, and expectations until only subconscious impressions (*samskaras*) remain.

Since there are no objects in the conscious mind to investigate and therefore, no insights to be had, this experience is referred to as *asamprajnata samadhi*, beyond insights (or beyond discerning).

Even when the yogi has attained these lower levels of *samadhi*[4] there is still the danger of losing the ground gained. Self-centered attachments form the slippery slope to unrealized yogic objectives:

1.19 Unresolved or unexpressed feelings and intentions can cause the individual to become melded with *prakriti* (through thoughts of continued existence) and subject to rebirth. This can be true even for celestial beings who are without gross physical bodies.

1.20 Others, aware of how attachments hinder progress, continue to strive to attain (the highest) *samadhi*, a state preceded by:

- Faith
- Courage to face obstacles and the persistence to carry on
- Remembrance of life's lessons and repeated recollection of the truths of sacred wisdom traditions
- (lower) States of contemplative absorption (*samadhi*), a clear, tranquil, one-pointed mind
- Intuitive insights which remove ignorance

Firm resolve and fervor build immunity to self-centered attachments:

1.21 Success is near for those whose resolve is unrestrained – fervent and unwavering.

1.22 Understanding the power of resolve, one can infer that nearness of success depends on the degree of its steadiness and intensity: mild, moderate, or fervent.

[4] The higher levels of *samadhi* are given later (see 1.47–1.51, 4.29)

Up to this point, the *Sutras'* primary focus is on the nature, activities, and habit patterns of the mind. In the next sutra, the scope of the path of Yoga is expanded to include the heart and its natural inclination toward devotion and selfless dedicated action. In this case, the object of devotion is God, *Ishvara*:[5]

1.23 Or *asamprajnata samadhi* can be attained by wholehearted devotion and dedication to God (*Ishvara*), which displaces self-centered personal desires and naturally fosters contemplative absorption.

1.24 *Ishvara* is a unique *Purusha*. It is never touched by the root causes of suffering (*klesas*), the entanglements created by actions, their reactions (karma), and the subconscious impressions (*samskaras*) produced by these actions.

1.25 There, in *Ishvara*, is the seed of omniscience, which surpasses all other sources of knowledge and ideas of omniscience. It is beyond what is known by gods, clergy, and philosophers.

1.26 Not bound by time, *Ishvara* is the Guru of even the most ancient Gurus.

1.27 *Ishvara* expresses as the primordial sound OM, also known as *pranava*.

Mantra repetition (mantra *japa*) is introduced. It is a powerful and often recommended practice that brings great benefit to those of a devotional nature and those not so inclined:[6]

1.28 Repeat it with focus, devotion, and right understanding and the purpose of this practice is revealed.

1.29 From this practice, awareness attains focus and naturally turns within. Not only that, obstacles that distract the mind and obstruct practice vanish.

[5] The path of *Bhakti Yoga*, the Yoga of devotion, insists on the freedom of devotees to worship the Divine in any name or form that resonates with them.

[6] Some mantras are strongly associated with specific deities; others are primarily repeated for the beneficial value of their sound vibration alone.

The obstacles that distract the mind from the path are presented.

1.30 The obstacles that distract the mind and disrupt practice are:
- Disease
- Dullness, complacency, narrow-mindedness
- Doubt
- Carelessness
- Laziness
- Addiction to sense experiences
- Confused, false, or shifting views on principles of life, wisdom teachings, and practice
- Failure to reach firm ground
- Slipping from the ground gained

1.31 These distracting obstacles are accompanied by:
- *Duhkha*: dissatisfaction, sorrow, suffering, and a pervasive, persistent feeling of precariousness
- Frustration from not having desires fulfilled
- Restlessness or trembling of the body
- Agitated or labored inhalation or exhalation

1.32 In order to prevent the distracting obstacles and their accompaniments, commit to the teachings and practices of one path.

In sutra 1.33 we come to the Four Locks and Four Keys, core teachings that help define the nature of the yogi's relationship with others. These are practical guidelines that can benefit anyone – yogis or not. The teachings in this sutra are gems of practical advice that cultivate undisturbed calmness of mind, on or off the mat or meditation cushion. They not only hasten progress in Yoga for the individual seeker, but also help generate harmony in society at large.[7]

1.33 The mind becomes calm, clear, and bright when it cultivates and abides in the unconditional virtues of friendliness, compassion, delight, and equanimity in conditions, respectively, of happiness, distress, virtue, and absence of virtue.

[7] Keep in mind that the keys to peace given should be applied to the individual yogi as well as to others.

Other methods for attaining undisturbed calmness of mind are listed:

1.34 Or by smooth, regulated exhalation and by retention of the breath.

1.35 Or clear steadiness of mind is attained when focus on a sense object causes a subtle sense perception to arise.

1.36 Or by contemplating the supreme radiant light in the heart that is beyond sorrow.

1.37 Or by contemplating the state of a great soul's mind that is free from attachments to sense objects.

1.38 Or by contemplating knowledge revealed through:

- A dream
- The tranquility of deep sleep
- The sense of individuality that persists through the states of wakefulness, dreamless sleep, and dreams

1.39 Or by meditating on any suitable object that inspires you.

1.40 When any meditation practice is mastered, the mind is freed from the distracting obstacles. Then the mind is able to focus its attention on anything from the smallest particle to the greatest magnitude.

The essential meditative practices have been outlined. Now we revisit *samadhi*, first presented in 1.17. Sutra 1.41 treats us to a clear foundational definition of *samadhi*. The sutras that follow offer details on the various levels of *samadhi*. Compare these with the descriptions given in sutra 1.17.

1.41 With regular practice and nonattachment, the whirling excursions of thought (*vrittis*) dwindle, weaken, and cease. As a result, the faculties of the mind become absorbed on the object of contemplation. The mind becomes like a naturally flawless transparent crystal that assumes the shapes and colors of objects nearby. This experience, called *samapatti* (or *samadhi*), is the union of knower, the object known, and the act of attaining knowledge.

1.42 There are levels of *samadhi*. In the first, mingling of the word, form, and knowledge regarding the object of contemplation persist. This is known as *savitarka samadhi*, or *samadhi* accompanied by concepts (of the object).

1.43 On the next level, the memory is completely cleared of all words, forms, knowledge, and concepts regarding the object of contemplation. It's as if the mind gives up its own intentions and identity so that only the object of contemplation shines forth in its own nature. This is called *nirvitarka samadhi*, the *samadhi* free of any concepts associated with the object.

1.44 The next two levels of *samadhi* are deeper, but can be explained in the same way as the previous two. They are practiced on the subtle nature of objects and are known as *savichara*, with insight, and *nirvichara*, beyond insight.

1.45 The subtlety of objects for contemplation ends only at what is undefinable: the unmanifest state of matter (*prakriti*). At this level, since matter has no distinguishing characteristics, there are no objects to perceive. There is just the primordial soup of *prakriti*.

1.46 These four *samadhis* still carry the seeds of subconscious impressions (*samskaras*).

1.47 As *nirvichara samadhi* fully matures, the luminous tranquil clarity of the supreme inner Self shines forth.

1.48 This state is truth-bearing. It grants intuitive insights into the cosmic order – the deepest realities of existence: self-identity, the mind, and the universe.

1.49 The purpose of this insight is different from the insights gained from inference or from hearing sacred wisdom teachings. Its unique purpose is to end false identification with the seen (nature, *prakriti*) by being able to discern the Seer (Self, *Purusha*) from the seen. (See 1.2–1.4)

1.50 The subconscious impression (*samskara*) born of this insight displaces all other *samskaras*.

The highest *samadhi* is now defined:

1.51 When even this impression (*samskara*) stills, all mental processes– conscious and subconscious - are stilled. This is the seedless (*nirbija*) *samadhi*, the state that transcends ignorance and brings liberation.

Looking ahead:

Having stated the goal of Yoga and outlined the fundamentals of Yoga practice and nonattachment, the next chapter describes a very compelling reason for living a Yoga life: transcending ignorance and the suffering it brings.

Chapter Two
Sadhana Pada: The Chapter on the Purpose of Practice

The chapter on practice provides the bedrock upon which the entire Yoga life and its practices are developed. It is summarized in three practices.

2.1 Kriya Yoga, the three elements that form the foundation of the Yoga life, are:
- *Tapas*: self-discipline and accepting hardship and pain as a help for purification
- *Svadhyaya*: repeated, deep study of sacred wisdom and the introspective search into the nature of the self; mantra repetition
- *Ishvara pranidhanam*: wholehearted devotion and dedication to *Ishvara*

2.2 Their purpose is to cultivate *samadhi* and to weaken and diminish the root causes of suffering (*klesas*).

The root causes of suffering are identified:

2.3 The root causes of suffering (*klesas*) are ignorance, egoism, attachment, aversion, and clinging to bodily life.

2.4 Ignorance is the origin of the other root causes of suffering (*klesas*), whether they are dormant, weakened, interrupted, or fully active.

2.5 Ignorance is rooted in misperception. It is due to experiencing:
- What changes as unchanging
- What is impure, colored by bias, and nonvirtuous as pure, free of bias, and virtuous
- What brings pain, restlessness, dissatisfaction, and distress as that which brings serenity, contentment, fulfillment, and happiness
- What is not the Self as the Self

2.6 Egoism arises from confusion – regarding the power of the Seer and the power of the instrument of seeing (mind/intellect) as the same thing.

2.7 Attachment arises from clinging to pleasurable experiences.

2.8 Aversion arises from clinging to painful experiences.

2.9 Clinging to life arises even in the wise and learned. It persists because it is innate.

The methods for overcoming the root causes of suffering are presented:

2.10 The root causes of suffering (*klesas*) are overcome in their subtle form (subconscious impressions) when the mind returns to its original, pure state. (See 1.45, 2.4, 4.34)

2.11 In their gross, active manifestations they can be overcome by meditation. (See 2.2)

Karma, the universal law of cause and effect, is introduced. Karma serves as one of Yoga's major lenses for viewing and making sense of the inner workings of life: the factors that determine the nature of our experiences – pleasant or unpleasant, beneficial or harmful. Karma is grounded in the root causes of suffering. This means that ignorance is karma's father (See 2.24). If we had to designate a mother, it would be *prakriti*. Ignorance of reality (father) plus the mesmerizing power of *prakriti* (mother) produces karma and the experiences we must face in this and future lifetimes.

Understanding karma helps us appreciate the powerful impact that our motives, decisions, and behavior have on the content and quality of our lives:

2.12 The residue of karma, the latent impressions produced by past actions, is rooted in the *klesas*. The effect of these impressions is experienced in present or future births.

2.13 As long as ignorance, the source of the root causes of suffering (*klesas*) exists, karma produces fruits in the form each birth takes, its life span, and its experiences.

2.14 These fruits can be either sweet or bitter – pleasurable or painful – depending on whether they were caused by virtuous or nonvirtuous acts.

This next sutra provides the ultimate reason for engaging in Yoga practices and living a yogic lifestyle: transcending suffering. Yoga, which can be translated as "remedy" offers a way out of fear, chronic anxiety, sorrow, and dissatisfaction. (See also 1.1)

2.15 Those who investigate the ways of life find that pain, sorrow, dissatisfaction, and a feeling of persistent, pervasive precariousness are surely a part of all experiences. This is *duhkha*. It is due to:

- Fear over losing what is gained
- The impermanence of all things
- Subconscious habit patterns (*samskaras*) created under the influence of ignorance that sustain craving and ignorance
- Changes of mood and mindset due to the interplay of the forces of nature (*gunas*) that vie for dominance in the mind

2.16 The *duhkha* that has not yet come can be avoided.

2.17 The dissatisfaction and suffering (*duhkha*) that can be prevented is caused by confusing the nature of the Seer with that of the seen.

We have learned that confusing the nature and powers of the seen (material nature, *prakriti*) with those of the Seer (Self, *Purusha*) is the immediate cause of suffering[8]. To help end this confusion, Patanjali now expands our knowledge of the nature – the identifying or characteristic factors – of Seer (Self, *Purusha*) and seen (*prakriti*):

2.18 The seen consists of the five elements and sense organs and has the qualities of translucence, activity, and inertia. Its purpose is to provide experiences and liberation.

2.19 There are four different stages of the evolution of the seen. They are, from gross to subtle:

- Discernible by the senses: gross elements
- Not discernible by the senses: subtle elements
- The discriminative faculty (*buddhi*), the first product of *prakriti*
- Undifferentiated matter, the *gunas* in equilibrium without any form

[8] Confusion is another way of describing ignorance.

2.20 The Seer is nothing but the sheer power of seeing – pure consciousness. Although it is pure and unchanging, it appears to have the qualities and contents of the mind.

2.21 The seen is worthwhile, beautiful, and pleasing since it has meaning– its nature and essence is truly for the purpose of experience and liberation.

2.22 For the liberated, the purpose of the seen – providing experiences and liberation – is fulfilled. It's as if it disappears, although it doesn't really vanish since the experience of its reality and its relevance is common to others.

2.23 Confusing the natures and powers of the Owner (Seer) and owned (seen) creates the condition for perceiving them as one.

Next, Patanjali reminds us that ignorance is the predecessor and foundation of all other causes of suffering:

2.24 Ignorance is the cause of confusing the Seer and seen as one.

2.25 Without ignorance, this confusion ceases to exist. The Seer stands apart from the seen as the Self. This is liberation (*kaivalya*).

If ignorance – *not knowing* – is the ultimate cause of suffering, then *knowing* is the ultimate remedy. *Viveka* is the unwavering discriminative discernment that yogis develop through practice and nonattachment. Through *viveka*, revelatory knowledge arises and ignorance is transcended.

2.26 The remedy that removes ignorance is an unwavering flow of discriminative discernment (*viveka*) which perceives the difference between the Seer and seen. (See 4.25–4.26 and 4.29–4.30)

2.27 For the yogi who attains this unwavering discernment (*viveka*), seveninsights arise that lead to the final stage – liberation.[9]

Attaining unwavering discriminative discernment is a lofty goal. The genius of Patanjali is that he provides practical straightforward teachings – a collection of holistic practices – that awaken deep, penetrating *viveka*. This compendium of practices forms the eight limbs of Yoga, the heart of Yoga practice and the Yoga life. Since it encompasses all of Yoga's essential practices, the *Yoga Sutras* are widely referred to as Ashtanga Yoga, the eight-limbed Yoga.

2.28 By integrating the limbs of Yoga into daily life, impurities – all born from the root causes of suffering (*klesas*) – dwindle away. The mind becomes illumined with the light of wisdom, culminating in unwavering discriminative discernment (*viveka*).

2.29 The eight limbs of Yoga are:

1. *Yama* = universal resolves that foster harmonious relationships to self, others, and life
2. *Niyama* = additional resolves taken on by yogis to encourage spiritual growth
3. *Asana* = posture
4. *Pranayama* = regulation of breath
5. *Pratyahara* = management and withdrawal of the senses
6. *Dharana* = concentration
7. *Dhyana* = meditation
8. *Samadhi* = absorption

2.30 *Yama* – the universal resolves – consists of:

- *Ahimsa* = harmlessness
- *Satya* = truthfulness

[9] Patanjali offers no details on the seven insights he is referring to, but here is a commonly accepted list:
1. Through *viveka*, the causes of suffering are recognized. Therefore, there is nothing more to be known on this subject.
2. The causes of suffering, having been identified, are progressively weakened.
3. Through *samadhi*, the causes of suffering are eliminated. There is nothing more to be gained in this area.
4. Mastery in *viveka* having been reached, there is nothing else self-effort can accomplish.
5. *Sattva* dominates the functioning of the mind-stuff.
6. The *gunas*, having fulfilled their purpose, lose their foothold like stones falling from a mountain peak, and incline toward reabsorption into *prakriti*.
7. The *Purusha* is realized as independent from the *gunas*. Liberation is attained.

- *Asteya* = nonstealing
- *Brahmacharya* = a life dedicated to self-mastery and liberation
- *Aparigraha* = freedom from craving to possess sense objects

2.31 The *yamas* are universal resolves for proper behavior in society. They are bright lights that reveal the way to a life of virtue and joy. Because they hold the capacity to bring peace and harmony, they apply to every being, regardless of social status, time, or circumstance.

2.32 *Niyama* – additional resolves yogis observe – consists of:

- *Saucha* = purity
- *Santosha* = contentment
- *Tapas* = accepting challenge, struggle, discomfort, and self-discipline as a help for purification
- *Svadhyaya* = repeated deep study of sacred wisdom and the introspective search into the nature of the self; mantra repetition
- *Ishvara pranidhanam* = wholehearted devotion and dedication to *Ishvara* (See 1.24)

The eightfold path offers supremely effective methods for self-transformation. Over the long haul, it's not always easy to be regular with our practices and resolves. Here, Patanjali provides two forms of *pratipaksha bhavana* – a powerful method for remaining on the yogic path.

2.33 When doubt or wayward thoughts disturb the cultivation of the *yamas* and *niyamas*, generate the opposite: a counterforce of thoughts, images, or feelings that have the power to uplift, invigorate, inspire, and steady the mind. This is *pratipaksha bhavana*.

2.34 Dubious reasoning and wayward thoughts such as causing harm, etc., whether done, incited, or approved of; whether arising from lust, anger, or delusion; and regardless of being mild, medium, or extreme in intensity, have ignorance and endless dissatisfaction and suffering (*duhkha*) as their fruits. Reflecting on this is also *pratipaksha bhavana*.

The rest of this chapter details some of the great benefits that can be attained when firmly established in the *yamas* and *niyamas*.

2.35 In the presence of one who is firmly established in nonviolence, hostility recedes.

2.36 On being firmly grounded in truthfulness, every thought, word, and deed will be an expression of the nature of *sat*: truth, existence; that which is good, real, authentic, wise, venerable and is in harmony with the essential nature of a being.

2.37 On being firmly grounded in nonstealing, all that is truly valuable comes near.

2.38 On being firmly grounded in a life of self-mastery and liberation (*brahmacharya*), one gains the power to endure, persevere, and succeed.

2.39 The meaning of life awakens when freedom from sense craving is unwavering.

2.40 From purity, one's instinctive protective intelligence awakens. Infatuation with one's own body, as well as sensual contact with others that is incompatible with the goal of Yoga, is naturally avoided.

2.41 Furthermore, when the mind is purified, it becomes clear and steady (*sattvic*). From this arises cheerfulness, one-pointedness, mastery of the senses, and fitness for Self-realization.

2.42 By contentment, the swift, easy flow of supreme joy is attained.

2.43 From the fire of self-discipline and the acceptance of life's inevitable hardships – and the lessons that can be learned from them – impurities evaporate and the full manifestation of the powers of the body and senses arise.

2.44 By the repeated study and integration of sacred wisdom, and the repetition of mantras, seekers create the condition for experiencing communion with their *Ishta Devata* – the symbol, image, or enlightened being that is their most cherished connection with divinity.

2.45 By wholehearted dedication to *Ishvara*, *samadhi* can be perfected or attained.

2.46 *Asana* should be steady and easeful.

2.47 *Asana* naturally becomes steady and easeful by relaxing physical effort and contemplating one's connection with the infinite. The yogi rests like the cosmic serpent Ananta, floating on the primordial waters, on whom rests Vishnu, the Lord of the Universe.

2.48 From this, one is undisturbed by dualities.

2.49 When a steady, easeful *asana* is achieved, *pranayama* can be practiced by regulating the movements of inhalation and exhalation.

2.50 The movements of the breath – inhalation, exhalation, and retention– are regulated according to the:

- Area of focus during practice
- Length of time of inhalation, exhalation, and retention
- Number of repetitions
- Perception that the breath, with practice, becomes subtle and penetrates deeply.

2.51 There is a fourth *pranayama* that transcends efforts to regulate the internal and external movements of the breath. It is a natural spontaneous suspension of breathing that occurs when the mind is steady.

2.52 Then the veil that obscures the inner light (*sattva*) dissipates.

2.53 And the mind attains *dharana*, the ability to hold focused attention. (See 1.34, 1.40)

2.54 When the mind is indrawn, the senses follow, withdrawing from sense objects. This is *pratyahara*, sense management.

2.55 From this practice, the highest mastery of the senses arises.

Looking ahead:

In the second chapter, we were given the essential theories and practices of Yoga. In the first twelve sutras of chapter three, Patanjali dives deeper into the meditative process and the levels of contemplation that can be attained. Following these sutras, he turns his attention to the extraordinary abilities (*siddhis*) that can be attained by a one-pointed mind.

For centuries, yogis have been admired and often feared for the supernormal powers they displayed.[10] Although Patanjali discourages efforts to attain most of these powers, he doesn't shy away from this topic. Instead, he includes a long list of some well-known powers and the ways to realize them. Why?

His motive might have been to demonstrate that such powers are not due to propitiating a deity, a bargain made with a disembodied spirit, or even more troubling – a deal with a demon.[11] Also, because of the long history of yogis' association with supernormal powers, his teaching could be regarded as incomplete without addressing this phenomenon.

Patanjali presents the powers as a result of an intention to attain a particular power coupled with a remarkable depth of mental focus (*samyama*).

The existence of these powers also serves to demonstrate that there is more to us and this universe than meets the eye.

See the preface to chapter three for more on the *siddhis*.

[10] Many times these powers were merely some form of tricks or illusions, used to attain some advantage through inspiring awe, wonderment, or intimidation of the wealthy and powerful.

[11] This may be the reason that among the some thirty definitions of the word Yoga, we find magical art, trick, and fraud.

Chapter Three
Vibhuti Pada: The Chapter on Accomplishments

This chapter begins by deepening our understanding of the theory and practice of meditation. We learn how *nirodha* progressively develops from concentration (*dharana*), to meditation (*dhyana*), to absorption (*samadhi*).

3.1 The practice of nurturing and holding a flow of attention toward one chosen object, place, or idea is *dharana*, concentration.

3.2 When the mind achieves an effortless unbroken flow of attention toward that one object, that is *dhyana* (meditation).

3.3 By continuing in this manner, the flow of attention becomes prolonged until *samadhi* - a state of mental integration and absorption - certainly arises. In this state, it's as if the mind gives up its own form so that the essence of the object alone shines forth.

3.4 When these three - *dharana*, *dhyana*, and *samadhi*, are all directed toward one object, it is called *samyama*.

3.5 With mastery of *samyama*, the penetrating light of intuitive insight arises.

3.6 Mastery of *samyama* progresses in stages.

3.7 Compared to the preceding five limbs, *dharana, dhyana*, and *samadhi* are more inwardly directed.

3.8 But even these three are external compared to the seedless (*nirbija*) *samadhi,* that transcends ignorance and brings liberation. (See 1.51)

3.9 This is how *nirodha* develops until it permeates the mind. Practice and nonattachment generate subconscious impressions of *nirodha*. As each moment of *nirodha* appears, it subdues the impressions that perpetuate the fluctuating, externalized states of mind.

3.10 When impressions of *nirodha* become strong and pervasive, a calm flow of *nirodha* is attained.

3.11 As all of the various distractions to *nirodha* dwindle, the one-pointed awareness that cultivates *samadhi* arises.

3.12 From repeated practice, the subsiding and arising thoughts become identical. Sustaining this one-pointed awareness develops *samadhi*.

The previous sutras described how the transformation of the mind occurs. Now, Patanjali reminds us that all of nature changes in a way that is akin to the changes that occur with the mind. By drawing this parallel, we are invited to see how the mind is not separate from nature and is subject to change just like a tree, a puppy, or a galaxy.

3.13 By understanding the transformations of mind, we can also understand the transformations of the form, characteristics, and condition of the elements of nature and the senses.

The *Yoga Sutras* emphasize that the yogi must be able to discern the difference between the mind, nature (*prakriti*), and the Self (*Purusha*). Here, Patanjali offers a more detailed examination of *prakriti* to help us become familiar with its nature and its limitations:

3.14 *Prakriti* is the substratum of the changes of form and characteristics that objects exhibit as they go through the succession of stages:

- Subsiding (past)
- Arising (present)
- Unmanifest (future)

3.15 The transformation of characteristics that manifest in objects is caused by the succession of these three phases. (However, there is only one underlying substance.)

Next begins a listing of supernormal powers (*siddhis*). Recall that *samyama* is when concentration, meditation, and *samadhi* are all brought to bear on an object of contemplation:

3.16 By *samyama* on these three phases of transformation, knowledge of past and future can be known.

3.17 A word, the object it refers to, and the ideas associated with that object are normally superimposed on one another, creating one unified impression in the mind. By *samyama* on the distinction between these three factors, knowledge of the meaning of the sounds produced by all beings is attained.

3.18 By *samyama* on the subconscious impressions that form the mind's deep-rooted tendencies comes direct perception of them. From this, knowledge of previous births is obtained.

3.19 By *samyama* on the ideas and intentions of others arises the ability to know their minds.

3.20 But this knowledge does not include the object on which the thoughts are based since it is not the purpose of this perception.

3.21 By *samyama* on the visible form of the body comes the understanding that vision is the ability to perceive the light that is reflected off of objects. Arising from this is the capacity to intercept the light from the eyes of observers, making one's body invisible to them.

3.22 In the same way, the disappearance of sound, touch, taste, smell, etc., is explained.

3.23 There are two categories of karma: karmas that are active during the present lifetime and karmas that are deferred for future births. From *samyama* on the distinction between these two, or on omens found in natural phenomena, knowledge of the time of death arises. (See 2.12 – 2.14 and 3.18)

Some *siddhis* are not razzle-dazzle. Here is a sweet one:

3.24 By *samyama* on friendliness, compassion, selfless joy, equanimity, and other such virtues, their full powers manifest.

Back to razzle-dazzle:

3.25 By *samyama* on the strength of elephants and other such animals, their strength is attained.

3.26 By *samyama* on the inner light (*sattva*) that illumines sense perception, one gains knowledge of objects that are subtle, hidden from view, or distant. (See 1.36, 3.5)

3.27 By *samyama* on the sun, knowledge of all planes of existence in the universe is attained.

3.28 By *samyama* on the moon, knowledge of the stars' alignment is attained.

3.29 By *samyama* on the pole star, knowledge of the stars' movements is attained.

3.30 By *samyama* on the navel plexus, knowledge of the body's constitution is attained.

3.31 By *samyama* on the pit of the throat, cessation of hunger and thirst is attained.

3.32 By *samyama* on the tortoise-shaped channel located in the chest, one's body and mind become steady.

3.33 By *samyama* on the light just below the crown of the head, vision (*darshan*) of the *siddhas*, perfected beings, can be attained.

***Siddhis* may arise unsought as a by-product of contemplative practices, devotion, and other yogic disciplines. Sincere yogis are well aware of the dangers of regarding the *siddhis* as objects – as personal possessions – that are used for self-centered purposes. Instead, yogis are counseled to maintain the attitude that the *siddhis* are God's powers and that God will use the powers through them if and when necessary. In other words, they are firm in the attitude that they are servants of the Divine Will.**

3.34 Or, any or all of the accomplishments listed in the previous seventeen sutras, can come spontaneously – without *samyama* – when the light of intuitive insight bursts forth in a pure, clear, steady mind. (See 3.53 – 3.55)

***Samyama* can also be used to arouse deep and complete knowledge of the mind.**

3.35 By *samyama* on the heart, the center of an individual's consciousness, there arises full knowledge of the mind and its source.

Here is a *siddhi* that has a major benefit – gaining the intuitive insight that leads to being able to discern the difference between the *Purusha* and *prakriti*:

3.36 *Sattva* (the pure, luminous intellect) and the *Purusha* (the power of awareness) are distinct realities. The intellect exists for the *Purusha*. The *Purusha*, beyond the limit of the intellect, exists to express its own inherent and true meaning. Failure to perceive the distinction between the two is the cause of all experiences of pleasure and pain. By *samyama* on this distinction, knowledge of the *Purusha* is attained.

3.37 From this knowledge, the powers of intuitive hearing, touch, sight, taste, and smell are born spontaneously, without the practice of *samyama*.

A break in the listing of *siddhis* is inserted here to warn of the danger of seeking them. Note that the warning comes after sutra 3.37, a possible by-product of the intuitive insight mentioned in 3.36. In sutra 3.37, we find a *siddhi* or Sutra 3.37 contains (or highlights or includes) a *siddhi* that brings the yogi close to omniscience, an attainment that could tempt the ego and arouse self-centered motivations and actions:

3.38 Although these powers may be considered as great accomplishments to an outwardly directed mindset, they obstruct the highest *samadhi*.

The detailing of the supernormal powers resumes:

3.39 When the subconscious impressions that bind the mind to the body are loosened, and the mind's pathway into and out of the body is perceived, one can join with (and function through) another's body.

3.40 *Two versions are possible for this sutra. The first is more literal and is the one found in virtually every translation of the Yoga Sutras. The second seems more in harmony with the overall intent of the Yoga Sutras:*

1) By mastery over *udana* (the upward moving current of *prana*) one moves, without obstruction, over the water, swamps, thorns. One rises above them.
2) By mastery over *udana*, the upward moving current of *prana*, one moves through the world free from nonvirtuous acts, moral impurity, and confusion. This uplifting of consciousness brings transformation.

3.41 *Samana prana* is the vital energy that governs physical and mental transformation. By mastering it, one gains radiance of body and mind.

3.42 By *samyama* on the relationship between hearing and *akasha*, one can perceive sounds (such as the *pranava*, OM) through which divine knowledge is gained. (See 3.37)

3.43 By *samyama* on the connection between the body and ether and from contemplative absorption (*samadhi*) on the lightness of cotton fiber, one can move unrestricted through space.

3.44 When the mind's activities are genuinely experienced as external – not limited – to the body, it is called the great bodiless awareness. From this experience, the veil that obscures the light of the pure *sattvic* mind is completely removed. (See 1.19, 2.52, 3.39)

3.45 Mastery over the elements is gained by *samyama* on their:

- Gross form – that which can be perceived by the senses
- Essential character – the special features that distinguish one element from another

- Subtle form – the essence or potential that gives rise to the material elements
- Relationship to the *gunas* – which are common to all objects
- Purpose for being – which is to bring experience and liberation to the *Purusha* (See 2.18)

3.46 From that *samyama* arises powers such as the ability to become minute, perfection of the body, and freedom from the limitations of the elements that form it.

The next *siddhi* can either be of practical use or it can devolve into a self-centered goal for those who want to look good to impress or attract others:

3.47 Perfection of the body is a physical form that is solid, well-proportioned, and stable. It possesses potent strength and radiates gracefulness.

The previous sutra dealt with the attainment of physical perfection. Patanjali now addresses perfection (or mastery) of the senses. It arises from *samyama* on the factors that are integral to the act of perception:

3.48 By *samyama* on the essential nature of the senses – the factors that work together to create sense perception – mastery over the sense organs is gained. These factors are:

- Reception of input: the mind (*manas*) responds to stimuli through the sense organs
- Illumination: *sattva*,[12] the precursor and essential nature of the sense organs. It illumines the process of perception with the light of consciousness.
- Ego sense: identification of sense experiences as self
- Interconnected relationship: as products of the *gunas*, the above three aspects work together
- Purpose: to give experiences and liberation to the *Purusha* (See 2.18)

3.49 From mastery over the senses, one gains swiftness of mind, a state with the capacity for sense perception without the aid of the sense organs – and mastery over primordial matter (*prakriti*).

[12] *Sattva* is the basis of the principle of perception.

Can there be a *siddhi* more tempting than the one presented in this next sutra?

3.50 One who attains the capacity to discern the distinction between the clear, luminous state of *sattva* and the *Purusha,* without confusing the nature of each, attains supremacy over all states of being and becoming (omnipotence) and knowledge of all (omniscience).[13] (See 4.25)

Omniscience and omnipotence open wide the door to incredible knowledge, a way to discover the highest truths of life and the universe. But omnipotence and omniscience alone can't take us to liberation. Nonattachment and *viveka* (unwavering discriminative discernment) are needed to usher the seeker to liberation. That is why the final six sutras focus on the highest states of nonattachment and *viveka* as the keys needed to attain full enlightenment, liberation (*kaivalya*).

For more details on nonattachment and *viveka*, see:

- **Nonattachment (*vairagya*) (See 3.51–3.52 and 1.15–1.16)**
- **Discriminative discernment (*viveka*) (See 3.53–3.56)**

3.51 By nonattachment to even omnipotence and omniscience, ignorance (the seed of all the root obstructions, *klesas*) is destroyed and liberation is experienced.

3.52 Invitations to display supernormal accomplishments (*siddhis*) should be rejected whether extended by those of high social status, those in authority, or by celestial beings who promise the joys of heaven. Fostered by adulation and flattery, such associations could generate undesirable consequences: renewed worldly attachment, arrogance, and pride.

Back in sutra 2.26, Patanjali identified *viveka*, discriminative discernment, as the means to overcome ignorance (*avidya*, not-knowing). In the following, the zenith of *viveka* is described.

[13] Omniscience is not knowledge of everything in the usual sense. Enlightenment does not bring knowledge of how to build a satellite, for example. In a spiritual context, omniscience means both knowing what needs to be known to ensure unshakable peace and freedom from suffering and knowing, through profound direct experience, the source and essence of all creation. Omnipotence is not having the strength of Superman, it is a deep direct understanding of the nature of the energy that permeates, animates, and sustains the universe. Knowledge brings with it some measure of control.

3.53 By *samyama* on the present moment and on the moments that follow, intuitive knowledge born of discriminative discernment (*viveka*) arises.

3.54 From this intuitive knowledge, arises the ability to discern the difference between two[14] things - *sattva* and *Purusha* – that are almost identical, that cannot be distinguished by origin, characteristics, and location.

3.55 Knowledge born of intuitive discernment (*viveka*) is transcendent and liberating. Free from the bonds of time, it encompasses all objects in all conditions simultaneously. (See 4.25–4.26, and 4.33)

3.56 When the mind attains purity of *sattva* that is equal to the purity of the *Purusha* (Self), liberation (*kaivalya*) dawns.

Looking ahead:

The final chapter of the *Yoga Sutras* serves as a summary of the main philosophical and practical aspects of Yoga. In addition, we are given tools to help us discern the difference between the mind and Self.

This chapter sparkles with descriptions of the origin of the mind and the yogi's experience of transcending time. As in chapters one and three, chapter four culminates with enlightenment (*kaivalya*), this time described as returning to the source of all life and creation (*pratiprasava*).

[14] The number two holds a special significance in Patanjali's teachings. The entirety of Yoga theory and practice can be understood as leading up to making the distinction between pure consciousness (*Purusha*) and *sattva* (pure mind).

Chapter Four
Kaivalya Pada: The Chapter on Liberation

Other ways that the *siddhis* can arise:

4.1 Supernormal powers (*siddhis*) may also be born from practices performed in previous births, by herbs, mantra repetition, asceticism, or as a side-effect of contemplative absorption (*samadhi*).

The next two sutras affirm that spiritual growth does not consist of attaining something outside us. Like a flower hidden within a seed, our True Nature is already and eternally within us. It is the *Purusha*, our heart of hearts, our True Nature, the Self. Indeed, all virtues are within, waiting for a yogi gardener to tend to them. With regular care, all virtues and attainments will bloom to their fullest, sweetest manifestation.

4.2 The transformations and attributes that manifest at each birth are the result of the inflow of the vast, innate potentials of *prakriti* under the influence of the individual's subconscious impressions (*samskaras*).

4.3 Efforts don't directly initiate this inflow. Effort, like a farmer removing obstacles to the flow of water, removes obstacles to the evolutionary streams of nature (*prakriti*).

Next, a lesson regarding the source of the mind:

4.4 Individual minds are created from the primary ego sense (*asmita matrat*) – the principle of individuation.

4.5 Although the activities of the many minds are diverse, the one primary ego sense is the origin of them all.

4.6 Of these activities, those born of meditation leave no subconscious karmic residue.

Sutra 4.6 returned us to the topic of karma. Recall that karma was described as determining experiences of pleasure and pain. Sutra 4.7, combined with 4.6, explains that fully matured yogis are beyond the workings of karma. Our actions and our personality (including what

we experience as inborn likes and dislikes, inclinations and aversions) are largely determined by subconscious character traits (*vasanas*) that emerge from past lifetime experiences. Even though we have been creating karma from many past lifetimes, sutra 4.8 tells us that only those character traits that are suitable for this present birth will manifest. Recall that sutra 4.4 stated that the many diverse minds that inhabit the universe have one origin. This means that although all minds move from birth to birth, place to place, and in circumstances that differ widely, the origin of all minds is one and the same (*asmita matrat*). This one origin is sometimes referred to as the Universal Mind or Cosmic Consciousness.

4.7 The actions of the yogi are neither white (good) nor black (bad); the actions of others are of three kinds: white, black, and mixed.

4.8 From the three categories of karma – white, black, mixed – only those subliminal traits (*vasanas*) that are suitable for this birth manifest.

More on *vasanas*. Recall that *vasanas* are a subclass of *samskaras* (subconscious impressions). *Vasanas* are essential building blocks of our personality. Some traits help our spiritual growth and some hinder it. Some *vasanas* rest largely inactive in the subconscious until conditions for their emergence arise. Factors such as our environment, occurrences, relationships, and our thoughts, words, and deeds can awaken them. For example, many Yoga practitioners have been surprised that a rather casual involvement with Yoga gradually transformed into a way of life. This shift and accelerated growth is due to the awakening of *vasanas* from past lifetimes. It can be experienced as a feeling of returning home, or a simple, yet strong sense of the rightness of the Yoga life for them. For such a practitioner, Yoga has morphed from something you do to someone you are.

4.9 Although the creation of the subliminal traits (*vasanas*) that manifest as an individual's present characteristics may be separated from each other by birth, place, and time, there is continuity of selfhood because the memories that form one's present traits are taken from the mind's storehouse of subconscious impressions (*samskaras*).

4.10 And these subliminal traits (*vasanas*) have no beginning since the desire for continued existence that sustains them is also without beginning. (See 1.19 and 2.9)

4.11 The *vasanas* are held together by the interdependence of:

- Cause and effect (karma), which leaves subconscious memories and desires
- The foundation (ignorance), the root of suffering and the major impediments to progress (*klesas*), as well as being the root of karma
- Support (sense experiences) that sustains desires through attachment and aversion

When these factors are absent, the *vasanas* disappear.

The next sutra can serve as an aid in developing nonattachment. It states that all forms of an object are already present within it in latent form.[15] Contemplating this truth and keeping it mind can teach us to be prepared to go with the flow of life's inevitable changes. When we become attached to any stage of the process of change, we set ourselves up for anxiety of every sort and of every degree of intensity. (See 2.15, *duhkha*)

4.12 The past and future characteristics of an object that manifest during the course of its existence are innate to its nature.

4.13 These characteristics, whether manifest or intangible, have the three fundamental components of nature (*gunas*) as their essence.

4.14 The transformations of these three fundamental components (*gunas*) are unique to the nature of an object. This is why the essential nature of an object remains consistent throughout all of its changes.

Patanjali is giving us another teaching on the nature of *prakriti*. There's the objective reality of an object and then there's how we perceive it and its value to us. Typically, an object is not experienced as it objectively is, but is overlaid by our past experiences, personal biases, hopes, and fears. This lesson continues in sutras 4.16 and 4.17. Then, in sutra 4.18, he gives us another nugget of information regarding the *Purusha*.

[15] If all forms of an object exist in that object, then past and future must also exist in the object. This applies to us as well. In other words, all facets of time are, in a mysterious way, here in the eternal now (which exists outside the flow of time). That is why evolved yogis do not experience time solely in a linear way. Look ahead to sutra 4.33. For the fully enlightened yogi, time is transcended.

4.15 Each mind perceives the same object differently. Even though the object is the same, perception of it is influenced by each mind's unique viewpoints, priorities, and experiences.

The existence of objects does not depend on our perception of them. There is an external reality that exists apart from our minds:[16]

4.16 An object's existence doesn't depend on a single mind's perception of it. If it did, what would become of that object when it is not being perceived by that mind?

4.17 An object is known or unknown depending on whether it colors the mind.

Here, we learn a bit more about the nature of the *Purusha* and its relation to the mind:

4.18 All of the mind's seesaw whirling excursions (*vrittis*), all its changes and fluctuations, are always known to the mind's transcendent sovereign – the eternal changeless consciousness (Seer, Self, *Purusha*).

An important teaching is offered here for our consideration and contemplation. The mind has no consciousness of its own... really:

4.19 The mind, like everything in nature, is an object of perception. Therefore, it is not self-illuminating; awareness is not its essential nature.

4.20 A further proof that the mind is not self-illuminating is that it cannot perceive both itself and an object at the same time.

4.21 If it is thought that each mind has a second that illumines the first, it would suggest that there is an endless series of intellects, each perceiving another. The result would be confusion of memory.

4.22 Transcendent unchanging consciousness (*Purusha*) reflects on the mind making it seem as if the mind possesses awareness of its own. (See 1.4, 2.17)

[16] *Ahamkara*, the "i-maker", does overlay a reality of hopes and fears onto the universe. It is in this sense that each of us creates an entire universe filled with truths, half-truths, and false perceptions. Patanjali encourages us to see the universe of matter as it is, and then discern it from the Self.

4.23 The mind, colored by both the Seer and the seen, can perceive all objects. (See 2.17–2.18)

4.24 The mind, a composite made up of several elements and streaked with countless subconscious impressions, desires, and tendencies, acts for the purpose of another (the *Purusha*). (See 3.36)

A central teaching is repeated here: the mind and the Self are not the same thing. Once we make the distinction between the mind and the Self (as a direct experience, not as an intellectual concept), a wonderful thing happens. We are drawn to enlightenment like iron to a magnet.

4.25 For one who discerns the distinction between the mind and the *Atma* (Self), false or limited notions of self-identity cease forever.

4.26 Then, the mind naturally inclines toward discriminative discernment and, not being far from liberation, gravitates toward it.

Practice needs to carry us past the conscious mind into the subconscious. The restructuring of the subconscious, which is a major determinative factor in our thoughts, words, and deeds, is essential. This restructuring involves cultivating consistency between the contents and activities of the conscious mind (which the yogi is systematically developing and refining) and the contents and influences of the subconscious mind (especially those that were developed before beginning the practice of Yoga).

4.27 The flow of discriminative discernment may be interrupted now and then by the force of subconscious impressions (*samskaras*), which cause distracting thoughts to arise.

4.28 These subconscious impressions (*samskaras*) can be removed in the same way as was described for the root causes of suffering (*klesas*):

- Meditation (2.11)
- Tracing them back to their cause (2.10)
- Uninterrupted discriminative discernment (2.26)

We now arrive at the *Yoga Sutras'* description of the concluding phase of the path to enlightenment. The same subject was presented from different perspectives in sutras 1.51 and 3.56. This time, the final phase of

spiritual growth is ushered in with the arrival of *dharmamegha samadhi* (the cloud of *dharma samadhi*). Note the reappearance of *viveka* in sutra 4.29 and the key role it plays:

4.29 One who does not seek personal gain from even the highest insights, remains in a state of discriminative discernment under all circumstances. From this, arises the cloud of *dharma samadhi* (*dharmamegha samadhi*). (See 1.16)

4.30 This *samadhi* ends the influences of the root causes of suffering (*klesas*) and past actions (karma).

4.31 At that time, knowledge that is boundless and eternal arises and all impurities and obstructions withdraw. Compared to this knowledge, what remains to be known is of no consequence to the attainment of liberation.

4.32 From this knowledge the purpose of the *gunas* and their succession of transformations is fulfilled. (See sutra 2.18)

Enlightenment can be characterized as a process of transcending the limitations of *prakriti*, including the body and mind. Here, we learn that time also needs to be transcended:

4.33 The series of transformations correlate to moments – time – which is transcended when the transformations end.

4.34 The three qualities of nature (*gunas*), having concluded their purpose for the *Purusha*, return to their original state of equilibrium. In other words, the power of pure consciousness stands steadfast and unchanging in its essential nature as the Self. This is liberation. (See 1.2–1.4)

It is thus.

Patanjali ends his magnificent discourse with one word: *iti: it is thus*. He began his teaching by telling us that now is the time for Yoga. He ends by declaring that all he teaches is true, real, and effective. He does this with one small word, *iti*.

The certainty of the power of Yoga for self-transformation, and for Self-realization, is confirmed.

Topic Index

This index is for finding information, stories, myths, and references to symbolism that are not directly stated in the sutras themselves. This is a place to discover some of the hidden treasures of Patanjali's *Yoga Sutras.*

A

Allowable desires: footnote to 2.18
Anxiety/aversion, fear: 2.8
Asana and the myth of Ananta, the Cosmic Snake: 2.47
Ashrams: 2.38
Atma, self/Self: 2.5
– as subjective experience of *Purusha*: 4.25
Availability: 2.28

B

Bandha: see footnote to 1.1
Belief vs. practice: 1.33
Bhava (in Buddhism), as process of creating and sustaining individuality: 4.11
Bodily perfection: 3.46
Body image: 2.39
Brahmacharya (continence), as guidelines for conduct: 2.38
Buddhi, intelligence, discriminative faculty: 2.19

C

Chakra (*Guru*, *jnana*, or *brahmarandhra chakra*): 3.33
Chakras: 3.30 *Citta* as understood in astrology: 1.1
– as the water snake, the entwiner: 1.2
– as opposed to *citi*: 4.34
Clinging as being out of step with the nature of life: 2.7
– to life is stubborn: 2.9
Clouds, symbolism: 4.29
Composites/compounds don't exist for themselves: 3.36
Contentment, as wedded to and arising from wisdom: 2.32
Counterforce thoughts: 2.33
Curiosity, as expanding the boundaries of the mind: 4.6

D

Darshan: 3.33
Deities: why Hindu deities are depicted as beautiful and benevolent: 1.48
Delight: 2.18
Deliverer, *viveka* (discriminative discernment) as deliverer: 3.55
Devotion: 2.45
Dharana and *dhyana* (concentration and meditation): 2.29, 3.1–3.2
Dharma: 3.13–3.14

H

I

J

K

L

M

N

O

P

Perceiving truth behind words and sounds: 3.17
Perception
– elements in the process of: 3.12
– as a darkening of the inner light: 4.17
Pleasure: 2.7
Power: masculine vs. feminine: 2.35
Practice, importance of regularity: 1.32
– sticking to one thing: 1.32
– don't reduce Yoga to its practices: 4.3
– as removing obstacles and not being ego-centered: 4.3
Prakriti, definition: 1.19
– as intelligent: 4.1
– nature of: 2.21
– as inflow and overflowing: 4.2
– as streams of the five elements: 4.3
Pratipaksha bhavanam, as a chance for new beginnings: 2.33
Pratiprasava, as real rest: 2.10
Priorities that shift as a result of *dharmamegha samadhi*: 4.31
Purity: 2.5, 2.39 – 2.41
– as light: 2.20, 2.32
– of *sattva* equal to *Purusha* brings liberation: 3.56
Purusha/prakriti relationship: 2.23, 4.18
– as master of *prakriti*: 4.18
– purpose of: 3.36

Q

Qualifications (four) of a seeker: 1.14

R

Remedy in Hindu astrology for difficult situations: 2.26
Requirements for *kaivalya* (expanded definition of *suddhi*): 3.56
Resentment: 1.33
Returning to the Source (*pratiprasava*), as goal of Yoga: 2.10, 4.34
Right, how focus on doing the right thing can be a way to try to control nature: 4.3
Right relationship with life, as like a dance: 4.3
Rudra, as deity metaphor for externalized and inward state of mind: 3.9

S

T

U

V

W

Y

Quotes Index

In this section, you will find a listing of all the quotes cited in this book. These quotes are from various faith traditions, sacred texts, spiritual masters, philosophers, and other notables. Their purpose is to help clarify difficult teachings, shine the wisdom of a different perspective on those teachings, and to demonstrate the universality of the challenges that mark the human condition, as well as the means to overcome those challenges and find lasting peace and meaning in life.

The sutra, or location of the quote, is on a separate line after the designation of the source of the quote.

Never cease to stand like curious children before the Great Mystery into which we were born.
– Albert Einstein
Page xi

Curiosity is lying in wait for every secret.
– Ralph Waldo Emerson
Page xi

The beginning of wisdom is the defining of words.
– Socrates
Page xiii

However many holy words you read, however many you speak, what good will they do if you don't act on them?
– The Buddha
Page xv

Silence is the language of God. All else is poor translation.
– Rumi
Page xv

Silence is more eloquent than words.
– Thomas Carlyle
Page xv

Somewhere we know that without silence words lose their meaning.
– Henri Nouwen
Page xv

The goal of Yoga is to have an easeful body, a peaceful mind, and a useful life.
– Sri Swami Satchidananda
Page 3

Let us enter into the house of knowledge of ourselves.
– St. Catherine of Siena
1.7

Be suspicious of what you want.
– Rumi
1.12

Thus, with patience I will strive with careful and persistent effort. For in such diligence enlightenment is found. If no wind blows then nothing stirs, and neither can there be a merit without careful and persistent effort.

That, if they bring forth the strength of perseverance even bees and flies and gnats and grubs will gain supreme enlightenment so hard to find.
– Shantideva
1.14

Without nonattachment there cannot be any kind of Yoga. Nonattachment is the basis of all the Yogas.
– Swami Vivekananda
1.15

Be aware of the ephemeral nature of material things. Lose your attachment to them.
– Shui-ch'ing Tzu
1.16

A glad spirit attains to perfection more quickly than any other.
– St. Philip Neri
1.22

Within the hearts of all beings resides the Supreme Lord (Ishvara) and by the Lord's power, the movements of all beings is orchestrated as if they were figurines on a carousel.
– Bhagavad Gita, 18.61
1.23

But seek first the kingdom of God and His righteousness, and all these things will be added unto you.
– Matthew 6:33
1.23

The dedicated immediately enjoy an unbroken state of supreme peace.
– Bhagavad Gita, 12.12
1.23

The teacher provides spiritual energy! Just like roots provide nutrients to the flowers.
– Master Choa Kok Sui
1.26

OM stands for the Supreme Reality. It is a symbol for what was, what is, and what will be. OM represents also what lies beyond past, present, and future.
– Mandukya Upanishad
1.28

Bhavana is the emotion with which the work is being done, the real motive with which the first move into the activity was made. Bhavana is the most basic factor of all activity.
– Sri Swami Santananda Saraswati
1.28

As seekers approach me, so I receive them. All paths, Arjuna, lead to Me.
– Bhagavad Gita, 4.11
1.32

And Peter opened his mouth and said, "Truly I perceive that God shows no partiality, but in every nation any one who fears him and does what is right is acceptable to him."
– Bible, Acts: 10.34-10:35
1.32

Confucius said... "in the world there are many different roads but the destination is the same. There are a hundred deliberations but the result is one."
– I Ching, Appended Remarks 2.5
1.32

At any time, in any form and accepted name, if one is shorn of all attachment, that one is you alone. My Lord! You are one although variously appearing.
– Anyayoga-Vyavaccheda-Dvatrimsika of Hemacandra
1.32

Be a rainbow in someone's cloud.
– Maya Angelou
1.33

Lead me from the unreal to the real, from darkness to light, from the fear of death to the knowledge of immortality.
– Brihadaranyaka Upanishad
1.36

Then the soul is in God and God in the soul, just as the fish is in the sea and the sea in the fish.
– St. Catherine of Siena
1.41

There are uses to adversity, and they don't reveal themselves until tested. Whether it's serious illness, financial hardship, or the simple constraint of parents who speak limited English, difficulty can tap unexpected strengths.
– Justice Sonia Sotomayer
2.1

Some people perform stern austerities that are not enjoined by the scriptures, but rather motivated by hypocrisy and egotism. Impelled by desire and attachment, they torment not only the elements of their body, but also I who dwell within them as the Supreme Soul. Know these senseless people to be of demoniacal resolves.
– Bhagavad Gita, 17.6
2.1

Anyone who truly loves God travels securely.
– St. Teresa of Avila
2.1

The important thing is not to stop questioning. One cannot help but be in awe when he contemplates the mysteries of eternity, of life, of the marvelous structure of reality. It is enough if one tries merely to comprehend a little of this mystery every day. Never lose a holy curiosity.
– Albert Einstein
2.1 (See footnote 50)

Thus, walking on this way with an awakened heart, not only do we escape the heavy cares of this world, but we are uplifted above ourselves and do taste of the divine sweetness.
– Blessed Angela of Foligno
2.2

When a superior person hears of the Tao,
She diligently puts it into practice.
When an average person hears of the Tao,
She believes half of it, and doubts the other half.
When a foolish person hears of the Tao,
She laughs out loud at the very idea.
If she didn't laugh, it wouldn't be the Tao.
– Tao Te Ching
2.3

Real knowledge is to know the extent of one's ignorance.
– Confucius
2.5

The doorstep to the temple of wisdom is knowledge of our own ignorance.
– Benjamin Franklin
2.5

Doesn't the Bible say, "Blessed are the pure in heart, they shall see God?" When? Only when there is purity in the heart; a heart peaceful and free from egoism – the "I" and the "mine." Purity of heart and equanimity of mind are the very essence of Yoga.
– Sri Swami Satchidananda
2.6

Although the sattva guna is pure, luminous, and without obstructions, still it binds you by giving rise to happiness and knowledge to which the mind readily becomes attached.
– Bhagavad Gita 14.6
2.7

Faith is a bird that sings when the dawn is still dark.
– Rabindranath Tagore
2.8

Faith is taking the first step even when you don't see the whole staircase.
– Martin Luther King, Jr.
2.8

Faith is the strength by which a shattered world shall emerge into the light.

– Helen Keller
2.8

And so… castles made of sand melt into the sea, eventually.
– Jimi Hendrix
2.15

Character cannot be developed in ease and quiet. Only through experience of trial and suffering can the soul be strengthened, ambition inspired, and success achieved.
– Helen Keller
2.15

Suffering is a short pain and a long joy.
– Blessed Henry Suso
2.16

Life is a succession of lessons which must be lived to be understood.
– Ralph Waldo Emerson
2.18

Praise the Lord from the earth,
All great sea creatures and ocean depths,
Lightning and hail, snow and clouds,
Powerful wind fulfilling His word,
Mountains and all hills,
Fruit trees and all cedars,
Wild animals and all cattle,
Crawling creatures and flying birds,
Kings of the earth and all peoples,
Princes and all rulers of the earth,
Young men and maidens,
Old and young together. Let them praise the name of the Lord.
– Psalm 148 (excerpt from the Berean Study Bible)
2.18

This is the unusual thing about nonviolence – nobody is defeated, everybody shares in the victory.
– Martin Luther King Jr.
2.35

Blessed are the peacemakers for they shall be called children of God.
– Matthew 5:9
2.35

Know the truth and the truth will set you free.
– John 8:32

2.36

The flowers and pearls and precious stones (which are angels, saints, and sages) ever cling to Hari (Narayana), the Remover of Sorrow.
– Bhagavata Purana, 10.238

2.37

It does not matter how slowly you go as long as you do not stop.
– Confucius

2.38

Ceasing to do evil, purifying the heart: This is the teaching of the Buddhas.
– Dhammapada, 1.83

2.41

Mastery of nature is vainly believed to be an adequate substitute for self mastery.
– Reinhold Niebuhr
2.41

If people knew how hard I worked to get my mastery, it wouldn't seem so wonderful at all.
– Michelangelo

2.41

Devotion complete culminates in knowledge supreme.
–Sri Ramana Maharishi
2.45

Pranayama without meditation can make the mind more restless.
– Hatha Yoga Pradipika

2.51

When the prana moves, the mind moves. When the prana is without movement, the mind is without movement.
– Hatha Yoga Pradipika

2.51

You can spend ten years in deep meditation gaining the ability to walk on water to cross the river, or you can pay the boatman ten cents.
– Adage from India
Introduction, Chapter 3

Practice meditation regularly. Meditation leads to eternal bliss. Therefore, meditate. Meditate.
– Sri Swami Sivananda
3.1

The yogi whose mind is truly peaceful (prasanta), who has subdued her/his passions and is free from the darkness of nonvirtue, attains ultimate happiness in Self-Realization.
– Bhagavad Gita, 6.27
3.10

In the beginning was Brahman with whom was the Word and the Word was the Supreme Brahman.
– Rig Veda
3.17

In the beginning was the word and the word was with God and the word was God.
– John 1.1
3.17

All the worlds rush into your mouths, like moths swiftly entering a blazing (jvalanam) fire to be destroyed.
– Bhagavad Gita, 11.28
3.41

Those that know others are clever. Those that know themselves have discernment.
– Tao Te Ching
3.54

Peace is your nature, do not disturb it.
– Sri Swami Satchidananda
4.18

I am the goal. I uphold everything; I am the Lord (prabhu), the witness, the abode, the refuge, the friend, the beginning and the end. I am the foundation, the infinite treasure house and indestructible seed of creation.
– Bhagavad Gita, 9.18
4.18

As you gain control of your mind, with the help of your higher Self, then your mind and ego become your allies. But the uncontrolled mind behaves as an enemy.
– Bhagavad Gita, 6.6
4.18 (See footnote 109)

God is more anxious to bestow His blessings on us than we are to receive them.
– Augustine of Hippo
4.26

. . . for we physicists believe the separation between past, present, and future is only an illusion, although a convincing one.
– Albert Einstein
4.33

Let the wise merge their speech into the mind, the mind into the intellect (buddhi), and the intellect into the Great Self (Atma), and the Great Self into the Peaceful Self.
– Katha Upanishad 1.3.13
4.34

Beyond the senses is the mind, higher than the mind is the intellect, higher than the intellect is the Great Self, higher than the Great Self is the unmanifested (undifferentiated prakriti, called maya by adherents of Vedanta). Beyond the unmanifested is the Purusha, all-pervading and devoid of identifying marks. Those who know this are liberated and obtain immortality.
– Katha Upanishad 2.3.7–8
4.34

If we only would look within, we would see the Light as if we were seeing our own image in a mirror.
– Sri Swami Satchidananda
4.34

Sanskrit Glossary

This glossary is divided into two sections, Sanskrit and English. It contains words that appear throughout the book and are key terms that relate to the practice of meditation as well as to Yoga, in general.

A

abhyasa – practice. Literally, to apply oneself toward. Continuous endeavor, vigilance, exercise, repetition, exertion.

advaita – nondualism; monism, Reality regarded as one and indivisible; beyond pairs of opposites, such as hot/cold, up/down, male/female, good/bad.

ahamkara – (*kri* = action + *aham* = "I." Literally, "the I-maker.") egoism, ego feeling; the sense of self identity.

ahimsa – non-injury; one of the *yamas.*

anahata – the unstruck, the continuous inner humming vibration, the heart *chakra.*

ananda – bliss

asamprajnata samadhi – the state of meditative absorption in which there are no objects in the conscious mind to contemplate. Only subconscious impressions remain.

asana – a steady, comfortable posture. It can refer to the various seated postures used for meditation and the bending and stretching practices of *Hatha Yoga.*

Ashtanga Yoga – refers to the eight limbs of *Raja Yoga*: *yama, niyama, asana, pranayama, pratyahara, dharana, dhyana, samadhi.*

asmita – egosim, from *asmi* = I am. Can be understood as an equivalent to *ahamkara* = I-maker, or it can be used as the primordial sense of individuality, the "birth" of the idea of I.

Atman – the Self or *Brahman* when regarded as abiding within the individual.

B

Bhagavad Gita – a Hindu scripture, a portion of the great epic the *Mahabharata* composed perhaps 2400 years ago, in which Lord Krishna instructs his disciple Arjuna in the various aspects of Yoga.

bhakti – (from *bhaj* = to partake of; to turn to) devotion

Bhakti Yoga – the Yoga of devotion to any name and form of the Divine.

bijam – seed, source

Brahma – God as creator of the universe. One of the Hindu trinity, which also includes Vishnu and Siva.

brahmamuhurta – the two-hour period before sunrise (roughly between four and six a.m.) that is especially conducive to meditation.

Brahman – (literally, greater than the greatest) the unmanifest supreme consciousness or God; the Absolute. In Vedanta, it refers to the Absolute Reality and is regarded as that which is beyond differences. It is considered *nirguna*, beyond nature, that which cannot be conceptualized. *Brahman* is pure absolute existence, knowledge and bliss. It is considered as the only absolute reality whereas the created universe is but an appearance.

buddhi – (from the root *budh* to enlighten, to know) intellect, discriminative faculty of the mind, understanding, reason. (See *mahat*)

C

chakra – (literally, wheel) one of the subtle nerve centers along the spine.

chit, cit – to perceive, observe; to know.

chitta, citta – (from *chit; see above.*) In the *Yoga Sutras*, *chitta* refers to the mind-stuff. In the nondualistic school of Vedanta (Advaita Vedanta) it refers to the subconscious.

citi – not to be confused with *citta*. *Citi* is a higher state of consciousness that arises when extraordinary one-pointedness, tranquility, clarity, and nonattachment occur.

D

darshana – the insight, vision or experience of a divine or enlightened being; any philosophical school. Yoga is traditionally considered one of six orthodox *darshanas* (philosophies) in India. To see or be seen by a holy individual or image of a deity, considered as a great blessing.

dharana – concentration; the practice of continually refocusing the mind on the object of meditation. The sixth of the eight limbs of Raja Yoga.

dharma (literally, that which holds together). Duty, righteousness, religion, virtue, characteristics, law, justice, universal law. It is the foundation of all order: religious, social and moral. Sri Swami Sivananda Maharaj defines *dharma* as that which brings harmony. In general there are two classifications of *dharma*: that which is common to all and that which is specific to a particular class or stage of life.

Dharma has been further broken down as follows:

- ***sanatana dharma***: the Eternal Truth (the more accurate name for what is now commonly called Hinduism)
- ***svadharma***: one's duty as dictated by inborn talents, traits, etc. One's purpose in this life
- ***apad dharma:*** duties prescribed in times of adversity
- ***uga dharma:*** the laws and codes of conduct appropriate to one's era in time
- ***sadharana dharma:*** the general obligations of common duties incumbent on everyone
- ***varna ashrama dharma:*** one's specific duty according to class and stage in life

In Buddhism, *dharma* is often used to refer to cosmic order, natural law, the teachings of The Buddha, codes of conduct, objects, facts, or ideas.

dharmamegha samadhi – a state of continuous discernment between the Spirit (Self, *Purusha*) and nature (*prakriti*). It is also a state of complete nonattachment to achieving the highest spiritual rewards. *Dharmamegha samadhi* is the last stage of spiritual development before full Self-realization.

dhyana – meditation; the easy, steady focus of the mind's attention on the object of meditation. The seventh of the eight limbs of the *Raja Yoga*.

diksha – translated as initiation, is central to all traditions of Yoga. It is the entrance into the Guru-disciple relationship. *Diksha* accelerates a student's spiritual potentials through the transmission of the teachings as well as a transmission of *shakti* (spiritual power) from the teacher to the student. Often, a mantra is given to the initiate as the primary object of meditation.

duhkha – suffering, pain, sorrow, grief. A persistent pervasive feeling of precariousness. Existential angst.

E

ekagrata - one-pointedness of mind. An uninterrupted flow of attention to the object of contemplation.

ekam – one; Reality. *Ekam* is the term used in the well-known phrase from the *Upanishads, "Ekam sat, vipraha bahudha vadanti," "The Truth is one (ekam); seers express it in many ways."* This principle is the basis of the nondualistic Advaita Vedanta philosophy, which proclaims that although we see many names and forms, they are all manifestations of the One Absolute Reality.

G

guna – literally, strand or thread. Quality, attribute, characteristic. One of the three qualities of nature: *sattva*, *rajas,* and *tamas* or balance, activity, and inertia.

Guru – the "weighty or venerable one." A spiritual guide or teacher. Scriptures such as the *Guru Gita* and the *Advaya-Taraka Upanishad* also state that the syllable, *gu* = darkness and *ru* = remover.

The sage Shankaracharya described a Guru as one whose mind is steadfast in the highest reality; who has a pure tranquil mind; and who has directly experienced identity with *Brahman.* Although it is understood that God is the true and only Guru, the human Guru acts as a conduit for the Divine teachings, grace, and guidance.

Guru-parampara – the lineage of teachers; the uninterrupted succession of teachers. Patanjali teaches in sutra 1.26, that *Ishvara* is *"the teacher of even the most ancient teachers."*

H

hatha – often poetically rendered as *ha* = sun; *tha* = moon.

Hatha Yoga – the physical branch of Yoga practice. It includes postures (*asanas*), breathing techniques (*pranayama*), seals (*mudras*), locks (*bandhas*), and cleansing practices (*kriyas*). Though known for its ability to bring health, flexibility, and relaxation, its ultimate objectives are the purification of the *nadis* (subtle nerve pathways) and uniting of the outgoing and incoming (or upward and downward) flows of *prana.* When the flow of *prana* is balanced and harmonious, the mind becomes still and tranquil and ready for the subtler practices of concentration, meditation and *samadhi.* Hatha Yoga helps return the body to its natural state of health and ease.

Hatha Yoga Pradipika – a classic in the teachings of *Hatha Yoga*, composed in the 15th century by Swami Swatmarama. It is considered to be the oldest text on *Hatha Yoga.*

I

ida - the subtle *nadi* (nerve current) that flows through the left nostril. It has the effect of cooling the system as opposed to *pingala*, the heating *nadi* on the right.

Integral Yoga – the Integral Yoga system, as taught by Sri Swami Satchidananda, is comprised of a synthesis of six classical branches of Yoga, utilizing an integrative approach. The branches are: Hatha, Raja, Japa, Karma, Bhakti, and Jnana Yoga. The aim is to purify and calm the body and mind in order to experience the peace and joy that is one's true nature. Integral Yoga practitioners bring that peace into the world by fostering interfaith harmony and leading service-oriented lives.

Ishta Devata – one's chosen deity. There is only one absolute God with the various deities being manifestations or representing aspects of that one Reality. In Hinduism and Yoga, seekers are free to choose whichever form is most meaningful to them for veneration and worship.

Ishvara – from the verb root *ish* = to rule, to own. Lord, God, the Divine with form, the Supreme Cosmic Soul.

There are several meanings for this term:

- The Supreme Ruler and Controller; both transcendent and immanent
- According to Advaita Vedanta, *Ishvara* is the Absolute (*Brahman*) as seen from within ignorance or illusion
- The material and efficient cause of the world
- According to Sri Patanjali: the Supreme *Purusha*, unaffected by afflictions, karmas or desires, the omniscient teacher of all teachers, expressed by the mantra OM

Ishvara pranidhanam – worship of God or self-surrender (one of the principles of Sri Patanjali's *Kriya Yoga* and one of the principles of *niyama*).

J

japa – repetition or recitation, usually of a mantra or name of God.

Japa Yoga – mantra repetition to calm, clear, and focus the mind. The repetition could be out loud, with lip movement only or mentally; or as a writing meditation (*likhita japa*).

jiva(tman) – an individual soul. According to Samkhya philosophy, *jivas* (souls) are infinite in number, conscious, and eternal. There is neither birth nor death for the *jiva*. According to Advaita Vedanta, the *jiva* is a blending of the Self and non-Self due to an incorrect identification of the Self with the body-mind. In Advaita Vedanta, *jivas* are considered essentially one, although in daily experience, they are perceived as many.

jivanmukta – liberated living soul. Liberation results from the discrimination between the *Purusha* and *prakriti* and the ultimate dissolution of ignorance (*avidya*).

jnanam – (from the root *jna* = to know) wisdom of the Self; knowledge, idea. The word is often used to refer to insights gained from meditation and *samadhi*.

Jnana Yoga – Yoga of Self-inquiry, knowledge and study. Characterized by contemplation on the True Nature of the Self, the constant effort to discriminate between what is real (permanent and unchanging) and what is unreal (that which changes).

K

kaivalya – From *kevala* = alone, one. Absolute freedom, independence, isolation, liberation.

karma – the universal law of action and reaction; cause and effect.

It is of four classes according to the effects the actions produce:

- White = happiness
- Black = unhappiness
- Black and white (mixed) = a mix of happiness and sorrow
- Neither black nor white = actions – like those of the yogi – which transcend karma, leaving the individual free

Karma can also be classified as follows:

- *Sanjita* = all the accumulated actions from previous births awaiting another lifetime to bear fruit
- *Prarabdha* = karmas manifesting in the present birth
- *Agami* = karmas currently being created

Karma Yoga – performing actions as selfless service without attachment to the results. Performance of one's duties without selfish expectation. Actions performed for the joy of serving.

karuna – mercy, compassion

klesa – from *klis* = to be troubled, to suffer distress. Misery, root obstruction. In Indian scriptural literature, *klesas* are also referred to as *viparyaya* or error.

kriya – (literally, action, practices) According to Sri Patanjali, it comprises the three preliminary steps in Yoga (*tapas, svadhyaya*, and *Ishvara pranidhanam*, or self-discipline and accepting of hardships as opportunities to grow, study, and self-surrender). The word also is used to refer to the cleansing practices of *Hatha Yoga*.

kumbhaka – breath retention. It could be voluntary as part of the practice of *pranayama* (as in the breathing practices of *Hatha Yoga*) or occurring naturally in deep meditative states (in which case it is referred to as *kevala kumbhaka*).

kundalini – (literally, coiled energy) the primordial energy stored at the base of the spine in the *muladhara chakra* of every individual. When awakened naturally through the one-pointed attentiveness and purification of selfishness, it begins to move upward within the subtle central channel (*sushumna*) of the spine, piercing and enlivening the *chakras* and initiating a total rejuvenation and spiritual evolution of the entire being. Because a forced, premature awakening of this energy can result in undesirable consequences, it is compared to a cobra that must be handled with great care.

L

Likhit japa – The practice of writing mantras. It is an aid to developing concentration (*dharana*).

M

maharishi – great sage. From *maha* = great + *drsh* = to see. Therefore, *maharishi* literally means, *great seer*, the one who has seen (experienced) spiritual truths.

mahat – great (in space, time, quality, or degree). Also a synonym for *buddhi*, the discriminative faculty of the mind. According to Samkhya philosophy, it is the cosmic aspect of the intellect and the first expression of *prakriti*. From, *mahat*, the ego evolves.

Mahat is also used as a term of respect and reverence for evolved spiritual individuals.

Mahavakya – four great statements from the *Upanishads* and *Vedas* that summarize their essence. They are all excellent as objects of meditation:

- Consciousness is *Brahman*
- This Self is *Brahman*
- Thou art That
- I am *Brahman*

mala beads - *mala* beads are useful aids for mantra repetition. There are 108 beads in the typical string with a 109th tied to a tassel. The number 108 is considered auspicious. The 109th, called the *meru*, represents the Highest. They are used like rosary beads, with the practitioner advancing one bead with each repetition. The right hand is used and held at heart level. In advancing the beads, the index finger is not used, since it represents the ego and should be kept out of the practice. The *meru* is never crossed. Instead, the beads are flipped around and the counting begins again.

Mala beads are also worn around the neck as reminders of the spiritual virtues and goal. In addition, they absorb the vibrations of the mantra and benefit the wearer by carrying the peace and clarity of meditation with them.

manas – (from the root *man*, to think) mind. This important term has several variations in meaning according to different schools of traditional thought. It emerges from the pure (*sattvic*) aspect of ego (*ahamkara*) and is regarded as the inner organ (*antahkarana*). As such, it receives and arranges input from the senses and conveys it to the *buddhi*.

mantra – (from *man* = to think + *tra* = protecting; a thought that protects) a sound formula used for meditation; a sacred word or phrase of great spiritual significance and power; scriptural hymns.

maya – illusion, the principle of appearance, the mysterious power of creation. It has several shades of meaning:

The force or quality that persuades us to misperceive the unreal as real, the temporary as permanent, the painful as pleasurable, the non-Self as the Self, and the unconditioned Absolute as having attributes.

According to Advaita Vedanta, it is the beginningless cause which brings about the illusory manifestation of the universe. It is not ultimately real and cannot function without *Brahman*. *Maya* is how the one reality can appear as many. Because it is illusory, it has significance only on the relative level.

mudra – sign, seal or symbol. In Hatha Yoga, it is a posture, or a gesture, or movement of the hands, which holds or directs the *prana* within. Many deities and saints are depicted performing *mudras* which grant benediction.

N

nada – sound. The sound heard within in deep meditation. The first vibration out of which all creation manifests. Sound is the first manifestation of the Absolute *Brahman* and is represented by the crescent shape in the Sanskrit script for OM.

nadi – subtle channels of energy flow in the body. There are 72,000 such conduits of vital energy in the body. The most important are *ida*, *pingala*, and *sushumna*. *Ida* functions as the cooling, receptive parasympathetic nervous system-like activities and is associated with the left nostril. *Pingala's* activities bring more movement, heat, and sympathetic nervous system-like functions and are associated with the right nostril.

The *sushumna* is associated with the hollow in the center of the spinal cord and is the channel through which the awakened *kundalini* energy moves in its journey from *chakra* to *chakra* until it reaches the crown of the head (*sahasrara*). The *Yoga Sutras* only mention *kurma nadi* (tortoise-shaped *nadi*) whose primary function is to bring stability to the body and mind.

Nirbija samadhi – without seed. *Nirbija samadhi* is the highest spiritual state since both conscious thought and *samskaras* (subconscious or seed impressions) are rendered inactive and transcended.

nirodha – from the verb root *rudh* = to obstruct, restrict, arrest, avert + *ni* = down or into. Stilling, restraint, cessation. It refers to both the process and attainment of stilling all activities of the mind (which obscure the experience of the *Purusha*). Traditionally, it is said to be applied on four levels: *vritti*, *pratyaya*, *samskara*, and *sarva*.

These four levels describe increasingly more complete and deeper attainments of *nirodha*.

- *Vrittis* – modifications of the mind-stuff; movements or currents of thought; thought processes
- *Pratyaya* – notions, beliefs; the thoughts that immediately arise in the mind when it is stimulated by an object. The individual thoughts that comprise *vrittis*
- *Samskara* – subconscious impressions
- *Sarva* – a complete cessation of all mental activity

nirvana – in Buddhist teachings, it refers to the state of liberation. It has also been referred to as unborn, unconditional, unchanging, indescribable: a state of nonattachment to either being or non-being; the state of absolute freedom.

nirvichara – *samadhi* that is beyond insight.

nirvikalpa – a term used in Vedanta for the *samadhi* that is without thought or imagination. It is analogous to *asamprajnata samadhi* in the *Yoga Sutras.*

nirvitarka – *samadhi* that is beyond examination.

niyama – observance (the second of the eight limbs of Yoga). Ethical principles adhered to by yogis.

O

OM – the cosmic sound vibration that is the source of, and includes, all other sounds and vibrations. OM is the absolute *Brahman* as sound and the foundation of all mantras. It is composed of the letters *A, U*, and *M*, which respectively represent creation, evolution and dissolution, or the waking, dreaming, and dreamless sleep states. Beyond these states is a fourth, the *anahata* or unrepeated.

P

pada – a one-fourth portion. Each of the four sections of the *Yoga Sutras* of Patanjali is referred to as a *pada.*

param – highest, supreme

Patanjali – the yogi and sage who compiled the *Yoga Sutras.* He is often referred to as the "Father of Yoga." Some identify him as also the author of the *Mahabhashya*, an important Sanskrit grammatical text, which dates to the second century B.C. There are also other works attributed to an author(s) named Patanjali, including texts on medicine.

In popular tradition, Sri Patanjali is considered an incarnation of the mythical serpent Ananta (or Sesha), on whom Lord Vishnu rests before the beginning of a new cycle of creation. Symbolically, snakes were said to be the guardians of esoteric teachings and Ananta, as Lord of the snakes, presided over them all. Ananta took on human form as Patanjali for the benefit of humanity.

In another version, Patanjali is said to have fallen from the sky as a newborn serpent into the hands of his mother as she was offering water in worship of the sun. She called him Patanjali from *pata* (meaning both serpent and fallen) and *anjali* (referring to hands cupped in worship).

prakriti – primordial nature. In Samkhya philosophy it is one of the two fundamental categories of existence, the other being *Purusha*. Although *prakriti* is active, consciousness is not intrinsic to its nature. In Advaita Vedanta, *prakriti* is a principle of illusion (*maya*) and is therefore not real.

prana – the vital energy, life breath, life force. Though one, *prana* is divided into five major categories according to its functions:

- *Prana*: rising upwards
- *Apana*: moving downwards. Governs the abdomen and excretory functions
- *Vyana*: governs circulation of blood
- *Samana*: the force that equalizes; also responsible for the digestive process
- *Udana*: directs vital currents upwards

pranava – OM, the basic hum of the vibration of the universe.

pranayama – the practice of controlling the vital force, usually through control of the breath. The fourth of the eight limbs of *Raja Yoga*.

pranidhanam – total dedication, self-surrender. In Buddhism, *pranidhanam* is taken to mean a vow and usually refers to the *Bodhisattva's* vow of helping all beings attain liberation.

prasadam – consecrated food offering, grace, tranquility.

pratipaksha bhavanam – practice of substituting positive thought forms for disturbing, negative ones.

pratyahara – management of the senses; withdrawal of the senses from their objects (the fifth of the eight limbs of the *Yoga Sutras*).

pratyaya – in the context of the *Yoga Sutras*, *pratyaya* is generally used to refer to the thought that instantly arises when the mind is impacted by an object of perception. As such, *pratyayas* form the content of *vrittis*.

While *vritti* refers to a fundamental mental process, *pratyaya* refers to the content of individual consciousness, including the insights (*prajna*) attained in all of the lower states of *samadhi*, which are not the result of *vritti* activity. In Samkhya philosophy *pratyaya* is equivalent to the intellect or *buddhi*.

puja – worship service

Purusha – the divine Self, which abides in all beings; individual soul. Depending on the context, texts might use "*Purusha*" to refer to the individual soul or to the Absolute God. In Samkhya philosophy, *Purusha* along with *prakriti* constitute the two basic categories of creation. It is pure consciousness, which is unchanging, eternal, and pure. The *Yoga Sutras* also use the word "Seer" and "Owner" to refer to the same reality. According to Advaita Vedanta, *Purusha* is One and is the eternal witness of all there is.

R

raga – attachment, liking, desire

raja – king

rajas – activity; restlessness (one of the three *gunas*).

Raja Yoga (literally, the Royal Yoga) – is another name by which the *Yoga Sutras* of Patanjali are known. Historically, the term was used to refer to paths capable of guiding seekers to the experience of highest *samadhi* (the superconscious state or enlightenment). Its use in connection with the *Yoga Sutras* was influenced by Swami Vivekananda, a great commentator on the Sutras and all branches of Yoga and the first Hindu monk to come to the United States in 1893.

S

sa-ananda samadhi – *samadhi* in which the *sattvic* mind is experienced.

sa-asmita samadhi – *samadhi* in which the ego alone is experienced.

sabda – sound, word, or name.

sabija – with seed

sadhana – spiritual practices, usually formal, but also refers to the cultivation of mindfulness and proper attitudes in life.

sahasrara chakra – the thousand-petaled lotus; the subtle center of consciousness at the crown of the head, where the awareness and energy go in the higher *samadhis*.

samadhi – (from *dha* = to hold + *sam* = together completely) contemplation, superconscious state, absorption (the eighth and final limb of the eight limbs listed in the *Yoga Sutras*).

Any of several states in which the mind is (to a greater or lesser degree) absorbed in a state of union with the object of meditation. It is beyond all thought, untouched by speech or words. It is the experience of unwavering stillness and awareness and leads to intuitive wisdom.

samapatti – coming together, meeting. A synonym for *samadhi.*

samprajnata samadhi – the state of meditative absorption in which information or understanding regarding the object of meditation is gained intuitively.

samsara – the continuing rounds of birth, death, and rebirth.

samskara – latent, subconscious impression; innate tendency due to past actions.

samyama – the combined practice of *dharana*, *dhyana,* and *samadhi* upon one object.

samyoga – connection, contact, perfect union

sangha – a community of like-minded individuals.

sankalpa – a resolve or vow.

sat – existence or Truth

Satchidananda, Sri Swami (1914 – 2002) – world-renowned Yoga Master and founder-spiritual head of the Integral Yoga® International and Satchidananda Ashram–Yogaville®. He created the LOTUS (Light Of Truth Shrine) in Virginia and inspired the LOTUS in South India. These are shrines dedicated to the One Truth that illumines all faiths.

satsang – literally, keeping company with the truth. It usually involves group activities centered on study of spiritual teachings through discourses or other activities, or on group practice.

sattva – purity, balanced state (one of the three *gunas*).

satya – truth; truthfulness (one of the principles of the *yamas*).

savichara samadhi – *samadhi* with insight

savitarka samadhi – *samadhi* with examination

shakti, Shakti – energy, power, capacity, the *kundalini* force; the divine cosmic energy which creates, evolves and dissolves the universe. As a proper name, Shakti is used to designate the consort of Lord Siva or the Divine Mother in general.

shanti – peace

shraddha – faith

Sivananda, Sri Swami (1887 – 1963) – great sage of the Himalayas, founder of the Divine Life Society; author of over 300 books on Yoga and spiritual life; Guru of Sri Swami Satchidananda and many other respected Yoga Masters.

Sri – eminent or illustrious. A prefix placed before names of scriptures and great women and men to show respect or reverence; a name of the Goddess of Divine Wealth.

sutra – (literally, thread) aphorism

svadhyaya – (from *sva* = self + the verb root *adhi* = to go over) study, scriptural study, study of the self, and the Self. One of the *niyamas*.

swami – one who has achieved self-mastery; in the Hindu tradition, a renunciate or monk; a member of the Holy Order of *Sannyas*.

T

tamas – inertia, dullness (one of the three *gunas*).

tanmatra – subtle essence, energy, or potential that gives rise to material elements. According to Samkhya philosophy, they evolve from the *tamasic* aspect of the ego. The five elements derived from the *tanmatras* are as follows:

- Sound – ether
- Touch – air
- Sight – fire
- Taste – water
- Smell – earth

Tantra Yoga – (*tantra*, from *tan* = do in detail + *tra* = to protect). Practices using rituals, *yantras*, and mantras to experience the union of Siva and Shakti (the masculine and feminine or positive and negative forces) within the individual. The practices are given the name *tantra* because they offer detailed explanations on the knowledge of mantras and the essence of things. Its practices are believed to have protective powers for its practitioners.

tapas – literally, to burn. Spiritual austerity; purificatory action, accepting but not causing pain (one of the *niyamas*).

tradak – the meditation practice of steady gazing at an object.

turiya – literally, the fourth. In the philosophy of Vedanta, it is the word that refers to the state that transcends the three states of waking, dreaming, and dreamless sleep. It is the eternal, unchanging state of witness consciousness.

U

Upanishads – literally, to devotedly sit close. The final portion of each of the *Vedas* which teaches the principles of the nondualistic Advaita Vedanta philosophy. The essential teaching of the *Upanishads* is that the Self of an individual is the same as *Brahman*, the Absolute. Therefore, the goal of spiritual life is presented as the realization of *Brahman* as one's True Identity or Self.

There are ten principle *Upanishads: Isha, Kena, Katha, Prasna, Mundaka, Mandukya, Taittiriya, Aitareya, Chandogya,* and *Brihadaranyaka.*

V

vairagya – literally, without color. Dispassion, nonattachment.

Vedanta – the culmination or end objective of knowledge; the final experience resulting from the study of the *Vedas*. There are two subdivisions of this philosophical school: complete and qualified nondualism.

Vedas – the primary revealed wisdom scriptures of Hinduism (*Rig, Sama, Yajur,* and *Atharva*).

vidya – knowledge, learning

viveka – discriminative discernment. Discrimination between the Real and the unreal, the permanent and impermanent, and the Self and the non-Self. A state of ever-present discrimination between that which changes and that which does not.

vritti – (from the verb root *vrt* = to turn, revolve, roll, move) modification or fluctuation of the mind-stuff in which the mind seeks to find meaning by linking together related pieces of information. According to Advaita Vedanta, *vritti* activity serves as the connecting link between knower (subject) and known (object) and is what makes knowledge of things within creation possible.

Vyasa (arranger or compiler) – the name of several great sages of Hinduism; his commentary on the *Yoga Sutras* is the oldest in existence, dating from the fifth century, C.E. He is also said to have compiled the four *Vedas*, the *Mahabharata*, the *Bhagavad Gita,* and the *Puranas*. Though tradition has it that one Vyasa compiled all these scriptures, it is not likely due to the large span of years involved. One reason for this could be that Vyasa was more of a title than a name.

vyutthana – externalization of individual consciousness. It is the orientation of the mind toward material or worldly values, such as status, wealth, acknowledgment, etc. It is the predominant characteristic of ordinary consciousness. *Vyutthana* implies the desire to know the nature of sense objects, believing that they are separate from the self. It also suggests the desire for gaining satisfaction or permanent happiness from the knowledge of those objects.

Y

yama – abstinence (the first of the eight limbs of *Raja Yoga*.)

Yoga – (literally, union) union of the individual with the Absolute; any course that makes for such union; a tranquil and clear state of mind under all conditions. The word also means remedy, discipline, and vehicle, among many other meanings.

English Glossary

attention – a prolonging of awareness directed toward any thought object, or image.

Cosmic Consciousness – unlimited, unbounded, omnipresent, omniscient awareness. See *Brahman* and *mahavakya* in the Sanskrit Glossary.

enlightenment – the state of knowing the Self as one's True Nature and as the essence of all life and objects in the universe. Also known as Self-realization, God-realization, and liberation among other terms. In Buddhism, it is known as *nirvana*; in Christianity, mystic union.

fervor – intensity, enthusiasm. It is an intense wish to achieve or attain an object of state. In meditation, we use the word to mean inspiration and motivation that is the result of recognizing the benefits of meditation.

God – the common name in English for the essence and source of creation. The origin of the word implies that which is invoked or poured out, or a spirit or power that rules a place of thing. The German origin of the word was originally gender neutral, but changed to masculine with the rise of Christianity.

ignorance – the state of being unaware of one's True Nature. See *avidya* in the Sanskrit Glossary.

initiation – the transmission of knowledge and empowerment that are part of the process of entering into the Guru-disciple relationship.

meditation – the practice of stilling the restless activity of the mind in order to experience deeper levels of being and inner peace.

nature – one of two principle aspects of creation, nature is the material aspect. See *prakriti* in the Sanskrit Glossary.

nonattachment – the mental state of absence of selfish expectations or desires. An objective, clear state of mind. See *vairagya* in the Sanskrit Glossary.

self – the individual self as opposed to the transcendent Self (*Atma* or *Purusha*).

Self – called, the *Atma* or *Purusha*, Self refers to our True Nature. It is called "true" because it is unborn, undying, and omnipresent. It is pure unbounded consciousness.

Self-realization – (see: enlightenment)

Spirit – one of two principle aspects of creation, Spirit is the principle of awareness. In Sanskrit, it can be called *Purusha*, *Atma*, or *Brahman*.

True Nature – the essence and ground of being. Seer, Self.

Sources

Below, you will find a partial list of the many resources that have contributed to this text. Among them are wonderful dictionaries, translations, and commentaries.

Not listed, are the many other books, articles, studies, and journals – whose names and whereabouts are now lost – that have been invaluable resources.

Dictionaries and Encyclopedias:

Ayto, John, *Dictionary of Word Origins*, Arcade Publishing, New York, NY, 2011.

Cappeller, C., *A Sanskrit-English dictionary: based upon the St. Petersburg lexicons*, Cambridge University Press, Cambridge, UK, 2009.

Denton, John M., *A Sanskrit Dictionary*, DFT, 2015.

Dowson, John, *A Classical Dictionary of Hindu Mythology and Religion: Geography, History and Literature*, D.K. Printworld Ltd., New Delhi, India, 2000.

Feuerstein, Georg, *The Shambhala Encyclopedia of Yoga*, Shambhala Publications, Boulder, CO, 1997.

Fischer-Schreiber, Ingrid and Ehrhard, Franz-Karl, *A Concise Dictionary of Buddhism and Zen*, Shambhala Publications, Boulder, CO, 2010.

Grimes, John, *A Concise Dictionary of Indian Philosophy*, State University of New York Press, Albany, NY, 1996.

Harvey, Van A., *A Handbook of Theological Terms*, Macmillan Publishing Company, New York, NY, 1964.

Integral Yoga International, *A Dictionary of Sanskrit Names*, Integral Yoga® International, Integral Yoga® Publications, Buckingham, VA, 2012.

Learn Sanskrit, learnsanskrit.org

Macdonell, Arthur A., *Sanskrit-English Dictionary*, Award Publishing House, Worksop, UK, 1979.

Melton, J. Gordon, *The Encyclopedia of Religious Phenomena*, Visible Ink Press, Canton, MI, 2008.

Monier-Williams, Sir Monier, *A Sanskrit-English Dictionary*, Searchable Digital Facsimile Edition, The Bhaktivedanta Book Trust, Sandy Ridge, NC, 2003.

Narayanaswami, Sri Chidambaram and Glashoff, Klaus, *Sanskrit Dictionary for Spoken Sanskrit*, spokensanskrit.org, Cochin, India, 2005.

Oxford Languages, *Oxford American Dictionary and Thesaurus*, Second Edition, Oxford University Press, New York, NY, 2009.

Prakashan, Prasad, Revised and enlarged edition of Prin. V. S. Apte's *The Practical Sanskrit-English Dictionary*, 1957-1959, https://dsal.uchicago.edu/dictionaries/apte/.

Ruppel, A. M., *The Cambridge Introduction to Sanskrit*, Cambridge University Press, Cambridge, UK, 2017.

Sharma, Amrita, *The Sterling Dictionary of Religion*, Sterling Publishers Private Limited, Uttar Pradesh, India, 1999.

Sivananda, Sri Swami, *Yoga – Vedanta Dictionary*, Divine Life Society, Rishikesh, India, 2012.

The University of Texas, Ancient Sanskrit Online, (https://lrc.la.utexas.edu/eieol_english_meaning_index/vedol/7), The University of Texas at Austin Linguistics Research Center.

Unknown Author, *English Sanskrit Dictionary*, lexilogos.com

Unknown Author, *Sanskrit Dictionary*, sanskritdictionary.com

Werner, Karel, *A Popular Dictionary of Hinduism*, NTC Publishing Group, Chicago, IL, 1997.

***Yoga Sutras* Translations and Commentaries**

Aranya, Swami Hariharananda, *Yoga Philosophy of Patanjali*, State University of New York Press, Albany, NY, 1983.

Balantyne, Dr. J.R. and Deva, Govind Sastri, *Yoga Sutras of Patanjali*, Book Faith India, Delhi, India, 2000.

Bryant, Edwin F., *The Yoga Sutras of Patanjali*, North Point Press, New York, NY, 2009.

Carrera, Reverend Jaganath, *Inside the Yoga Sutras*, Integral Yoga® Publications, Buckingham, Virginia, 2008.

Chapple, Christopher, *Yoga and the Luminous: Patanjali's Spiritual Path to Freedom*, State University of New York Press, Albany, NY, 2008.

Chapple, Christopher and Viraj, Yogi Ananda, *The Yoga Sutras of Patanjali: An Analysis of the Sanskrit with Accompanying English Translation*, Sri Satguru Publications, Delhi, India, 1990.

D'Andrade, Hugh, *The Royal Yoga*, Samuel Weiser, Inc., New York, NY, 1971.

Dass, Baba Hari, *The Yoga Sutras of Patanjali: A Study Guide for Book I, Samadhi Pada*, Sri Ram Publishing, Santa Cruz, CA, 1999.

Feuerstein, Georg, *The Yoga-Sutra of Patanjali*, Inner Traditions, Rochester, VT, 1979.

Govindan, Marshall, *Kriya Yoga Sutras of Patanjali and the Siddhas*, Kriya Yoga Publications, Eastman, Quebec, Canada, 2000.

Hartranft, Chip, *The Yoga-Sutra of Patanjali*, Shambhala Publications, Boulder, CO, 2003.

Houston, Vyaas, *The Yoga Sutra Workbook: The Certainty of Freedom*, American Sanskrit Institute, Collingswood, NJ, 1995.

Iyengar, B.K.S., *Light on the Yoga Sutras of Patanjali*, Thorsons, London, UK, 1993.

Jha, Ganganatha, *Yoga-Darshana: Sutras of Patanjali with Bhasya of Vyasa*, Asian Humanities Press, Berkeley, CA, 2002.

Leggett, Trevor, *Sankara on the Yoga Sutras*, Motilala Banarsidass, Delhi, India, 2017.

Malhotra, Ashok Kumar, *An Introduction to Yoga Philosophy: An Annotated Translation of the Yoga Sutras*, Ashgate, Surrey, UK, 2001.

Miller, Barbara Stoler, *Yoga Discipline of Freedom: The Yoga Sutra Attributed to Patanjali*, Bantam Books, New York, NY, 1998.

Mishra, Ramamurti S., *Yoga Sutras*, Anchor Books, New York, NY, 1973.

Prabhavananda, Swami and Isherwood, Christopher, *How to Know God: The Yoga Aphorisms of Patanjali*, Vedanta Press, Hollywood, CA, 2007.

Prasad, Rama, *Patanjali's Yoga Sutras*, Munshiram Manoharlal Publishers, New Delhi, India, 2002.

Ranganathan, Shyam, *Patanjali's Yoga Sutras*, Penguin Random House, New York, NY, 2009.

Ravikanth, B., *Yoga Sutras of Patanjali*, Sanskrit Works, sanskritworks.com, 2012.

Satchidananda, Sri Swami, *The Yoga Sutras of Patanjali*, Integral Yoga® Publications, Buckingham, VA, 2012.

Swami, Shree Purohit, *Patanjali's Path to Yoga*, Rupa Publications, New Delhi, India, 2003.

Taimini, L.K., *The Science of Yoga*, Theosophical Publishing House, Wheaton, IL, 1961.

Tola, Fernando and Dragonetti, Carmen, *The Yoga Sutras of Patanjali*, Montilal Publishers, Delhi, India, 2001.

Venkatesananda, Swami, *The I-dea of I*, The Chiltern Yoga Trust, Cape Province, South Africa, 1973.

Villoldo, Ph.D., Alberto, *Yoga, Power, and Spirit: Patanjali the Shaman*, Hay House, Carlsbad, CA, 2007.

Vivekananda, Swami, *The Yoga Sutras of Patanjali*, Divine Life Society, Rishikesh, India, 2001.

Whicher, Ian, *The Integrity of the Yoga Darsana*, State University of New York Press, Albany, NY, 1998.

White, David Gordon, *The Yoga Sutras of Patanjali: A Biography*, Princeton University Press, Princeton, NJ, 2014.

Woods, James Haughton, *The Yoga System of Patanjali*, Motilal Banarsidass Publishers Private Limited, Delhi, India, 1998.

Yoga

Carrera, Reverend Jaganath, *Awaken: Inside Yoga Meditation*, Yoga Life Publications, Woodland Park, NJ, 2012.

Eliade, Mircea, *Yoga, Immortality, and Freedom*, Princeton University Press, Princeton, NJ, 2009.

Feuerstein, Georg, *The Yoga Tradition: Its History, Literature, Philosophy and Practice*, Hohm Press, Chino Valley, AZ, 1998.

Mandelkorn, Philip, Edited by, *To Know Your Self: The Essential Teachings of Swami Satchidananda*, Integral Yoga® Publications, Buckingham, VA, 1988.

Nikhilananda, Swami, Ramakrishna-Vivekananda Center, New York, NY, 1953.

Sivananda, Sri Swami, *All About Hinduism*, Divine Life Society, Rishikesh, India, 1977.

Sivananda, Sri Swami, *Bliss Divine*, The Divine Life Society, Rishikesh, India, 1974.

Sivananda, Sri Swami, *Concentration and Meditation*, The Divine Life Society, Rishikesh, India, 1975.

Sivananda, Sri Swami, *Mind, Its Mysteries and Control*, Divine Life Society, Rishikesh, India, 1997.

White, David Gordon, *Yoga in Practice*, Princeton University Press, Princeton, NJ, 2012.

Sacred Texts

Chinmayananda, Swami, *Kathopanishad*, Chinmaya Mission Trust, Mumbai, India, 2006.

Easwaran, Eknath, *The Upanishads*, Nilgiri Press, Tomales, CA, 1995.

Narayananda, Swami, *Sri Guru Gita*, Divine Life Society Publications, Rishikesh, India, 2005.

Prabhavananda, Swami and Manchester, Frederick, *The Upanishads: Breath of the Eternal*, Vedanta Press, Hollywood, CA, 1971.

Saraswati, Swami Satyananda, *Shree Maa: The Guru and the Goddess*, Devi Mandir Publications, Napa, CA, 1996.

Satchidananda, Sri Swami, *The Living Gita: The Complete Bhagavad Gita*, Integral Yoga® Publications, Buckingham, VA, 1988.

Schweig, Graham M., *Bhagavad Gita*, Harper Collins, New York, NY, 2006.

Sivananda, Sri Swami, *The Principle Upanishads*, Divine Life Society, Rishikesh, India, 1998.

Sundaram, P.S., *Tiruvalluvar: the Kural*, Penguin Books, London, UK, 2005.

Tirth, Swami Shivom, *Shri Guru Gita: The Divine Song of the Guru*, Swami Shivom Tirth Ashram, Pond Eddy, NY, 2006.

Tripurari, Swami B.V., *Bhagavad Gita: Its Feeling and Philosophy*, Mandala Publishing, San Rafael, CA, 2001.

Symbolism and Mythology

Cooper, J. C., *An Illustrated Encyclopedia of Traditional Symbols*, Thames & Hudson, New York, NY, 1978.

Chevalier, Jean and Gheerbrant, Alain, *Dictionary of Symbols*, Penguin Books, New York, NY, 1982.

Danielou, Alain, *Myths and Gods of India*, Inner Traditions International, Rochester, VT, 1991.

Eliade, Mircea, *Images and Symbols: Studies in Religious Symbolism*, Princeton University Press, Princeton, NJ, 1991.

Jansen, Eva Rudy, *The Book of Hindu Imagery: The Gods and Their Symbols*, Binkey Kok Publications, Diever, Holland, 1997.

Nityananda, Swami, *Symbolism in Hinduism*, Central Chinmaya Trust, Mumbai, India, 2008.

Other Resources

Abbott, Elizabeth, *A History of Celibacy*, Da Capo Press, Cambridge, MA, 2001.

Armstrong, Karen, *The Great Transformation: The Beginning of Our Religious Traditions*, Alfred A. Knopf, New York, NY, 2006.

Babb, Lawrence A., *Understanding Jainism*, Dunedin Academic Press, London, UK, 2015.

Beck, Guy L., Editor, *Sacred Sound: Experiencing Music in World Religions*, Wilfrid Laurier University Press, Ontario, Canada, 2006.

Beck, Guy L., *Sonic Theology: Hinduism and Sacred Sound*, The University of South Carolina Press, Columbia, SC, 2008.

Bhalla, Prem P., *Hindu Rites, Rituals, Customs, and Traditions*, Pustak Mahal, Mumbai, India, 2006.

Eck, Diana L., *India: A Sacred Geography*, Harmony Books, New York, NY, 2012.

Filliozat, Peirre-Sylvain, *The Sanskrit Language: An Overview – History and Structure, Linguistic and Philosophical Representations, Uses and Users*, Indica Books, Varanasi, India, 2000.

Frawley, David, *Yoga and Ayurveda: Self-Healing and Self-Realization*, Nataraj Books, Springfield, VA, 1999.

Ganeri, Jonardon, *Artha: Meaning*, Oxford University Press, New York, NY, 2006.

Ganeri, Jonardon, *Philosophy in Classical India: The Proper Work of Reason*, Motilal Banarsidass, Delhi, India, 2001.

Girard, Rene, *Violence and the Sacred*, John Hopkins University Press, Baltimore, MD, 1977.

Graham, William A., *Beyond the Written Word: Oral Aspects of Scripture in the History of Religion*, Press Syndicate of the University of Cambridge, New York, NY, 1993.

Juergensmeyer, Mark, Kitts, Margo, Jerryson, Michael, eds., *The Oxford Handbook of Religion and Violence*, Oxford University Press, Oxford, UK, 2013.

Khan, Sufi Inayat, Ashraf, SH. Muhammad, *Music*, Lahore, Pakistan, 1971.

Klostermaier, Klaus K., *A Short Introduction to Hinduism*, Oneworld Publications, Boston, MA, 1998.

Ricard, Matthieu, *Altruism*, Back Bay Books, New York, NY, 2013.

Ricard, Matthieu, *Happiness*, Little Brown & Company, New York, NY, 2007.

Rohr, Richard, *The Divine Dance*, Whitaker House, New Kensington, PA, 2016.

Sacks, Rabbi Jonathan, *Not in God's Name: Confronting Religious Violence*, Schocken Books, New York, NY, 2015.

Schmidt, Frederick W., Editor, *The Changing Face of God*, Morehouse Publishing, Harrisburg, PA, 1989.

Shankman, Richard, *The Experience of Samadhi: An In-depth Exploration of Buddhist Meditation*, Shambhala Publications, Boston, MA, 2008.

Svoboda, Dr. Robert E., *Prakriti: Your Ayurvedic Constitution*, Geocom Limited, Albuquerque, NM, 1989.

Whicher, Ian and Carpenter, David, *Yoga: The Indian Tradition*, Routledge, London, UK, 2003.

White, David Gordon, *Sinister Yogis*, University of Chicago Press, Chicago, IL, 2009.

Reverend Jaganath Carrera

Reverend Jaganath has shared the joy and practical wisdom of the *Yoga Sutras* with students since 1974. Known as Guruji by his students, he is the founder and spiritual head of the Yoga Life Society. He is the author of the best selling, *Inside the Yoga Sutras* and *Awaken: Inside Yoga Meditation.*

A direct disciple of of Sri Swami Satchidananda, he has taught all facets of Yoga at universities, prisons, Yoga centers, and interfaith programs. He established the Integral Yoga® Ministry and was chief administrator of Satchidananda Ashram – Yogaville® and founded the Integral Yoga® Institute of New Brunswick, New Jersey, where he was director for fourteen years.

Reverend Jaganath has developed several teacher training programs in Raja Yoga and meditation, and established the Yoga Life Ministry.

For more information on trainings, workshops, or classes with Reverend Jaganath Carrera, please go to www.yogalifesociety.com.